ANDEAN ARCHAEOLOGY
Papers in Memory of Clifford Evans

Edited by

Ramiro Matos M., Solveig A. Turpin, Herbert H. Eling, Jr.

Monograph XXVII

Institute of Archaeology

University of California, Los Angeles

Library of Congress Cataloging-in-Publication Data

Main entry under title:

  Andean Archaeology.

  (Monograph / Institute of Archaeology, University of California, Los Angeles ; 27)
  Bibliography: p.
  1. Indians of South America—Andes—Antiquities—Congresses. 2. Excavations (Archaeology)—Andes—Congresses. 3. Andes—Antiquities—Congresses. I. Matos Mendieta, Ramiro. II. Turpin, Solveig A. III. Eling, Herbert H. IV. Series: Monograph (University of California, Los Angeles. Institute of Archaeology) ; 27.
  F2229.A.56   1986   980'.01   85-11854
  ISBN 0-917956-52-4

Monographs of the Institute of Archaeology include preliminary and final excavation reports, symposia papers, and accounts of research in such wide-ranging subjects as archaeometry, ethnoarchaeology, paleodemography, and rock art.

This publication was made possible in part by a grant from the Institute of Andean Research, New York.

Editor: Ernestine S. Elster
Associate Editors: Timothy Earle, Clement W. Meighan, Merrick Posnansky, James R. Sackett
Director of Publications: Ernestine S. Elster
Cover Design: Christine Choe

Contents

Foreword from the Honorary Chairman

Over the years, whether abroad or in this country, the exchange of research information is a necessary but all too infrequent result of the gatherings of Andeanists. Fortunately, the Andean Archaeology 1981 symposium, convened more or less spontaneously on the felicitous inspiration of Ramiro Matos Mendieta, Visiting Professor at the University of Texas at Austin, achieved the needed objective to an unusual degree. To a large extent, this may have been due to the generous mix of graduate students and junior professionals, a relaxed discussion atmosphere, and the minimal presence of "sacred cows."

The only excuse I have for injecting this introductory note to the publication of this highly productive Andeanist conference is that Dr. Matos was my surrogate while I was on leave in Hamburg. Since I have been intimately concerned with the University of Texas Andean Program for many years, even in absentia I was allowed to identify myself with its patronage.

Needless to say, I heartily approve ex post facto the homage paid to Clifford Evans whom I have known since graduate student days.

Richard P. Schaedel
Professor, University of Texas at Austin

Preface

Increasingly, archaeologists, anthropologists, and ethnologists have turned to the Andean area as one of the few parts of the world where it is still possible to come in contact with ancient ethnic traditional groups, their technology, their native social organization, their economic systems, and, above all, their complex ideologies. Every year more researchers spread throughout the Andes tracing ancient settlement patterns, excavating the pre-Hispanic structures, and studying documents and oral traditions. At times, a veritable flood of national and foreign colleagues are studying Andean cultures.

The eight million inhabitants of the Andes who still speak Quechua and Aymara, or other minor language groups, constitute an inexhaustible source of linguistic ethnic information on Andean life, its nature, its rites, and its customs. The rich archives dating from the sixteenth to the twentieth century, inherited information from the Spanish colonies, may explain the social and political relationships of the people that form Andean society. The antiquated idea of writing Peruvian history from afar, utilizing only such sources as the Archive of the Indies in Seville, has been replaced largely through the efforts of such ethnohistorians as John V. Murra. Since the 1950s he has recognized the importance of these documents, even those purely bureaucratic in content. Maria Rostworowski de Diez Canseco has also uncovered a large variety of sources, offering us a better way of visualizing Andean history. Today, many others follow this course with optimal results.

The archaeological panorama is not as praiseworthy. It is one thing to study Andean archaeology in its real dimensions and quite another to create archaeological cultures to discuss in theory. Objective contributions have been few. The fieldwork, the empirical data, the treatment of the data, and the presentation and synthesis of the data do not equal the numbers of field workers or the money expended. In many cases the models designed, while of some theoretical importance, are of debatable value in the reconstruction of Andean process or development. At times, the ideas overshadow the data, especially where ideas are emphasized to the neglect of the informational content. Nonetheless, the intent to explain Andean history within the nomenclature of the social sciences and to find the Andean sense and dimension must be recognized. This volume, however, is oriented toward the presentation of data in support of the conclusions offered. We hope this will place theory in its proper perspective.

Of course, the list of contributions to Andean archaeology is long. The essays in this volume and the others which were presented at the 1981 Andean Conference at the University of Texas at Austin form only part. Many of our Peruvian colleagues were absent or silent because of financial limitations or field commitments in Peru and Ecuador. Meticulous work, like that of Duccio Bonvia in Los Gavilanes, of Rogger Ravines in Garaguy and Jequetepeque, of Kasou Terada in Huacaloma, is an example to others involved in recent research.

Paralleling the development in field research is the greater interest on the part of universities in the United States. Several academic departments have sponsored programs and special seminars; libraries have increased their holdings; and several institutions have dedicated organizations solely to Andean research. In addition to the traditional AAA and SAA meetings, numerous conferences have been convened to discuss Andean themes. In the spring of 1981, availing ourselves of the opportunity to invite Andean specialists attending the SAA meeting in San Diego, we organized the Andean Colloquium in homage to the recently deceased Dr. Clifford Evans. This meeting was held at the University of Texas at Austin on April 28 and 29, 1981.

The Andean Colloquium was an unprecedented success, largely due to the attendance of many distinguished scientists, professors, and students of the University of Texas and other institutions. We were honored and enlightened by the presence of the president of the Institute of Andean Studies in New York, the late Junius Bird, Robert Bird, Teresa Gisbert, Terence Grieder, William H. Isbell, Daniel G. Julien, Margaret J. Kluge, Donald Lathrap, Thomas F. Lynch, William Meyer-Oakes, Elias Mujica, Jeffrey Quilter, Mario A. Rivera, Abelardo Sandoval M., Helaine Silverman, Karen E. Stothert, Teresa Topic, Paul Trawick, Lux Vidal, and James Vreeland. Chairing the five sessions were Drs. Jeremiah Epstein, Gideon Sjoberg, Greg Urban, Larry Patrick, and Richard N. Adams, all of the University of Texas at Austin. Special recognition should go to the graduate students of the University of Texas, Herbert H. Eling, Jr., Gordon McEwan, and Richard Watson. They showed not only the ability to perform the research but also a vocation for the Andes. The program was rich and informative, and the contributions outstanding. We regret that due to financial considerations we are unable to include all the papers in this edition. The difficult choice to emphasize those papers which dealt with original, recent field research had to be made to accommodate the projected size of its volume.

The colloquium was organized soon after the death of Clifford Evans. The homage paid to Evans and his work by his colleagues was immediate and unanimous. In addition to the loss of a great scholar of American archaeology in general and Andean archaeology in particular, we were deprived of a tireless researcher, a great teacher, and an excellent friend. The publication of papers delivered at the colloquium dedicated to his memory is a well-deserved recognition of this work.

The Institute of Latin American Studies, under its director William Glade, and the Department of Anthropology, under the chairmanship of Chad Oliver, gave their support and patronage. Terence Grieder, Department of

Fine Arts, also deserves recognition for his complete support of the project. Dr. Richard N. Adams generously hosted an evening of Andean music. Many special thanks go to Carole Smith, Department of Anthropology, who handled all the administrative tasks.

This volume was organized and edited by Solveig Turpin, Herbert H. Eling, Jr., and me. Timothy Earle of UCLA deserves special thanks for his assistance in the review process and for making much of this publication possible. The able assistance of Dr. Ernestine Elster of the Institute of Archaeology at UCLA is acknowledged. The support of John V. Murra, President, and Craig Morris, Secretary, of the Institute of Andean Studies in New York deserves special recognition. Without their help, publication may have been impossible. The essays are arranged in chronological order according to their topics. All work is original and the result of ongoing fieldwork. It is our hope that this emphasis will be emulated and this volume will be only the first of many to make a substantial contribution to the empirical basis for interpretation of Andean culture.

Ramiro Matos Mendieta

In Memoriam
Clifford Evans (1920-1980)

The premature death of Clifford Evans, a terrible loss for his family, leaves the archaeologists studying South American civilizations without an advocate before many of the foreign boards deciding on the relevance of local endeavor. The scholarly contribution of Clifford Evans and Betty Meggers to Brazilian and Andean archaeology will be evaluated by other, more competent, hands. Here I would like to stress the understanding Evans displayed, long before many of his compatriots, in the natural interest we as students of the Andean past had in the professional and technical growth of our disciplines in every American republic. I can think of only George Kubler, John H. Rowe, and Richard P. Schaedel as comparable animators of archaeology practiced not only in South America but also by South Americans.

Year after year the Smithsonian, and specifically the laboratories of Clifford Evans and Betty Meggers, welcomed one or more colleagues from the hemisphere for substantial stays. The library, the technical staff, and the experience of the hosts were put at the disposal of the visiting scholars. These scholars were encouraged to travel to other institutions, to attend the meetings of the Washington Anthropological Society, to exchange ideas over staff lunches. Some had to learn English, others followed courses in quantitative techniques at local universities, and all were painlessly shown the advantages of a stay at the Smithsonian. Most visitors came from Brazil but virtually every South American country was represented at one time or another. Away from the Smithsonian, Clifford Evans and others organized short, intensive seminars in some of the countries where they conducted research--years later I would meet colleagues whose brighter professional moments referred to seminars in Colombia, Brazil, or Puerto Rico. The absence of postgraduate training in some of the republics made these seminars particularly valuable.

When possible, Cliff would also see to it that a local scholar should receive material support for his field investigations. I remember how significant such modest support could be in one of the republics after a particularly repressive regime came to power. Many of our colleagues lost their jobs, at least temporarily; others remained unemployed for a year or more. This had no effect on the visible support provided by the Smithsonian since the jeep they had entrusted to the fired colleague continued at his disposal and permitted the continuation of his research. At another level, the only way, for years, of getting the original in Spanish of Vasquez de Espinoza's description of the Andes in the early seventeenth century was to ask for it from Cliff; it arrived soon, properly registered, under the Smithsonian's frank. In 1970, at the Lima gathering of the International Congress of Americanists, Evans and Meggers proposed the publication of an international journal of American archaeology in Spanish, a forum we still desperately need. Unfortunately, the international posture of the United States at that time made this a politically unacceptable proposition, where in 1960 it may well have been welcomed. Similarly, the effort to set up a postgraduate school of archaeology for the Andean countries, efforts in which Evans was a decisive element, were similarly turned down in 1974. Few universities in those days could afford to be known as accepting funds from the United States.

Although I had met Evans years earlier, I got to know him well in the early sixties when I was preparing the Huanuco study. Without his support and that of the Institute of Andean Research of which he was then president, there would have been no Huanuco study. He was concerned about the scholarly competence of the staff, but he was also supportive of including funds for five students from the Universidad Mayor de San Marcos. The National Science Foundation also paid the consultant fees to colleagues such as Manuel Chavez Ballon and Ramiro Matos Mendieta. The Institute, under his direction, subsidized the publication of an important sixteenth-century inspection by Garci Diez de San Miguel (1964 [1567] Casa de la Cultura, Lima) and Inigo Ortiz de Zúñiga (1967 and 1972 [1562]). A few years later, Betty Meggers translated and the Smithsonian published the English edition of Luis G. Lumbreras's The Peoples and Cultures of Ancient Peru.

I remember Evans's last appearance at the annual board meeting of the Institute of Andean Research, late in 1980. Among the issues before us was the delayed release of Toribio Mejía Xesspe's report on Paracas. This was the fourth volume of the Julio C. Tello's legacy which Mejía had prepared and the Institute of Andean Research had financed. It is still the Institute's only publication. The printing was completed in the summer of 1979, but the work had not been released because the family had objected to Mejía's name appearing, at last, as co-author. Evans led the discussion of the ways the hostage-book could be released; Tello, after all, had been one, if not the, founder of the Institute of Andean Research. Publishing his work and encouraging him to write up his studies had been a priority since the 1930s (see Kroeber 1944). At the board meeting Evans had before him one of the very few copies of the Paracas volume in circulation; it reposes now in the Smithsonian library and awaits a serious review. To the end of his life, Cliff was concerned that the book, although printed, could not circulate. This unique catalogue raisonne of the excavations at Paracas, based on Mejía's Xesspe's notebooks, links Evans's and our days with those of the founders.

The Institute of Andean Research, whose president Clifford Evans was at a sensitive, transitional time, joins you in mourning South American archaeology's loss.

John V. Murra
President,
Institute of Andean Archaeology

Bibliography of Clifford Evans

1947   Book review of Junius B. Bird: Excavations in Northern Chile. American Antiquity 12(4):278-79.

1948   Book review of Marshall T. Newman: Skeletal Material from Central Coast of Peru. American Antiquity 14(1):68-69.

1950   A report on recent archaeological investigations in the Lagôa Santa region (Minas Gerais). American Antiquity 15(4):341-43.

Book note on H. V. Walter: The Pre-History of the Lagôa Santa Region (Minas Gerais). American Anthropologist 52(1):108.

The Archaeology of the Territory of Amapá (Brazilian Guiana). Ph.D. diss. Ann Arbor: University Microfilms.

(with Betty J. Meggers)
Preliminary results of archaeological investigations in the mouth of the Amazon. American Antiquity 16(1):1-9.

1951   Book review of James A. Ford and Gordon R. Willey: Surface Survey of Virú Valley, Peru. American Antiquity 16(3):270-72.

The territory of Amapá: land in Dispute. Archaeology 4(3):175-80.

(with Betty J. Meggers)
American table d'hôte. Américas 3(7):16-19.

(with Betty J. Meggers)
Cardápio americano. Américas 3(8):16-19. (Portuguese edition).

(with Betty J. Meggers)
La Mesa Americana. Américas 3(8):16-19. (Spanish edition).

(with Betty J. Meggers)
Book review of Helen C. Palmatary: The Pottery of Marajó Island, Brasil. American Anthropologist 53(3):396-98.

1952 (with William Duncan Strong)
Cultural Stratigraphy in the Virú Valley, Northern Peru: The Formative and Florescent Epochs. Columbia Studies in Archaeology and Ethnology 4. New York: Columbia University Press.

1953 (with C. G. Holland and Betty J. Meggers)
The East Mound. Quarterly Bulletin of Archeological Society of Virginia 7(3).

1954 Book review of Charles Wagley: Amazon Town: A Study of Man in the Tropics. American Anthropologist 56(3):508-10.

Letter to editor re Spaulding's review of Ford's "Measurements of Some Prehistoric Design Developments in the Southeastern States." American Anthropologist 56(1):114.

(with Betty J. Meggers)
Uma Interpretação das Culturas da Ilha de Marajo. Publication 7, Instituto de Anthropologia e Etnologia do Pará, Museu Paraense Emílio Goeldi, Belém, Brazil.

1955 New archeological interpretations in northeastern South America. In New Interpretations of Aboriginal American Culture History, 75th Anniversary Volume of Anthropological Society of Washington, D.C., 82-94.

A Ceramic Study of Virginia Archeology. With an Appendix An Analysis of Projectile Points and Blades by C. G. Holland. Bureau of American Ethnology, Bulletin 160. Washington, D.C.

Book review of Edward Weyer: Jungle Quest. Americas (English edition) 7(7):40-41; (Spanish and Portuguese editions) 7(8):41-42.

Book review of Junius Bird and Louisa Bellinger: Paracas Fabrics and Nazca Needlework, 3rd Century B.C. to 3rd Century A.D. Scientific Monthly 81(3):150-51.

Filiações das culturas arqueológicas no Território do Amapá. Anais do XXXI Congresso Internacional de Americanistas 2:801-12. São Paulo.

(with Betty J. Meggers)
Life among the Wai Wai Indians. National Geographic Magazine 107(3):329-46.

(with Betty J. Meggers)
The Wai Wai of Guiana. In National Geographic on Indians of the
Americas, 345-55. Washington D.C.: National Geographic Society.

(with Betty J. Meggers)
Resumenes: Las Culturas de Marajó. Ciencias Sociales, Union
Panamericana 32(6):116-21. Washington D.C.

(with Betty J. Meggers)
Preliminary report on archeological investigations in the Guayas
Basin, Ecuador. Cuadernos de Historia y Arqueología, Año IV,
4(12):1-12. Guayaquil, Ecuador.

(with Betty J. Meggers)
Informe preliminar sobre las investigaciones arqueológicas realizadas
en la cuenca del Guayas, Ecuador. Cuadernos de Historia y Arqueología, Año IV, 4(12):1-18. Guayaquil, Ecuador.

(with Betty J. Meggers)
Preliminary results of archeological investigations in British Guiana.
Timehri: The Journal of the Royal Agricultural and Commercial
Society of British Guiana 34:5-26.

(with Betty J. Meggers)
Preliminary results of archaeological investigations in British Guiana
(abstract). Anais do XXXI Congresso Internacional de Americanistas
2:761-62. São Paulo.

(with Betty J. Meggers)
Culture areas of South America: an archeological point of view
(abstract). Anais do XXXI Congresso Internacional de Americanistas
2:683-84. São Paulo.

1956 Book review of A. Kroeber: Proto-Lima: A Middle Period Culture of
Peru. American Anthropologist 58(1):204-5.

Tendencias actuales de la investigación arqueologica en América
Latina. Ciéncias Sociales, Pan American Union 7(38):85-95.

The culture area concept in an exhibition of Latin American archaeology, United States National Museum, Washington (text in English and
French). Museum UNESCO 9(4):215-25.

(with Junius B. Bird)
Book review of Wendell C. Bennett: Ancient Arts of the Andes and 32
Masterworks of the Andes, A Supplement. American Antiquity
21(4):438-39.

(with Betty J. Meggers)
The reconstruction of settlement pattern in the South American
tropical forest. In Prehistoric Settlement Patterns in the New World,
edited by G. R. Willey. Viking Publications in Anthropology 23:156-
64.

1957   Book review of Greta Mostny: Culturas Precolombinas de Chile. Hispanic American Historical Review, February, 111.

Book review of F. L. Cornely: Culture Diaguita Chilena y Cultura de el Molle.   Hispanic American Historical Review, February, 110.

Book review of Harold S. Gladwin: A History of the Ancient Southwest.   American Scientist 45:394A.

(with Betty J. Meggers)
Formative Period cultures in the Guayas Basin, coastal Ecuador. American Antiquity 22(3):235-47.

(with Betty J. Meggers)
Book review of: Program of the History of America, Indigenous Period.   American Antiquity 22(3):306-9.   (Spanish translation printed in Revista del Museo Nacional 26 [1958]:299-302.)

(with Betty J. Meggers, as contributing editors)
Archeology of western and southern South America.   In Handbook of Latin American Studies 191:24-36.   Gainesville: University of Florida Press.

(with Betty J. Meggers)
Archeological Investigations at the Mouth of the Amazon.   Bureau of American Ethnology Bulletin 167.   Washington, D.C.

1958   Book review of G. H. S. Bushnell: Peru.   American Antiquity 23(3):328-29.

Archaeology: Western Hemisphere.   In The Americana Annual,   42-44. New York: Americana Corp.

(Compiler and editor).   Anthropological activities in the United States, 1956.   Boletín Bibliográfico de Antropología Americana 19-20(1):31-65.   Mexico City.

Book review of Doris Stone: The Archeology of Central and Southern Honduras.   American Journal of Archaeology 62(4):461-62.

Comments on Rydén's review of Heyerdahl and Skjölsvold: Archeological Evidence of Pre-Spanish Visits to the Galápagos Islands. American Antiquity 24:189.

Book review of Michael Swan: The Marches of El Dorado: British Guiana, Brazil, Venezuela.   Hispanic American Historical Review, November,   570.

(with Betty J. Meggers)
La Mesa Americana.   Revista de Información y Cultura Michoacán 41 (January):6-9.   (Reprinted from Spanish edition of Americas, August 1951, without credit to source.)

(with Betty J. Meggers)
Archaeological research in Eastern Ecuador: Report to the Committee

on Research, Grant No. 2012 (1956). Yearbook 1957, pp. 376-77.
Philadelphia: American Philosophical Society.

(with Betty J. Meggers)
Valdivia, an early formative culture of Ecuador. Archaeology
11(3):175-82.

(with Betty J. Meggers)
Archaeology: South America (except Colombia and Venezuela). In
Handbook of Latin American Studies 20:25-35. Gainesville:
University of Florida Press.

(with Betty J. Meggers)
Book review of Gordon R. Willey and Philip Phillips: Method and
Theory in American Archaeology. American Antiquity 24:195-96.

(with Betty J. Meggers)
Archaeological evidence of a prehistoric migration from the Rio Napo
to the mouth of the Amazon. In Migrations in New World Culture
History. University of Arizona Social Science Bulletin 27(2):9-16.

(with Betty J. Meggers)
Present status and future problems of archaeological investigations in
Ecuador. Miscellanea Paul Rivet Octogenario Dictata, 2:353-61.
Universidad Nacional Autónoma de Mexico.

(with Betty J. Meggers)
Identifacação das áreas culturais e dos tipos de cultura na base da
cerâmica das jazidas arqueológicas. Arquivos do Museu Nacional
46:9-32. Rio de Janeiro.

1959   Archeology: Western Hemisphere. In The Americana Annual, 44-45.
New York: Americana Corp.

Book review of Estevão Pinto: Etnologia brasileira (Fulniô—os últimos
Tapuias). Hispanic American Historical Review 39(2):340-41.

Book review of Alfonso Vinci: Samatari (Orinoco-Amazoni). Hispanic
American Historical Review 39(2):358-59.

Book review of Gastão Cruls: Hiléia Amazonica: Aspectos da Flora,
Fauna, Arqueología e Etnografía Indígenas, 3d ed. Hispanic American
Historical Review, August, 482.

Book review of Antonio Serrano: Manual de la Cerámica Indígena.
Hispanic American Historical Review, August, 483.

(with Betty J. Meggers)
O emprêgo do método comparativo na interpretação arqueológica.
Revista Sociologia 20(3):397-409. São Paulo.

(with Betty J. Meggers)
Archaeology: South America (except Colombia and Venezuela). In
Handbook of Latin American Studies 21:16-26. Gainesville:
University of Florida Press.

(with Betty J. Meggers and Emilio Estrada)
Cultura Valdivia. Publicación del Museu "Victor Emilio Estrada" 6.
Guayaquil, Ecuador.

1960   Inca. In The World Book Encyclopedia, 79-82.   Chicago.

Archaeology: Western Hemisphere. In The American Annual, 43-45.
New York: Americana Corp.

Book review of Julian H. Steward and Louis Faron: Native Peoples of
South America. American Antiquity 26(1):123-24.

Book review of Helen C. Palmatary: The Archeology of the Lower
Tapajós Valley, Brazil. The Hispanic American Historical Review,
November, 628-29.

Book review of Annette Laming and José Emperaire: A Jazida José
Vieira: Um Sitio Guaraní e Pre-Cerâmico do Interior do Paraná.
American Antiquity 26(2):292-93.

(Assistant editor). Guianas, Ecuador and Brazil. In Abstracts of
New World Archaeology 1:104-6, 109-11. Washington, D.C.: Society
for American Archaeology.

(with Betty J. Meggers)
Archeological Investigations in British Guiana. Bureau of American
Ethnology Bulletin 177. Washington, D.C.

(with Betty J. Meggers)
A new dating method using obsidian, part II. An archeological
evaluation of the method. American Antiquity 25(4):523-37.

(with Betty J. Meggers, contributing editors)
Archaeology: South America (except Colombia and Venezuela). In
Handbook of Latin American Studies 22:17-26. Gainesville:
University of Florida Press.

(with Betty J. Meggers and Jose M. Cruxent)
Preliminary results of archeological investigations along the Orinoco
and Ventuari Rivers. Actas del XXXIII Congresso Internacional de
Americanistas, 359-69. San José, Costa Rica.

(with George Quimby)
American Indian. In The World Book Encyclopedia,   108-39.
Chicago.

1961   Book review (Spanish translation) of Julian H. Steward and Louis
Faron: Native Peoples of South America. Revista Interamericana de
Ciencias Sociales, segunda epoca 1(1):219-20. Washington, D.C.: Pan
American Union.

Book review of Wesley R. Hurt and Oldemar Blasi: Os Sambaquí do
Macedo, A. 52.B - Paraná, Brasil. American Antiquity 27(1):122-23.

Book review of Hans Feriz: Ecuador 1960: Verslag van een Ar-
chaeologische Studiereis. American Antiquity 27(2):262-63.

(Assistant editor). Guianas, Ecuador and Brazil. Abstracts of New World Archaeology 2:156-59, 162-64. Washington, D.C.: Society for American Archaeology.

Book review of José Cruxent and Irving Rouse: An Archeological Chronology of Venezuela, vols. 1 and 2. American Journal of Archaeology 65:88-89.

(with Betty J. Meggers, contributing editors)
Archaeology: South America (except Colombia and Venezuela). In Handbook of Latin American Studies 23:24-37. Gainesville: University of Florida Press.

(with Betty J. Meggers)
Book review (Spanish translation) of Gordon R. Willey and Philip Phillips: Method and Theory in American Archeology. Revista Interamericano 1(1):220-22.

(with Betty J. Meggers)
An experimental formulation of horizon styles in the tropical forest area of South America. In Essays in Pre-Columbian Art and Archaeology, 372-88. Cambridge: Harvard University Press.

(with Michael J. Harner, contributing editors)
Ethnology: South America. In Handbook of Latin American Studies 23:42-57. Gainesville: University of Florida Press.

1962 Book review (in Spanish) of: Etnología y Arqueología, Lima, 1960, Actas y Trabajos del Epoca PreHispánica del Segundo Congreso Nacional de História del Perú, Lima, 1959; and Antiguo Peru, Espacio y Tiempo, Lima, 1960. Revista Interamericana de Ciéncias Sociales, segunda época 1(3):435. Washington D.C.: Pan American Union.

Book review (in Spanish) of Serafin Cordero: Los Charruas: Sintesis Etnográfica y Arqueológica del Uruguay Montevideo, 1960. Revista Interamericana de Ciéncias Sociales, segunda epoca 1(3):437. Washington D.C.: Pan American Union.

(with Betty J. Meggers)
Use of organic temper for carbon-14 dating in lowland South America. American Antiquity 28(2):243-45.

(with Betty J. Meggers, contributing editors)
Archaeology: South America (except Colombia and Venezuela). In Handbook of Latin Studies 24:27-39. Gainesville: University of Florida Press.

(with Betty J. Meggers)
The Machalilla culture: an early Formative complex on the Ecuadorian coast. American Antiquity 28(2):186-92.

(with Betty J. Meggers and Emilio Estrada)
Possible transpacific contact on the coast of Ecuador. Science 135(3501):371-72.

(with Gordon Ekholm)
The interrelationships of New World cultures: a coordinated research program of the Institute of Andean Research. In Akten des 34 Internationalen Amerikanistenkongresses, 233-78. Vienna.

1963   (with Betty J. Meggers, editors)
Aboriginal Cultural Development in Latin America: An Interpretative Review. Smithsonian Miscellaneous Collections 146, Publication 4517. Washington, D.C.

(with Betty J. Meggers, contributing editors)
Archaeology: South America (except Colombia and Venezuela). In Handbook of Latin American Studies 25:26-34. Gainesville: University of Florida Press.

(with Emilio Estrada)
Cultural development in Ecuador. In Aboriginal Cultural Development in Latin America: An Interpretative Review. Smithsonian Miscellaneous Collections 146(1):77-88. Washington, D.C.

1964   Book review of: Edición Extraordinaria en Homenaje al Cincuentenario del Descubrimiento de Machupicchu: Revista del Museo e Instituto Arqueológico, Universidad Nacional del Cuzco. American Antiquity 29(3):398.

Book review of Frederic Engel: A Preceramic Settlement on the Central Coast of Peru: Asia, Unit I. American Anthropologist 66(1):197-98.

Lowland South America. In Prehistoric Man in the New World, edited by Jesse D. Jennings and Edward Norbeck, 419-50. Chicago: University of Chicago Press.

Book review of Robert L. Stephenson and Alice L. L. Ferguson: The Accokeek Creek Site, A Middle Atlantic Seaboard Culture Sequence. American Anthropologist 66(2):446-47.

Book review of José M. Cruxent and Irving Rouse: Arqueología Cronológica de Venezuela, 2 vols. The Hispanic American Historical Review 44(2):269-70.

Book review of Philip C. Hammond: Archaeological Techniques for Amateurs. American Antiquity 30(1):126-27.

Book review of Gwyn Jones: The Norse Atlantic Saga; Being the Norse Voyages of Discovery and Settlement to Iceland, Greenland, America. American Anthropologist 66(4): pt. 1, 948-49.

Book review of S. K. Lothrop: Archaeology of the Diquis Delta, Costa Rica. American Anthropologist 66(5):1218.

Book review of Donald Robertson: Pre-Columbian Architecture. American Anthropologist 66(6): pt. 1, 1441.

(with Betty J. Meggers)
Genealogical and demographic information on the Wai Wai of British

Guiana. In Beiträge zur Völkerkunde Südamerikas Festgabe für Herbert Baldus zum 65 Geburtstag, edited by Hans Becher. Völkerkundliche Abhandlungen Band I, Des Niedersächsischen Landesmuseum Abteilung für Völkerkunde, 199-207. Hannover, Germany.

(with Betty J. Meggers)
British Guiana Archaeology: A Return to the Original Interpretations. American Antiquity 30(1):83-84.

(with Betty J. Meggers)
Book review of Irving Rouse and José Cruxent: Venezuelan Archaeology. American Antiquity 30(2):227-28.

(with Betty J. Meggers)
Especulaciones sobre rutas tempranas de difusión de la cerámica entre Sur y Mesoamerica. Hombre y Cultura 1(3):1-15.

(with Betty J. Meggers and Emilio Estrada)
The Jambelí culture of south coastal Ecuador. Proceedings of the U.S. National Museum 115(3492):483-558. Washington, D.C.

1965 Book review of S. K. Lothrop: Treasurers of Ancient America: The Arts of Pre-Columbian Civilizations from Mexico to Peru. American Anthropologist 67(1):159-60.

Book review of Seiichi Izumi and Toshihiko Sono: Andes 2, Excavations at Kotosh, Peru. American Anthropologist 67(1):160-62.

Book review of Sprague de Camp and Catherine C. de Camp: Ancient Ruins and Archaeology. ISIS, 56.2.184: 236.

The dating of Easter Island archeological obsidian specimens: Report No. 18. In Reports of the Norwegian Archaeological Expedition to Easter Island and the East Pacific. Miscellaneous Reports 2. Monographs of the School of American Research and the Kon-Tiki Museum 24, pt. 2:469-95. Santa Fe, New Mexico.

(with Betty J. Meggers)
Cronología relativa y absóluta en la costa del Ecuador. Cuadernos de História y Arqueología, Año XI, no. 27 (1961):3-8. Casa de la Cultura Ecuatoriana, Núcleo del Guayas, Guayaquil.

(with Betty J. Meggers)
Guia para prospecção arqueológica no Brasil. Museu Paraense Emílio Goeldi, Guia 2. Belém, Brazil.

(with Betty J. Meggers, contributing editors)
Archaeology: South America. In Handbook of Latin American Studies 27:56-75. Gainesville: University of Florida Press.

(with Betty J. Meggers and Emilio Estrada)
Early Formative Period of Coastal Ecuador: The Valdivia and Machalilla Phases. Smithsonian Contributions to Anthropology 1. Washington, D.C.

1966 Book review of: Homenaje a Fernando Márquez-Mirada, Arqueólogo e Historiador de America. American Antiquity 31(4):593-94.

(with Betty J. Meggers)
A transpacific contact in 3000 B.C. Scientific American 214(1):28-35.

(with Betty J. Meggers)
Mesoamerica and Ecuador. In Handbook of Middle American Indians 4:243-64. Austin: University of Texas Press.

(with Betty J. Meggers)
Transpacific origin of Valdivia Phase pottery in coastal Ecuador. In Actas y Memorias, XXXVI Congreso Internacional de Americanistas España, 63-67. Seville, Spain.

(with Betty J. Meggers)
Beginnings of food production in Ecuador. In Actas y Memorias, XXXVI Congreso Internacional de Americanistas España, 201-7. Seville, Spain.

(with Betty J. Meggers)
A transpacific contact in 3000 B.C. Japan-America Forum 12(6):44-57. (Japanese translation of 1966 Scientific American article.)

1967 Book review of G. H. S. Bushnell: Ancient Arts of the Americas. American Antiquity 32(2):255-56.

Introdução. Program Nacional de Pesquisas Arqueológicas: Resultados Preliminares do Primeiro Ano 1965-1966, Museu Paraense Emílio Goeldi, Publicações Avulsas 6:7-13. Belém, Brazil.

Amazon archeology, a centennial appraisal. Actas do Simpósio sôbre a Biota Amazônica 2:1-12. Rio de Janeiro.

(with Betty J. Meggers, contributing editors)
Archaeology: South America. In Handbook of Latin American Studies 29:75-104. Gainesville: University of Florida Press.

(with Betty J. Meggers)
Potsherd language and how to read it. Mimeograph. Washington, D.C.: Smithsonian Institution.

1968 The lack of archeology on Dominica. In Proceedings of the Second International Congress for the Study of Pre-Columbian Cultures in the Lesser Antilles, July 24-28, 1967, Barbados Museum, 93-102. Barbados.

Obituary: Rafael Larco Hoyle, 1901-1966. American Antiquity 33(2):233-36.

Obituary: James Alfred Ford, 1911-1968. American Anthropologist 70:1161-67.

Archaeology and diplomacy in Latin America. Foreign Service Journal 45(6):35-37, 50.

(with Betty J. Meggers)
Archeological Investigations on the Rio Napo, Eastern Ecuador.

Smithsonian Contributions to Anthropology 6.   Washington, D.C.

(with Irving Friedman)
Obsidian dating revisited.   Science 162:813-14.

1969   Book review of Hans Dietrich Disselhoff: Daily Life in Ancient Peru.
       American Antiquity 34:97-98.

       (with Betty J. Meggers)
       Introdução.   Programa Nacional de Pesquisas Arqueológicas,
       Resultados Preliminares do Segundo Ano, 1966-1967.   Museu Paraense
       Emílio Goeldi, Publicações Avulsas 10:7-10.   Belém, Brazil

       (with Betty J. Meggers)
       Speculations on early pottery diffusion routes between South and
       Middle America.   Biotropica 1:20-27.

       (with Betty J. Meggers)
       Como Interpretar el Lenguaje de los Tiestos.   Translated from
       revised edition of Potsherd Language by Víctor A. Núñez Regueiro
       (multilith).

       (with Betty J. Meggers)
       Introdução.   Programa Nacional de Pesquisas Arqueológicas,
       Resultados Preliminares do Terceiro Ano, 1967-1968.   Museu Paraense
       Emílio Goeldi, Publicações Avulsas 13:7-11.   Belém, Brazil.

       (with José Proenza Brochado, Valentin Calderon, Igor Chmyz,
       Ondemar Ferreira Dias, Silvia Maranca, Betty J. Meggers, Eurico Th.
       Miller, Nássaro A. de Souza Nasser, Celso Perota, Walter F. Piazza,
       José Wilson Rauth, and Mário F. Simões)
       Arqueologia Brasileira em 1968; Um Relatório Preliminar sôbre o
       Programa nacional de Pesquisas Arqueológicas.   Museu Paraense
       Emílio Goeldi, Publicações Avulsas 12.   Belém, Brazil.

1970   Book review of: Bibliografía Indígena Andina Peruana (1900-1968),
       Vols. 1 and 2, by Hector Martinez, Miguel Cameo C., and Jesus
       Ramirez S. Lima.   American Anthropologist 72(3):640.

       (with Betty J. Meggers)
       Como Interpretar a Linguagem da Cerâmica.   Translated from the
       revised edition of Potsherd Language by Alroino B. Eble (multilith).

       (with Betty J. Meggers, contributing editors)
       Archaeology: South America.   In Handbook of Latin American Studies
       31:68-94.   Gainesville: University of Florida Press.

       (with José Proenza Brochado, Valentin Calderon, Igor Chmyz,
       Ondemar Ferreira Dias, Silvia Maranca, Betty J. Meggers, Eurico Th.
       Miller, Nássaro A. de Souza Nasser, Celso Perota, Walter F. Piazza,
       José Wilson Rauth, and Mário F. Simões)
       Brazilian archaeology in 1968: an interim report on the national
       program of archaeological research.   American Antiquity 35(1):1-13

1971   Book review of Donald Lathrap: The Upper Amazon.   American
       Anthropologist 73:1414-16.

(with Betty J. Meggers)
Introducão. Programa national de Pesquisas Arqueológicas, Resultados Preliminares do Quarto Ano, 1968-69. Museu Paraense Emílio Goeldi, Publicações Avulsas 15:7-9. Belém, Brazil.

(with Betty J. Meggers)
Especulaciones sobre rutas tempranas de difusión de la cerámica entre Sur y Mesoamerica (translation of Biotropica article). Revista Dominicana de Arqueología y Antropología, Año 1, 1(1):137-49.

(with Betty J. Meggers, contributing editors)
Archaeology: South America. In Handbook of Latin American Studies 33:67-102. Gainesville: University of Florida Press.

1973 (with Betty J. Meggers)
A reconstituicão de pré-história amazónica. Algumas consideracões teóricas. O Museu Goeldi no Ano do Sesquicentenário. Museu Paraense Emílio Goeldi, Publicações Avulsas 20:51-69. Belém, Brazil.

(with Betty J. Meggers)
Site survey at the mouth of the Amazon. Reprint from BAE Bul. 167:6-11. In In Search of Man, edited by Ernestine L. Green, 43-48. Boston: Little Brown and Co.

(with Betty J. Meggers)
United States "imperialism" and Latin American archaeology. American Antiquity 38:257-58.

(with Betty J. Meggers)
An interpretation of the cultures of Marajó Island (Revised English translation of 1954 article). In Peoples and Cultures of Native South America, edited by Daniel R. Gross, 39-47. New York: Natural History Press.

(with Betty J. Meggers, contributing editors)
Archaeology: South America. In Handbook of Latin American Studies 35:49-69. Gainesville: University of Florida Press.

1974 Book review of Charles R. McGimsey III: Public Archeology. Museum News 52(8):49-50.

(with Betty J. Meggers)
Introducão. Programa Nacional de Pesquisas Arqueológicas, Resultados Preliminares do Quinto Ano, 1969-70. Museu Paraense Emílio Goeldi, Publicações Avulsas 26:7-10. Belém, Brazil.

(with Betty J. Meggers)
Imperialismo norteamericano y arqueología latinoamericana (translation of 1973 article). Boletin del Instituto Montecristeño de Arqueología 1:11-13. Montecristi, Dominican Republic.

(with Betty J. Meggers)
A transpacific contact in 3000 B.C. In New World Archaeology: Theoretical and Cultural Transformations, edited by Ezra B. W. Zubrow, Margaret C. Fritz, and John M. Fritz, 97-104. San Francisco: W. H. Freeman and Co. (Reprint of 1966 article)

(with Betty J. Meggers)
A reconstituicão de pré-história amazónica: Algumas considerações teóricas. Paleoclimas 2, Instituto de Geografía, Universidade de Saõ Paulo. (Reprint of 1973 article).

1975 (with Betty J. Meggers)
La "seriación Fordiana" como método para construir una cronología relativa. Revista de la Universidad Católica, Año 3, 10:11-40. Quito.

(with Betty J. Meggers, contributing editors)
Archaeology: South America. In Handbook of Latin American Studies 37:52-84. Gainesville: University of Florida Press.

1976 Background and introduction. Symposium: New Research Designs Applied to Paleoindian Problems: Some Preliminary Results. Actas del XLI Congreso Internacional de Americanistas 3:458-61. Mexico City.

(with Betty J. Meggers)
Some potential contributions of Caribbean archaeology to the reconstruction of New World prehistory. In Proceedings of the First Puerto Rican Symposium on Archaeology, edited by Linda Sickler Robinson, 25-32. Informe No. 1, Fundación Arqueológica, Antropológica e Histórica de Puerto Rico, San Juan.

(with Owen S. Rye)
Traditional Pottery Techniques of Pakistan: Field and Laboratory Studies. Smithsonian Contributions to Anthropology 21. Washington, D.C.

1977 (with Betty J. Meggers)
Early Formative Period chronology of the Ecuadorian coast: a correction. American Antiquity 42:266.

(with Betty J. Meggers)
Las tierras bajas de Suramérica y las Antillas. Estudios Arqueológicos (Centro de Investigaciones Arqueológicas), Ediciones de la Universidad Católica, Quito, 11-69. (Complete translation of Meggers and Evans 1978, In Ancient Native Americans.)

(with Betty J. Meggers, contributing editors)
Archaeology: South America. In Handbook of Latin American Studies 39:73-109. Gainesville: University of Florida Press.

1978 (with Betty J. Meggers)
Accomplishments of the Proyecto Andino de Estudios Arqueológicos, 1967-1971. National Geographic Society Research Reports, 1969:163-71.

(with Betty J. Meggers)
Aspectos arqueológicos de las tierras bajas de Suramérica y las Antillas. Cuadernos del Cendia 258(4). Universidad Autónoma de Santo Domingo. (Complete translation of Meggers and Evans, 1978, In Ancient Native Americans.)

(with Betty J. Meggers)
Lowland South America and the Antilles. In Ancient Native Americans, edited by Jesse D. Jennings, 543-91. San Francisco: W. H. Freeman and Co.

(with Betty J. Meggers)
Apresentacão. Areas da Amazônia Legal Brasileira para Pesquisa en Cadastro de Sitiós Arqueológicos, by Mario F. Simões and Fernanda Araujo Costa. Museu Paraense Emílio Goeldi, Publicações Avulsas 30:5. Belém, Brazil.

1979 (with Betty J. Meggers)
An experimental reconstruction of Taruma Village succession and some implications. In Brazil: Anthropological Perspectives, edited by Maxine L. Margolis and William E. Carter, 39-60. New York: Columbia University Press.

1980 (with Betty J. Meggers)
Archaeology: South America. In Handbook of Latin American Studies 41:68-106. Austin: University of Texas Press.

(with Betty J. Meggers)
Un Metodo Cerámico para el Reconocimiento de Comunidades Pre-Históricas. Boletín del Museo del Hombre Dominicano, Año 9, 14:57-73.

1.

Monte Verde:
An Early Man Site in South-Central Chile

Tom Dillehay and Mario Pino Q.

Archaeological and geological research conducted at Monte Verde, an early man site in south-central Chile, has revealed an early and minimally modified pebble tool assemblage, a well-preserved wood industry, and diverse ecofactual materials in direct association with the osteological remains of at least five to six individual mastodons and the residue of an architectural structure. Radiocarbon dates from the site show that this single cultural episode took place no less than 12,000 to 14,000 years ago.

This paper introduces the site, discusses the research problems and methods, and reviews implications of the research findings, including the results of three field seasons. Three levels of data interpretations are provided: (1) context and form, (2) classification and tentative function, and (3) interpretative implications. Most of the discussion pertains to the first two, including discussion of contextual association of distinct artifact categories and of methodological procedures designed specifically to define and classify cultural form and function. When considered conclusive, the function of specific artifact specimens and/or assemblages will be given. General observations on the overall activity structure represented by the data and their local, regional, and continental implications will be made.

At present, the analysis of ecofactual and artifactual materials from the Monte Verde site remains incomplete; that, combined with the lack of space, precludes a detailed and thorough report here. This presentation of data must be considered only as an interim report on the research focus and methodological procedures employed at Monte Verde.

Research Problem

The purpose of research at Monte Verde was to establish the history, organization, and function of human activity at the site. The main emphasis has been on the technological and economic processes by which early man adapted to the subantarctic forest of south-central Chile, as reconstructed and interpreted through the excavated inorganic and well-preserved organic artifactual and ecofactual materials, and on the behavior reflected in their spatial patterning. A corollary emphasis has been to examine the specific activity structure of the early man occupation at the site and the organization of the cultural event. The results of the research will provide a basis for the comparative study of adaptation in other late Pleistocene environmental contexts in the New World.

One data set for early man that has not been adequately pursued comprises resources such as pebbles and tree branches that required little or no cultural modification for use as a tool. To date, most archaeologists have maintained reservations on the validity of minimally modified tools (such as pebble implements) owing to (1) the dubious cultural-geological context of materials, or (2) the chance that modification occurred as the result of natural processes.

Given the nature of the artifactual materials recovered from Monte Verde, research has been extended to include naturally occurring resource "forms" suitable for immediate use. In this sense, once the artifactual collections from Monte Verde have been analyzed and interpreted, their substantive contribution will lie in providing insight into the validity of assemblages of minimally modified lithic and wooden materials from elsewhere in the New World which, at best, have been accepted with reservations because they cannot be defined by extant technological paradigms.

General Research Design

In response to the research difficulties—that is, the presence of minimally modified stone implements and a well-preserved wood industry in a late Pleistocene geological context—during our first season at Monte Verde, we used an archaeological and geological excavation procedure to aid interpretation of ecofactual and artifactual materials and the natural and cultural actions that account for their deposition and form. In order to test the type, composition, and spatial distribution of naturally deposited stone and wood specimens along the creek and to compare these patterns with those recorded in the buried cultural context, 12 m^2 block units were excavated in natural context, concentrating on materials in the same stratigraphic layer that contains cultural materials at Monte Verde. This allowed us to compare, quantitatively and qualitatively, the composition and distribution of inorganic and organic materials in both the cultural context and in active and buried natural contexts. By employing this specific complementary method, we were best able to (1) detect and define the morphological similarities and differences between artifacts and ecofacts, and (2) define and explain the often vague boundary between the human processes and the natural mechanisms that alter inorganic and organic elements.

Background on Previous Research at Monte Verde

Monte Verde is located 55 km southwest of Puerto Montt in south-central Chile. Cultural materials at the site are buried in the banks of Chinchihuapi Creek, a southern tributary of the Río Maullin, located at about 40° 30' S, 73° W (fig. 1.1). The stream drains from a wet boggy area in a humid subantarctic forest that has existed at least since Late Pleistocene times.

The site was first called to my attention in 1976 by local woodcutters and a student who reported large molars eroding from the banks. In January 1978, students of the Universidad Austral de Chile and I established a 1 m^2 grid. Additional survey and excavation at Monte Verde have defined three

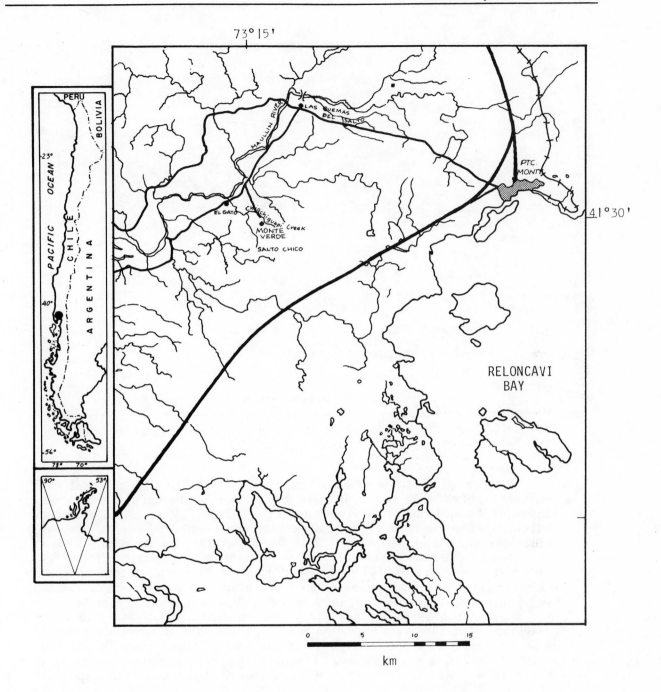

Figure 1.1.   Location of the Monte Verde site.

distinct areas: Area A, along the north side of the creek, where the heaviest concentration of wood, bone, and lithics were found; Area B, about 350 m downstream from Area A, where dental remains of an infant mastodon were recovered; and Area C, along a sandy ridge on the south side of the creek, where modified pebbles and the remains of a hearth were excavated.

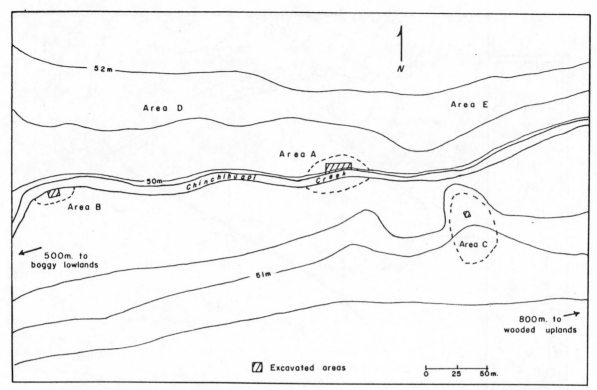

Figure 1.2.   Specific location of the Monte Verde site along Chinchihuapi Creek, including Areas A, B and C.

In area A, 18 m² were excavated (fig. 1.2). Artifactual material was recovered between .95 to 1.1 m below the surface in the ancient creek bed. This work defined the nature of the general geological deposits and recorded the direct buried association of modified lithic and wood artifacts and the osteological remains of mastodons (fig. 1.3). Excavation was by natural levels and, where possible, by microstrata within the natural strata. Some 117 individual bone elements, 181 modified lithics, and 85 worked pieces of wood were excavated during the 1978 season. Another 112 bone elements, which had been washed out of the site, were collected from the modern creek bed.

During the 1979 and 1981 field seasons, 110 m² of the site were excavated. Test pits were placed on the slopes and tops of surrounding ridges in an attempt to discover additional activity areas. These tests yielded two modified flakes, a percussion-split pebble of basalt, and the remains of a hearth on a ridge (Area C) about 80 m southeast of the main site area (fig. 1.2).

In addition, a group of multidisciplinary specialists studied the geological and ecological context in which the cultural event took place. Pino conducted the geological investigations, and local biotic zones near the site were defined and mapped by Professor Claudio Briones of the Instituto de Botánica, Universidad Austral de Chile. The recovered faunal materials were analyzed by Dr. Rodolfo Casamiquela of the Centro de Investigación Científica, Viedma, Argentina. Dr. Juan Díaz-Vaz O. of the Instituto de Tecnología de Madera, Universidad Austral de Chile, examined the paleo-organic remains from the site. In 1980, Dr. Michael B. Collins of the University of Kentucky was asked to participate in the edge-wear analysis of lithic materials.

O   50 cm.

Figure 1.3.   In situ association of lithic, wood, and bone at the Monte Verde site.

In January 1981, an additional 12 m² of the site were excavated. A wishbone-shaped foundation of a structure was found in direct association with the bone, wood, and lithic remains in Area A. A modified log, in a V-shaped vice-like implement also made of wood, was excavated about .5 m southwest of the structure. Four modified pebble tools were recovered in direct association with the modified log and vice-like implement. Burned clay patches and charcoal indicated hearths on the floor of the structure and in the vicinity of the log.

Geology of the Site

Although Pino's geologic study is still in progess, his preliminary conclusions are as follows: Eight geologic strata are distinguished in the immediate area of the Monte Verde site (fig. 1.4). The lowest five strata, MV-4 through MV-8, are of primary interest here. MV-7 and MV-8, the lowest strata, are deposits of gravel and a gray, heavy-grained sand with lenses of volcanic ash. MV-6, a 4 m wide creek bed deposit overlying a narrow strip of MV-7, consists of 4 to 37 cm of medium-grained brown sand and gravel. The ancient creek, MV-6, cuts through the upper level of MV-7; these two strata were contemporaneous surfaces at the time of the cultural event. Strata MV-6 and MV-7 contain the buried archaeological component in Area A—the evidence of the cultural event

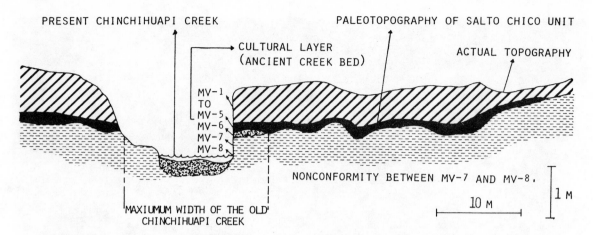

PRESENT CHINCHIHUAPI CREEK

PALEOTOPOGRAPHY OF SALTO CHICO UNIT

CULTURAL LAYER
(ANCIENT CREEK BED)

ACTUAL TOPOGRAPHY

MV-1
TO
MV-5
MV-6
MV-7
MV-8

NONCONFORMITY BETWEEN MV-7 AND MV-8.

10 M

1 M

MAXIMUM WIDTH OF THE OLD
CHINCHIHUAPI CREEK

Figure 1.4.   Stratigraphic section of the Monte Verde site.

that took place at the top of these strata. Cultural materials recovered from the test pit on the sandy knoll to the southeast were found in the upper part of MV-7, while the dental remains found downstream were lying on top of MV-6. Core drilling and test pits outside of the site area show that at the time stratum MV-6 was deposited, the stream was flanked by low sandy knolls and small bogs. Access to the creek bed was restricted; entrance in the immediate site area was achieved only by descending the hearth-bearing sandy ridge on the southside of the creek. Later, the bogs, represented by stratum MV-5, expanded to cover the stream, creating a peat deposit 1 to 25 cm thick that overlaid and sealed in the archaeological materials. All bone, lithic, and wood materials are contained within a 15 cm thick layer comprised of the upper part of MV-6 (the ancient creek channel) and MV-7 (the channel's sandy bank). Some bone elements have been washed out of their in situ location by the modern creek which has recut a channel alongside the ancient creek bank and buried artifacts. Nevertheless, about 80-90% of the buried deposits are still intact. In some excavated units of Area A, the organic artifacts are differentially preserved by the uneven thickness of the peat layer. For instance, the larger and thicker bones, which lie on MV-6, are not completely covered by the peat and are not well preserved. Overlying MV-5 and MV-4 is a stratum of small pebbles and sand 4 to 26 cm thick, above which lie about 60 cm of more recent sediments, MV-1 through MV-3.

Pino's preliminary analysis indicates that MV-7 and MV-8 were surface strata of the Salto Chico Unit, a high terrace formed by the Río Maullin drainage during Late Pleistocene times. The Salto Chico Unit is made up of sand and gravel; matrices of sandy silt with some volcanic ash are a common characteristic of the unit. The age of these deposits has not yet been determined.

Stratum MV-6 was formed by erosional noncomformity of strata MV-7 and MV-8 of the Salto Chico Unit. The gravel pebbles that comprise the ancient stream bed are not the direct product of initial transport or sedimentation by the Río Maullin drainage system but, rather, are the result of later local outwash of the smaller sized particles (e.g., sand, smaller gravels, etc.) from the upper levels (MV-7 and MV-8) of the unit. The fractured nature of pebbles in the MV-6 stratum is accounted for by sedimentary processes that occurred during the formation of MV-7 and MV-8, not during the later development of MV-6. Biotite, tonalite, and hornblend granite are the most common rock types in the creek bed. Basalt and andesite occur less frequently.

The sole postdepositional disturbance of strata MV-4 through MV-8 occurred in recent times. The modern stream reincised a channel, exposing one edge of the ancient MV-6 creek bed which contains the materials.

Stream action as a possible agent for modification of stone, wood, and bone has been negated by Pino. Detailed geological analysis shows that the creek banks of MV-6 were about 20 cm high and that the maximum depth of water passing through the site was about 15 cm.

Through the examination of the inclination of gravels in the stream and of the sediments, Pino has also been able to determine that the ancient creek was low in energy and not likely to have flaked or created edge retouch on pebbles or to have cut and worked wood and bone. The low-energy flow of the creek is also evidenced by piles of wooden twigs that were carried by the creek and deposited against one side of the thicker pieces of bone and wood artifacts. Any rapid creek flow after the cultural event would have carried all wood downstream.

Although Professors Briones, Pino, and Díaz-Vaz are only beginning to reconstruct the paleoenvironment, they have tentatively concluded that cold and wet conditions, much like the present-day environment, prevailed in the region some 12,000 to 16,000 years ago. Similar conditions for the same time span have also been postulated by the geologists Heusser (1966, 1974) and Mercer (1972), who have worked independently just north of the Monte Verde site.

Radiocarbon Chronology

One sample of wood from the base of MV-4, four samples of wood and charcoal from MV-5, one bone sample from the top of MV-6, and a wood fragment from the modified log close to the architectural feature on the surface of MV-7 were submitted for radiocarbon analysis. Both the corrected and uncorrected dates for samples from all strata are listed in table 1.1.

As can be determined from table 1.1, the sequence of the radiocarbon data is congruent with the geological stratigraphy at the site. The single cultural event at Monte Verde is estimated to date between 12,000 to 14,000 years ago. Two humanly altered materials from the cultural layers are dated. Sample Tx-3760 from bone in stratum MV-7 places the cultural event approximately between 12,350 to 13,030 years old. A minor problem exists with the Tx-3208 date of 13,965 ± 250; stratigraphically it lies at the top of MV-6, about 5 cm above the Tx-3760 date from the top of MV-6 and the Tx-4437 date from the top of MV-7, but it is much earlier. This may indicate that the Tx-3208 wood sample represents depositional lag of older material in the cultural area. On the other hand, the Tx-3760 date on bone may be younger than the cultural event. Additional radiocarbon dates on wood from MV-5 and on both bone and wood artifacts from MV-6 and MV-7 will hopefully resolve this problem.

The geological evidence, as analyzed at the time of this writing, is compatible with radiocarbon dates. The dating of these geological strata are in general agreement with Mercer's (1972), Heusser's (1966, 1974), and Hoganson and Ashworth's (1982) radiocarbon dates for similar contexts.

Cultural Material

Four categories of cultural materials have been excavated at Monte Verde. These include architecture, lithics, wood, and bone. Analyses of these materials are incomplete, and thus only preliminary comments will be provided here. With the exception of one bifacial implement, which had eroded from

Table 1.1.   Radiocarbon dates from stratum MV-4, MV-5, MV-6, and
MV-7 at the Monte Verde site.

Sample No.	Material	Total Carbon Counted	Counting Time	Age BP, 5730 Half-Life
Non-Culture Bearing Deposits				
Lower Layer of MV-4				
Tx-4436	Wood	3.500 gm	2800 min	8,270±130
Upper Layer of MV-5				
Tx-3207	Wood and Charcoal	2.409 gm	2700 min	11,155±130
Tx-3210	Wood	0.551 gm	5500 min	12,115±470
Lower Layer of MV-5				
Tx-3208	Charcoal	1.592 gm	5600 min	13,965±250
Tx-3472	Wood	2.412 gm	3700 min	11,950±120
Culture Bearing Deposits				
Upper Layer of MV-6				
Tx-3760	Bone	1.682 gm	2700 min	12,350±200
Upper Layer of MV-7				
Tx-4437	Wood	6.000 gm	2800 min	13,030±130

stratum MV-6 of the creek bank, only the cultural materials are discussed below. The osteological remains collected from the modern creek bed will be reported in a later publication. Distinct activity areas are also observed at Monte Verde, and, although the analyses of these data are also inclusive, the spatial patterning of activity structure will be briefly discussed.

Architectural Artifacts

The foundation of a wishbone-shaped structure, comprised of compacted gravel and sand, was located on the buried surface of MV-7, below stratum MV-5 (the peat layer). The structure has a semirectangular platform protruding from the exterior side of its base (fig. 1.5). An entryway opens to the southeast. Two hearths were found on the floor of the structure. In addition, the remains of a 42 cm long center "pole" were located inside the structure and near the inner face of the platform. The buried end of the pole had been cut and pointed. The upper end was preserved only as far as it extended up into the MV-5 peat layer. No modified lithics were recovered from the floor of the structure, although numerous "stains" were observed. Also, vertically arranged branches about 3 to 8 cm in length were recovered from the middle of the side walls. These specimens are interpreted as the remains of walls made of branches.

Lying along the southwestern side of the structure was a 1.2 m long log which had been heavily modified by burning and scraping. The upper part of the log had been scraped on three sides to form a semi-flat surface (fig. 1.6a),

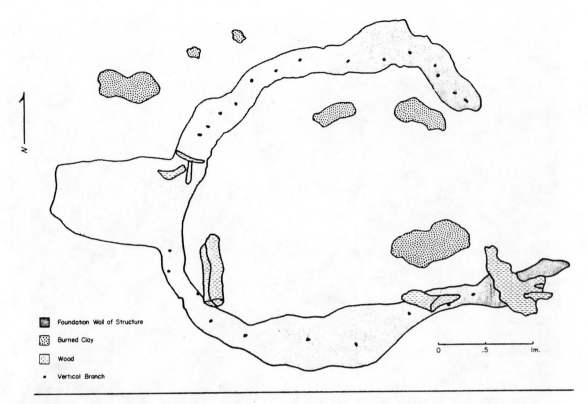

Foundation Wall of Structure

Burned Clay

Wood

• Vertical Branch

0   .5   1m.

Figure 1.5.   General plan of the architectural feature at Monte Verde.

the bottom side had a 5 cm wide groove running down its full length; and, midway down the groove, a bridge was cut perpendicular to the groove (fig. 1.6b).

One end of the log was positioned in a heavily modified, V-shaped wooden implement, which possibly served as a "vise" to hold the log in place while it was being worked. The V-shaped object measures about 90 cm in length and 30 cm in width. Four wooden pegs were found placed in the sand against the east side of the log.

Lithic Artifacts

Most lithics from Monte Verde exhibit minimal cultural modification and use, thus creating an intriguing problem in defining the type and form of stone technology at the site. Although stones that can be morphologically identified as cultural implements exist, a significant quantity of pieces do not show clear evidence of cultural use to the naked eye. Based on their form, edge-wear characteristics, and context, human utilization is suspected. At least three lithic specimens are of unquestionable human production—a grooved stone, a biface, and a core—and at least six others exhibit forms much more easily explained as a result of human rather than natural processes—a chopper, another grooved stone, a split cobble, and three edge-battered stones.

No bifacially flaked tools have been excavated at the site. We have attempted to recover microlithic debitage by passing the excavated portions of strata MV-5 and MV-6 through fine screens (1/6 in.), but no chipping debris was discovered, suggesting that various tools made from secondary and tertiary flakes, including projectile points, were not manufactured. Of course, it is

0   .5 m.

Figure 1.6a.   *Modified log and associated "vise"-like implement in situ about*
0.4 m south of the architectural feature.

0   .5 m.

Figure 1.6b.   *Underside of the log showing the cut canal and perpendicularly*
cut "bridge".

possible that such tool types were produced outside of the kill site area, for instance, on the sandy knoll to the southeast. If this were the case, however, we would also expect that these tools would have been utilized to process the plant materials and the hide and meat of the animals in Area A. The same reasoning applies to the absence of bifacially flaked stone projectile points.

One notable artifact is the bifacial chopper made of nonlocal quartzite. This tool was found at the edge of the modern creek bank. It is the most technologically "advanced" tool in the lithic assemblage. Unfortunately, its surface context restricts our interpretation. Surface microcleavages in the quartzite contain both MV-6 sands and MV-5 peat, suggesting that the tool had eroded from the buried cultural site exposed in the MV-6 stratum of the modern creek bed. Pino has identified the nearest source of this quartzite as an area some 80 km to the north.

The remaining lithic artifacts at Monte Verde belong to an industry which incorporates only minimal modification of the raw material. It is the process of selection of natural form (either for immediate use or for minimal alteration prior to use) rather than bifacial manufacture that is the key to understanding the lithic artifact assemblage. The selection is believed to have been carried out in two steps: the first is the collection of specific natural forms which are later used, and the second is the selection of specific attributes of those forms either for direct use or for use through some degree of manufactured modification. Thus, one of the hypotheses that we are testing is that the individuals at Monte Verde selected certain forms and types of rock for utilization. The null hypothesis is that there is a random distribution of stone forms within the cultural site area. The hypotheses are being tested in part by statistically comparing the frequency and distribution of the lithic forms and types from the area identified as the site with the naturally occurring gravels.

Focusing on this problem, we excavated twelve 1 m^2 control units of the buried stratum MV-6 in distant "natural" areas. All stones from these units were counted. All fractured stones were catalogued and classified according to size, form, weight and type of stone. In total, 128,457 stones were counted, and, of these, some 1,842 fractured ones were classified and analyzed in terms of the above-mentioned characteristics. For comparative purposes, the same technique was applied to stones recovered from excavation in the forty-two 1 m^2 control units in cultural area A. About 3,834 stones were counted and, of these, 843 were fractured.

Our preliminary analysis of these materials shows that about eighteen different forms of fractured stones (Sanzana 1980) are available in the natural context of the ancient stratum MV-6. These eighteen forms occur randomly in the natural areas, but tend to be clustered in specific locales in the cultural area where concentrations of wood and bone are found. Statistical analysis of both the "natural" collection and the "cultural" assemblage will aid in our interpretation of lithic form and function.

Experiments on lithic replication were also performed on stones from the "natural" area in an attempt to establish associations between the edge characteristics of the different forms of naturally occurring fractured pebble when applied to different types of wood and to ox and horse bone. Pressure and angle of application, length of flake, motion and number of scraping or cutting strokes applied on experimental bone, wood, and other stone materials will be quantified to verify any correlations between the various forms of edge-wear attributes on fractured pebble flakes and specific tasks and material type. The data recovered from these experiments will also aid analysis of lithic use wear.

The site lies on an old terrace that is composed of poorly sorted fluvio-glacial materials. Since nearly all of the specimens from the site range from pebbles to small cobble-sized igneous and metamorphic rocks, the cultural-natural boundary is vague. M. B. Collins, the project's primary lithic analyst, is approaching the lithic collection exclusively from a morphological attribute perspective. Below are his general procedure and tentative conclusions.

Collins and Dillehay (1981) have defined the 207-member lithic "collection" from the Monte Verde site "as those pieces which, on contextual evidence, <u>could</u> have been employed culturally." These are specimens that were recovered among the modified wood and bone elements contained in the upper levels of MV-6 and sealed in by the overlying peat (MV-5) or, in the case of two pieces, in the upper level of MV-7, the adjacent sandy bank which was contemporaneous with the ancient creek bed (MV-6). Within the collection are (1) definite artifacts–objects exhibiting contextual and/or morphological characteristics indicative of human intervention, and (2) the majority of stone of which cultural status is problematic. Collins has established eleven descriptive categories based upon morphological criteria. The objects in each category have been examined and described in terms of morphology, lithology, and wear. His work has been aided by experimental replication using stones from natural areas to shape replicas of grooved, wooden artifacts.

Collins and Dillehay's preliminary analysis reveals that a minority of the stone objects from Monte Verde are unquestionably human products, including a biface and core. Both are made of probable foreign materials. Two spherical, grooved stones (fig. 1.7) and a hafted split pebble clearly are man-made of local materials. The majority of the stones may be natural but have attributes or contexts that show cultural use. Upon completion of the comparative edge-wear analysis on the archaeological specimens, the experimentally replicated objects, and the naturally occurring fracture stones, we will have more reliable sets of data to determine the number and diversity of the man-modified stones and to define the cultural boundaries of lithic technology at Monte Verde.

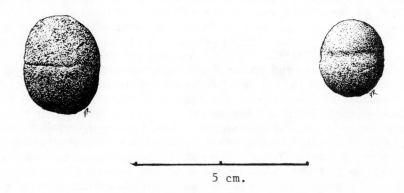

5 cm.

Figure 1.7.   Full-groove "bola" stones.

Nevertheless, we can conclude that selectivity of naturally occurring stones was the primary task. Evidence of direct percussion is limited to the biface and core. Pecking/abrading and fracturing of dense crystalline material as well as flaking of the brittle, finer grained piece seem to have been other techniques for stone working.

Wooden Artifacts

The wooden artifacts include two hafts on which are mounted end-scrapers made of quartzite, two modified branches with full-length grooves and associated subtriangular gouges in situ, and about eighty-five pieces of wood with cuts, grooves, modified edges, and abrasions. The hafted scrapers were attached with bitumen.

In addition, four branches of wood show worked and utilized segments. Each specimen exhibits cuts and utilized tips with similar edge angles (38% to 45%) and thinned, curved "handles." These four artifacts were found in close association with the bone remains of the torso area of three individual mastodons. Three of the specimens average about 40 cm in length. The largest branch is about 1.3 m long.

Nine other wood artifacts are of particular concern here. One is a lanceolate piece of wood with its interior portion gouged and scraped in a concave form. The base is also concave and the distal end has been diagonally cut to form a sharp point which is burned at the tip. The tool, 7.7 cm long, is made of luma wood, a highly resistant hardwood found locally.

Dr. Juan Díaz-Vaz has determined that these alterations were not caused by natural processes, such as stones being pressed or mashed into the wood, thus creating depressions, but rather the wood had been "cut." This conclusion was derived from analysis of the cellular structure of the wood.

Eight burned pieces of reed (Juncus bufonius, Briones MS.) were concentrated in a 1 m² area. These specimens measure 4.5 to 5 cm in length. Three of them exhibit conical-shaped tips.

A varied array of plant specimens, including the wooden artifacts, were preserved by the overlying peat. The preserved floral materials include leaves and branches of trees, seeds of fruits, flowers, and pods, and pollen. Dr. Carlos Ramirez, Director of the Instituto de Botánica, and Professor Claudio Briones, both of the Universidad Austral de Chile, have conducted a preliminary analysis of these materials. They have identified most of the species determining that the paleoenvironment at the time of the cultural event was similar to that of present day, a humid, subantarctic forest with cold, wet conditions. The most common plant remains recovered at Monte Verde are branches of the luma tree (Amomyrtus luma) and large quantities of fruits (Aristotelia chilensis, Rubus contrictus, and Berberis busifolia) and other shrubs (Briones, MS.).

The archaeologically recorded floral materials were compared to specimens obtained from excavations in "natural" areas. There is a marked quantitative and qualitative distinction between the number of species found in both areas. The natural area rendered species local to the creek bank microenvironment, whereas the items from the cultural context are selected hardwoods (luma and alerce) from nearby and distant microenvironments. In addition, a higher quantity and greater diversity of edible plant types (such as hackberry seeds and unidentifiable fruits) occur in the cultural area. Plant remains in the cultural context are of species from different locales in the area and from different seasons of the year.

Osteological Remains

All bone recovered represents the mastodon (<u>Cuvieronius sensu</u>) (Casamiquela n.d.). The sample includes one hundred and twelve surface-collected bone elements that had eroded from the site and another fifty four excavated bone specimens. Based on analysis of both the surface collected and excavated molars from the site, Dr. Casamiquela has estimated that at least five to six individuals are represented including two young, one sub-adult, one adult, and two old animals. His estimation is based on the minimal number of bone elements.

Several excavated bone elements exhibit modifications (fig. 1.8). An ilium that had a modified branch attached to its center with bitumen was recovered from the top of MV-7 and the base of MV-6, about 10 cm below the level with other cultural materials; however, the vertically placed wood protruded up through the cultural stratum. The bone exhibits numerous shallow, narrow grooves approximately 3 mm in width on the surface which holds the wood.

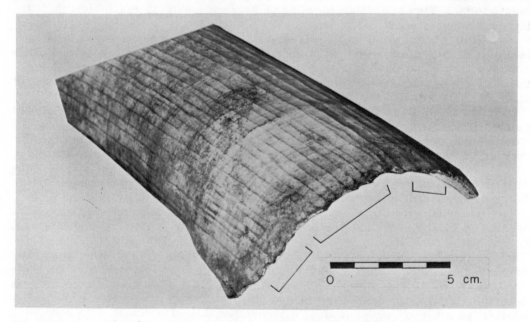

Figure 1.8.   Tusk fragment of mastodon showing modification along one edge. Brackets indicate heavy polish and diagonal striations.

Four other bones (2 femora, 1 skull fragment, and 1 long bone fragment) display grooves. Dr. Casamiquela has determined that these grooves were produced by human activity. He also noted that the tip of one long bone fragment from Area A exhibits several cuts and depressions similar to modifications made on flakers recovered from the lower levels of the Tagua-Tagua site.

The partial skeletons of the individual mastodons recovered from Area A are disarticulated, and 95% of the bones are fractured. Only the limb, torso, and head portions are represented in the collection. The disturbed nature of these skeletons can best be explained by butchering and food processing. No strong evidence suggests that natural mechanisms (e.g., frost fracture,

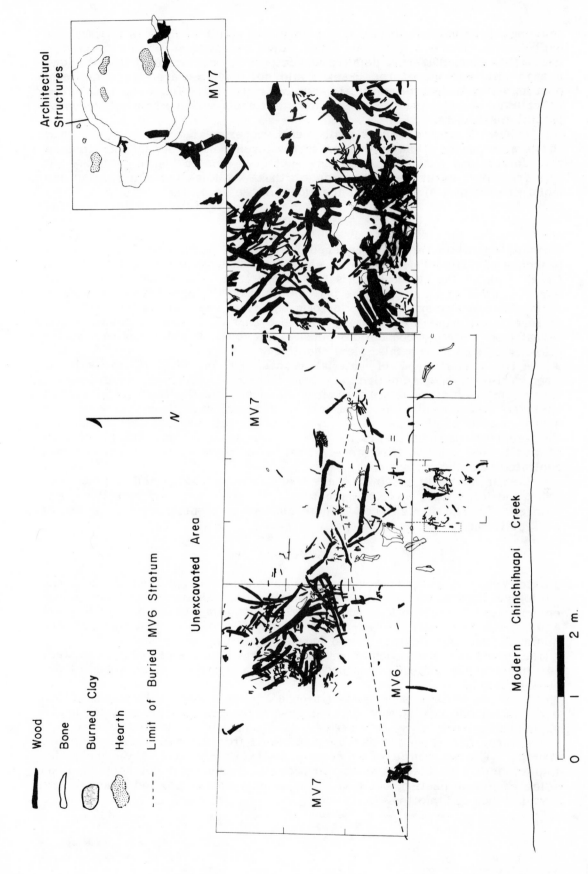

Figure 1.9.   Area A excavation showing distribution of bones, wood and architectural feature. Lithic materials are not shown here. Note the distinct clusters of materials forming a semi-circle. Areas outside of the block enclosures have not been excavated.

scavengers, or postdepositional disturbance as a result of flooding or wash) can explain the observed patterns. The combined studies of the ecological specialists Pino, Díaz-Vaz, Ramirez and Briones have determined that the low-energy environment of the creek could not have created any significant postdepositional disturbance of the cultural materials. The wood and leaves, of course, would have been the first materials to have been displaced by natural mechanisms.

Eight fractured mollusk shells were also excavated at the site. These shells were packed in clay inside one of the femur bones. As yet, biologists at the Universidad Austral de Chile have not been able to identify the species. The fractured nature and location of these shells at the site suggest that mollusks were part of the diet of the Monte Verde people.

Activity Areas

Archaeological materials recovered from Area A, B, and C indicate the presence of different activity areas along a 400 m long stretch of Chinchihuapi Creek. As all the cultural debris from these areas is contained in the upper part of MV-6 or on the surface of MV-7, and as the artifactual assemblages from these areas are similar in form and type, one can assume that these different activities are culturally related. Further archaeological work may reveal more concrete connections between Areas A, B, and C, as well as the presence of additional locales along the creek.

The spatial layout of materials recovered from the 42 m² excavated in Area A takes on a semicircular form (fig. 1.9). As yet, no geological formations, such as sloughs, depressions, or embankments, which might suggest that this layout resulted from natural mechanisms, have been observed. The northern side of this partially revealed semicircle has not been excavated. The semicircle is comprised of the architectural structure and multiple clusters of wood, bone, and modified stone. Most of the osteological remains are concentrated near the ancient creek bank.

Four spatially distinct clusters of modified wood, small fragments of bone, and lithic tools have been recorded. The wood artifacts exhibit cut and pointed tips and forked ends. These clusters are tentatively interpreted as work platforms at the water's edge.

Conclusions

Monte Verde is an archaeological site that provides significant cultural and ecological data to enable us to reconstruct and to explain not only the paleo-environmental conditions of south-central Chile some 12,000 to 15,000 years ago but also how early man adapted to them. The data suggest that both the minimally modified stone and wood industry were utilized to maintain a diversified economy. In addition, Monte Verde offers a unique opportunity to study the architecture of early man and the activity structure of an apparent occupational site.

Monte Verde is an important archaeological site not only because of its early date, but also because it is the first early man location reported in the subantarctic forest of South America. It is a unique site in that we have architecture, lithic, wood, and bone artifacts from an early site in the New World. The presence of a wood industry at the site is of particular importance. We also have the opportunity to document not only the wood selected for utilization, but also the chance to correlate wood function with certain types of lithic tools.

16

Acknowledgments

The research described was supported by the Universidad Austral de Chile, Valdivia, Chile; the University of Kentucky, Lexington, Kentucky; the National Science Foundation; the National Geographic Society; and the University Research Institute, the University of Texas, Austin, Texas. Professor Mauricio Van de Maele, Director, Museo de Historía y Antropología, Universidad Austral de Chile, Valdivia freely gave me his support and encouragement. I am also grateful to many Chilean colleagues for sharing their knowledge of Chilean prehistory. I am deeply indebted to my numerous Chilean friends and students who were patient, bold field workers often working under very harsh conditions. I also thank Michael B. Collins, William Brown, Lawrence Keely, Eric Gibson, Richard Boisvert, Susan Graham, and David Pollack for their assistance in the analysis of cultural materials, and my Andean colleagues for their discussions of the site. This paper is dedicated to the late Mr. Ivan von Leifner, a Hungarian-Chilean, who diligently worked with enthusiasm on the conservation of the wooden artifacts.

References

Briones, Claudio.
  n.d.   La vegetación de Monte Verde, Chile. Manuscript in possession of the author.

Casamiquela, Rodolfo.
  n.d.   Informe preliminar sobre los restos vertebrados de Monte Verde, Chile. Manuscript in possession of the author.

Collins, M. B., and Tom D. Dillehay.
  1981   The implications of the Lithic assemblage from Monte Verde, Chile, for Early Man Studies. In A. L. Bryan (editor) New Evidence for the Pleistocene Peopling of the Americas. Orono: Center for Early Man Studies.

Heusser, C. J.
  1966   Late Pleistocene pollen diagrams from southern Chile. Manuscript in possession of the author.

  1974   Vegetation and climate of the southern Chilean Lake district during and since the last interglaciation. Quaternary Research 4:290-315.

Hoganson, John W., and A. C. Ashworth.
  1982   The late-glacial climate of the Chilean Lake region implied by fossil beetles. Third North American Paleontological Convention.

Mercer, J. H.
  1972   Chilean glacial chronology 20,000 to 11,000 carbon-14 years ago: some global comparisons. Science 176:1118-1120.

Sanzana, Patricio.
  1980   Analísis geoarqueológico en gravas fracturadas de Monte Verde I, X Región, Chile. Tesis de Licenciatura en Filosofía y Ciencias Sociales. Universidad Austral de Chile, Valdivia.

2.

The Lomas of Paloma:
Human-Environment Relations in a
Central Peruvian Fog Oasis:
Archaeobotany and Palynology

Glendon H. Weir and J. Philip Dering

Abstract

The preliminary results of archaeobotanical, coprolite, and palynological studies of the central coastal Peruvian site of Paloma suggest that increasing human utilization between about 7,700 and 5,000 B.P. degraded the fragile lomas site's resources and environment, and that this degradation was human induced rather than due to climatic factors. This may have forced the Palomans to emphasize exploitation of a wider range of resource zones, including the littoral, riverine valleys and western flanks of the Andes, all within 50 km of the coast. The interpretation that human-caused environmental stress led to this degradation is supported by the plant remains and coprolite data recovered from the original archaeological context in close association with human burials, huts, and other features, including probability samples. Human pressure on plant and other resources of the lomas, coupled with the decreasing availability of local moisture due to gradual removal of the shrub and tree cover, led to a more intensive manipulation of some plants and exploitation of marine resources. The site settlement pattern indicates increasing sedentism, as do the findings of beans, curcurbits, and other early potential economic plants such as the tuberous begonia. The coprolite and archaeological plant data also suggest changing diets on the central coast of Peru. Ultimately, littoral and riverine resources appear to have become emphasized more than those of lomas and arid floodplain settings, with implications for the later emergence of social complexity outside of the lomas. Thus, problems of environmental degradation may have required solutions including greater emphasis on sedentism and an eventual transition to food production and complex societies on the central coast of Peru.

Introduction

The Paloma Project, carried out by an international team of researchers, is an interdisciplinary study of the human-environment relations of an Archaic (Preceramic) central Peruvian coastal settlement. Conceived in 1975, its objective, both then and now, is the holistic study of a well-preserved, extensive approximately 7,700- to 5,000-year-old site in order to gain a better understanding of a major stage of human history—the transition to dense settlement, food production, and increasing social complexity on the arid Peruvian coast.

Heretofore, our understanding of human occupation of the arid central Andes of western South America in Post-Pleistocene times was known primarily from work in the various caves and rockshelters of the highlands. Among these were Bird's (1965, 1967) work in Patagonia, and that of others in the Argentine cordillera (Gonzalez 1960), the highlands of Peru (Cardich 1958, 1964, 1974; Engel 1968; Lynch 1970; MacNeish 1969, 1970) and various caves of northern Chile and southern Peru (Engel 1968, 1981).

However, the lower arid coastal regions have not been as well understood. Our studies focus on a unique environmental and cultural setting, the lomas areas of the Andean foothills. These areas, called "fog oases" (Ellenberg 1958, 1959), have been the subject of intensive ongoing studies by our team since 1976. Our preliminary results suggest that the lomas areas were the loci of early human settlement along the Pacific coast of South America and were capable of supporting semisedentary settlements in the past.

Today the lomas are arid, barren habitats during part of the year, but, during the southern winter, they blossom into verdant vegetational zones which support brief but intensive grazing of livestock by transhumant highland herders. This is possible because of the phenomenon of the garua (or camanchaca as it is called further south)—a dense winter fog—which deposits moisture on the lomas between June and December in good years. These seasonally lush areas are now much degraded by intensive grazing, overcutting for firewood, and, we believe, by the past overuse of lomas resources during prehistoric and historic times.

Our studies and those of the other members of our interdisciplinary team of the Paloma settlement are providing new insights into Holocene occupations on the Peruvian coast. Data from the site, which was intermittently occupied over almost a 3,000-year time span from approximately 7,700 B.P. to later than 5,000 B.P., suggest that the environmental degradation was human induced rather than being due to climatic factors. In former times, apparently as recently as 35 years ago (Engel, personal communication), the lomas were covered with trees which enhanced retention of the fog-deposited moisture and formed lush, green habitats surrounded by arid coastal desert. As these unique habitats were increasingly exploited by human populations through time, the resulting degradation forced more intensive exploitation of a wider range of resource zones within a few kilometers of the site. As the Palomans' increasing population caused the floral and faunal resources of the lomas to become insufficient for their needs, they increasingly came to rely on marine resources, more intensive encouragement and management of plant foods, and, we believe, an eventual transition to food production elsewhere in the riverine valleys.

We believe our studies of the Paloma site are important in showing that the lomas were occupied at an early date, at least periodically, and apparently increasingly so over time until abandonment of the site. Our data also suggest that the Palomans may have initially been following a seasonal round of exploitation periodically using lomas, western flanks, riverine valley, and marine

resources.   Then, as populations grew and their needs for food increased, they
turned to a more sedentary lifestyle which included preadaptation to food
production.   The Paloma settlement spans a period of time critical to our understanding of the processes involved in this transition to sedentism and has
implications for subsequent increases in social complexity on the coast of Peru.

The Site of Paloma

The site of Paloma is located just north of the Chilca Valley, about 65 km
south of Lima (fig. 2.1), 4.5 linear km east of the Playa la Tiza on the Pacific
coast, and 7.5 linear km north of the central valley of the Quebrada de Chilca
(fig. 2.2).   The site begins at an altitude of 250 m, situated just below the
lower limits of a severely degraded lomas vegetation formation which extends
today to an elevation of 600 m, overlooking the Chilca Valley.

Figure 2.1.   Location of the Paloma settlement site (12b VII 613).

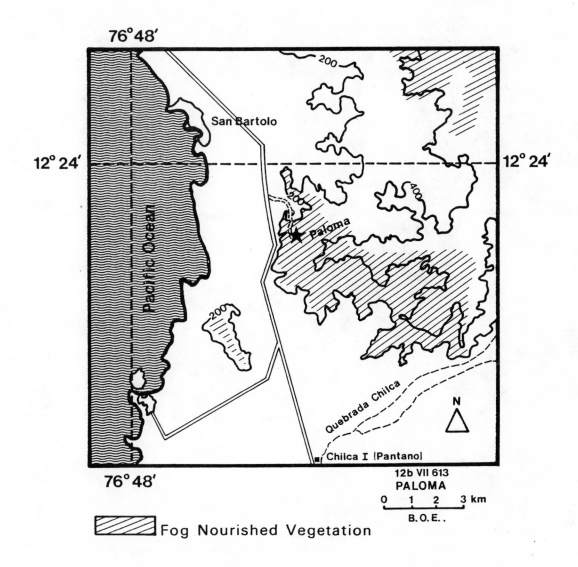

Fog Nourished Vegetation

Figure 2.2.   *Paloma site located just below the lower limits of a severely
degraded lomas vegetation.*

During its heyday, the Paloma settlement was culturally and ecologically
associated with the nearby Chilca Valley. The valley and the Lurin River
which enters the Pacific 18 km to the northwest form a catchment area which
included at least four exploitable resource zones in addition to the coastal
desert: (1) the littoral zone, (2) the river valleys, (3) the lomas and (4) the
western flanks of the Andes, all within 50 km of the coast. The Paloma site
is located at the edge of the Chilca Valley and has previously been recognized
by Engel (1968) as an ancient and excellent access route to the Peruvian
highlands. More recently, MacNeish (1977) has emphasized the strategic
location of the Paloma site within the Chilca-Lurin drainages.

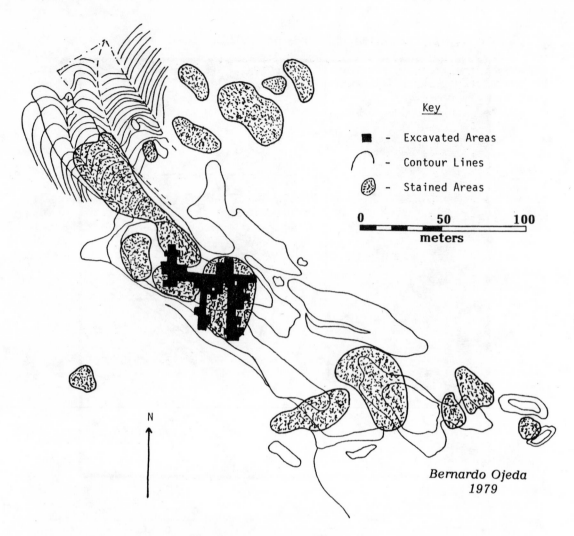

Key

■ - Excavated Areas

⌒ - Contour Lines

▧ - Stained Areas

0   50   100
meters

N

Bernardo Ojeda
1979

Figure 2.3.   *Map of the Paloma site (12b VII 613). Contour intervals indicate depth of deposits as determined by auger tests and excavations.*

The settlement of Paloma occupies some 15 hectares (Engel 1981) situated on a series of low hills in a then-lomas area at the very edge of the Chilca drainage system. Just below the modern lomas zone is a series of deeply stained, oval areas that represent the site (fig. 2.3), designated numerically as 12b VII 613, an Archaic (Preceramic) site according to Lumbreras's (1974) terminology.

The period of site occupation lasted from about 7,700 to later than 5,000 B.P., according to several series of radiocarbon dates; a recent extreme date is 7,735 ± 100 radiocarbon years (uncorrected). The sample on which this date is based was taken from a provisional lower level at the site. This level, however, is not the lowest area of the site. A series of radiocarbon dates by Engel in the general area of the Paloma site ranges from as old as 8,000 to 9,000 radiocarbon years (Engel, personal communication). The site appears to have been abandoned between 4,500 and 5,000 years ago but was periodically and briefly reoccupied in later times.

The oval, stained areas depicted in figure 2.3 are the remains of dwellings and human occupation debris, as well as unconsolidated shell midden some 4.5 linear km from the ocean. Each cubic meter of the shell-midden deposits weigh approximately 1,000 kg, of which about 300 kg are shell; the rest is composed of various plant, animal, cultural and sediment materials. The Paloma site is exceptionally rich in human burials, structures, and plant and animal remains preserved in a complex stratigraphy by the extreme aridity of the adjoining coastal Peruvian desert.

History of the Paloma Project

Engel (1981) located the site during a survey of the archaeological resources of the Chilca Valley area and conducted preliminary excavations there between 1973 and 1975. Lacking the necessary specialists for ecological and demographical analyses of the exceptionally well-preserved site and the numerous human burials, Engel invited Robert Benfer of the University of Missouri, Columbia to organize a research team. One of us (Weir) then became associated with the project. In 1976, the National Science Foundation funded both a pilot project to establish the feasibility of a longer term study of the human ecology, demography, and health of the Palomans, and also the archaeological excavations to provide these data. Later, in 1978, the other author (Dering) joined the project as a consultant in archaeobotany.

The 1976 fieldwork was accomplished as a cooperative project with the Center for Investigation of Arid Zones (Centro de Investigaciones de Zonas Aridas--C.I.Z.A.) of the National Agrarian University (Universidad Nacional Agraria--U.N.A.) of Peru. It involved researchers and students from a number of institutions in both Peru and the United States (C.I.Z.A., U.N.A.; University of Missouri, Columbia; Texas A&M University; University of Texas, Austin; and the University of California, Santa Barbara).

Based on the results of the 1976 excavations, the National Science Foundation funded a continued interdisciplinary research program in 1979 focusing on the excavation of more human burials and recovery of the associated plant remains and ecological evidence. Most recently, the National Science Foundation supported a further two-year program of analyses and syntheses of the rich and varied data base from the thirteen months of fieldwork from 1976 through 1980. Our paper presents an overview of our study of the archaeobotanical and palynological material and our preliminary findings to date.

Environment, Ecology and Plant Use of the Palomans

The lack of paleoenvironmental data from the arid western coast of South America, especially the coastal and Andean areas of Peru and Chile, has caused investigators to rely on data from other areas of South America. Vehik (1977) has suggested that the Paloma site may have been occupied in a warmer period following a cool and moist time. However, based on our more recent studies of the best available climatological evidence (Weir and Dering 1980), and the environmental indicators present in the plants and other evidence from the Paloma site, we now believe that the main period of the Archaic (Preceramic) occupation of the Paloma site more likely took place during a cool period, from about 6,500 to 5,000 B.P. This immediately followed a climatic optimum on the west coast of South America which began before 7,700 B.P. and lasted to about 6,500 B.P. We are currently planning to conduct a separate investigation in order to resolve the matter by coring a number of mid-Andean lakes and studying their environmental pollen data.

However, at this time, the lack of locally specific paleoenvironmental data has caused other investigators to rely on indirect ecological indicators in order to assess the evidence for any possible past patterns of environmental change during the various periods of site occupation on the coast and in other areas of Peru. Such indicators have included shifting settlement patterns (Moseley 1975; Cohen 1977), changing artifact assemblages, and isolated environmental observations (Lanning 1967; Lynch 1971). These indirect approaches to environmental reconstruction carry with them the risk of producing oversimplified models of past climatic change and their cultural correlates which have little or no basis in biological reality (Parsons 1970).

More recently, however, other investigators have begun pioneering the use of environmentally sensitive bioindicators, consisting of various flora and fauna, as a means of identifying local changes in ecology (Sarma 1974; Llagostera 1979). The approaches range in generality from inductions based on secondary evidence, as in Cohen (1977), or preliminary analyses of bioindicator data, as in Craig and Psuty (1968), to the construction of paleoenvironmental chronologies in restricted geographical regions (Sarma 1974; Llagostera 1979).

At Paloma, a wide range of floral and faunal indicators are preserved at the site permitting us to reconstruct more precisely the nature of the paleoenvironment during the period of occupation. The bioindicators consist of fossil pollen associated with the archaeological context of the site as compared to nonsite pollen data; plant macrofossil remains; charcoal and wood; and vertebrate and invertebrate animals, including shellfish which are preserved in great numbers. In addition, pollen studies of the modern environment are being conducted in order to establish a modern baseline for comparison with the past environmental data (Weir 1976; 1978). The data recovered from human coprolites at the site, including fossil pollen, plant macrofossils, and evidence for human endoparasites, are also being studied and will provide direct evidence of the foodstuffs consumed by the Palomans and the state of their health (see Benfer, this volume).

The Paloma site lies at the interface of several different ecological and vegetation zones (the lomas, western Andean flanks, riverine valleys, coastal desert, and the littoral), offering us the opportunity to compare the human exploitation of these different areas and their resources and to examine their relationships to the Paloma settlement.

The plant use practices of the Palomans may be viewed from the perspective of previous models of the origins of food production and of the introduction of cultigens to the Peruvian coast. In Peru, hunting and gathering societies developed into economies based on food production between about 6,000 and 3,000 B.P. (Cohen 1975). During this period, the hunting and gathering populations of the Andes and the coast became increasingly sedentary, and many cultigens appeared for the first time (MacNeish 1977). However, the details of this economic shift have not yet been adequately described, although several essentially undocumented hypotheses have been proposed to explain its cause.

Heretofore, there appears to be no convincing evidence that plants were domesticated early on the coast of Peru (Cohen 1975). Thus, the data in table 2.1 clearly document a time lag between the early appearance of cultigens in the Andean highlands and their later introduction on the coast as full-fledged domesticates. For example, all of the cultigens from the Ancon-Chillon area of the central Peruvian coast, the most completely studied sequence to date, appear in advanced domesticated form (Cohen 1975). In table 2.1, the first appearance of five major cultigens in the highlands, on the coast, and at the Paloma site are compared. We are still awaiting definitive dating results for some of these cultigens pending final stratigraphic interpretations of recently

Table 2.1.   First appearance of five major cultigens in Highlands, on
coast and at Paloma.

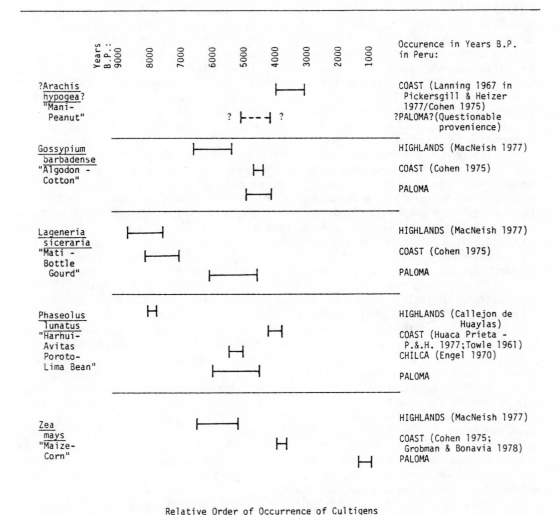

Relative Order of Occurrence of Cultigens

received radiometric dates.   Nonetheless, our preliminary data on the timing of the introduction of cultigens do tend to support the interpretation of delayed coastal acceptance.   During the excavations at Paloma, preliminary evidence for the early introduction of two such cultigens was at first thought to exist.   Several ears of Zea mays (corn or maize), which were found in association with a canine burial in one area of the site, appeared to be of considerable antiquity, based on the formation of some 20 cm of a thick, calichelike layer covering the deposit.   However, preliminary evaluation of the corn by Robert M. Bird (personal communication) suggested that the corn was from a considerably later period.   This was subsequently confirmed when radiocarbon determinations showed that the corn dated from about 1,830 ± 85 years B.P. (uncorrected).   Apparently, the rate of formation of the calichelike material covering the corn cache was considerably faster than at first estimated and only gave the impression of the presence of early Preceramic corn in this instance. The other cultigen involved the possibility of a single, apparently unique, and highly fragmentary specimen of Arachis hypogea (peanut or mani) fruit which was found in a peripheral deposit at the edge of the Paloma site. The field identification of this plant specimen as that of a possible cultigen was made by a knowledgeable Peruvian workman, since deceased, associated with the Paloma excavations. However, since neither of the authors was present when the specimen was found, the workman could not be interviewed, and the sample was too fragmentary for laboratory analyses, we were unable to confirm the identification. No other remains of corn or peanuts have been identified to date from any other materials excavated at Paloma. Our considered opinion of these two unique instances of possible early cultigens is that they were probably intrusive from later periods of occupation in the area of the site.

However, the knowledge of the timing of the spread of cultigens from the highlands to the coast is poor. We believe that it is possible that cultigens could have appeared on the coast in areas beyond the Ancon-Chillon drainage earlier than is usually accepted. The Chilca Valley to date does have two interesting, if controversial, dates for cultigen occurrence: the appearance of Phaseolus lunatus (lima bean) on the coast at 5,300 B.P. and the potato (Solanum tuberosum) at 10,000 B.P. high above the Chilca Valley at the Tres Ventanas cave site (Engel 1970). Thus, the possibility exists that cultigen introductions occurred earlier in this region than in other areas of coastal Peru.

In addition, the Paloma site has been recognized by MacNeish (1977) as a strategic location occupied during the crucial time of the beginnings of agriculture on the coast, between 4,500 and 6,000 B.P. In the area of the Chilca Valley and the nearby Lurin River drainages, the coastal mountains rise rapidly, compressing the life zones into relatively compact geographical areas. Although the Paloma site is somewhat more than a half-day walk from the western highlands (MacNeish 1977), it is clearly located in a strategic position from which the local seasonal resources could be supplemented by other resources in the nearby Chilca Valley, the littoral zone, and the nearby flanks of the coastal mountains (all within 50 km of the site) if they were unoccupied and available to the Palomans. The possible early occurrence of cultigens in and around the Chilca Valley, and the area's strategic location adjacent to the river valleys, ocean, and the western Andean flanks, suggest that the Paloma site could have been an early conduit of cultigen diffusion between the centers of highland domestication and the coast.

Another line of evidence suggests the possibility that the Chilca-Lurin area may have been a center of early coastal agriculture. Cohen (1975:113) reports that, on the coast, in particular the Ancon-Chillon region, "there is no evidence of any independent experimentation with domestication of lesser local crops..." However, at Paloma there is now an indication of local experimentation with Begonia geraniifolia, a lomas plant which has a substantial edible tuber with "eyes" similar to that of the potato, Solanum tuberosum. In certain areas of the site, B. geraniifolia tubers are the most frequently encountered plant macrofossil, and the "eyes" are the most common part.

In spite of the fact that this plant now grows wild in all lomas surrounding the Ancon-Chillon area (Ferreyra 1953; Torres-Guevara 1979), B. geraniifolia was not reported from the Ancon-Chillon region by Cohen (1975). This plant is quite common today even in the most heavily degraded lomas, including that of modern Paloma. There are three possible explanations for why this plant was absent from the report of the Ancon-Chillon studies: (1) it was overlooked as a food source by the prehistoric populations, which we doubt because of its ubiquitous nature; (2) the plant was overlooked by Cohen; or (3) the Encanto complex sites were not located on extinct lomas. Of these possibilities, it appears most likely that Cohen overlooked the plant remains, as fragments of B. geraniifolia appear to be present in the debris from exposed cuts at the site. However, we have not examined the Ancon-Chillon sites intensively to test this proposition.

Since there appears to be no modern, historical, or ethnographic record of the use of this plant for food, we have experimented with various means of preparing this plant. However, to date, the acrid taste, regardless of the method of cooking, has defeated our attempts to make it palatable to modern tastes as food. Our investigations are continuing, however, and our ultimate results will be reported later in detail.

At Paloma, the modern distribution of both B. geraniifolia and another lomas plant, Hymenocallis amancaes (amancay), is also closely associated with ancient terraces of Lapa-Lapa origin, a prehistoric occupation of the quebradas just above the site, but of a later period (Engel 1981). This distribution, along with the fact that B. geraniifolia remains constitute one of the most common plant remains at Paloma, suggest that the prehistoric occupants may have encouraged and managed it as an economic plant, if not as a semicultigen.

To test this hypothesis we have successfully experimented with reproducing B. geraniifolia from tuber eye fragments, as is commonly done with the domesticated potato. Since B. geraniifolia can be reproduced in the same manner as Solanum tuberosum, the possibility exists that the plant was managed as an economic plant by the prehistoric inhabitants at Paloma, and such management or encouragement could indicate a form of preadaptation to agriculture at this site and possibly, by extension, to the coast.

Archaeobotany

Yet another line of evidence concerning the plant use practices of the Palomans is the plant macrofossil remains excavated in intimate archaeological association with a broad range of burials, houses, features, and apparent food processing areas. These plant remains are bioindicators of past plant utilization practices, as well as of possible past environmental conditions. Because of the tremendous amount of material recovered from the site, the sample studied to date is still relatively incomplete in comparison to the materials yet to be analyzed.

A total of well over six thousand plant macrofossil remains from the three major occupation levels at Paloma (Levels 200, 300 and 400) have been examined. This preliminary data base contains some thirty-two hundred pieces of wood and charcoal, nineteen hundred seventy-three seeds, and hundreds of fragments of culms, fruits, leaves, roots, and tubers. To date, thirty six different plant taxa have been identified in the macrofossil sample, although a number of others remain unidentified, and more are being recovered from hundreds of probability samples at our laboratories.

The identified plants recovered from the Paloma archaeological sample (table 2.2) can be placed in four general categories on the basis of their modern distributions (table 2.3): (1) plants that still occur in the Paloma lomas, (2) plants common at other nearby coastal lomas but no longer at Paloma, (3) modern riverine and coastal plants that probably were collected from the environs of the Chilca Valley in the past, and (4) plants that occur today, and presumably in the past, from higher elevations along the western slopes of the Andes. (An exception to this categorization is Tillandsia species—cardo and others—one of the few genera of plants that grows today and grew previously in the coastal desert between the littoral zones and the flanks of the coastal mountains.)

Table 2.2.   Plant specimens identified from La Paloma archaeological samples.

Wood:	Seeds, Fruits:
Croton alnifolius	Lycopersicon peruvianum
Piqueria sp.	Armatocereus matucanensis
Heliotropium sp.	Neoraimondii macrostibis
Caesalpinia sp.	Carica candicans
Prosopis sp.	Asclepias sp.
Trixis paradoxica	Schinus molle
Cestrum auriculatum	Stenomesson sp.
Salix sp.	Loxanthocereus sp.
Gynerium saggitatum (woody monocot)	Hymenocallis amancaes
	Galvezia fruticosa
Herbaceous Plants (Vegetative parts):	Lageneria siceraria
Tillandsia spp.	**Domesticate Plant Remains:**
Scirpus sp.	
Cyperus sp.	Psidium guayaba
Typha sp.	**Arachis hypogea
Eragrostis sp.	*Cucurbita ficifolia
*Stipa sp.	*Phaseolus sp.
Sporobolus virginicus	**Zea mays
*Festuca sp.	
Oxalis sp.	
Begonia geraniifolia	* tentative
Nolana sp.	** from intrusive deposits

Table 2.3.   Present distribution of plants recovered from Paloma site archaeological samples.

Loma Paloma:	Coastal Desert:
Croton alnifolius	Tillandsia spp.
Piqueria sp.	
Heliotropium sp.	**Riverine Chilca Valley:**
Trixis paradoxica	
Tillandsia spp.	Salix sp
Oxalis sp..	Gynerium saggitatum
*Begonia geraniifolia	Scirpus sp.
Nolana humifosa	Cyperus sp.
Carica candicans	Typha sp.
Loxanthocereus sp.	Sporobolus virginicus
Hymenocallis amancaes	Schinus molle
Valeriana sp.	Lageneria siceraria
Eragrostis sp.	Galvezia fruticosa
Stipa sp.	Menthostachys mollis
	Prosopis sp.
Other Coastal Lomas:	Baccharis sp.
Caesalpinia spinosa	**Western Andean Flanks:**
Capparis sp.	
Cestrum auriculatum	Neoraimondia macrostibis (800 m)
Stenomesson sp.	Armatocereus matucaensis (1000 m)
	Haagocereus sp. (1800 m)

*not present in ecological zones outside of the lomas

Many plants not now present at the Paloma site have been identified in the archaeological sample (table 2.3). Possible explanations for the contrast between the botanical components of the past and those of today are presented in the discussions below of the modern distributions of plants across the various ecological zones.

The Lomas of Paloma

Fourteen of the plants identified from the Paloma archaeological record still grow in the modern lomas. The most abundant of these plant remains include stems of the common lomas shrubs Piqueria sp., Croton alnifolius, Heliotropium sp. and Trixis paradoxica. These plants were obviously used for firewood, as evidenced by their charred remains and the archaeological context, as were the bromeliads Tillandsia latifolia and T. purpurea. These plants grow throughout the coastal desert immediately below the margins of the modern lomas of Paloma (table 2.4), and are used in folk medicine as antidepressants and other purposes (Vasquez-Nuñez 1974).

Lomas grasses were also a prominent component of building materials at Paloma, especially for the roofs of huts, and were often encountered on house floors and in midden deposits at the site. Identification of the lomas grasses is still tentative in some cases, but their prominence should be emphasized.

Other plants used as food which were included in the archaeological sample were the columnar cactus Loxanthocereus, and the fruits of the mito (Carica candicans). Loxanthocereus has a very tasty fruit that ripened sporadically during our observations between August 1979 and February 1980. The fruit of the mito tree is still consumed in the countryside and was observed in association with contemporary human habitations in the mid-range elevations of the western Andean slopes between 2,700 and 3,200 m. The last trees which occur in the Paloma lomas today are mitos, and they are also a plant common at other Peruvian coastal lomas that we have visited over the last few years.

One other plant which may have had economic usage in the past is Valeriana pinnatifida (alberjilla). Vasquez-Nuñez (1974) lists a Valeriana species that was historically used as a tranquilizer in folk medicine on the Peruvian coast.

Common Plants in Other Central Peruvian Lomas

The trees Capparis prisca (chaydo) and Caesalpinia spp. are common at other central Peruvian lomas that are not as heavily degraded as are the modern lomas at Paloma. These two trees, along with the shrub Cestrum auriculatum (chamo or tundio) were present archaeologically in the earlier levels at Paloma (Levels 400 and 300), but had disappeared by the time of Level 200 about 4,920 B.P. The possibility that the lomas were heavily degraded by the prehistoric inhabitants of Paloma, through stripping of the arboreal overstory for firewood, is discussed below. Caesalpinia spinosa (tara or taya), one of the common lomas trees, is used as a remedy for gastrointestinal illnesses on the coast of Peru (Vasquez-Nuñez 1974), and it may have been similarly used in the past.

Riverine Chilca Valley

The residents of Paloma apparently drew heavily on the resources of the nearby Chilca Valley. Even allowing for some radical and unlikely changes in precipitation patterns, several plants in the archaeological record at Paloma obviously grew in a riverine valley environment. Among these were important building materials at the site such as Salix sp. (sauce), Gynerium saggitatum (cana brava) and other as yet unidentified canes, and Scirpus spp. (junco). Junco was commonly twined into burial mats and wrappings. Salix sp. and Galvezia fruticosa (curi or pitau) are both phreatophytes with deep tap roots which prefer river margins and other areas where there is an extensive underground reservoir of water. The canes also thrive best in swales, and junco must grow in standing water for at least part of the year.

Three other valley economic plants identified from the Paloma samples were Schinus molle (molle), Mentostachys mollis (muna), and Baccharis sp. (probably chchilca). Although comparatively infrequent in the archaeological sample, molle is one of the most prominent trees of the western slopes of the Andes today. It is most common in the sunnier inland portions of the modern Chilca Valley, where underground water is available. Molle fruits are an excellent antispasmodic for a severely upset stomach and can also be used to treat colds, coughs, and rheumatism (Cerrate 1979; Horkheimer 1973). Mentostachys mollis is similarly used to treat gastrointestinal problems, and species of Baccharis are taken as an infusion to treat coughs (Vasquez-Nuñez 1974).

The fruits of Prosopis spp. (algarrobo) are frequently used as a tonic in Peru and are a well known traditional food source of hunter-gatherers in both Peru and the southwestern United States. Horkheimer (1973) also mentions that P. limensis fruits were used as an emergency food by later agricultural groups. Judging from its archaeological distribution at Paloma, it was probably used as an occasional food staple. Based on its present distribution, algarrobo (or algarroba) is the most likely of all the plants listed in table 2.3 to have grown outside riverine valley environments in the lomas of the past. On the other hand, the remains of Prosopis were not among the most frequent plant remains in the Paloma samples, suggesting that the tree may have been extra-local even then.

Western Andean Flanks

Three cacti from this resource zone provide the most convincing evidence yet uncovered that the inhabitants of Paloma were familiar with, and commonly used, plants from the higher elevations of the western Andean slopes. This suggests a vertical economy, at least in part, with perhaps seasonal utilization of these and similar upslope plant resources during certain periods of the occupation of the Paloma site. Neoraimondia macrostibis is a giant columnar cactus that grows inland and upslope from the coastal fog belt at elevations as low as 800 m, but it is most common around 1,100 m according to our observations. Armatocereus matucanensis (cuchi) grows at a slightly higher elevation today, from perhaps 1,000 m upwards. On the central coast of Peru in the general area of the Paloma site, Haagocereus (pitahaya) was found growing at about 1,800 m.

During the Paloma occupation, the distribution of these cacti could have been different than it is today. For example, a very slight increase in available moisture from precipitation at lower elevations could have significantly extended their vertical distribution. However, the ability of cacti to actually grow in a lomas area that typically remains shrouded in dense winter fog for several months of the year would probably be limited by such factors as fungal growth and the other rigors of a cloudy, humid, and cool environment. Our judgement is that the past distribution of these cacti was essentially similar to the modern distributions, and prompted a vertical harvesting pattern for the fruits and other parts of these plants from the upland slopes. Today the cacti of the upper edges of the coastal desert are about 12 to 15 km from the Paloma site, and, in the case of Haagocereus, is a 25 to 30 km walk.

Table 2.4. Modern plant specimens from the Paloma Site area today.

Name	Herbarium	Pollen	Seed/Fruit	Wood
Croton ruizanus	x	x		
Piqueria peruviana	x	x		
Heliotropium arborescens	x	x		x
Tillandsia latifolia	x	x		
Commelina fasiculata	x	x		
Oxalis sp.	x	x		
Hymenocallis amanacaes	x	x		
Begonia geraniifolia	x	x	x (tuber)	
Nicotiana paniculata	x	x		
Lycopersicon peruvianum	x	x	x	
Cereus (Armatocereus) sp.	x	x	x	
Caesalpinia tinctoria	x	x	x	x
Carica candicans	x	x	x	x
Croton alnifolius	x	x	x	x
Nolana humifosa	x	x		
Bromus catharticus	x	x		
Pepperomia atoconga	x	x		
Pepperomia hillili	x	x		
Vicia lomensis	x	x		
Solanum sp.	x	x		
Solanum tuberiferum	x	x		
Eragrostis peruviana	x	x		
Chenopodium petiolare	x	x	x	
Anthericum eccoremorrhizum	x	x		
Loasa urens	x	x		
Nicandra physaloides	x	x		
Anagallis arvensis	x	x		
Sicyos baderoa	x	x		
Heliotropium angiospermum	x	x		x
Silene sp.	x	x		
Piqueria pubescens	x	x	x	x
Lycopersicon hirsutum	x	x		
Trixis paradoxa	x	x		x
Coldenia ferreyrii	x	x		x
Geranium limae	x	x		
*Alnus jorulensis	x	x		x
Pluchea chingoyo	x	x		
Begonia octopetala	x	x	x (tuber)	
Mentzelia cordifolia	x	x		
Cyperus sp.	x	x	x	
Scirpus sp.	x	x	x	
Tillandsia purpurea	x	x		
Prosopis chilensis	x	x	x	x
Salix chilensis	x	x	x	x
Valeriana pinnatifida	x	x		

*Normally highland plant, but also occurs in coastal river valleys.

This does suggest that at least certain past distributions of these plants may have included areas closer to the Paloma lomas than is currently the case, since the immediate catchment area of the site is a more likely procurement source than the more distant desert loci.

Interestingly, cacti of the western slopes usually flower and fruit in the Austral summer, a time when the garua winter fog is absent from the coast. The possibility of determining seasonality of usage from this observation is, however, reduced by the ease with which cactus fruit may be dried, stored and presumably transported in this area. We believe it is quite possible that, for example, the fruit may have been dried and stored in March and possibly consumed by the Palomans in June or later. However, because the seeds recovered from food storage contexts at the site are in the process of having their identifications confirmed, this remains speculation on our part.

Our preliminary assessment of the plant macrofossil record at the site demonstrates that the inhabitants of Paloma were exploiting several different ecological and resource zones, apparently at different times of the year. The Palomans were not restricting themselves to gathering plants from only the lomas, they were also seasonally collecting plants from the river valleys, the higher elevations of the Andean slopes, and from the coastal desert floor.

Charcoal and Firewood

We have recently completed a study of the firewood and charcoal remains recovered from hearths at the Paloma site (Dering and Weir n.d.). In contrast to many of the other plant remains at the site, the contents of the hearths show that most firewood was collected from the lomas of Paloma. Although some recycling of woody house construction materials was observed, the woody lomas plants were predominant.

This significant finding demonstrates a potential for overusing and thus damaging the delicate relationship that exists between vegetation structure and the capture of available moisture from fog precipitation by these plants. A woody overstory is critical to the viability of the lomas vegetation formation, since trees and shrubs act as vertical condensation and collection surfaces for the thick winter fogs which roll in from the sea. Today, tree-covered modern lomas on the central coast of Peru receive 500 to 900 mm of total precipitation from this source during the Austral winter (Torres-Guevara 1979; López-Ocaña, personal communication, 1980). This is more than six times the amount of moisture captured by treeless lomas vegetation alone, such as is the case at Paloma today. The degradation or removal of the tree and shrub cover would result in an almost instantaneous reduction in the amount of available or effective moisture retained in a lomas formation.

We believe that even a stable, much less an increasing population at Paloma could have severely strained the woody lomas overstory vegetation over time through use as firewood. Thus the importance of a woody overstory to the stability of the lomas vegetation formation would have been at cross-purposes to its role in a village economy as an important source of fuel for the fires. Firewood is a precious commodity even today in western Peru. The river valleys and lomas have often been stripped of Prosopis, Caesalpinia, Capparis and Schinus spp., in addition to a number of other comparatively minor woody species of plants. For example, at the lomas of Iguanil, several kilometers up the coast, a Caesalpinia woodland has disappeared over the last fifteen years; all that remains is a maze of stumps, and even these are being carefully rooted out of the ground for firewood. The past inhabitants of Paloma may have overused their lomas firewood resources, and for this reason alone have seriously degraded their local environment over time. Reversing such a trend would have been difficult or impossible even if the population remained stable. It is apparent that the firewood factor alone was sufficient to have had a severe impact on the local ecology and environment direct Paloma lomas.

Table 2.5. Species composition of woody plants from Paloma hearths listed in descending order of abundance.

LEVEL 400:	LEVEL 300:	LEVEL 200:
Piqueria	Piqueria	Piqueria
Croton	Heliotropium	Croton
Heliotropium	Tillandsia	Tillandsia
Tillandsia	Gynerium	Gynerium
Capparis	Croton	Heliotropium
Gynerium	Caesalpinia	
Caesalpinia		
Cestrum		
Prosopis		

At many modern central Peruvian lomas, the species abundance of the woody overstory is linked directly to the condition and stability of the vegetation. A slightly degraded area retains a richer species composition of the woody overstory, while a heavily degraded lomas which has been cut over for firewood is depauperate in woody species (Torres-Guevara 1979). By charting changes in the plant macrofossil assemblages of firewood and charcoal through time, it was possible to monitor the condition of the lomas from the times of Levels 400 through 200 (table 2.5).

The wood and charcoal identified from Levels 200, 300 and 400 at Paloma show that a reduction in abundance of woody species took place over time. The most heavily exploited firewood was found to be an aromatic Compositae shrub, Piqueria spp. (chichis), that grows no higher than 1.5 m. In studies conducted by other members of our research team, this shrub was found to be highly flammable (Stocker personal communication, 1979), apparently as a result of the volatile oils in the woody stems and leaves (Dering and Weir n.d.). The most interesting aspect of the firewood study is the finding that not even during early Level 400 times did the Paloma hearths yield many branches or twigs larger than a few centimeters in diameter, although apparently a reduction in stem diameter in wood took place from Level 400 through 200 times (table 2.6).

Thus we concluded that there was a loss of woody species over time coupled with a reduction in the stem diameter of Paloma firewood. Apparently not only were tree species disappearing from the lomas, but those available for firewood were becoming smaller. A reduction in the woody overstory on a lomas can also be equated with a reduction in the available moisture from the winter fog, which, in a delicately balanced, marginal environment, means slower growth for all associated plants. As a result, the firewood shortage which plagues Peru today also confronted the inhabitants of Paloma several thousand years ago.

The exact causes and complete history of this shortage of wood has yet to be completely elucidated and detailed at the Paloma site. The key lies in many hundred more samples of plant remains and pollen samples from the lower level deposits at Paloma which have yet to be completely analyzed.

Table 2.6.   Average stem diameters of woody plants
from the Paloma site fire hearths.

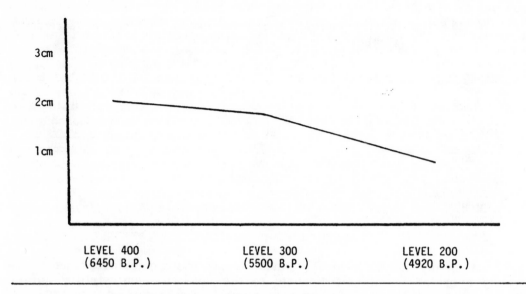

LEVEL 400	LEVEL 300	LEVEL 200
(6450 B.P.)	(5500 B.P.)	(4920 B.P.)

Archaeological and Environmental Palynology

Over six hundred fossil and modern pollen samples have been recovered from a wide variety of archaeological contexts, including burials, house floors, and food processing implements (such as batan grinding stones and others), as well as from archaeological and modern sediments.   In addition, atmospheric samples and modern comparative pollen collections have been compiled to provide a measure of the modern environmental and floral parameters in order that a modern data baseline may be used with which to compare the fossil pollen data (Weir 1976, 1978).   Several hundred additional fossil pollen samples from probability squares have also been collected and are undergoing laboratory analyses.

Our pollen studies to date show that some of the modern atmospheric and surface samples which were collected in order to establish a modern pollen rain baseline (representing the plants there today) are relatively depauperate in pollen, as are certain categories of fossil pollen samples collected at the site. This is not an unexpected or unusual phenomenon in certain types of arid land soils (Weir 1976), such as are present at the Paloma site today.

Only in anaerobic conditions typically present in bogs, or in sediments below water tables, are conditions ideal for preservation of pollen.   Under these conditions, in which the pollen is not exposed to the oxidizing effects of the atmosphere and other agents of pollen degradation, there is a reasonable expectation that most pollen grains representing the fossil pollen rain and the past vegetation (and cultural activities) will be preserved.   On the other hand, in most arid land surface sediments such as those that exist today in the area of the Paloma site, the likelihood of the pollen being preserved in representative amounts precisely reflecting all components of the vegetation is not good. Biological, chemical, and physical agents of pollen degradation are more active in these soils, and result in the likelihood that only a portion of the pollen grains deposited over time will survive in the fossil pollen record.

The majority of pollen grains produced by the plants in most plant communities come from anemophilous, or wind-pollinated, species. Various trees, shrubs, and other plants produce relatively prodigious amounts of pollen (as compared to entomophilous species, pollinated by insects, and plants pollinated by other means), which are widely dispersed by the prevailing wind patterns. Wind-pollinated plants typically make up over 90% of the pollen rain in such communities. Other plants, such as insect-pollinated herbaceous plants, produce relatively fewer pollen grains which make up only a few percent of the pollen rain.

Interestingly, we have found that the vegetation of many lomas areas typically has a much higher component of various insect-pollinated plants, which produce relatively much smaller amounts of pollen, most of which remains localized in the immediate vicinity of the plants. Such is the case in the lomas of Paloma today, where much of the modern pollen rain from the local vegetation is composed of insect-pollinated herbaceous plants, representative of the modern distribution of the vegetation in spite of the preservation biases of arid land soil (Weir 1978).

The atypically high distribution of entomophilous pollen types which we have found in the modern, and in some past, pollen spectra from the Paloma site suggests that it may be related both to the unusually high species diversity of the insect-pollinated component of the lomas vegetation, as well as to our inferred degradation of the woody plant component of the Paloma lomas over time. This is so because the majority of the woody species are usually anemophilous, or wind-pollinated, and thus the relative scarcity of these pollen types supports our hypothesis of the reduction of woody plants over time at Paloma.

The atypical distribution of insect-pollinated plants also attests to the long period of time that insect pollinators have had to develop their specialized pollinator-plant relationships (Aguilar, personal communication). Thus, we infer that the lomas type of vegetation formation has been stable for the relatively long period of time during the Holocene and terminal Pleistocene needed to evolve these specialized relationships. This observation also suggests that the species diversity of the insect-pollinated plants in the lomas vegetation formation is of some antiquity, regardless of the relative presence or absence of the shrub and tree overstory over time. Since such specialized adaptations typically appear and persist in a relatively narrow range of environmental conditions, it is possible to infer that significant alterations in climatic patterns have not been a feature of the regional climate of the lomas areas for at least thousands of years. Table 2.7 shows the species composition of modern Paloma lomas plants and their pollination vectors or means of dispersal.

Thus, today the vegetation of the Paloma lomas is composed mainly of insect-pollinated herbs and shrubs; this is also reflected in the modern pollen rain collected from surface sediments at the site. Apparently, however, this was not always the case during the period of human occupation in the past. Instead, our data show that then the anemophilous, or wind-pollinated, tree pollen types represented a much larger component of the fossil pollen rain in the area. Some of these high-frequency pollen types are shown in table 2.8, and represent parent plants that were present in the past at the site, but are either absent or present in much-reduced numbers today.

Some of these fossil pollen types represent various trees, including <u>Prosopis</u> and <u>Salix</u> species, Compositae (composite) Family shrubs and herbs, <u>Gramineae</u> (grass) Family grasses, and Chenopodiaceae (chenopod) Family plants and others, implying that the past vegetation of the Paloma lomas region was far richer in certain trees, shrubs and grasses than is the case today. These fossil pollen types were found in association not only with culturally sterile sediments, but also with archaeological sediments and artifacts such as grinding stones, from house floors and in coprolites.

Other fossil pollen types found in archaeological contexts also probably reflect the use of economic plants by the Palomans. These include the fossil pollen types of the Euphorbiaceae (euphorb) Family, including such representatives as Croton sp.; Cactaceae (cactus) Family with two different pollen types; Cyperaceae (sedge) Family; Typhaceae (cattail) Family; Bromeliaceae (bromeliad) Family such as Tillandsia spp.; and three different pollen types of

Table 2.7.   Modern Paloma plants and their pollination methods, agents, or vectors.

Plant Species:	Primary Pollination Methods, Agents or Vectors: Entomophilous, etc. or self:	Anemophilous:
Piqueria sp.		x
Trixis sp.		x
Eragrostis sp.		x
Stipa sp.		x
Peperomia sp. (in part ?)		x
Parietaria sp. (in part ?)		x
Croton alnifolius	x	
Heliptropium sp.	x	
Tillandsia	x	
Oxalis sp.	x	
Begonia geraniifolia	x	
Nolana humifosa	x	
Carica candicans	x	
Loxanthocereus sp.	x	
Hymenocalles amancaes	x	
Valeriana sp.	x	
Stellaria media	x	
Heliotropium angiospermum	x	
Urocarpidium peruvianum	x	
Capsella bursa-pastoris	x	
Euphorbia sp.	x	
Calandrinia ruizii	x	
Passiflora suberosa	x	
Tigridia lutea	x	
Solanum phyllanthum	x	
Bowelsia palmata	x	
Cryptantha granulosa	x	
Fortunatia biflora	x	
Anthericum eccremorrhizum	x	
Tetragonia crystallina	x	
Commelina jamesonii	x	
Cacabus prostrata	x	
Salvia rhombifolia	x	
Stenomesson coccineum	x	
Crassula connata	x	
Lycopersicon peruvianum	x	
Dicliptera tomentosa	x	

Table 2.8.   Archaeological or past Paloma Lomas plants not present today and their pollination methods.

Plant Species	Primary Pollination Methods, Vectors or Agents:	
	Entomophilous, etc. or self	Anemophilous
Gramineae spp. (several types)		x
*Gynerium sp.		x
*Scirpus sp.		x
Compositae spp. (Low Spine type)		x
Chenopodiaceae-Amaranthus pollen types		x
*Typha sp.		x
*Cyperaceae sp.		x
Asclepias sp.		x
*Prosopis sp.		x (Secondary)
*Salix sp.		x (Secondary)
Solanaceae (three pollen types)	x	
*Schinus sp.	x	
Capparis sp.	x (in part ?)	
Caesalpinia sp.	x (in part ?)	
Cestrum auriculatum	x	
**Armatocereus sp.	x	
**Neoraimondii sp.	x	
*Galvezia sp.	x	
*Lageneria sp.	x	
*Menthostachys sp.	x (in part ?)	
*Baccharis sp.	x	
**Haagocereus sp.	x	

*Riverine valley or littoral zone plant today in distribution.
**Western Andean slopes plant today in distribution.
No asterisk.   Known from other coastal lomas today but not present at site.

the Solanaceae (nightshade or potato) Family. In addition, fossil pollen types of the Anacardiaceae (sumac) Family, possibly Schinus species, and the Capparidaceae (caper) Family Capparis species were present, as was the fossil pollen type of Carica of the Caricaceae (carica) Family.

While not conclusive in themselves, the presence of these pollen types in the sediments and archaeological contexts of Paloma, in conjunction with the plant macrofossil remains discussed above, tends to support the conclusion that a significant range of economically useful plants was available to, and probably used by, the Palomans. Although our pollen studies are in a preliminary interpretive stage, it is still possible to conclude that the past plant environment of Paloma was considerably different from that of today, and that it changed over time in significant ways, becoming relatively depauperate in woody species and plants which are no longer found in the Paloma lomas. These data also suggest the local plant environment was under increasing stress from long-term human occupation and use, rather than from changing climatic regimes in the region. In addition, the presence of the fossil pollen types of potentially economic plants, along with the plant macrofossil remains, suggests the exploitation of a number of plant species with well-documented uses today, in the historic past, and elsewhere archaeologically. Finally, these data also imply that the insect-pollinated component of lomas vegetation is of some antiquity, suggesting the stability of the lomas formation over time, and tends to confirm the absence of major fluctuations in regional climatic regimes over long periods of time. Once a wider range of environmentally oriented pollen data has been analyzed, we expect the fossil pollen spectra from the environs and the larger region surrounding the Paloma site to contribute significantly to our understanding of past patterns of environmental stability or change in this area and, more generally, on the central coast of Peru.

Coprolite Studies

Some two hundred seventy-six human coprolites associated with a wide range of human habitations, features, and burials have been recovered from the Paloma site and are being studied to improve our understanding of past patterns of food consumption and health of the Palomans. A wide range of fossil pollen was found associated with many of these coprolites, including many of the significant environmental and possible economic pollen types discussed above.

In general, the degree of preservation of the fossil pollen in the coprolites was good to excellent, and compared favorably with or better than the pollen recovered from archaeological contexts and sediments. The coprolites also included faunal and floral macrofossils which proved to be a rich source of information about the foods that the Palomans preferred. Prominent among these data in table 2.9 are numerous plant fibers, shellfish fragments, bone fragments, and seeds from all levels of the Paloma site.

Apparently one of the major plant foods consumed by the ancient Palomans was grass caryopses (grass "fruits" or "seeds") which may have been typically ground on batan grinding stones and ingested in a variety of ways. Both the fossil grass pollen and the grass plant parts strongly support our interpretation of the habitual use of this food resource. Seeds of other plants present in the coprolites included chenopods (Chenopodiaceae), solanaceous (Solanaceae) seeds, and seeds of the composites (Compositae). The fossil pollen types of these plant families were also found in many of the coprolite residues. Taken together, this suggests that certain species of these plant families—particularly the fruits or other plant parts of the chenopod and solanaceous parent plants—were probably consumed by the Palomans as part of their diets, at least seasonally.

Other dietary components included shellfish (<u>Aulacomia</u> and other species), various fish (vertebral and scale remains of indeterminate species in coprolite residues), and a variety of mammal and bird bone, hair, and feather fragments. These preliminary data from the coprolite studies suggest that the Palomans were exploiting and consuming a wide variety of plants and animals as foodstuffs from a number of different resource zones within the catchment area of the site. The presence of charcoal and fragments of the stone materials of which batan grinding stones were made also provided evidence of the food preparation techniques associated with the Paloma populations.

Conclusions

Each biological, physical, and human environment presents human populations with specific sets of problems which they must solve in order to adapt. At Paloma, in order to address more precisely the processes of change and adaptation, our objective has been to document and describe the nature of the prehistoric environments and the solutions that the populations of the lomas found to the environmental challenges. Thus, the orientation of our research

Table 2.9.   Floral and faunal macrofossil components of
Paloma site coprolites.

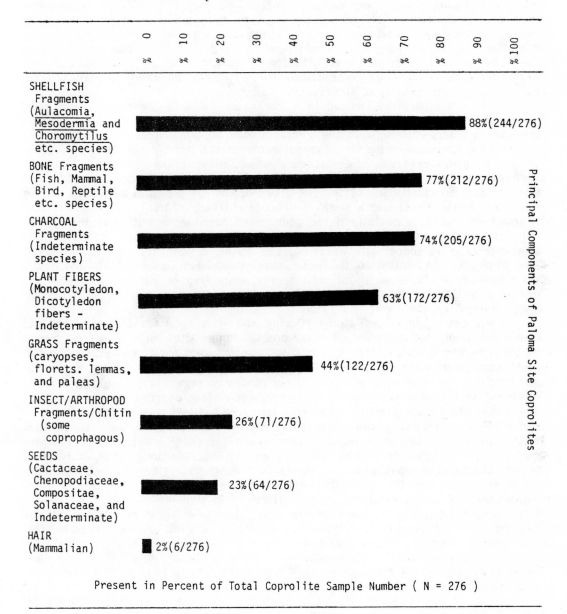

| | 0% | 10% | 20% | 30% | 40% | 50% | 60% | 70% | 80% | 90% | 100% |

SHELLFISH Fragments (Aulacomia, Mesodermia and Choromytilus etc. species) 88%(244/276)

BONE Fragments (Fish, Mammal, Bird, Reptile etc. species) 77%(212/276)

CHARCOAL Fragments (Indeterminate species) 74%(205/276)

PLANT FIBERS (Monocotyledon, Dicotyledon fibers - Indeterminate) 63%(172/276)

GRASS Fragments (caryopses, florets. lemmas, and paleas) 44%(122/276)

INSECT/ARTHROPOD Fragments/Chitin (some coprophagous) 26%(71/276)

SEEDS (Cactaceae, Chenopodiaceae, Compositae, Solanaceae, and Indeterminate) 23%(64/276)

HAIR (Mammalian) 2%(6/276)

Principal Components of Paloma Site Coprolites

Present in Percent of Total Coprolite Sample Number (N = 276)

to the human-environment relations of the people of Paloma frames each of our questions in terms of the problems faced and the responses to these problems. Answers to these questions will guide us in integrating the resulting data.

We believe that the data from our analyses of the botanical materials at the Paloma site will provide the first reliable paleoecological description of this time period on the central Peruvian coast. These data can then be compared and integrated into existing paleoecological schemes from other nearby areas of South America (Llagostera 1979; Sarma 1974; Heusser 1974).

As Engel (1981) has pointed out, aside from the arid coastal desert, the ancient Palomans and their contemporaries had only four possible settlement locales: (1) the rainy highlands of the western Andean flanks, (2) the lomas fog oases, (3) riverine valleys, and (4) along the Pacific coast littoral, where brackish water is available as seeps and in shallow wells. Our data suggest that the ancient Palomans were utilizing all of these resource zones from the earliest times, but that over time, the emphasis changed to littoral zone resouces, and ultimately, to the riverine valleys.

The Paloma site, located in a lomas fog oasis in the past, would have provided sufficient water and plant foods during the Austral winter, as well as marine resources throughout the year. Based on our observations of modern Peruvian herders following the shortest route to the nearby sea, Paloma is only 15 to 30 minutes from the littoral. As Benfer (this volume) points out, through careful control of population sizes, or emigration of surplus population, and by careful monitoring of the resources of the lomas, the inhabitants of the Chilca-Lurin catchment area could have lived comfortably at Paloma throughout much, if not all, of the year. The possible exception is during disruptions in the cycles of fog and fish caused by El Niño. This phenomenon is characterized by abnormally warm surface water, destruction of marine fauna, and abnormal precipitation from the coast inland (Prohaska 1973). Although its occurrence is rare in modern times, only five or six times in the last century, El Niño could have been a factor in periodic past episodes of environmental stress on the coast.

We have found for Paloma (Dering and Weir n.d.) what Engel (personal communication) has observed at other coastal lomas sites—significant decreases in the size and quality of the woody plant species used for firewood. Once the overstory vegetation of shrubs and trees was stripped beyond a certain threshold point, the ability of the lomas plants to regenerate would have been at least temporarily disrupted. However, even after overuse and degradation, the local plant environment could have recovered if left unused for a period of time (López-Ocaña, personal communication, 1980). Thus, on a short-term basis, El Niño could have caused famines and forced the Paloman populations to disperse over other nearby resource zones; over the long-term, it is more likely that the occupation of the lomas by even the most careful peoples could have stressed the fragile habitat to the breaking point, forcing a more permanent relocation to the nearby littoral and riverine valleys. As Benfer (this volume) points out, the Paloman populations over time were apparently in the process of gradually adapting to their changing circumstances. Our continuing studies of the excavated materials from the site will test this proposition and demonstrate whether or not a threshold effect might have effected such drastic changes in the lomas setting as to have rendered it uninhabitable.

Our interpretation of the preliminary archaeological and palynological data is that the lomas were probably wooded during the earliest occupation at Paloma, just as they were elsewhere as recently as thirty-five years ago (Engel, personal communication, 1978). Then, over time, the lomas apparently began to degrade under the impact of longtime human overutilization of its plant and other resources, only to revive when the pressure was removed after the abandonment of the site between approximately 5,000 and 4,500 B.P. Superimposed on this human-lomas interaction was the long term nature of the local environment and its patterns of stability and change. Thus, a moist, favorable climate of the wooded lomas would have enhanced the ability of the lomas to sustain human impact; a drying trend, resulting from the removal of the woody overstory, would have reduced the resiliency of the lomas vegetation to long-term human exploitation. As a result, we feel that it is unnecessary to postulate long-term or sudden changes of climate in order to explain the abandonment of the lomas. Instead, our data tend to suggest that the degradation was human-induced and may have forced the Palomans to emphasize exploitation of the littoral and riverine valleys over time. Ultimately, when the lomas were no longer able to support their increasing numbers, the inhabitants of this part of the central coast lomas may have begun to relocate in more permanent, small settlements closer to the riverine valleys. Engel (1981) has documented similar movements during this period away from the alluvial fans of the Andean foothills to the nearby riverine valleys. The semi-cultivation or cultivation of plants there for carbohydrates as the primary source of food may have begun earlier as plant encouragement and management in the lomas, if not as full-fledged introduction of domesticates. This process would have intensified in the comparatively water-rich local environments of the valleys with their increasing populations. The later development of increasingly complex societies may have been the logical consequence of increasing control over diet and local environments which had its beginnings in the ancient lomas of the central Andean foothills.

Thus, it appears that the primary resources of the lomas—firewood, water, and plant carbohydrates—became less available (or dependable) over time, while exploitation of marine and cultigen plant resources intensified. These changes inevitably led from the ancient harvesting way of life in resource zones such as the ancient lomas and littoral zones, to a transition to food production ending in the central coastal riverine valleys with the development of increasingly complex societies. The extremely well-preserved floral and faunal remains of the Paloma settlement allow us to better describe and understand the processes involved in the transition from gathering to food production during the Archaic (Preceramic) period on the arid central coast of Peru.

Acknowledgments

The research reported in this paper was supported by National Science Foundation Grants NSF BNF76 12316, NSF BNS78 07727a/b and NSF BNS81 053940, Robert A. Benfer, Director. To our friend and colleague, Robert A. Benfer, our thanks for his optimism, support, and insight into matters mundane and intellectual. Our colleagues and hosts in Peru, Frederic A. Engel and Carlos López-Ocaña, Directors of C.I.Z.A. of the National Agrarian University of Peru, have given us support, assistance, and intellectual enthusiasm. We owe them a debt of gratitude, both personally and professionally. To our other colleagues from Peru and the United States who have participated in this work, we offer our sincere appreciation. Bernardino Ojeda E., Miriam Vallejos, Juan Torres G., Pilar Valverde, and other colleagues, friends, and "family" from the staff of C.I.Z.A. and the National Agrarian University have our personal and professional admiration and thanks.

References

Aguilar, P.
  1976 Personal communication, November. Centro de Investigaciones de Zonas Aridas, Universidad Nacional Agraria, Lima, Perú.

Bird, J. B.
  1965 The concept of a "pre-Projectile Point" cultural stage in Chile and Peru. American Antiquity 31(2):262-270.

  1967 Fell's cave. Boletin de la Sociedad Arquelogica de Santiago.

Cardich, A.
  1958 Los yacimientos de Lauricocha. Studia Prehistórica 1. Buenos Aires: Centro Argentino de Estudios Prehistóricos.

  1964 Lauricocha. Studia Prehistórica. Buenos Aires: Centro Argentino de Estudios Prehistóricos.

  1974 Los yacimientos de la estapa agrícola de Lauricocha. Sociedad Argentina de Antropología, Nueva Serie 8:27-48.

Cerrate de Ferreyra, E.
  1979 El Molle. Boletin de Lima 2:28-32.

Cohen, M. N.
  1975 Population pressure and the origins of agriculture: an archaeological example from the coast of Peru. In Population, Ecology and Social Organization, edited by S. Polgar, 79-122. The Hague: Mouton.

  1977 The food crisis in prehistory: overpopulation and the origins of agriculture. New Haven: Yale University Press.

Craig, A. K., and N. P. Psuty.
  1968 Marine desert ecology of southern Peru. The Paracas Papers 1(2). Reconnaissance report. Occasional Publications of the Geography Department of Florida Atlantic University.

Dering, J. P. and G. H. Weir.
  n.d. Bioindicators from the coastal preceramic village of Paloma, Chilca Valley, Peru. Manuscript.

Dering, J. P.
  n.d. Analysis of plant remains from the preceramic site of La Paloma, Chilca Valley, Peru. Manuscript on file at the University of Missouri, Columbia (1979).

Ellenberg, H.
  1958 Neleloasen in der Kustenwuste Perus. Universitat of Gotingen.

  1959 Uber des wassergehalt tropischer neleloasen in der Kustenwuste Perus. Geobotanische Forshunginstitut Berlin 12:47-74.

Engel, F. A.
  1968 La grotte du Megatherium a Chilca. In Echanges et Communications: melanges offerts a Claude Levi-Strauss, edited by J. Pouillon and P. Maranda, 413-535. The Hague: Mouton.

  1970 Exploration of the Chilca Canyon, Peru. Current Anthropology 11(1):55-58.

1978 Personal communication, June. Centro de Investigaciones de Zonas Aridas, Universidad Nacional Agraria, Lima, Peru.

1981 Prehistoric Andean ecology: man, settlement and environment in the Andes. Papers of the Department of Anthropology, Hunter College of the City University of New York. New York: Humanities Press.

Ferreyra, R.
1953 Communidades vegetales de alguna lomas costaneras del Peru. Estación Exp. Agricola de la Molina, Boletin 53.

Gonzalez, A. R.
1960 La estratigraphía de la gruta de Intihuasi. Revista del Instituto de Antropología 1. Universidad Nacional de Córdoba, Argentina.

Grobman, A., and Duccio Bonavia.
1978 Pre-ceramic maize on the north-central coast of Peru. Nature 276(5686):386-87.

Heusser, C. J.
1974 Vegetation and climate of the southern Chilean lake district during and since the Late Interglaciation. Quaternary Research 4:290-315.

Horkheimer, H.
1973 Alimentación y obtenación de alimentos en el Perú prehispánico. Comentarios del Peru 13. Universidad Nacional Mayor de San Marcos, Lima, Peru.

Lanning, E. P.
1967 Peru Before the Incas. Englewood Cliffs, N.J: Prentice Hall.

Llagostera, M. A.
1979 9,700 years of maritime subsistence of the Pacific. American Antiquity 44:309-324.

López–Ocaña, C.
1980 Personal communication, March. Centro de Investigaciones de Zonas Aridas, Universidad Nacional Agraria, Lima, Perú.

Lumbreras, L. G.
1974 The Peoples and Cultures of Ancient Peru. Translated by B. J. Meggars. Washington, D.C: Smithsonian Institution Press.

Lynch, T. F.
1970 Excavations at Quisci Puncu, Callejon de Huaylas, Peru. Occasional Papers of the Idaho State Museum.

1971 Preceramic transhumance in the Callejon de Huaylas, Peru. American Antiquity 36:138-48.

MacNeish, R. S.
1969 First Annual Report of the Ayacucho Archaeological-Botanical Project. Andover, Massachusetts: Peabody Foundation.

1970 Second Annual Report of the Ayacucho Archaeological-Botanical Project. Andover, Massachusetts: Peabody Foundation.

1977 The beginning of agriculture in central Peru. In Origins of Agriculture, edited by C. Reed. The Hague: Mouton.

Moseley, J. E.
1975 The Maritime Foundations of Andean Civilization. Menlo Park, California: Cummings.

Parsons, M. H.
1970 Preceramic subsistence on the Peruvian coast. American Antiquity 35:292-304.

Pickersgill, B., and C. B. Heiser.
1977 Origins and distributions of plants in the New World Tropics. In Origins of Agriculture, edited by .C. Reed. The Hague: Mouton.

Prohaska, F. J.
1973 New evidence on the climatic controls along the Peruvian coast. In Coastal Deserts: Their Natural and Human Environments, edited by P. H. Amiran and A. W. Wilson. Tucson: University of Arizona Press.

Sarma, A. V. M.
1974 Holocene paleoecology of south coastal Ecuador. Proceedings of the American Philosophical Society 18:93-134.

Stocker, Terrence
1979 Personal communication, November. Centro de Investigaciones de Zonas Aridas, Lima, Perú.

Torres-Guevara, J.
1979 Quantification and analysis of the physico-environmental factors that determine the vegetation of the lomas of central Peru. Thesis on file at the Centro de Investigaciones de Zonas Aridas and the Department of Biology, National Agrarian University, Lima, Peru.

Towle, M. A.
1961 The Ethnobotany of Pre-Columbian Peru. Viking Fund Publications in Anthropology 30. Chicago: Aldine.

Vasquez-Nuñez, N.
1974 Algunos aspectos actuales sobre el uso de plantas medicinales en la costa Peruana. Anales Científicos 13:32-52.

Vehik, S. C.
1977 Climate, population, subsistence and the central Peruvian lomas between 8000 and 2500 B.P. Report on file with Paloma Project and in Report to the National Science Foundation.

Weir, G. H.
1976 Palynology, flora and vegetation of Hovenweep National Monument: implications for aboriginal plant use on Cajon Mesa, Colorado and Utah. Unpublished Ph. D. dissertation, Texas A&M University, College Station, Texas.

1978 Diet and environment in preceramic coastal Peru. Report on file with the Paloma Project and in Report to the National Science Foundation.

1977 The beginning of agriculture in central Peru. In Origins of Agriculture, edited by C. Reed. The Hague: Mouton.

1970 Second Annual Report of the Ayacucho Archaeological-Botanical Project. Andover, Massachusetts: Peabody Foundation.

Weir, G. H., and J. P. Dering.
1980 Analyses of plant remains from the preceramic site of La Paloma, Chilca Valley, Peru. Report on file with the Paloma Project and in Report to the National Science Foundation.

3.

Holocene Coastal Adaptations: Changing Demography and Health at the Fog Oasis of Paloma, Peru, 7,800-5,000 B.P.

Robert A. Benfer

Archaeologists have documented a dramatic change in human experience--the adoption of sedentary life and food production by foragers in many different parts of the world—beginning approximately 8,000 to 10,000 years ago (Cohen 1977). The associated biological adjustments of both individuals and populations have scarcely been systematically studied. Attempts to infer Holocene adaptations in contemporary populations have not always been successful, perhaps because recent movements of peoples and stresses (Crosby 1972) have obscured previous adaptations. Therefore, the physical remains of the actual people who underwent these stresses must be examined for the information they preserve about prehistoric adaptations.

The Paloma Project, for which preliminary results will be reported below, has been guided by principles of human ecology which differ somewhat from archaeological perspectives. A review of this perspective is followed by a description of the Paloma Project and its results.

Human Ecology

While American studies of human remains have greatly increased in recent years (see Buikstra and Cook 1980), the work which most influenced the present study has been in the Old World. That work is Angel's (1971) study of adaptation in Hellenistic Greece, relevant to all studies of adaptation to sedentism. Angel found that newly sedentized peoples were beset with problems of inadequate diet and disease. Over centuries, the problems were solved, and the skeletal indicators of stress confirmed that the decline in the quality of life which accompanied sedentism was reversed. The young, especially, achieved improved health, which, combined with the more favorable circumstances of sedentism, led to population growth. Angel explains much of the Greek Hellenistic florescence as a consequence of the initial adoption of sedentism and the successful practice of food production.

In recent years, archaeologists have more often adopted an ecological framework which assumes interdependencies among our own and other species, often following the general orientation of Odum (1971), and more recently, the explicitly evolutionary approach of Pianka (1978). In doing so, recent works (such as Jochim 1981; Winterhalder and Smith 1981; Hayden 1981) have reexamined earlier work. Jochim (1981), for example, cites Dobzhansky's (1974) suggestion that human adaptation is the possession of a valid set of solutions to problems of survival. But Jochim (1981:19) extends this definition of adaptedness to refer to solutions to "...a variety of problems. Guiding these solutions are diverse goals, only one of which may be reproductive success." This kind of extension of the meaning of adaptation has been a source of misunderstandings among investigators. In this sense, all human populations guided by goals must be considered "adapted," ignoring the possibility of actual extinctions (Laughlin 1978) or maladaption. Reynolds (1980:40) challenges us to imagine what it would mean to say that no cultures have valid solutions, that "many, perhaps most cultures have run amok". It should be apparent that a useful theory of adaptation must have a criterion of success. Rather than assume, as cultural relativists might, that all populations have an equally "valid" set of solutions (usually evaluated by economic models), I prefer to look at adaptation with respect to evolution. Durham (1981:218) states this meaning for any particular attribute: "For human populations, an attribute is adaptive when it can be shown in comparison with alternative character states to confer the likelihood of maximum survival and reproduction for its carriers." Populations which did not long reproduce, of course, will not be represented in the archaeological record. Thus a "strategies for survival" approach (Jochim 1981) must be viewed as the natural histories of successful populations. Note that neither Durham nor I insist upon genetic adaptation as the sole meaning of the word (although see Neel 1958, for a review with that orientation). An individual's fitness is his or her proportionate contribution to the next generation. Genetic fitness is the proportionate contribution which is somehow related to possession of a particular allele. Adaptation, the relative fitness of an individual (or, by extension, a gene or a population), is a more general process. Williams (1981) notes that fitness ("adaptative fitness") is sometimes determined by relative comparisons to other individuals who have other alleles or traits or by the rate of increase or decrease of specified genotypes (or phenotypes) across generational time. But in either case, the necessity for genetic adaptation is not an issue here.

Short-term studies of contemporary populations, even those living in extreme environments, sometimes lead to the conviction that most mechanisms for human adaptations are social or cultural rather than acclimatory, developmental, or genetic (see Moran 1981, for such a claim for Eskimos). Some studies have detected slight genetic adaptations. The work of Baker (1968) and his associates is illustrative (but see Stewart 1973:89).

Examination of human skeletal materials which sample thousands of generations have produced numerous examples of genetic and/or acclimatization effects. Notwithstanding cultural/social adaptations, Newman (1960) has demonstrated that, American Indians, an extremely homogeneous people (Stewart 1973), conform reasonably well to Allen's and Bergmann's rules. Durham (1981:218) proposes not to apply genetic theories of natural selection to human behavior, lest we end up with sociobiology rather than with "good and solid human ecology," as if there was some conflict between ecology and evolution. Even Wilson (1975), in his synthesis of sociobiology, considered human societies too flexible to admit simple genetic explanations except that genes promoting flexibility in social behavior must have been selected (1975:548-49).

Recent syntheses of human adaptation studies in living peoples focus sometimes on the population and genetic variability (Moran 1979:9) and sometimes on individual homeostasis, achieved by attaining a "beneficial adjustment to the environment" (Frisancho 1979:2).

The topic of investigation in this paper is the adjustment to sedentism and food production over a period of thousands of years in central coastal Peru. Angel's work in Greece (1975) has been mentioned. A series of recent Ph.D. dissertations have been summarized by Buikstra and Cook (1980). These works document elevated disease levels and/or nutritional stress among native American agriculturists compared with pre-agricultural groups. Paloma, spanning the beginning stages of food production, with well preserved human and ecological remains, is ideally suited for the exploration of this process through time. There are several ways to approach the problem. One might focus on individual human remains, and hence, homeostasis. Another approach would be to study populations of human remains and their possible equilibria. Yet a third approach could focus on the external evidence for adaptation--the archaeological and ecological materials. Whatever sources of evidence are available, each may be evaluated by consideration of one or more of the mechanisms of adaptation:

1. Individual behavior, idiosyncratic if not shared

2. Shared behavior (whether widely shared or kept by specialists) which is passed across generations as well as laterally among groups.

3. Physiological shifts during growth and development and acclimatization.

4. Notwithstanding the preceding in a number of generations, genetic changes can easily produce adaptation. Genetic adaptations are most probable from stresses by which less than perfect adjustments are possible by the first three mechanisms.

5. However, in all four cases adaptation will be considered as a degree, measured on a scale from maladaptation to optimal adaptation. At any level, drift, inbreeding, and even gene flow from differently adapted peoples can lead to less than perfect adaptation.

Human Adaptations to Sedentism at Paloma, Peru

While sedentism was not the only new stress imposed upon the Palomans, it was a significant one. The following assumptions will guide the analysis of the effects of sedentism at Paloma:

A. If settlement of seasonally favorable habitats, such as the fog oases and intermittant stream banks of the central coast of Peru, resulted from immigration of peoples whose subsistence had been based on a semi-sedentary hunting and gathering economy, then settlement in the fog oases and the intermittent streams of the Chilca Valley of coastal Peru would have been marginal habitats because of the lack of knowledge of resources.

B. Thus, a satisfactory adjustment--both to the natural environment as well as to other human groups—would take some time after initial settlement, if indeed it was ever attained for the lomas and littoral resources.

C. Successful long-term inhabitants of these fragile habitats would need to know the range of resources and how to best harvest them, as well as how to adapt to occasional failure of these resources as would occur during El Niño events which cause the Peruvian current to shift. The inhabitants would also have to control their rate of population increase if no other suitable alternative resources were available.

D. Skeletons and soft tissues should show indicators of acclimatization and decreasing stress if a successful adjustment occurred.

E. Culturally, the means to preserve and store resources, as well as alternative subsistence strategies or migration routes, would be developed as familiarity with disruptive cycles, such as El Niño, increased.

F. Demographic curves should show (1) enhanced survival of infants with increasing sedentism and (2) delayed marriage and/or increased birth spacing if consequent population growth were to be avoided.

G. Environmental indicators should not show degradation, such as the elimination of shrub and tree cover, if a stable adjustment was achieved.

Origins of Sedentism and Civilization in Coastal Peru

Throughout the world at the close of the Pleistocene, some peoples moved to coastal and/or riverine settings (Binford 1968; Cohen 1977). Some groups migrated to the coasts as a direct result of population pressure in the interior, perhaps due to a decrease in the numbers of easily hunted herbivores (Martin 1967). Rick (1980) proposes that at least a base camp form of sedentism was practiced by Peruvian highland hunters at an early date due to the availability of Camildae. Willey proposed that the early users of the lomas camps near the coast, about 6,500 B.P., were highland hunters who followed the game there during the winter (see also Patterson 1971) and, over time, replaced seasonal camps with villages "whose inhabitants depended largely on plants" (Willey 1971:68). MacNeish, Patterson and Browman (1975) suggest that the central highlands of the Andes provided a large region in which early Holocene human bands moved about widely. Engel (1968) found marine shells in Tres Ventanas cave high above the Chilca Valley, documenting some connections with the coast, two days' walk down from the site.

Once the coast was discovered, the peoples who exploited the resources of the coastal setting may have found a rich habitat. Lanning (1967) and, even more emphatically, Moseley (1975) have pointed to the extreme richness of the marine resources which would have permitted coastal peoples to live in at least semipermanent hamlets or villages throughout much of the year for thousands of years before becoming dependent on cultigens. This view has been challenged recently (Osborn 1977; Wilson 1981; Raymond 1981) with reinterpretations of the meager published data. Paloma is probably unique in providing the evidence to answer these and related questions, because it may be one of a very few such sites now accessible. Richardson (1980) reviews the evidence and concludes that the existing coast was covered with water about 5,000 years ago, removing most of the archaeological evidence from the critical period of 9,000 to 5,000 B.P. Sites on the coast tend to be situated either in one of the river valleys near the streams or in alluvial fans near the fog oases, scattered from the central Peruvian coast to Chile (see Engel 1980). Since many of the riverine sites might have been at former confluences, and thus today would be covered by the Pacific, and others might have been removed by periodic flooding (Nials et al. 1979), sites in the fog oases (which begin 200 m or more above the modern sea level) contain what is left of the archaeological record. The site of Paloma is the largest Precotton, Preceramic period site yet discovered on the coast of Peru (although Rivasplata (1978) offers a brief report on a similar site).

Some of the inhabitants of the western slopes of the central Andes lived and, on occasion, died at the site of Paloma, between 5,000 and 7,700 years ago. Over 200 graves were excavated with care; most were supervised by a physical anthropologist. The health, diet, marriage patterns, and especially the demography--the most objective measure of adaptation--can be inferred from the 175 well-preserved individuals who were buried in and around the simple huts of the site (see Engel 1980: fig. 5-25).

Thirteen months of fieldwork under my direction followed several seasons of work by Frederic Engel and Bernardino Ojeda. Here I want to present some hypotheses and data as to how improved adaptation may be determined and help to explain cumulative changes in social complexity (see Quilter 1979).

A review of the natural setting and the history of investigations at the site of Paloma will be followed by some of our preliminary findings from study of the human remains. Weir and Dering (this volume) discuss some of the more exciting botanical and environmental findings. Detailed zooarchaeological studies under the direction of Elizabeth Wing of the Florida State Museum and Elizabeth Reitz of the Department of Anthropology, University of Georgia, and final archaeological interpretations are also in progress.

Natural Setting

The west coast of central and southern Peru is a barren desert which is bordered by one of the richest marine resource bases known. The complex interactions of the Andean mountains, trade winds, and the Coriolis force produce a uniquely rich marine environment in contrast to a barren coast that has almost no rainfall (Moseley 1975). Periodic El Niños (failure of the Peruvian current) lead to rare cataclysmic rainfalls. Most streams in the coastal valleys are dry part of the year. The climate is homogeneous; the temperature rarely goes much above or below 20° C. Sparse vegetation has often been further reduced by man, producing a dismal denuded landscape. How long this area has been dry is a matter of considerable debate (Lanning 1967:48; Craig and Psuty 1968:123), but the relationship between humans and nature is seen clearly in arid coastal Peru (Willey 1971:82). Engel (1980) notes that on these arid western slopes of the central Andes, the availability of water constrains human habitation to the rainy highlands, fog oases (lomas), streams, and regions of the coast where lenses of brackish water can be found in shallow wells.

The Site of Paloma

The lomas of Paloma are on a series of low hills 3 km from the Pacific Ocean on the central coast of Peru, on the outer limit of the Chilca Valley, and on the edge of the more fertile Lurin Valley. The Paloma fog oasis almost never experiences rain; instead, a heavy fog and mist nourish the vegetation which turns the barren landscape above the site green during the southern winter months (see Weir and Dering, this volume). In the summer, lomas regions dry up (Lanning 1967; Lynch 1970; Patterson 1971) and assume their barren aspect. The site of Paloma, on the northern edge of the lomas of Paloma, is close to the Chilca River which today is dry in the winter at the same time the lomas produces water. The site is also close to the brackish water found near the modern town of San Bartolo at the archaeological site of Curayaco.

The site of Paloma is presently just below the limits of the modern lomas zone and appears as a series of deeply stained oval areas (see fig. 2.3, p. 22). The village (site 12b-VII-613 in the catalog of the Centro de Investigaciones de Zonas Aridas de la Universidad Nacional Agraria, Camilo Carrillo 300A, Lima) occupies an alluvial plain approximately 250 X 600 m, or some 15 ha in extent. The plain is between 200 and 250 m above sea level.

The stains depicted in figure 2.3 are the surface indications of dwellings, human burials, incredible amounts of shell midden, and numerous plant remains. A small probability sample shows houses and burials associated with all substantial surface debris.

After discovery of the site, Frederic Engel (1980) and Bernardino Ojeda conducted test excavations, emphasizing settlement patterns. Realizing the opportunity but lacking the specialists, Engel invited me to organize a joint University of Missouri/National Agrarian University of Peru research team for the study of the demography, health, and ecology of the well-preserved remains. The National Science Foundation funded a pilot project (six months of excavations in 1976), and later, a larger project (six months of more intensive excavations in 1979). Recently, the same agency sponsored analyses of materials recovered from 55 excavated houses, 200 excavated human graves, and 2,860 m² of excavated area.

The preliminary results presented here are based upon the work completed by the summer of 1981; final analyses of stratigraphy and histological indications of age may slightly alter these results. The data from Paloma which bear on the question of adaptation of hunter-collectors to the coastal setting are now presented.

Results

Table 3.1 presents the demographic data from the burials of Paloma. In figure 3.1, the survivorship curves are presented according to the three major stratigraphic divisions which Engel (1980) suggests are the three superimposed

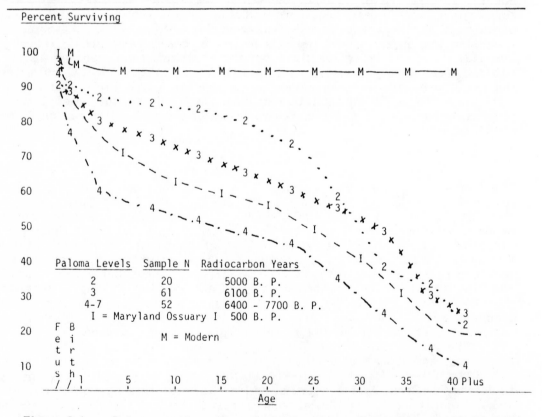

Paloma Levels	Sample N	Radiocarbon Years
2	20	5000 B. P.
3	61	6100 B. P.
4-7	52	6400 - 7700 B. P.
I = Maryland Ossuary	I	500 B. P.
M = Modern		

Figure 3.1. *Paloma graduated survivorship curves. Both sexes combined, (r=0).*

Table 3.1.   Paloma demography–1981.   Based on study of gross indicators of age and sex.

AGE	RADIOCARBON AGE: 5000 B.P. LEVEL: #200				RADIOCARBON AGE: 6000 B.P. LEVEL: #300/230				RADIOCARBON AGE: 6500+ B.P. LEVEL: #400				AGE AND LEVEL TO BE DETERMINED				GRAND TOTALS			
	M	F	?	TOTAL	M	F	?	TOTAL	M	F	?	TOTAL	M	F	?	TOTAL	M	F	?	TOTAL
FETUS	0	0	2	2	0	0	4	4	1	1	1	3	0	1	1	2	1	2	8	11
0 – 1	1	0	0	1	0	3	7	10	3	5	6	14	2	1	4	7	6	9	7	32
1 – 4	0	0	0	0	0	0	2	2	0	2	1	3	1	0	0	1	1	2	3	6
5 – 9	0	0	1	1	3	0	2	5	1	1	3	5	0	0	3	3	4	1	9	14
10 – 14	1	0	0	1	2	0	3	5	0	0	0	0	1	0	0	1	4	0	3	7
15 – 19	0	0	0	0	0	2	0	2	2	0	0	2	0	0	0	0	2	2	0	4
20 – 24	1	0	0	1	1	1	0	2	2	1	0	3	0	0	0	0	4	2	0	6
25 – 29	3	0	0	3	3	2	0	5	2	1	0	3	0	1	1	2	8	4	1	13
30 – 34	0	2	0	2	4	3	1	8	3	5	0	8	0	0	0	0	7	10	1	18
35 – 39	1	3	0	4	1	2	0	3	1	2	0	3	0	0	0	0	3	7	0	10
40 – 44	2	0	0	2	7	3	0	10	1	1	0	2	0	0	0	0	10	4	0	14
45 – 49	1	1	0	2	1	3	0	4	1	1	1	3	0	0	0	0	3	5	1	9
50 +	1	0	0	1	1	0	0	1	1	2	0	3	2	1	0	3	5	3	0	8
	11	6	3	20	18	22	12	61	22	22	12	52	6	4	9	19	58	51	43	152
CHILD (1–14)	0	0	0	0	0	0	10	10	0	0	4	4	0	0	8	8	0	0	22	22
ADULT (14 +)	0	1	1	2	2	1	5	8	1	1	0	2	1	2	6	9	4	5	12	21
TOTALS			2/22				18/79				6/58				17/36				43/195	

Note: Does not include 14 individuals encountered in the 1979–1980 probability sample excavations nor a number of pre-1976 remains not yet assignable to a specific burial or tomb.

51

occupations. These curves show the probability of surviving from any given age to the next age, as inferred from the percentages that died in each age period. Ages are based on gross osteological observations of dental eruption, modification of the pubic symphysis, etc. (see Bass 1971, for descriptive methods of inferring sex). For comparisons, figure 3.1 also presents a curve for a modern population, Hungary, as well as one for a sample of protohistoric North American Indian horticulturalists from a Maryland ossuary (Ubelacker 1980, Ossuary I).

A difficult obstacle in applying Life Table methods to osteological materials is the possible systematic underenumeration of infants and newborns due to differential preservation and the relative rarity with which they are buried in cemeteries (see Weiss 1973). Even today, stillborns are not always claimed for burial at American hospitals. This problem is probably not troublesome for the Paloma data. Preservation is excellent, and the burials are in houses rather than in a cemetery. The percentage of infants (21% overall; infants + fetuses = 28%) is in fact higher than, for example, that of the Libben site (17.5% infants) where preservation is also excellent (Lovejoy et al. 1977:293), but the remains there are from a formal burial area. Lovejoy et al. state they did not overlook any substantial number of infants but do not discuss the possibility that they may not have been buried in the ossuary. Ubelacker (1980) describes a sample from Ecuador. Treated as a single series, Ubelacker found that only 15% of the sample was comprised of infants who died before one year. Ubelacker (1980:18), as well, notes that some types of individuals may not have been buried in the cemetery or their remains may not have survived to be discovered by the archaeologist. This is a serious problem in paleodemography. Jaffe and Medina (1979) propose to solve this problem by estimating life expectancy at birth from pooled prehistoric series. They predict that e(0) will be less than, or at most equal to, e(20). However, combining all levels at Paloma and including fetal deaths, e(0) equals 21 and is much greater than e(20), which equals 17. Thus, adult estimates will not always be of help in assessing infant mortality and fetal wastage, both of which are very sensitive to environmental stresses. Another problem, the underestimation of the aged where gross indicators of age at time of death are employed, has not been corrected for in figure 3.1. Preliminary histological investigations of bone at the University of Missouri (Jackson 1981) and of root transparency at the University of Florida (Maples 1978) have found that gross estimators of age may underestimate the age of older adults by as much as fifteen years. On the other hand, studies using the Miles method of dental aging (Daniel S. Edwards, personal communication) find good agreement between age estimates by dental wear and pubic symphyseal change of Paloman individuals who died in their 20s and early 30s. Histomorphometric standards developed from Europeans may be inappropriate for other populations (Thompson and Gunness-Hey 1981), but a revised formula, based on standards from prehistoric North American Indians (data from Stout 1976) also overestimated Paloman ages when compared to traditional gross indicators. Sexual dimorphism is pronounced, so that sex attribution is likely to be very accurate. All individuals have been studied in the laboratory. Thus, with the possible exception of underaging of the old, which are relatively few in number, the data are quite accurate. The presumed slight increase in population has not been adjusted for at this time.

The results obtained are remarkable. Figure 3.1 shows a clear improvement in child, juvenile, and young adult mortality from the earliest inhabitants (sixty-five hundred or more years ago) until the latest occupations at the site (five thousand years ago). These results are more extreme than could be attributed to chance if the skeletons are viewed as random samples from the levels. If they are a proper sample, the results must be attributable to steady improvements in diet and health.

For a stationary, stable population, such as the total sample of Palomans, the average expected life span at birth is twenty-one years. This is a long life span for archaeological populations. The late prehistoric Libben Ossuary, even with a possible deficit of infants, only had an e(0) of twenty years. The overall Paloman survivorship curve more nearly resembles those of horticulturalists than hunter-collectors (see Weiss 1973).

From the survivorship curves, a large proportion of individuals did not survive childhood (42%; note that this sample includes fetal remains rarely recovered at most archaeological sites). However, the percentage that did survive appears to have steadily increased through time. For example, the percentage of fetuses and infants (up to one year of age) decreased from 33% in the earliest level to 23% in level 300 and to 19% in level 200. The same trend (L400 = 6%, L300 = 3%, L200 = 0%) is found in the number of children who died between ages 1 and 4 (table 3.1), the time when weanling diarrhea often causes a childhood peak, for example, in modern South American peasant death rates (see Blakely 1971:49 for an archaeological example). The same trend is repeated in the 5 to 9 age group (L400 = 10%, L300 = 8%, L200 = 5%). Thus, a gradual improvement in the health and nutrition is supported by the consistency in diminishing death rates over time in the pre-adolescent age groups.

These survivorship curves would seem to strongly support a steadily increasing adaptation to the resources of the coast. However, it is possible that a bias in burial or recovery of the skeletons has influenced the results. For example, what if Paloma were settled as a village (colonists usually are young and produce an excess of children, some of whom die, compared to less rapidly growing populations) and later became an extractive station frequented more by adults than children? Paloman demographic profiles could be indicative of either a growing population or a stationary one whose child mortality is diminishing. Thus, another line of evidence which is independent of possible demographic bias, such as health, is needed. If demography is potentially the strongest indicator of the continuing adaptive success of a population, the health of individuals should reflect the degree of adaptive success in an age biased sample.

Health

There are difficulties in learning the population structure of modern technologically simple peoples before the introduction of Western diseases. Crosby (1972) documents the dramatic demographic changes which took place in both hemispheres after Columbus. Prior to colonial exploration, the Bering and Panamanian land bridges may have protected South Americans from many infectious diseases, including tuberculosis, malaria, influenza, measles, smallpox, and poliomyelitis (Black 1975).

Cockburn (1971) noted that less virulent pathogens or those which can also live outside of hosts are the most likely to survive among small groups. Diseases which could quickly immunize a majority of the population would not have survived in virulent form through most of prehistory. However, there are diseases, such as typhoid fever, amoebic dysentery, pinta, trachoma, and leprosy, in which the host remains infective for a long time. Others, such as malaria and schistosomiasis, not only persist in the host, but also have an intermediate host or outside vector, and could survive in small human populations. But as Cockburn notes, this is largely conjectural since there is little in the way of precise and well-documented data on infections in small groups of isolated hunters and gatherers. Extant populations everywhere have already acquired the bitter experience of exposure to Western diseases. Dunn (1968) summarizes the available knowledge of hunters and gatherers. Chronic diseases, especially of the aged (who are few), are relatively infrequent.

Patterson (1971:201) has postulated a model for early Coastal Peru that is in many ways similar to Angel's model for Greece. Patterson suggests that nutritional levels rose as a result of more efficient utilization of plant resources. However, this heavier utilization led to overexploitation of a fragile habitat, thereby causing a drop in nutritional levels and higher stress. In an attempt to maintain the population and to reduce stress, more emphasis was placed on marine resources. This led to partial sedentism and prepared coastal populations for the use of domesticated plants that had been brought into the area from outside (Pickersgill 1969:54). With both domesticates and marine resources available, another rise in nutritional level and reduction in stress would have occurred.

Can stresses predicted by Patterson's model (see also Cohen 1981) be detected in human skeletal remains? If Cockburn (1971) and Black (1975) are correct that in small scale societies chronic diseases are more likely to persist than acute forms, then we are fortunate, because chronic diseases are much more likely to leave their mark on surviving bone. Acute stress, such as illness or starvation, may also be detected by some indicators.

Harris lines, lines of "arrested growth," are one of the indicators being studied for the Paloman series to address this question. Increased density of mineral deposition at the point of arrest results. For example, I have two growth arrest lines in my tibiae, which, by projecting backwards from their location in the adult bone to the age at which they would have represented the growing ends, should have occurred at ages eight and twelve years. At eight I had measles complicated by pneumonia, and at twelve, scarlet fever. Remodeling can remove the lines, but for comparative purposes, Harris lines can provide a reliable relative measure of morbidity.

Figure 3.2 shows, by levels, the number of Harris lines found in a small sample of adult tibiae. These data were obtained by Gehlert (1979) and I reorganized them according to stratigraphic levels. Gehlert (1979) found that, taken as a single sample, the Paloma series has an unusually large number of lines compared to most other Peruvian series. But pooling data in this manner can be deceptive. As can be seen from figure 2, morbidity at Paloma as measured by Harris lines decreases through time. The Palomans were probably never more than a few hundred individuals, and, even as a sedentary group, one would not have expected such a small population to suffer from many of the infectious diseases that plague larger groups of settled peoples. Moreover, the worldwide exchange of diseases which has taken place since the 15th century (Crosby 1972) had not yet transplanted disease organisms into the Andes. More likely then, the growth arrest lines from Paloma represent periods of stress, perhaps due to insufficient nourishment. Within or directly outside many of the huts at Paloma are storage pits, often filled with evidence of food. It seems likely that, over time, the people that lived in this region learned to preserve and store food for the cyclical disruptions that El Niño must have caused in each generation. The Harris lines support, as an independent line of evidence, the changes depicted in the survivorship curves—the Palomans were solving the problems of fashioning a healthy environment for themselves.

Saul (1974) has explained the collapse of the Mayan civilization as a consequence of failing to solve health problems. Work done among the modern Maya (Furbee et al. n.d.) found that, even today, their life span is extremely

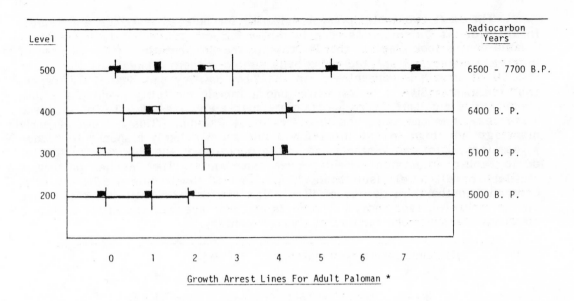

Level — Radiocarbon Years

500 — 6500 - 7700 B.P.

400 — 6400 B. P.

300 — 5100 B. P.

200 — 5000 B. P.

0 1 2 3 4 5 6 7

Growth Arrest Lines For Adult Paloman *

*Each male value had had 1.2 subtracted from it (the average difference between males and females. Filled squares represent males; open squares, females.

Figure 3.2.   *Paloman growth arrest lines plotted against strata.*

short, perhaps the shortest of living peoples.

On the other hand, a potential for population growth, not decrease, is suggested for Paloma. The argument as to the importance of population growth in Mesolithic and Archaic population adaptation is well known—predictions exist for the human skeletal indicators. Cohen (1981:532) predicts that Mesolithic populations should show increasing stress if such "populations were increasingly forced to rely on these resources (r-selected, abundant but not preferred species) because of growing population and increasing spatial limitations." Hayden (1981:523), on the other hand, predicts that "human skeletal remains should show little trend toward increasing stress over time."

The Paloman human data show decreasing, not increasing, stress; they support Hayden's view. The degree and amount of adjustment to excess population, implied by increasingly effective adaptation (see Angel 1971), can also be evaluated by the Paloman materials. The most obvious adjustment—dispersal—cannot, of course, be easily documented from a single site. Engel's atlas (1980) of intensive surveys of the coast may resolve that question. However, the question of cultural control of population growth can be tested by the Paloman sample.

Hassan (1979:147) notes that cultural methods of population control do not necessarily suggest equilibrium, but would be especially important compensations for "recurrent scarcities and occasional overpopulation over the perceived span of environmental variability." Since the fog oasis habitat is fragile, one would predict extreme population control if other locations were unavailable for outmigration of human surpluses, a prediction of the population pressure hypothesis.

The next two tables present evidence for delayed marriage and female infanticide at Paloma. As seen in tables 3.2 and 3.3, about twice as many female deaths took place in the 30s than in the 20s, but this is the reverse of most archaeological and technologically simple modern populations where the risk of childbirth is concentrated in the 20s. Owsley and Bass (1979) report that the Larson Site, a historic site, had a female mortality peak in the late teens and early 20s. These people were extremely stressed—41% of the dead were less than one year, double the rates at Paloma. This pattern of early marriage and high infant mortality would seem a likely response to sudden stress (e.g., European contact) and is the opposite of the Paloman pattern of demographic adjustment to long-term constraints. The Paloman pattern is similar for all levels (see table 3.1). Most of the female deaths are concentrated in the third decade of life. Marriage delayed until the 30s is rare but not unknown, even today. The Scots and Irish are well known for such late marriage ever since the famines of the last century.

Table 3.2.   Evidence for delayed marriage.

Paloma Male-Female Differential Mortality

In the Second and Third Decade

(1979 Sample Pooled Over All Levels)

Age At Death	Male	Female	
20 - 29	10	5	Chi-Square = 6.50, p<.02
30 - 39	11	21	

Table 3.3.   Evidence for female infanticide.

Number of Deaths By Sex and Level

Levels	Infants (Birth - 1 Year)		Non-Infants (1 - 70 Years)	
	Male	Female	Male	Female
400 - 700	3	5	15	17
300	0	3	23	9
200	1	0	11	6
TOTAL	4	8	49	32

In table 3.3, the evidence for female infanticide is presented. As can be seen, the number of baby girls who died in their first year is double that of males (using sexing criteria of Weaver 1980). Kramer (1982) reports similar ratios among modern peoples not practicing infanticide. Paloman non-infants show about 1.5 times as many males as females, a predictable consequence of female infanticide if a nearly 50:50 birth ratio is assumed. Thus, population control mechanisms, even without emigration, may have been strong enough to remove population pressure as an adaptive problem for survival and reproductive success.

Discussion

Survivorship curves document increasing adaptation to the coastal habitat. Harris lines indicate improved resistance to periodic disruptions. Male-female ratios and mortality rates seem to suggest cultural control of birth rate. The paleodemographic results bear directly on modern health. Today, acute weanling diarrheal disease is a leading cause of death in the young of South America (anonymous 1956). For example, Berlin and Markell (1977) report 32% of the Aguaruna Jivaro die between the ages of 1 and 5 years, which is triple the percentage in Paloma. Maybe present-day infant mortality rates are due to colonialism bringing European diseases (Weiss 1973:78) to peoples not adapted to them. The implication is that the "demographic transition" is a new phenomenon, based on more recent increases in infant mortality.

The paleobotanical evidence also bears consideration with respect to ongoing attempts to reforest the fog oases. Weir and Dering (this volume) have found significant decreases over time in both numbers and diameters of the shrubs and trees from the lomas used for firewood. Once stripped, the regeneration capacity of the shrubbery overstory and the water retention qualities of the lomas would be disrupted. It appears that the primary resources of the lomas--water, firewood, and carbohydrates—became less available over time, and fishing and use of marine resources was intensified. Yet, at the same time, the population was becoming healthier. Although restrained in its growth by infanticide and late marriage, perhaps, as responses to limitations of resources, the population potential for growth was great at Paloma.

If Richardson (1980) is correct that the sea level rose to its modern level 5,000 years ago, this might explain the abandonment of Paloma and other fog oases when mollusk beds were flooded. Strontium levels in Paloman bone (Benfer, Vogt, and Schlagel n.d.) are very low—lower than any reported populations--suggesting a very high protein element of the diet; mollusks, fish, and sea mammals must have been major components. These results support the preliminary findings from studies of intestinal contents and coprolites (Weir n.d.). The necessity to occupy presumably already utilized riverine settlements, such as the site of Chilca I (Engel 1970), may have led to temporarily exceeding the carrying capacity, and then to shifts in plant management from those species more useful to fishermen (Pozorski and Pozorski 1979) to plants which directly provided food. This adjustment may have been decisive in increasing the carrying capacity for peoples sufficiently organized to efficiently manage water control.

Whatever the ultimate cause or causes, the lomas camps were abandoned in favor of riverine settings, such as the Chilca River, between about 5,000 and 4,500 B.P., where today cultigens sprout during the summer when the Chilca River produces moisture near its banks and then complete their growth cycle during the winter using moisture condensed from the thick fog (Bernardino Ojeda, personal communication). This phenomenon was observed in the Chilca

Valley in the sixteenth century (Cieza de Leon 1971). The knowledge of cultivation using fog for moisture was undoubtedly known in the prehistoric past. Clearly, former inhabitants of lomas settings would find more intensive horticulture of carbohydrate-producing plants a feasible method of dealing with an increased population dependent on the river valley. Trace element study of human bone from sites such as Chilca I is needed to confirm this shift in diet, but it seems plausible that a sedentary life in the lomas, with increasing sophistication in water control methods, could have led to some of the social mechanisms necessary to control water more efficiently in the riverine setting. Coercive social measures would have been necessary to control overexploitation of the fragile lomas habitat and thus may have "preadapted" people to the need for similar and more stringent controls for the sharing of limited riverside fields.

Individual desires to maintain health, to obtain food and water by access to known resource areas, and to have children were satisfied by sedentism, a dietary, technological, and social adaptation to the coastal environment. Slowly, knowledge was accumulated for fishing and hunting of sea mammals, preservation of fish against shortages, and management of water control and native lomas (such as the Tuberous begonia, Begonia geraniifolia) as well as imported plants (such as lima beans, Phaseolus lunatus; squash, Cucurbitacae, and the bottle gourd, Lageneria siceraria; see Weir and Dering, this volume).

These adjustments would have been useless without efficient social controls on population growth. Over many centuries, a people with increasing options in food procurement became increasingly healthy. Tremendous population and cultural potential was building. The next evolutionary stage in adaptation to the arid coast was possibly precipitated by rising sea levels, but not, as far as the data available from Paloma indicate, due directly to population increases. A more important component was the potential rate of expansion of peoples whose lomas/littoral equilibrium was disturbed. Intensified exploitation of the riverine environment may have been followed, not preceded, by dramatic population increases, since the skeletal indications document the ability of the Paloman peoples to control their rate of increase, at least for several millennia.

Acknowledgments

Many of the participants in the Paloma Project have been cited in this report. My co-directors, Frederic Engel, Alice N. Benfer, and Glendon H. Weir have contributed the most. Many of the better ideas in this paper and most of the results are due to them. Frederic Engel deserves the warmest acknowledgement. He has shared his site, his research laboratory, his knowledge, his companionship, and most of all, his enthusiasm with me and coinvestigators who have had the pleasure of working with him.

The National Science Foundation provided most of the funding (NSF BNS76 12316, NSF BNS78 07727a/b, and NSF BNS-81053940), with additional funds provided by the University of Missouri Research Council. C.I.Z.A. provided laboratories, colleagues, and friendship for all of us. The Swiss scientific foundation Terres Aride (F.E.P.T.A.) has, since 1977, helped support Engel's archaeological investigations through C.I.Z.A. Solveig Turpin read and made valuable editorial improvements to this paper for which I would like to express my thanks.

References

Angel, J. Lawrence.
 1971   The People of Lerna.   Washington, D.C.: Smithsonian Institution Press.

 1975   Paleoecology, paleodemography and health.   In Population, Ecology, and Social Evolution, edited by Steven Polgar, pp. 167-190.   The Hague: Mouton.

Anonymous
 1956   Pan American sanitary bureau: summary of reports on the health conditions in the Americas, 1950-53.   Scientific Publication 25.   Washington, D.C.: Pan American Sanitary Bureau.

Baker, Paul T., ed.
 1968   High Altitude Adaptation in a Peruvian Community.   Occasional Papers in Anthropology 1.   University Park: Department of Anthropology, Pennsylvania State University, Pennsylvania.

Bass, William M.
 1971   Human Osteology.   Columbia: Missouri Archaeological Society.

Benfer, Robert A., James A. Vogt, and Steve Schlagel.
 n.d.   Instrumental neutron activation analysis of ancient Peruvian bone: the effects of soil, strata, demography, and disease.   Paper presented to symposium: Biogeochemistry in Archaeology.   John Ericson, organizer, Society for Archaeological Science, San Diego, 1981.

Berlin, Elois Ann, and Edward K. Markell.
 1977   An assessment of the nutritional and health status of an Aguaruna Jivaro community, Amazonas, Peru.   Ecology of Food and Nutrition 6:69-81.

Binford, L. R.
 1968   Post-Pleistocene adaptations.   In New Perspectives in Archaeology, edited by S.R. Binford and L.R. Binford, 314-341.   Chicago: Aldine.

Black, Francis L.
 1975   Infectious diseases in primitive societies.   Science 187:515-18.

Blakely, Robert L.
 1971   Comparison of the mortality profiles of Archaic, Middle Woodland, and Middle Mississippian skeletal populations.   American Journal Of Physical Anthropology 34:43-54.

Buikstra, Jane E., and Della C. Cook.
 1980   Paleopathology: An American account.   Annual Review of Anthropology 9:433-70.

Cieza de Leon, Pedro de.
 1971   La Cronica Del Peru.   Ediciónes de La Revista Ximenez de Quesada.   Ministério de Educacion Nacional.   Instituto Columbiano de Cultura Hispánica XXIV.

Cockburn, T. A.
1971 Infectious diseases in ancient populations. Current Anthropology 12:45-54.

Cohen, Mark N.
1977 The Food Crisis in Prehistory. New Haven, Connecticut: Yale University Press.

1981 Comment on research and development in the Stone Age: Technological transitions among hunter-gatherers, by Brian Hayden. Current Anthropology 22:532.

Craig, A. K., and N. P. Psuty.
1968 Marine Desert Ecology of Southern Peru. The Paracas Papers 1(2). Reconnaissance report. Occasional Publication of the Geography Department, Florida Atlantic University. Boca Raton.

Crosby, A. W., Jr.
1972 The Columbian Exchange. Westport, Connecticut: Greenwood Press.

Dobzhansky, T.
1974 Chance and creativity in evolution. In Studies in the Philosophy of Biology, edited by F. J. Ayala and T. Dobzhansky, 309-39. Berkeley: University of California Press.

Dunn, F. L.
1968 Epidemiological factors: Health and disease in hunter-gatherers. In Man The Hunter, edited by R. B. Lee and Irven DeVore, 221-28. Chicago: Aldine.

Durham, William H.
1981 Overview: Optimal foraging analysis in human ecology. In Hunter-Gatherer Foraging Strategies, edited by Bruce Winterhalder and Eric Alden Smith, 218-31. Chicago: University of Chicago Press.

Edwards, Daniel S.
1983 Dental Attrition and Subsistence at the Pre-Ceramic Site of Paloma, Peru. Master's thesis, Department of Anthropology, University of Missouri-Columbia.

Engel, Frederic-Andre.
1968 La Grotte du Megatherium a Chilca. In Communications: Melanges Offerts a Claude Levi-Strauss, edited by J. Pouillon and P. Maranda, 413-35. The Hague: Mouton.

1970 Exploration of the Chilca Canyon, Peru. Current Anthropology 11:55-58.

1980 Paloma, Village 613. In Prehistoric Andean Ecology, edited by Frederic-Andre Engel, 103-35. New York: Humanities Press.

Frisancho, A. Robert.
1979 Human Adaptation: A Functional Interpretation. St. Louis: C. V. Mosby Company.

Furbee, Louanna, Harry K. Lynch, John S. Thomas, and Robert A. Benfer.
    n.d.   Tojolabal: Maya Population Response to Stress. In Ethnographic Profile of the Tojolabal, edited by Jill Brody and John S. Thomas. Geoscience and Man Series. Louisiana State University, Baton Rouge, Louisiana. In progress.

Gehlert, Sarah G.
    1979   Dental asymmetry in two Peruvian populations. Master's paper, University of Missouri-Columbia.

Hassan, Fekri A.
    1979   Demography and archaeology. Annual Review of Anthropology 8:137-60.

Hayden, Brian.
    1981   Research and development in the Stone Age: Technological transitions among hunter-gatherers. Current Anthropology 22:519-531.

Jackson, Barbara E.
    1981   Histomorphometric analysis of twenty-two human rib segments from the preceramic site of Paloma, Peru. Master's paper, University of Missouri-Columbia.

Jaffee, A. J., and C. M. Medina.
    1979   Statistical notes on mortality and fertility in prehistoric American populations. Paper presented to the XLIII International Congress of Americanists, Vancouver, August, 1979.

Jochim, Michael A.
    1981   Strategies For Survival: Cultural Behavior In An Ecological Context. New York: Academic Press.

Kramer, Patricia L.
    1982   Infant mortality: A cohort study in a northern Italian industrialized population. Abstract in American Journal Of Physical Anthropology 57:203-4.

Lanning, Edward P.
    1967   Peru Before The Incas. Englewood Cliffs, N. J.: Prentice Hall.

Laughlin, Charles D., Jr., and Ivan A. Brady, eds.
    1978   Extinction and Survival in Human Populations. New York: Columbia University Press.

Lovejoy, C. Owen, Richard S. Meindl, Thomas R. Pryzbeck, Thomas S. Barton, Kingsbury G. Heiple, and David Kotting.
    1977   Paleodemography of the Libben site, Ottawa County, Ohio. Science 198:291-93.

Lynch, Thomas F.
    1970   Preceramic transhumance in the Callejon de Huaylas, Peru. American Antiquity 36:139-148.

MacNeish, R.S., T. C. Patterson, and D. L. Browman.
 1975 The Central Peruvian Prehistoric Interaction Sphere. Papers of the Robert S. Peabody Foundation For Archaeology 7. Andover, MA: Phillips Academy.

Maples, William R.
 1978 An improved technique using dental histology for estimation of adult age. Journal of Forensic Sciences 23:764-770.

Martin, Paul S.
 1967 Prehistoric overkill. In Pleistocene Extinctions: The Search for a Cause, edited by P. S. Martin and H. E. Wright. New Haven, CT: Yale University Press.

Moseley, Michael E.
 1975 The Maritime Foundations Of Andean Civilization. Menlo Park, CA: Cummings.

Moran, Emilio F.
 1979 Human Adaptability: An Introduction to Ecological Anthropology. North Scituate, MA: Duxbury Press.

 1981 Human adaptation to arctic zones. Annual Review of Anthropology 10:1-25.

Neel, James V.
 1958 The study of natural selection in primitive and civilized human populations. American Anthropological Association Memoir 86:43-72.

Newman, Marshall T.
 1960 Adaptations in the physique of American aborigines to nutritional factors. Human Biology 32:288-313.

Nials, Fred L., Eric E. Deeds, Michael E. Moseley, Sheila G. Pozorski, Thomas G. Pozorski, and Robert A. Feldman.
 1979 El Niño: The catastrophic flooding of coastal Peru, part 2. Bulletin of the Field Museum of Natural History 50:4-10.

Odum, E. P.
 1971 Fundamentals of Ecology. Philadelphia: W. B. Saunders.

Osborn, Alan J.
 1977 Strandloopers, mermaids, and other fairly tales: Ecological determinants of marine resource utilization—the Peruvian case. In For Theory Bulding In Archaeology, edited by L. R. Binford, 157-206. New York: Academic Press.

Owsley, Douglas W., and William M. Bass
 1979 A demographic analysis of skeletons from the Larson Site (39WW2) Walworth County, South Dakota: Vital statistics. American Journal of Physical Anthropology 51:145-54.

Page, John W.
 1974 Human evolution in Peru: 9000-1000 B.P. Ph.D. diss., University of Missouri-Columbia.

Patterson, Thomas C.
  1971 The emergence of food production in central Peru. In Prehistoric Agriculture, edited by S. Struever, 181-207. New York: Natural History Press.

Pianka, E. R.
  1978 Evolutionary ecology. New York: Harper & Row.

Pickersgill, Barbara.
  1969 The archaeological record of chili peppers (Capsicum spp.) and the sequence of plant domestication in Peru. American Antiquity 34:54-61.

Pozorski, Sheila and Thomas Pozorski.
  1979 Alto Salaverry: A Peruvian coastal preceramic site. Annals Of The Carnegie Museum 48:337-375.

Quilter, Jeffrey.
  1979 Mortuary practices at the preceramic site of Paloma. Ph.D. diss., University of California, Santa Barbara.

Raymond, J. S.
  1981 The maritime foundations of Andean civilization: A reconsideration of the evidence. American Antiquity 46:806-821.

Reynolds, Vernon
  1980 The Biology Of Human Action. San Francisco: W. H. Freeman.

Rick, John W.
  1980 Prehistoric Hunters of the High Andes. New York: Academic Press.

Richardson, James B., III.
  1980 Modeling the development of sedentary maritime economies on the coast of Peru: A preliminary statement. Annals Of Carnegie Museum 50:139-50.

Rivasplata, J. Deza.
  1978 El excedente en la economía marina del Arcaico Tardío. In El Hombre y la Cultura Andina, Tomo I., edited by Ramiro Matos M. III Congreso Peruano. Lima, Peru: San Marcos University.

Saul, Frank.
  1974 The Human Skeletal Remains of Altar de Sacrificios. Papers of the Peabody Museum of Archaeology and Ethnology 36. Cambridge, MA: Peabody Museum.

Stewart, T. D.
  1973 The People of America. New York: Charles Scribner's Sons.

Stout, S. D.
  1976 Histomorphometric analysis of archaeological bone. Ph.D. diss., Washington University, St. Louis.

Thompson, D. D., and M. Gunness-Hey.
1981   Bone mineral-osteon analysis of Yupik-Inupiaq skeletons.   American Journal of Physical Anthropology 55:1-7.

Ubelaker, Douglas A.
1980   Human skeletal remains from Site OGSE-80, a preceramic site on the Sta. Elena Peninsula, Coastal Equador.   Journal of Washington Academy of Science 70:3-24.

Weaver, David S.
1980   Sex differences in the ilia of a known sex and age sample of fetal and infant skeletons.   American Journal of Physical Anthropology 52:191-95.

Weir, Glendon H.
n.d.   Preliminary fossil pollen and macrofossil analyses of coprolites and sediments from La Paloma Village Site area, Chilca Valley Drainage, Peru.   Manuscript.

Weiss, Kenneth M.
1973   Demographic models for anthropology.   Memoirs of the Society for American Archaeology 27.

Willey, Gordon R.
1971   An Introduction to American Archaeology.   Vol. 2, South America. Englewood Cliffs, N.J.: Prentice Hall.

Williams, B. J.
1981   A critical review of models in sociobiology.   Annual Review of Anthropology 10:163-92.

Wilson, David J.
1981   Of maize and men: A critique of the maritime hypothesis of state origins on the coast of Peru.   American Anthropologist 83:93-120.

Wilson, E. O.
1975   Sociobiology;   The New Synthesis.   Cambridge: Harvard University Press.

Winterhalder, Bruce, and Eric Alden Smith.
1981   Hunter-Gatherer Foraging Strategies.   Chicago: University of Chicago Press.

4.

Early Organizational Diversity in the Peruvian Highlands: Huaricoto and Kotosh

Richard L. Burger and Lucy Salazar-Burger

Introduction

In the Peruvian highlands within the last two decades, a number of early temples and shrines have been discovered whose principal architectural feature is a repetitive sequence of elaborately constructed buildings with semi-subterranean hearths preserved intact by "temple entombment." This pattern appears to have been initiated toward the end of the third millennium B.C. and to have continued in some regions into the first millennium B.C. The unexpected similarity between these pre-Chavín highland centers is an exciting development in Andean prehistory. It has been interpreted as reflecting a widely held set of religious beliefs expressed through similar rituals emphasizing the presentation of burnt offerings; the varied expressions of this religious ideology through time and space can be referred to collectively as the Kotosh Religious Tradition (Burger and Salazar Burger 1980).

The recent documentation of the Kotosh Religious Tradition for the Upper Huallaga, the Callejón de Huaylas and the Chuquicara should not be construed as implying equivalence or even similarity between the early societies of these areas. On the contrary, the temples and shrines in question are located in quite different ecological settings and the populations which constructed, maintained, and worshipped in them were necessarily supported by dissimilar patterns of production. A corollary of this observation is that the density of population in these areas may have been very different. The way in which these groups were organized to support the religious centers in question should therefore not be assumed to be the same. If not, some reflection of organizational diversity might be encountered in the archaeological record.

Numerous differences do, in fact, exist among the religious centers of the Kotosh Religious Tradition. It is the differences, rather than the similarities that are the focus of this article. Moseley (1975:94), in his study of early public architecture on the Peruvian coast, suggested that distinctions in size and elaboration of monumental architecture, where not mitigated by functional variation, generally reflect differences in the degree and nature of corporate power. The repetitive character of the ceremonial structures at sites like Kotosh suggests that each of these buildings may have fulfilled similar or identical functions, and that some of the differences between them might be profitably understood as the result of the way in which labor was organized and directed. This approach would seem equally valid whether making comparisons between structures of apparently homologous functions at a single site or from different sites. We will explore this theme by comparing the temples from the centers of Kotosh and Shillacoto in the Upper Huallaga Valley with the ceremonial hearths at the shrine of Huaricoto in the Callejón de Huaylas. Alternative models of labor organization and control will be delineated as a possible explanation of the observed differences between the ritual structures of these two areas. It is suggested that the support communities of centers like Kotosh produced and renewed their temples by corporate labor projects under the direction of a permanent authority, while shrines like Huaricoto were the product of societies in which authority and responsibility for the construction and maintenance of ceremonial hearths rotated among individuals representing the smaller social units of society, such as households or lineages.

Models of Labor Mobilization and Control

In the Central Andes, corporate labor projects were traditionally carried out within the context of asymmetrical reciprocity between the authorities who usually provided direction, food, corn beer, and coca, and supporting communities which provided labor. The work force was mobilized by means of the mita or faena (Alberti and Mayer 1974:21-3; Isbell 1978:176). The mita was an annual labor service owed by taxpayers and used for the completion of public goals. This tax was levied in Inca times on the basis of decimal divisions of the population, and on the basis of residential communities in Colonial, and perhaps earlier, times (Rowe 1946:267-68; Kubler 1946: 372). The effectiveness of mita organization is attested to by constructions like that of Sacsahuaman in Cuzco where thirty thousand men at a time were reported to have worked (Rowe 1946:267-268). The faena was obligatory communal labor levied when necessary in post-Conquest times for the completion of specific public projects (Isbell 1978:176-177). Both the faena and the mita concentrated the productive forces of dispersed hamlets and villages for the completion of a common goal under the direction of a single authority generally not residing in the small rural residential units. The purpose of these mechanisms was to distribute equitably the burden of labor over administered areas where slave and wage labor was absent or rare. The Peruvian government abolished mita and faena undertakings in order to eliminate abuses of power and to encourage wage labor, but both systems persist in modified form on a reduced level (Isbell 1978:176-177).

A frequent characteristic of the mita system of labor mobilization was the division of large projects into small repetitious segments, each of which could be assigned to a particular labor group. Moseley (1975a) and Day (1982:342) have argued that the resulting "segmentation" can be observed in pre-Inca monuments, like the Huaca del Sol, Pampa Grande and Chan Chan. Largely on this basis, mitalike systems can be traced back at least two thousand years into Peruvian prehistory. Moreover, Moseley suggests that mitalike systems were probably more pervasive and of greater antiquity than can be currently demonstrated (Moseley 1978:505). Pozorski (1980:104) and Feldman (1977:15) have gone further suggesting that mitalike (corvée) labor may have been employed in the construction of much older sites like Aspero or Huaca de los Reyes, which date to the late Preceramic and the Initial Period, respectively.[1] We consider it possible that corporate labor might also have been utilized to build early highland temples like Kotosh and Galgada.

On the other hand, systems, such as the mita or faena, would not have been necessary or even appropriate for the construction of small shrines like Huaricoto. What alternatives might have existed for mobilizing the work force necessary for the creation of these modest centers? Presently, among the traditional highland communities of Peru, the cargo system is probably the most common way of accomplishing many public goals, especially religious ones, without taking recourse in permanent authorities or corporate labor. The cargo system rotates authority and responsibility for the completion of tasks from individual to individual on a calendric basis. Participation in the cargo system is, in theory, voluntary but refusal to accept a cargo may undermine the right of the individual to essential communally controlled resources like agricultural land, pasture, and water for irrigation, not to mention the loaned labor of others (Fonseca 1973:9). The person accepting the cargo usually utilizes mechanisms of private reciprocity, such as ayni or minka, in order to assure that consanguineal, affinal, and fictive kin help him with the burden of the task (Fonseca 1973:70; Isbell 1978:168).

The cargo system, as currently practiced in most highland communities, bears a resemblance to the cofradía system which flourished in Spain during the sixteenth and seventeenth centuries. For this reason, the cargo system has sometimes been dismissed as culturally intrusive (Kubler 1946:405). Certain aspects of the cargo system, such as the alternation of cargos between civil and religious posts, or the hierarchically ordered set of positions through which an individual advances during his lifetime, may have been introduced by the Spanish or have been elaborated locally following the Conquest. Other features of the cargo system probably existed long before that time, which would partially explain the rapid and widespread "adoption" of the cofradía-like system even in parts of Peru and Mesoamerica resistant to Spanish institutions. The cargo system has been embraced in highland communities uncongenial to other non-Quechua institutions and ideas. For example, the authors have visited communities in the Callejón de Conchucos which support cargo systems but have little familiarity with basic Catholic concepts. A similar process occurred in Colonial Mexico. Missionaries in early Colonial times denounced the rotating sponsorship of rituals and feasts as an example of the continuation of idolatrous pre-Hispanic customs (Carrasco 1961:492).

Coe (1965), drawing upon ethnohistoric documents, described one late pre-Hispanic cargolike system from the Yucatan in which ritual and civil power was annually rotated counter-clockwise from one lineage to another. Bricker (1978) has drawn upon different documentary and ethnographic sources from the southern Maya area to demonstrate that while the sharp division between church and state responsibilities, as manifested in the current civil-religious hierarchy, appears to be a post-Conquest development, the rotation of combined local religious and political authority is indigenous. Zuidema (personal communication) has also found evidence in Peruvian ethnohistoric documents to support the existence of pre-Hispanic rotational systems of ritual responsibility at local shrines in highland Peru.

The possibility that organizational features might have been held in common by pre-Hispanic Peru or Mesoamerica and sixteenth-century Spain should not be surprising, since the annual rotation of political-religious authority and responsibility has worldwide distribution and is found in such diverse societies as the Berbers and the Khumbu Sherpas (Rhoades and Thompson 1975:541; Coe 1965:112). In fact, Rhoades and Thompson (1975:541-546) recently argued that social mechanisms like the cargo system and its relatives, may evolve as a response to the demands of high altitude agro-pastoral activities, thus explaining the presence of similar institutions in the Andes, Himalayas, Alps, and Atlas mountain ranges.

The social benefits of cargolike systems are widely recognized, especially for small or dispersed populations. These systems of rotating political and ritual responsibilities reinforce social cohesion and integration by insuring that each segment of the society participates in the social system without being subordinated to the other segments. Cargolike systems tend to inhibit institutionally the concentration of power and, in some cases, wealth in the hands of a single individual lineage, or community (Coe 1965:112; Haviland 1966:627; Rhoades and Thompson 1975:541-42; Webb 1975:180). Some anthropologists have observed that cargo systems can reinforce economic stratification, translating it into prestige and authority (Cancian 1965). This view, while applicable to some modern peasant communities, may not be relevant to the prehistoric societies being considered here because of the absence of pan-regional market systems and nation states that provide the framework for localized stratification.

The limitations of cargolike systems are self-evident, though less frequently mentioned. The social network upon which the cargoholder (carguyoq) draws for support is small, especially compared to the number of in-dividuals who could be mobilized through a mita or faena system. The car-goholder can only call upon his own resources and those of the segment of society with reciprocal obligations to him. Moreover, the authority of the carguyoq is temporary and lacks coercive power. His resource base is inherently more limited than that of a permanent authority and consequently an upper limit is placed on the scale of projects which can be carried out.

The limited resources of a carguyoq and his social network make him vulnerable to the unpredictable harvests or personal hardships (e.g., illness or death of relatives) which may require the expenditure of resources earmarked for the cargo. His organizational ability, charisma, and other factors also play a role in determining the upper limits of labor input which may be mobilized in a given year. In the Peruvian highlands, the ecological and climatic variability often results in localized crop failures, a reality against which farmers hedge by exploiting many small fields at different locations. In a mita or faena system, all communities participate collectively, thereby dampening variations in the resources available each year; they are, in effect, cost-sharing systems, based on labor rather than money. Moreover, organizational ability is generally held constant in corporate labor systems which are predicated on the existence of some permanent authority. If one accepts the above arguments, it would be expected that annual or short-term fluctuations of labor input should be more notable in a cargolike system than in a centrally directed system of corporate labor.

The annual rotation of authority also limits the knowledge and experience available to the individual or individuals in charge. This problem is aggravated by the widespread rule that an individual may hold a specific cargo only once. The difficulties of information transfer between cargoholders may be partially mitigated by ladder systems in which the carguyoq has already held cargos at lower levels before he is responsible for the more complex and costly upper cargos. Also, in some cargo systems part-time specialists serve as ritual advisors. They provide some continuity and esoteric knowledge without assuming responsibility for the undertaking in question (Bricker 1978:42). However, even with these features, the enterprises of a cargolike system might be expected to be characterized by less complex and more variable results than those directed by a single permanent authority.

The expected variability in cargolike systems would only partly be due to the discontinuity of knowledge or the absence of full-time specialized personnel to develop and maintain large bodies of esoteric lore and ritual. Competition is one of the basic features of modern cargo systems and the rivalry between past and present cargoholders reinforces and amplifies the already existing tendency towards variability, spurring the cargo-holder to outdo past cargoholders by dedicating even greater resources to the task, although such expenditures may not be necessary for its completion from a purely ritual standpoint. Mishkin (1946:468), for example, notes that in Kauri, Cuzco cargoholders will double or triple the normal expenditures of resources when possible. During our three seasons of excavations at Huaricoto, we had the opportunity to witness the way in which the annual cargoholder decorated the shrine of the Señor de Chaukayán for the annual festival. In one case, innovations were made to accommodate unusually high expenditures by a prosperous carguyoq, while in other years, less prosperous cargoholders added new features in order to give a special "personal" character to the completion of the cargo, thereby distracting attention from the limited resources actually expended.

The above discussion attempts to delineate some of the characteristics of cargolike systems which might be recognizable in the archaeological record. Unfortunately, these remarks must be considered tentative since few ethnographers have studied the material aspects of the cargo system. However, if our suggestions are generally correct, then the products of cargolike systems of authority and labor mobilization should differ from projects carried out by coporate labor projects in regard to (1) absolute size, (2) fluctuations in labor input, (3) the complexity of the undertaking and (4) the degree of short-term variability.

Most ritual activities do not necessarily require permanent, or even temporary, constructions. Even when altars or rooms for religious ceremonies are necessary, the effort extended for their construction may be relatively insignificant when compared to the total labor expended during the festival. The annual construction of altars and other ritual structures by cargoholders is known ethnographically from Mesoamerica (Redfield 1941:279) and Peru (Mishkin 1946:465; Aranguren 1977). In Kauri, Cuzco, a lower level cargoholder is responsible each year for building the altar and also for providing music (Mishkin 1946:465). Unfortunately, outlays made to support feasting, dancing, and other ceremonial activities are difficult to document archaeologically. The quantitative and qualitative study of short-term variation in the nature and extent of such prehistoric activities would be very laborious, if not impossible to establish. On the other hand, ritual constructions can be studied and should reflect the forces described in general terms for corporate undertakings or cargolike systems of sponsorship.

Size and Fluctuations of Labor Input

The late Preceramic (Mito phase) constructions at Kotosh consist primarily of temple structures on elevated platforms. The larger of the two mounds at Kotosh, mound KT, was intensively studied. In Mito times, KT consisted of three main platforms. The upper one was not excavated. The middle platform yielded the remains of the Templo de los Nichitos (ER-11) which had been built on top of an earlier temple, the well-known Templo de las Manos Cruzadas (UR-22). Excavations were not continued below UR-22, although earlier temples are presumed to exist below it. A sequence of seven temple buildings was uncovered on the lower platform level and additional temples are believed to be buried underneath the Templo Blanco (ER-27 and ER-28), the oldest excavated structures at Kotosh. Approximately five to seven meters of Preceramic cultural materials remain beneath the studied strata of mound KT. Nearly three quarters of the mound received little attention. A limited study of the nearby 6.5 m high KM mound ,found only a thin post-Mito phase occupation covering additional late Preceramic constructions, two of which resembled the Mito temple buildings of the KT mound (Izumi and Terada 1972:284). On the basis of the known sample of Mito constructions, it would appear that the temple buildings uncovered by the University of Tokyo constitute only a small fraction of literally dozens of similar structures. If the density of these buildings is representative for the unexcavated areas of KT and KM, there could easily be a hundred Mito period temples at Kotosh.

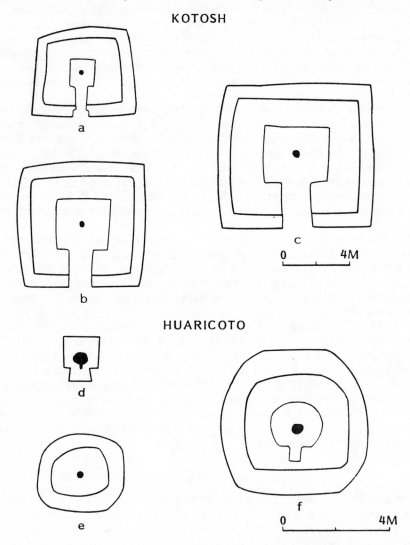

Figure 4.1. Kotosh: (a) ER-20; (b) ER-23; (c) ER-19. Huaricoto: (d) Ceremonial Hearth XII; (e) Ceremonial Hearth VII; (f) Ceremonial Hearth IV.

The eleven extant Kotosh temple buildings hold a number of architectural features in common: 1) a stone perimetric wall with a subrectangular shape, 2) a single entryway, 3) a split-level floor, 4) a centrally located semi-subterranean hearth, and 5) one or more sub-floor "flues" with outlets beyond the superstructure (Izumi and Terada 1972:129-76).[2] These buildings were apparently roofed with logs and clay. The perimetric walls were 1.5 to 2 m high, at least in those instances where the buildings were buried intact, and the excavators believe this to be the original roof level. Since most Kotosh temples were interred with only the lower courses of the perimetric wall remaining, it is not possible to determine whether in all cases the walls had been made entirely of stone, as in UR-22, or whether the upper courses might have been built of adobe or other perishable materials. There were conspicuous differences between the Kotosh temple buildings in terms of the number and arrangement of secondary architectural elements (e.g. wall paintings, clay modeling). These features, however, do not lend themselves to comparison since they can only be considered in the few instances where the perimetric walls are fairly complete.

Despite the contrasts which exist between the Kotosh constructions, the fundamental similarity in ground plan (fig. 4.1) and general construction technique make it reasonable to assume, for our purposes, that the labor investment required to construct them would have been roughly proportional to their size. We will use the surface area covered by a temple as a convenient measure, although a number of alternative methods could have been chosen. The larger the surface area covered by a temple, the more materials were necessary for walls, split-level floors, roof and so forth, and the more time necessary for gathering and transporting the raw materials, and for the construction activities.

The labor investment required to construct the older Kotosh temples is not great. The average Kotosh temple covers almost the same area as the Quechua homes studied by Mishkin in Kauri, Cuzco (49 m²). According to Mishkin (1946:440), four or five men working intermittently for several months can build a home in Kauri. Though the Kotosh temples are more elaborate in their design and finish than the houses, it is problable that a dozen people working full-time could finish a small temple structure in less than a month. The labor investment required to construct a Kotosh temple building was small compared to the time invested in Initial Period constructions like La Florida or Garagay which required millions of man-days (Ravines 1979; Patterson 1985:66).

A considerable size range, however, exists among the Mito buildings. The seven temples of the lower platform of KT can be ordered chronologically on the basis of detailed descriptions of their architecture and stratigraphic profiles. The temples on this platform show a clear trend towards increased size during the Mito phase. The oldest known structure on the platform covers 21 m², and the most recent covers 76 m² (fig. 4.2). The two structures known from the middle platform of KT are similar to each other in size, both being larger than any of the temples on the lower platform. It is difficult to interpret the stratigraphic relationship betweeen the structures on the lower and middle platforms because of the absence of direct superposition, the poor preservation of certain critical loci, and the incomplete excavation of the lower strata of the middle platform area. The excavators, however, concluded that the two levels functioned simultaneously, with access between them provided by a staircase (Izumi and Terada 1972:174-5). If this conclusion is correct, then there was not a simple unilinear increase in the size of Kotosh temple structures throughout the site during the Mito phase, although this may have been the trend on each of the platforms. The difficulty in determining

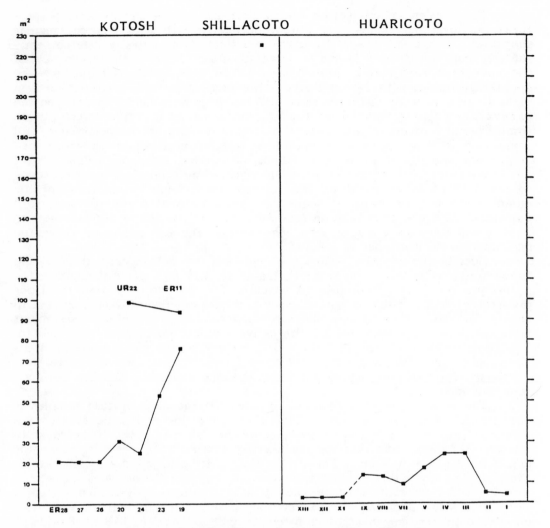

Figure 4.2. Variation of surface area of ceremonial architecture structures at each site ordered from oldest (left) to youngest (right).

the relative ages of structures in different sectors of the site prevents a consideration of the KM temple buildings in this regard.

The Kotosh Religious Tradition continued in the upper Huallaga River Basin after the Mito phase, although there is no clear evidence for its persistence at Kotosh. However, 4 km to the northeast, at the site of Shillacoto, a Mito-like temple was found associated with early Initial Period ceramics (Kano 1972:139-40; Izumi, Cuculiza, and Kano 1972:30, 75; Burger and Salazar Burger 1980:30). This structure is superimposed above at least three other temple buildings (Izumi, Cuculiza, and Kano 1972:72). The early Initial Period "Templo" of Shillacoto was only partially excavated, but it definitely resembles the Kotosh Mito temples in construction and ground plan. The stone perimetric wall of the Shillacoto temple is .5 to 1 meter higher than those at Kotosh and the building covers more than twice the area of the largest known Kotosh temple. The contrast in scale between the last of the late Preceramic temples at Kotosh and the early Initial Period temple at Shillacoto reinforces the impression that there may be a real diachronic trend in the upper Huallaga toward larger temple buildings which would have allowed the attendence of more people at the rituals, but would also have required a greater outlay of labor for the constructions.

At Huaricoto we have tentatively identified thirteen ceremonial hearths, nine of which were excavated almost in their entirety. The term "ceremonial hearth" is used to refer to the architectual feature constructed for the inciner-ation of offerings; the term subsumes the hearth and the elements framing it (floors, walls, etc.). We resort to this additional term because the word "temple" is inappropriate for many of the very modest constructions at sites like Huaricoto, although "ceremonial hearths" and temples of the Kotosh Religious Tradition are envisioned as parts of a continuum. The ceremonial hearths at Huaricoto span the late Preceramic, Initial Period, and Early Horizon. Most of those dating to the late Preceramic and Initial Period show no evidence of large imperishable walls (fig.4.3a). The modest Preceramic and Initial Period cermonial hearths would have required a fraction of the labor necessary to build even the smallest temple at Kotosh (fig. 4.2). Six other ceremonial hearths dated to the late Initial period (fig. 4.3b) and Early Horizon (fig. 4.3c) were enclosed by perimetric walls, several of which were preserved

Figure 4.3   *Ceremonial hearths from Huaricota. (a) Hearth XII, late Preceramic, lacked a stone-based perimetric wall and air duct. (b) Hearth VII, late Initial Period, had a perimetric wall of cobbles and quarried stone but lacked a lower floor. (c) Hearth IV, Early Horizon, had two air ducts, a lower floor, and a perimetric wall of dressed stones.*

due to ceremonial entombment. However, even the best conserved of the buildings shows evidence of only three or four courses of stonework. It would appear that even the largest ceremonial hearths at Huaricoto were constructed mainly of perishable materials such as adobe, using masonry only for the foundations or base and, in rare instances, for the lower part of the perimetric wall.

Like Kotosh, the Huaricoto ritual architecture varies considerably in scale. The ceremonial hearths, lacking stone foundations and evidence of superstructures, are assumed to represent the low end of the spectrum, despite the difficulties they present in quantification. Those features with their partially conserved walls cover areas ranging from as little as 5 to 24 m². Clearly, the Huaricoto ceremonial features were built on a smaller scale than their Kotosh counterparts. The largest of the Huaricoto hearths which dates to the Early Horizon, barely equals the smallest and the oldest of the excavated late Preceramic Kotosh temples. The smallest ceremonial hearths at Huaricoto have no known equivalent at Kotosh, just as the large stone temples dating to the middle and later part of the Mito phase at Kotosh have no equal at Huaricoto. The early Initial period "Templo" of Shillacoto is approximately ten times the size of thé largest Huaricoto temple construction.

The variability in the dimensions of the Huaricoto ceremonial hearths does not seem to follow a pattern of linear growth. There is relatively little noticeable change in the magnitude of the late Preceramic hearths. The fluctuations which do occur during the late Initial Period and Early Horizon do not seem to be explicable in purely diachronic terms. There seems to be a pattern of dramatic shifts from large to small buildings within a relatively short time. The contrasting size of these ritual features would have been visible to visitors to the religious center. For example, Ceremonial Hearth II was constructed half a meter to the east of the slightly earlier Ceremonial Hearth IV, but it was one-fifth as large as the neighboring structure. Despite such fluctuations, the local capacity for building large-scale ceremonial hearths does seem to increase through time. The largest of the late Initial period ceremonial hearths are bigger than the largest of their Preceramic antecedents at Huaricoto, just as the largest of the Early Horizon ceremonial hearths surpasses the most impressive of the Initial Period buildings.

Table 4.1. Construction housing ceremonial hearths: Kotosh and Huaricoto.

Architectural features		Kotosh	Huaricoto
Utilize stone-based perimeter wall		92%	54%
Utilize a split-level floor		100%	42%
Utilize air ducts		100%	62.5%
Architectural style			
Perimetric wall form:	sub-rectangular	100%	14%
	circular	–	57%
	other	–	28%
Sunken lower floor form:	composite	100%	60%
	round	–	20%
	sub-rectangular	–	20%
Hearth form:	circular	100%	86%
	semi-circular	–	14%

Variability in Style and Construction

The variability characteristic of Huaricoto ceremonial hearths contrasts markedly with the repetitious and somewhat standardized temple buildings of Kotosh (fig. 4.1). Future detailed publication of the Huaricoto results will facilitate such comparisons but some of the most striking differences have been summarized in table 4.1.

Table 4.1 documents some of the options open to the builders of a ceremonial hearth at Huaricoto. Some decisions, whether to build substantial perimetric walls may in part have been determined by labor constraints. Other construction features may have been dictated by practical concerns, such as the use of air ducts in order to get sufficient oxygen into sunken hearths when the normal flow of air was restricted by the surrounding superstructure. Purely stylistic decisions, whether to construct a circular or composite shaped lower floor, need not have significantly affected the amount of labor required for construction and must have been dictated by other considerations. It is clear, however, that the changes in these variables did not follow a simple progression of stylistic change through time. At Huaricoto, within a single epoch, it was acceptable to build a number of very different structures for the same ritual. Some of these "stylistic" decisions may have been dictated by considerations of local social organization, such as ayllu or lineage affiliation.

The final variable to be examined here is the orientation of the religious structures at Kotosh and Huaricoto. Among the cultures of the New World there was generally some rationale, astronomical or otherwise, for the positioning of ritual structures. The temple buildings at Kotosh are clearly oriented in relation to the cardinal directions (fig. 4.4), the ones on the lower platform to the south and the ones on the middle platform to the north. Fluctuations of a few degrees which occur around the cardinal axes at Kotosh are not unusual for people using unsophisticated methods of alignment (Johh Carlson, personal

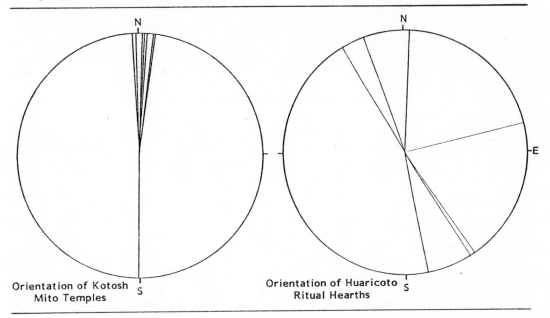

Orientation of Kotosh Mito Temples

Orientation of Huaricoto Ritual Hearths

Figure 4.4. *Orientations of ceremonial features at Kotosh and Huaricoto.*

communication). The ability to achieve even this degree of orientation to the cardinal directions requires some method, probably the observation of solstices and equinoxes (Carlson 1976:111). Orientation of buildings and sites to the cardinal directions is one of the most frequent types of astronomically determined orientations in antiquity. The temples at Kotosh are among the earliest examples known in the New World.

Determining the orientation of the Kotosh structures is a straightforward procedure since the temples are sub-rectangular in shape and have a single entrance. An imaginary axis can be drawn through the middle of the entrance which will be parallel to the lateral perimetric walls and run through the middle of the semi-subterranean hearth of the structure, dividing the building into bilaterally symmetric halves. Unfortunately, it is not possible to follow the same procedure at Huaricoto because of the lack of unambiguous entrances. However, it is possible in all but the circular buildings, to delineate a central axis which crosses the hearth and divides the structure into bilaterally symmetric parts. At Kotosh, the narrower portion of the lower floors always faced the entrance. If this is also true for Huaricoto, the orientations of ceremonial hearths I, II, IV, XI, XII, and XIII can be provisionally determined. The air ducts in these structures run out of the hearth in the direction of the hypothetical entrance and orientation. If this positioning of flues were characteristic of the remaining hearths as well, it would become possible to suggest the orientations of those with circular superstructures. The orientations of the Huaricoto ceremonial hearths and the Kotosh temples are illustrated together in figure 4.4 for comparative purposes.

The ceremonial hearths at Huaricoto do not point towards the cardinal directions. Most of the orientations are to the southeast or the northwest, roughly the direction of the valley floor in this part of the Callejón de Huaylas. Several of the later ceremonial hearths at Huaricoto are aligned to the northeast, perhaps in deference to one of the snow-capped peaks of the Cordillera Blanca (e.g., Nevado Carhuacatac, 6,171 meters elevation). No matter what, if any, interpretation of the orientations of the Huaricoto buildings is followed, it would seem clear that there is substantially more variability in building orientation at Huaricoto than at Kotosh and that the somewhat esoteric knowledge of astronomical matters like solstices was not employed at Huaricoto to orient the ceremonial hearths.

Discussion and Conclusions

At the outset of this article, an attempt was made to delineate the way in which the ritual architecture built by a cargolike system of authority and labor mobilization might be distinguished archaeologically from constructions of a similar function built by corporate labor. The absolute scale of the structures, the fluctuations in labor input, the complexity of the undertakings, and the degree of short-term variability were specified as being potentially sensitive to such organizational differences. Since our consideration of these organizational factors was stimulated by our work at Huaricoto and the contrast which the site presented with Kotosh, it should not surprise the reader that the archaeological evidence from Huaricoto was, for the most part, consistent with the rotational model of organization. We would still argue, however, that the organizational factors discussed here are useful for explaining the empirical differences between the sites of Kotosh and Huaricoto, and will be equally serviceable for the understanding of differences between centers of the Kotosh Religious Tradition, to be investigated in the future.

Izumi and Terada (1972:306) suggested that the well-planned, large-scale Mito architecture found at Kotosh must have been built by a highly organized society in which powerful leaders or priests could compel the people to work for religious purposes. The regularity and conservatism in the design of the Kotosh temples over several centuries, along with the standardized orientation of these buildings to the cardinal directions, is consistent with the notion that the undertakings were organized and directed by recognized leaders capable of subordinating the will of individual households in order to ensure the continuity of ritual patterns. While corporate labor was probably responsible for the constructions at Kotosh, there does not appear to be evidence of the segmentation attributed to mitalike labor systems in later times.

The ceremonial hearths at Huaricoto show a remarkable diversity in form and construction. Such variability is difficult to reconcile with a permanent, although not necessarily full-time, source of authority. The unique characteristics of most ceremonial hearths, along with the multiplicity of orientations, suggests that responsibility for their construction may have devolved upon many different individual units (e.g., households), as occurs among modern societies having rotational systems of ritual authority and responsibility. The erratic fluctuations that occur in size and, by implication, in labor investment also conform to the expectations stated at the outset in contrast to the situation at Kotosh, which would have been constructed on a cost sharing basis. The construction of the ceremonial hearths at Huaricoto is well within the capacity of a household and does not require the postulation of corporate labor.

Some differences betweeen Huaricoto and Kotosh can be accounted for by the organizational dichotomy presented here, but a number of alternative hypotheses also come to mind. The most obvious of these would be to attribute the disparity in scale and variability to factors of space or time, thereby reducing Huaricoto to a "regional" variant or later version of Kotosh. Light is shed on this possibility by the site of Galgada, which is located 115 km from Huaricoto and 265 km from Kotosh. Despite Galgada's greater proximity to Huaricoto, the late Preceramic Galgada temple buildings are strikingly similar to those at Kotosh in size, ground plan, and construction (Grieder and Bueno 1981). This resemblance appears to continue into the Initial Period, when comparing Shillacoto with the upper levels at Galgada. Thus, it would seem that temporal and spatial dimensions are not responsible for the sharp contrasts between Huaricoto and Kotosh.

The dissimilarity of Huaricoto would also be understandable if the assumption were incorrect that the ceremonial hearths at Huaricoto served the same function as temples at the larger sites. However, the archaeological context and associations of these features militates against this alternative. It could also be suggested that Huaricoto held a different position in some hypothetical hierarchy of ceremonial centers, sites like Kotosh or Galgada being primary ceremonial centers while sites like Huaricoto being secondary (Burger and Salazar Burger 1980:29). Such an approach is compatible with, but not implied by, the argument that the specific differences between them are principally a function of organizational factors. The evaluation of regional hierarchies of religious centers would require additional information on other poorly understood "formative" sites in the Callejón de Huaylas, at least half a dozen of which could contain the remains of centers like Huaricoto, or even Kotosh.

A number of architectural features in Kotosh and Huaricoto have not been considered up to this point, but they are germane to the discussion. At Kotosh there appears to have been the simultaneous operation of temple buildings on the different platforms. Moreover, there are considerable variations in secondary architectural elements (Izumi and Terada 1972:29), although the ground plan remained roughly the same. A comparable situation was encountered at the late Preceramic center of Aspero. Moseley (1975:94) has suggested that such differences might imply that early corporate authority on the coast was essentially pluralistic. A similar interpretation might be applied to Kotosh. If corporate authority at Kotosh was pluralistic, the gap between it and the rotational system of authority postulated for Huaricoto would be narrowed.

At Huaricoto there were several large-scale undertakings which shaped, ordered, and preserved the mound upon which the ceremonial hearths were built. Most notable among these were the central stone platform built during the late Preceramic period, the narrow stone terraces used to consolidate the north edge of the shrine during the Initial Period, and the massive stone walls which partitioned the shrine during the Early Horizon. Each of these projects must have drawn a work force from a number of households. Such occasional activities, however, do not imply the existence of corporate authority, since non-corporate group activities, such as the construction of terraces and the cleaning of canals, are well documented in the present ethnographic record for highland Peru.

The variability at Kotosh and the large-scale activities at Huaricoto raise some interesting questions about the limitations of our hypothesis. Perhaps the most notable incongruity between the expectations outlined at the beginning of the article and the archaeological patterning at Kotosh and Huaricoto is the failure of the hypothesis to account for the apparent increase in the scale of the temple structures. The original model proposed that corporate labor was less vulnerable to short-term fluctuations in labor expenditure than cargolike systems of organization which were presumably based upon smaller social units. Using Moseley's original formulation, the former system of labor mobilization might be expected to show little change through time if the degree and nature of authority remained fixed. However, the possibility of population change must be taken into account when dealing with long time spans, and such considerations are especially pressing with the late Preceramic and Initial Periods. These are frequently correlated with the diversification and intensification of agriculture and with marked population growth on the coast and highlands of Peru (Patterson 1971; Cohen 1978; MacNeish, Patterson and Browman 1975). An expanding population would permit additional labor to be incorporated into existing systems of organization without necessarily changing either the degree or nature of authority. This circumstance would produce a corresponding increase in total labor expenditure. We have already noted that the temples in the upper Huallaga appear gradually to increase in size, and Grieder (personal communication) has reported comparable increases in the size of the Galgada temples. At Huaricoto, the capacity for building ceremonial hearths also seems to develop, although this pattern is somewhat obscured by erratic short-term fluctuations. A parallel increase at Huaricoto is registered in other constructions, with the erection of the Early Horizon megalithic walls representing the greatest single expenditure of energy during the history of the site.

A dichotomy has been drawn here between early societies utilizing corporate labor and those using one possible alternative, a system of rotating ritual authority within which labor is mobilized through ties of blood marriage, ritual kinship, and friendship. These systems have been presented as two options which may have been exercised by the early societies of highland Peru during the second and first millennia B.C. But these organizational arrangements are not static over time. Under various types of stress, cargolike systems give way to other forms of organization such as cost-sharing, just as the importance of cargo systems in recent centuries is probably the result of the Colonial destruction of the upper levels of traditional indigenous authority and the concurrent depopulation of the Andes and Mesoamerica. The dynamic processes leading to these organizational transformations are rarely documented but Mesoamerican ethnography has provided some interesting leads. Cancian (1965), for example, has shown the way in which rapid population growth undermined the cargo system of Zinacantan, while Brandes (1981) has related the local decline of the cargo system in Tzintzunzan to the emergence of social stratification.

Childe (1944:23) observed that "the archaeological record is, to put it mildly, vague as to the social organization of preliterate communities" and archaeologists in the Andes have been understandably loath to become involved in the inference of what admittedly are intangible institutions. Yet as Carneiro (1974:179) and many others have concluded, the transformation at the core of the emergence of complex societies may be primarily organizational. Thus, the nature and variety of early organizational arrangements, and the causes of transitions between them are of critical importance to archaeologists and deserve far more scrutiny than they have received.

The archaeological evidence considered here is uneven and sparse. We hope, however, that our discussion will stimulate debate and eventually lead to a better understanding of early systems of Andean organization and the way in which they can be inferred from the archaeological record.

Acknowledgments

The research at Huaricoto was conducted with the support of the National Geographic Society, the Organization of American States, the Museo Nacional de Antropología y Arqueología and the Instituto Nacional de Cultura. Clifford Evans unflinchingly embraced open and good-natured controversy and this article is dedicated to him.

Notes

1. Ravines and Isbell (1976:267) proposed that the monumental late Initial Period center of Garagay may have been built using a cargolike system, but no attempt was made to evaluate this possibility using the archaeological record.

2. EFI-25 is an apparent exception to this description. It consists of a split-level floor with a semi-subterranean hearth and sub-floor flues, but there is no indication of a perimetric wall. The excavators believe that EFI-25 may have been built without a surrounding wall (Izumi and Terada 1972:162.

References

Alberti, Giorgio, and Enrique Mayer.
   1974 Reciprocidad andina: Ayer y hoy. In Reciprocidad e Intercambio en los Andes Peruanos, edited by Giorgio Alberti and Enrique Mayer, 13-33. Lima: Instituto de Estudios Peruanos.

Aranguren, Angélica.
   1977 Las creencias y ritos mágicos-religiosos de los Pastores. Allpanchis Phuturinqa 8(1975): 103-32.

Brandes, Stanley.
  1981 Cargos versus cost sharing: Mesoamerican fiestas with special references to Tzintzuntzan. Journal of Anthropological Research 37(3): 209-25.

Bricker, Victoria.
  1978 Symbolic representations of protohistoric social stratification and religious organization in a modern Maya community. In Codex Wauchope: A Tribute Roll, edited by Marco Giardino, Barbara Edmonson and Winifred Creamer, 39-56. Human Mosaic Vol. 12. Tulane University.

Burger, Richard L., and Lucy Salazar Burger.
  1980 Ritual and religion at Huaricoto. Archaeology 33:26-32.

Cancian, Frank.
  1965 Economics and Prestige in a Maya Community: The Religious Cargo System of Zinacantan. Stanford University Press.

Carlson, John.
  1976 Astronomical investigations and site orientation influences at Palenque. In The Art, Iconography, and Dynastic History of Palenque, Part III: Proceedings of the Segunda Mesa Redonda de Palenque, edited by Merle Greene Robertson, 107-22. Pebble Beach, CA: Pre-Columbian Art Research, The Robert Louis Stevenson School.

Carneiro, Robert.
  1974 A reappraisal of the roles of technology and organization in the origin of civilization. American Antiquity 39(2): 179-86.

Carrasco, Pedro.
  1961 The civil-religious hierarchy in Mesoamerican communities: Pre-Spanish background of the colonial development. American Anthropologist 63:483-97.

Childe, V. Gordon.
  1944 Archaeological ages as technological stages. Journal of the Royal Anthropological Institute 74:7-24.

Coe, Michael.
  1965 A model of ancient community structure in the Maya lowlands. Southwestern Journal of Anthropology 21:97-114.

Cohen, Mark N.
  1978 Population pressure and the origins of agriculture: An archaeological example from the coast of Peru. In Advances in Andean Archaeology, edited by David L. Browman, 91-132. The Hague: Mouton.

Day, Kent.
  1982 Storage and labor service: A production and management design in the Andean area. In Chan Chan: Andean Desert City, edited by Michael E. Moseley and Kent Day, 333-49. University of New Mexico Press.

Feldman, Robert A.
  1977   Life in ancient Peru.   Field Museum of Natural History Bulletin 48(6):
         12-17.

Fonseca, Cesar.
  1973   Sistemas económicos andinos.   Lima: Seminario de Historia Rural
         Andina.

Grieder, Terence, and Alberto Bueno Mendoza.
  1981   La Galgada: Peru before pottery.   Archaeology 34:45-51.

Haviland, William A.
  1966   Social integration and the Classic Maya.   American Antiquity 31(5),
         pt. 1:625-31.

Isbell, Billie Jean.
  1978   To Defend Ourselves: Ecology and Ritual in an Andean Village.
         Institute of Latin American Studies, The University of Texas, Austin.

Izumi, Seiichi, Pedro Cuculiza, and Chiaki Kano.
  1972   Excavations at Shillacoto, Huanuco, Peru.   The University Museum,
         Bulletin No. 3.   Tokyo: University of Tokyo.

Izumi, Seiichi, and Kazuo Terada.
  1972   Andes 4:   Excavations at Kotosh, Peru 1963 and 1966.   Tokyo:
         University of Tokyo Press.

Kano, Chiaki.
  1972   Pre-Chavín cultures in the central highlands of Peru: New evidence
         from Shillacoto, Huanuco.   In Cult of the Feline, edited by Elizabeth
         P. Benson, 139-52.   Washington: Dumbarton Oaks Research Library
         and Collection, Trustees for Harvard University.

Kubler, George.
  1946   The Quechua in the Colonial world.   In Handbook of South American
         Indians 2, edited by Julian Steward, 331-410.   Washington: United
         States Government Printing Office.

MacNeish, Richard S., Thomas Patterson, and David Browman.
  1975   The Central Peruvian Interaction Sphere.   Papers of the Robert S.
         Peabody Foundation 7.   Andover, Mass.

Mishkin, Bernard.
  1946   The contemporary Quechua.   In Handbook of South American Indians
         2, edited by Julian Steward, 411-70.

Moseley, Michael.
  1975   The Maritime Foundations of Andean Civilization.   Menlo Park, CA:
         Cummings Publishing Company.

  1975a Prehistoric principles of labor organization in the Moche Valley, Peru.
         American Antiquity 40:191-96.

1978   The evolution of Andean civilization. In Ancient Native Americans, edited by Jesse D. Jennings, 491-541. San Francisco: W. H. Freeman and Company.

Patterson, Thomas C.
1971   Central Peru: Its population and economy. Archaeology 24:316-21.

1985   The Huaca La Florida, Rimac Valley, Peru. In Early Ceremonial Architecture in the Andes, edited by Christopher Donnan, 59-69. Washington, D.C.: Dumbarton Oaks Research Library and Collection.

Pozorski, Thomas.
1980   The Early Horizon site of Huaca de los Reyes: Societal implications. American Antiquity 45:100-10.

Ravines, Rogger.
1979   Garagay como arqueología experimental. In Arqueología Peruana: Investigaciones arqueológicas en el Perú 1976, edited by Ramiro Matos, 75-80. Lima: Centro de Projección Cristiana.

Ravines, Rogger, and William H. Isbell.
1976   Garagay: Sitio ceremonial temprano en el Valle de Lima. Revista del Museo Nacional 41:253-75.

Redfield, Robert.
1941   The Folk Culture of Yucatan. University of Chicago Press.

Rhoades, Robert, and Stephen Thompson.
1975   Adaptive strategies in Alpine environments: Beyond ecological particularism. American Ethnologist 2(3): 535-51.

Rowe, John Howland.
1946   Inca culture at the time of the Spanish conquest. In Handbook of South American Indians 2, edited by Julian H. Steward, 183-330. Washington D.C: Smithsonian Institution, Bureau of American Ethnology Bulletin 143.

Webb, Malcolm.
1975   The flag follows trade: an essay on the necessary interaction of military and commerical factors in state formation. In Ancient Civilization and Trade, edited by Jeremy Sabloff and Carl Lamberg-Karlovsky, 155-209. Albuquerque: University of New Mexico Press.

5.

C14 and Cultural Chronology on the
North Coast of Peru:
Implications for a Regional Chronology

Richard P. Watson

Numerous chronologies have been applied to the North Coast of Peru. The major difficulty in using these chronologies for regional comparison is that most were developed for specific valleys (Willey 1953; Donnan and Mackey 1978; Rodriquez Suy Suy n.d.; Hecker and Hecker 1977; Zevallos Quiñones 1971; Matos Mendieta 1965-66; Izumi and Terada 1966) or represent Pan-Andean chronologies (Rowe 1962; Lanning 1967; Willey 1971). While the latter suffer from overgeneralization, making them insensitive to changes and developments which occurred largely or entirely on the North Coast, the former are so specific that multivalley or regional continuities and commonalities are obscured.

The chronology presented here (fig. 5.1) is patterned after the "master sequence" approach of Rowe (1962). The horizon and period designations of Rowe have been retained; however, the beginning and ending dates have, in some cases, been modified to coincide more closely with the North Coast evidence. In addition, letters have been substituted for numerals in the subdivision of the various periods and horizons in order to avoid confusion with the numerical division of the Early Intermediate Period, Moche phase.

Although no single valley on the North Coast has a well-dated sequence extending from the Preceramic Period to the Late Horizon, the combination of archaeological and C14 evidence from the Chicama, Moche, and Virú valleys is sufficient to develop a master sequence for the North Coast (fig. 5.1). A more complete discussion of this sequence and the evidence upon which it is based is presented below.

Periods and Horizons

The Preceramic Period on the North Coast is characterized by a wide range of cultural adaptations and developments extending over a very long period of time, in excess of 8,000 years (Padre Aban, Tx-1935, Tx-1933, Tx-1934,Tx-1936; Huaca Prieta, C-318a, C-318b, C-321, C-315, L-116B(1), L-116A, L-116B(2), C-362, C-313, C-598, C-316) (see tables 5.7b, 5.7c, 5.8b, 5.8c). The most obvious defining characteristic of this period is the lack of ceramics, which are not found in this region until about 2100-2000 B.C. Dated materials from this period place the first occurrence of cotton textiles at some time around 2500-2400 B.C. The appearance of cotton textiles has been used on the Central and South coasts to define the Cotton Preceramic (Engel 1957; Moseley 1975b). This division is not used in the chronology proposed here, although some means of subdividing this excessively long period would be useful.

The Initial Period, marked by the first occurrence of ceramics, appears to have begun about 2100-2000 B.C. and to have lasted until around 1400 B.C. Ten C14 dates from three sites can be associated with this period (Caballo Muerto, Tx-1937, Tx-1938; Gramalote, Tx-1930A, Tx-1929A, Tx-1929B, Tx-1931B, Tx-1931A, Tx-1930B; Huaca Prieta, C-322—2 assays) (see tables 5.7a, 5.7b, 5.8b).

S. Pozorski (1976; Pozorski and Pozorski 1979) has documented an early occurrence of maize on the North Coast during this period on the basis of two cobs and a husk fragment recovered from the site of Gramalote. On the basis of evidence for the intial mound construction at Caballo Muerto, the construction of ceremonial structures requiring corporate labor was first initiated during this period (T. Pozorski 1976, 1980; Pozorski and Pozorski 1979).

The Early Horizon is characterized by the appearance of a jaguar cult which, on the North Coast, is represented on ceramics and in monumental architecture (Larco Hoyle 1941; T. Pozorski 1976, 1980). This horizon begins about 1400 B.C. in the Moche Valley. On the basis of a series of uncalibrated C14 dates, T. Pozorski (1980) estimates that the initial construction at Huaca de los Reyes occurred about 1350 B.C. (Huaca Herederos Chica, Tx-1937, Tx-1938; Huaca de los Reyes, Tx-2181, Tx-2180, Tx-1973, Tx-1972, Tx-1974; Huaca Guavalito, Tx-1939) (see table 5.7a). The dendrochronologically calibrated dates presented here, however, indicate that a date between 1500 B.C. and 1400 B.C. might be a better estimate. In his initial discussion of C14 dates from Caballo Muerto, Pozorski states that Tx-1974 seems to be too early (T. Pozorski 1976; Valastro, Davis, and Varela 1978). Such a date would, however, be consistent with an Initial Period occupation and may merely represent carbon from an earlier construction.

From the Chicama, a wooden roof timber from a subterranean structure in Huaca Prieta, which was associated with Cupisnique ceramics and maize, has been dated to the middle of this period (C-75) (see table 5.8b).

West has obtained three dates from carbon associated with Early Horizon materials and architecture in the Virú Valley (V-127, UCLA-1976A, UCLA-1976B; V-434, UCLA-1974E) (see tables 5.6a, 5.6b). The latest of these dates, UCLA-1974E, coincides well with the end of the Early Horizon and the beginning of the Early Intermediate Period, both contextually and chronologically (West, personal communication).

The Early Intermediate Period (EIP) on the North Coast is probably most easily defined as beginning with the appearance of white-on-red ceramics (Salinar and Puerto Moorin) and ending with the disappearance of the Moche V style and the introduction of highland (Huari ?) characteristics (Schaedel 1978). On the basis of recent radiocarbon assays from Puerto Moorin phase materials (Early Intermediate Period-A) from the Virú Valley (West, personal communication), this period begins somewhat earlier than has generally been assumed. The Early Intermediate Period on the North Coast can be subdivided into three phases on the basis of ceramic, iconographic, settlement, mortuary, metallurgical, and agricultural evidence: the Salinar/Puerto Moorin phase (A), the

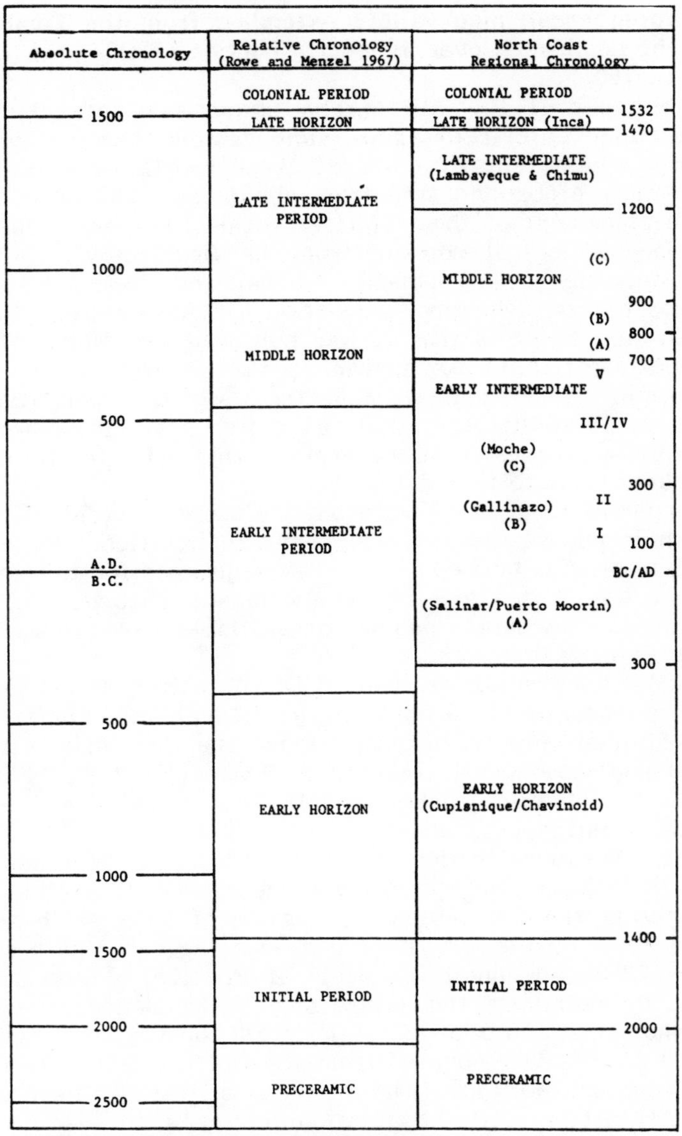

Figure 5.1.   *Comparative chronological chart: Pan-Peruvian chronology to North Coast regional chronology.*

Gallinazo phase (B), and the Moche phase (C). The Salinar/Puerto Moorin phase lasted from about 300 B.C. until some time between A.D. 1 and A.D. 100. The Gallinazo phase appears to have lasted about 100 to 150 years in the Chicama and Moche valleys, from about A.D. 1 to A.D. 100-150. In the Virú Valley, however, the Gallinazo phase persisted for 200 to 300 years, beginning from some time between A.D. 1 and A.D. 100 and lasting until about A.D. 300. During the last 150 to 200 years of this period (A.D. 100-150 to A.D. 300), the first two subphases of the Moche phase developed in the Chicama and Moche valleys.

About A.D. 300, the Gallinazo phase of the Virú Valley comes to an abrupt end. At this time, archaeological evidence indicates that the Moche of the Chicama and Moche valleys expanded their hegemony out of their homeland. This expansion, apparently accomplished through military conquest, ultimately encompassed nine valleys extending from the Lambayeque to the Nepeña. Moche dominance over at least a portion of this area was maintained until about A.D. 700.

The subphases of the EIP Moche phase are defined on the basis of stylistic differences apparent in ceramic vessels (Larco Hoyle 1948). The exact temporal placement of each of these subphases is unknown, but the entire Moche phase probably lasted from about A.D. 300 to A.D. 750. Some feeling for the placement of the subphases within this period can be gained by looking to the archaeological evidence from the Virú Valley.

Moche ceramics from subphases I-II have not been recovered from the Virú Valley in contexts suggesting occupation. Evidence from the Santa Valley (Donnan 1973) also suggests that it was not until the Moche III-IV subphases that there was significant expansion to the south. Excavations by West (personal communication) indicate that the Gallinazo occupation of the Virú Valley lasted until about A.D. 300, at which time there was an apparent incursion of Moche peoples from the north. This indicates that subphases I-II must have occured prior to that date.

As is apparent from this discussion, the use of several valleys to develop a master chronological sequence poses serious difficulties. In order to resolve the obvious discrepancies between the valley sequences for this period, the Virú Valley sequence was chosen to serve as the master sequence for the Early Intermediate Period. The larger number of available C14 dates relevant to this period was the defining criterion.

The Middle Horizon begins about A.D. 700 with the demise of the Moche phase and the introduction of a constellation of highland (Huari ?) traits. This period is subdivided into three phases along the lines originally proposed by Stumer (1956) and subsequently revised by Schaedel (1978). Phase (A) lasted only about 50 to 100 years, between A.D. 700 and A.D. 800. This phase is marked by the simultaneous occurrence of both old local styles and intrusive highland styles. In reviewing figures 5.2 through 5.7, it becomes apparent that very few of the illustrated sites show the presence of a Middle Horizon (A) occupation, giving the erroneous impression of large-scale depopulation or massive relocations. While the latter has been suggested as a Middle Horizon trait (Schaedel 1978), an equally plausible alternative, or corollary, hypothesis may be found by examining the nature of the archaeological evidence. This apparent chronological gap probably stems from the fact that few purely Huari style ceramics have been recovered from the North Coast. Even fewer of the known examples come from identifiable contexts. As has been pointed out by Schaedel (1978), little work has been conducted to discover and isolate nonceramic traits which are directly attributable to highland influences. As a result, only those sites from which Middle Horizon (A) ceramics have been recovered were assigned to this phase. Undoubtedly, as more Middle Horizon diagnostics are enumerated, these gaps will be filled.

Phase (B) represents the fusion of old local styles with highland styles which produces new local styles along with what Stumer (1956) refers to as "decadent Wari" (Wari Norteño B: Larco Hoyle 1948). This phase begins about A.D. 800 and lasts until A.D. 900 or 1000.

The final phase (C) of the Middle Horizon is characterized for ceramic remains by Stumer (1956) as:

> one of elimination of the last vestiges of the 2 main original strains, local and highland intrusive, in anything approaching their pure forms. There is also the consolidation of various original elements with those having arrived during the previous period, thus achieving a sound and almost completely formed basis for the future regional style. This stage is also one of elimination

of many design and form elements which were prominent during the extreme fusion of the second stage. At this time as well, form analysis of ceramics reveals a tendency to go back to a number of forms in general use during the pre-Tiahuancoid days and in comparative eclipse during the fusional epoch's height. (Stumer 1956:67)

Schaedel (1978) reaffirms the significance of this phase as a precursor to regional styles and polities which developed in the Late Intermediate Period.

Julien (1980:68-71) reports four radiocarbon dates from the Middle Horizon site of V-358 in the Virú Valley (Tx-3788, Tx-3790, Tx-3787, Tx-3789) (see table 5.6b). The assignment of this site to the Middle Horizon was accomplished on the basis of excavated utilitarian ceramics and is well supported by the C14 dates.

The Early Middle Horizon is known so far from only a single site in the Chicama Valley—Pelenque (Donnan 1968). Radiocarbon dates directly relating to this horizon in the Virú, Moche, and Chicama valleys are unfortunately lacking. The definition of these periods was made from ceramic and architectural seriations resulting from reconnaissance data (Kluge, Rabinowitz, and Watson 1976; Kosok n.d.).

The Late Intermediate Period (LIP) begins about A.D. 1200, with the founding of the Chimu Imperial Dynasty. This date follows Schaedel's (1978) argument that the Late Intermediate Period be defined on ethnohistoric evidence to include only ethnohistorically documented pre-Inca peoples and polities. Published C14 dates from architectural contexts for this period, and for the following Late Horizon, are all but nonexistent. The largest number of LIP dates is from the Chicama-Moche Intervalley Canal (Kus 1972) (UCLA-1711I, UCLA-1711G, UCLA-1711H, UCLA-1711E, UCLA-1711F, UCLA-1711C, UCLA-1711A, UCLA-1711B) (see table 5.8a). A single date has also been reported for materials from the Uhle Compound at Chan Chan (Moseley 1975a) (Gx-3253) (see table 5.7b). There are no published dates for Late Horizon contexts from any of the North Coast valleys.

The Late Horizon on the North Coast, as in the Ica sequence, is defined as beginning with the Inca conquest, sometime between 1470 and 1480, with the most likely date being 1476. This period ends with the arrival of the Spanish in 1532, which also marks the beginning of the Colonial period.

Statement of Purpose

This paper is not presented as, nor was it ever intended to be, the definitive solution to the problems of cultural chronology on the North Coast of Peru. Rather, it is an attempt to provide a common ground from which a discussion of North Coast chronology can begin. The compilation of calibrated and raw dates is intended to provide a corpus of readily available dates to which new and unpublished dates can be compared. The presentation of sources for each date, and in many cases, supplementary references to the dated sites, should greatly facilitate the use of this material. Only within a well defined chronological framework can the processual problems now concerning archaeologists be addressed. This paper is an attempt to stimulate the development of such a framework.

Figures 5.3 through 5.7 compile the local chronologies, where available, for the individual valleys extending from the Casma Valley in the south to the Tumbes Valley in the north. In those valleys for which a published chronology or sequence was lacking (Casma, Nepeña, and Saña), I have used the regional chronology developed by Schaedel (n.d.; Shimada 1979). All chronologies are drawn to a single scale for ease of comparison. Four sites from the near North Highlands for which several radiocarbon dates are available were also included for comparative purposes (fig. 5.2).

In addition to the local chronologies, selected archaeological sites from each valley have been included in their appropriate temporal position: the temporal placements of these sites are based on dendrochronologically calibrated radiocarbon dates and/or on the basis of archaeological evidence where absolute dates are not available (see figs. 5.2-5.7 and tables 5.1-5.15).

Tables 5.1 through 5.15 represent a summary of the radiocarbon and archaeological evidence used in the temporal placement of these sites, as well as the sources from which the evidence is derived. As can be seen from figures 5.3 through 5.7, there is considerable variation in the temporal placement of chronological periods on the North Coast.

Notes for Tables 5.1–5.15.

1. Unless otherwise noted the original date (B.P.) is given first, standardized to 1950, and is followed by dendrochronologically calibrated B.P. and calendar dates. Calibrations accomplished using the procedure presented by Damon et al. (1974). The calibrated standard deviation was calculated as the square root of the sum of the variances, see Damon et al. (1974:365). All original dates are reported using the 5568 half-life.

2. Chronological periods represented at each site or with C14 sample: Colonial period (C), Late Horizon (LH), Late Intermediate Period (LIP), Middle Horizon (MH), Early Intermediate Period (EIP), Early Horizon (EH), Preceramic (PC).

3. Original date reported was standardized to 1960, it has been calibrated accordingly.

4. Sample numbers reported by Cárdenas (1979) are from the C14 laboratory at the Universidad Católica del Perú.

5. This date was determined using a solid state assay technique. Refinements in the methods of assay indicate that solid state measurements may contain substantial error.

6. Assay beyond the range of calibration tables. Calendar date reported is corrected to the 5730 half-life.

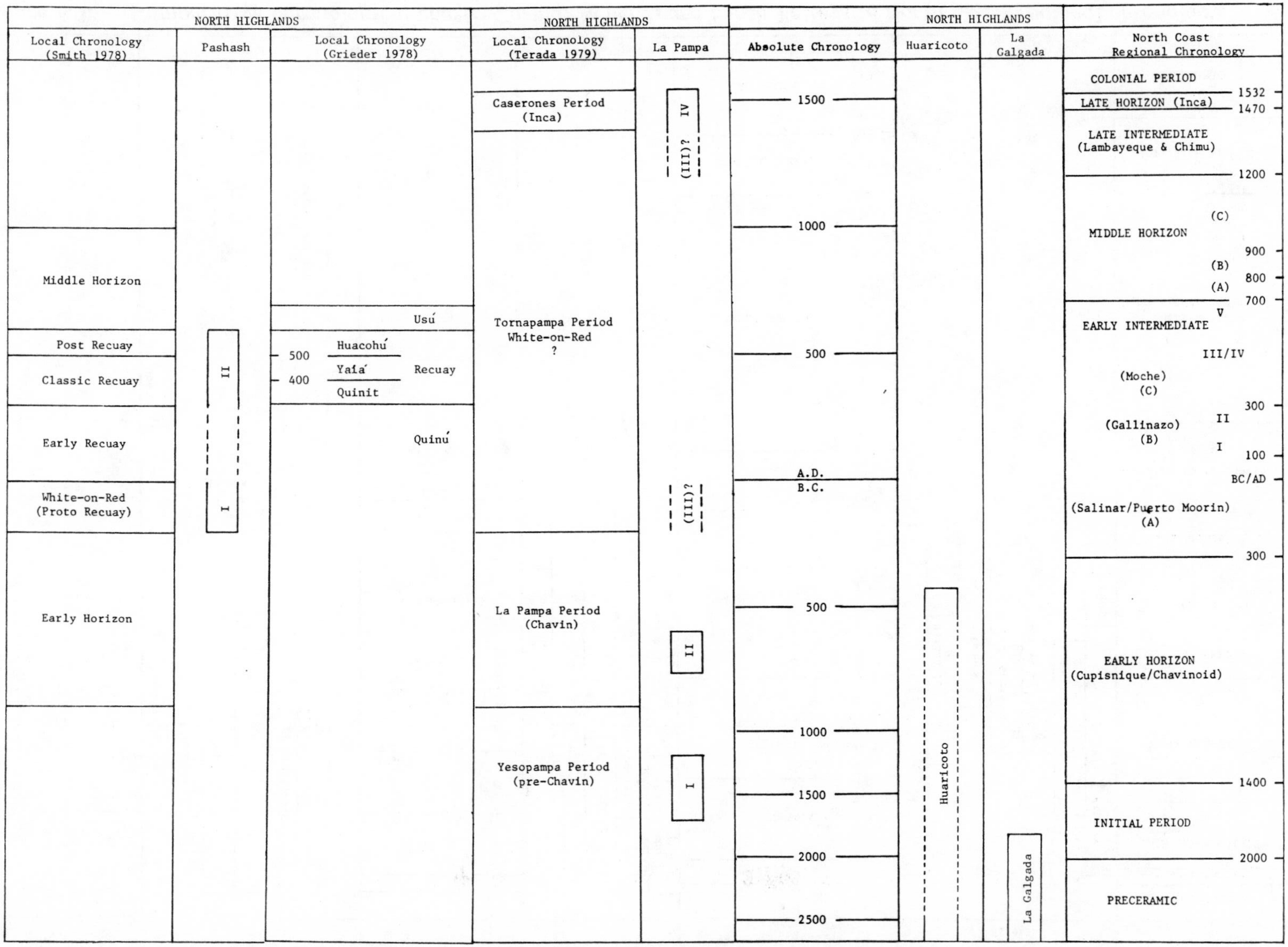

Comparative chronological chart columns:

North Coast Regional Chronology

- COLONIAL PERIOD
- LATE HORIZON (Inca) — 1532, 1470
- LATE INTERMEDIATE (Lambayeque & Chimu) — 1200
- MIDDLE HORIZON (C) 900, (B) 800, (A) 700
- EARLY INTERMEDIATE — V, III/IV, (Moche)(C), II (Gallinazo)(B) 300, I 100, (Salinar/Puerto Moorin)(A), BC/AD, 300
- EARLY HORIZON (Cupisnique/Chavinoid) — 1400
- INITIAL PERIOD — 2000
- PRECERAMIC

NORTH HIGHLANDS — La Galgada

- La Galgada

NORTH HIGHLANDS — Huaricoto

- Huaricoto

Absolute Chronology

- 1500, 1000, 500, A.D. / B.C., 500, 1000, 1500, 2000, 2500

La Pampa

- IV ¿(III)
- ¿(III)
- II
- I

NORTH HIGHLANDS — Local Chronology (Terada 1979)

- Caserones Period (Inca)
- Tornapampa Period — White-on-Red ?
- La Pampa Period (Chavin)
- Yesopampa Period (pre-Chavin)

Local Chronology (Grieder 1978)

- Usú
- Huacohú — 500
- Yafá — 400
- Quinit
- Recuay
- Quinú

NORTH HIGHLANDS — Pashash

- II
- I

Local Chronology (Smith 1978)

- Middle Horizon
- Post Recuay
- Classic Recuay
- Early Recuay
- White-on-Red (Proto Recuay)
- Early Horizon

Figure 5.2. *Comparative chronological chart: North Highlands (Pashash, La Pampa, Huaricoto, La Galgada) to North Coast regional chronology.*

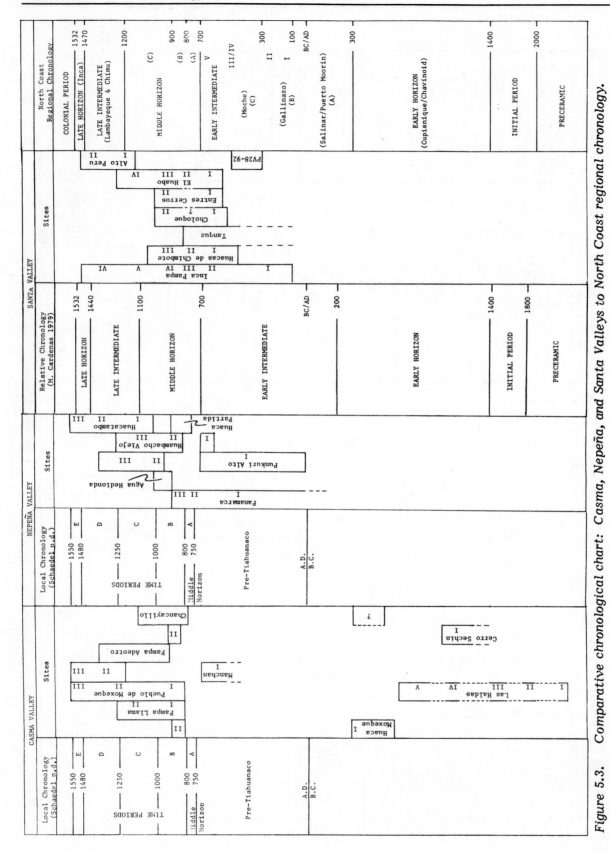

Figure 5.3.   Comparative chronological chart: Casma, Nepeña, and Santa Valleys to North Coast regional chronology.

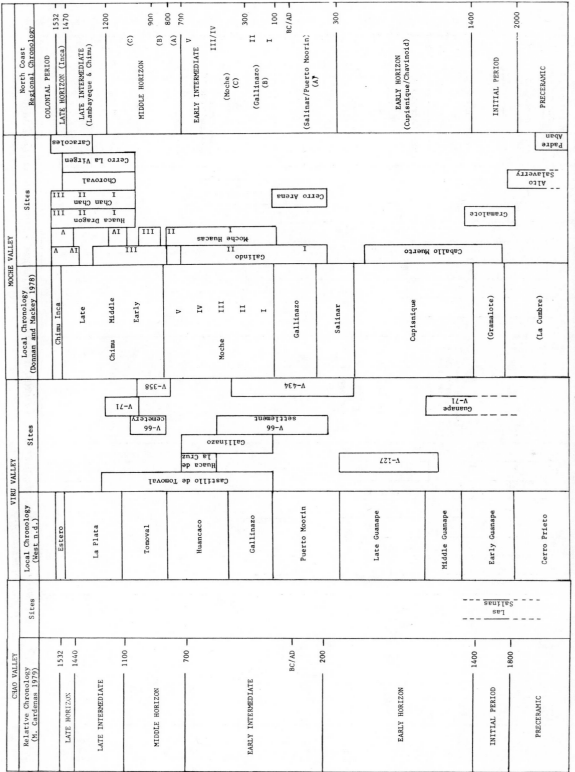

Figure 5.4. *Comparative chronological chart: Chao, Virú, and Moche Valleys to North Coast regional chronology.*

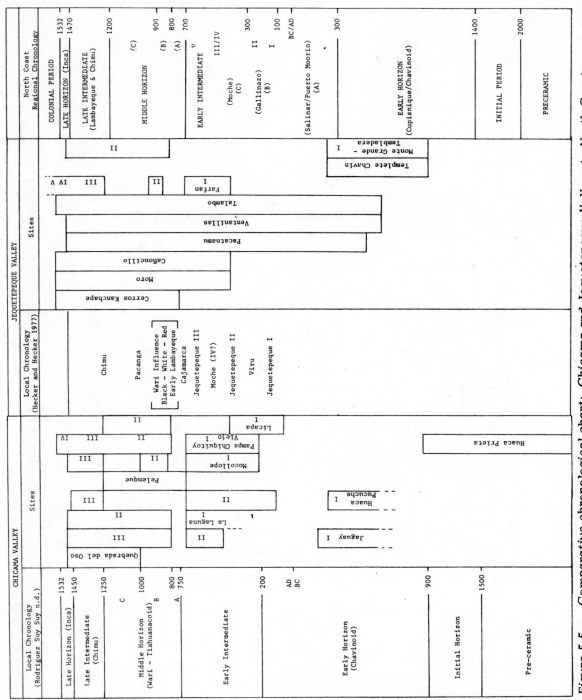

Figure 5.5. *Comparative chronological chart: Chicama and Jequetepeque Valleys to North Coast regional chronology.*

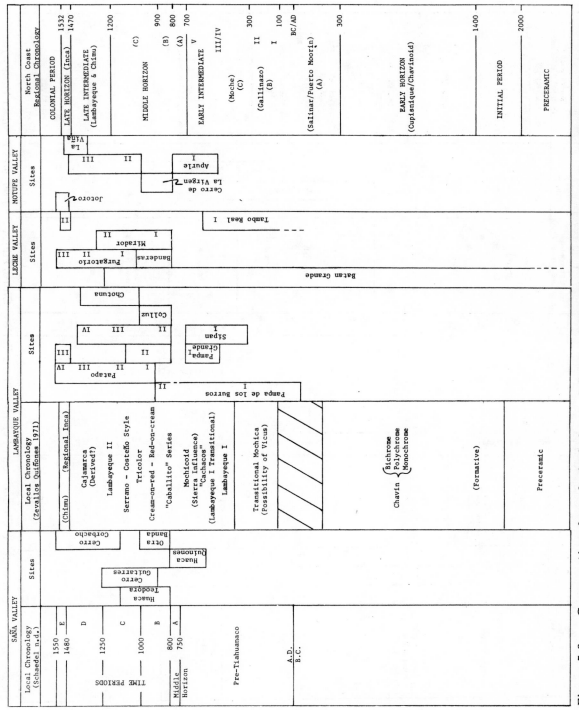

Figure 5.6. Comparative chronological chart: Saña, Lambayeque, Leche, and Motupe Valleys to North Coast regional chronology.

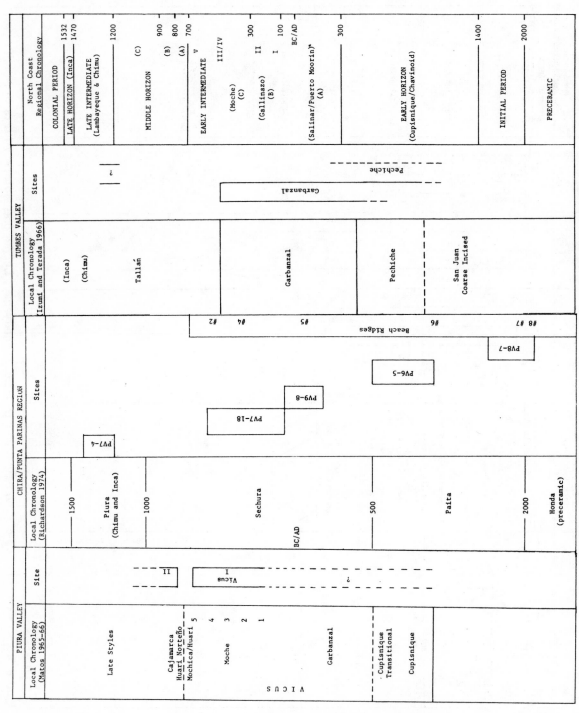

Figure 5.7. *Comparative Chronological chart: Piura Valley, Chira/Punta Region, and Tumbes Valley to North Coast regional chronology.*

Table 5.1a. Chronological evidence for selected sites in the North Highlands.

VALLEY	SITE	RADIOCARBON EVIDENCE			ARCHAEOLOGICAL EVIDENCE②			COMMENTS
		SAMPLE #	AGE①	REFERENCES	CERAMICS	ARCHITECTURE	REFERENCES	
North Highlands	Pashash	Tx-1330	420 ± 80 (456 ± 89) (AD 1494)	(Valastro, Davis, and Varela 1975)	EIP	EIP	(Grieder 1978; Smith 1978)	Grieder believes that this date is the result of buried colonial period material covered by debris from modern erosion (1978).
		Tx-1331	1100 ± 270 (1083 ± 275) (AD 867)	(Valastro, Davis, and Varela 1975)	EIP	EIP	(Grieder 1978; Smith 1978)	"...fill must be mixed; date too recent for red-on-white..." (Valastro, Davis, and Varela 1975).
		Tx-943	1380 ± 100 (1358 ± 102) (AD 592)	(Valastro, Davis, and Varela 1975)	EIP	EIP	(Grieder 1978; Smith 1978)	"This specimen should be compared with Tx-940 and 942 from Level 2 of the same cut, which tested as older despite their position nearer the surface." (Grieder 1978:192).
		Tx-1329	1400 ± 60 (1379 ± 64) (AD 571)	(Valastro, Davis, and Varela 1975)	EIP	EIP	(Grieder 1978; Smith 1978)	"Dates offering of stone, pedestal bowls, Recuay effigy pottery, copper bells, and megalithic revetment wall." (Valastro, Davis, and Varela 1975:94).
		Tx-941	1490 ± 70 (1471 ± 73) (AD 479)	(Valastro, Davis, and Varela 1975)	EIP	EIP	(Grieder 1978; Smith 1978)	Roof beam from Recuay period house.
		Tx-940	1500 ± 90 (1481 ± 93) (AD 469)	(Valastro, Davis, and Varela 1975)	EIP	EIP	(Grieder 1978; Smith 1978)	"...date plausable, and agrees with Tx-942 (below) as it should, but in reverse sequence with Tx-943 (below) suggesting redeposition of slope wash on small structures flanking El Caseron." (Valastro, Davis, and Varela 1975:93).
		Tx-942	1580 ± 70 (1563 ± 75) (AD 387)	(Valastro, Davis, and Varela 1975)	EIP	EIP	(Grieder 1978; Smith 1978)	See Tx-940 and Tx-943.
		Tx-1824	1590 ± 60 (1574 ± 66) (AD 376)	(Valastro, Davis, and Varela 1977)	EIP	EIP	(Grieder 1978; Smith 1978)	This sample was expected to date the same as Tx-1329, such an early date suggests that it was not in primary context when collected. See (Grieder 1978:192).
		Tx-1332	1610 ± 170 (1595 ± 172) (AD 355)	(Valastro, Davis, and Varela 1975)	EH,EIP	EH,EIP	(Grieder 1978; Smith 1978)	"...agrees with Tx-944 above, but-like that date-surprisingly late for terminal Chavin." (Valastro, Davis, and Varela 1975:94).
		Tx-944	1640 ± 80 (1627 ± 84) (AD 323)	(Valastro, Davis, and Varela 1975)	EH,EIP	EH,EIP	(Grieder 1978; Smith 1978)	"...appropriately early relative to other dates in series, but surprisingly late for end of Chavinoid." (Valastro, Davis, and Varela 1975:94).

Table 5.1b. Chronological evidence for selected sites in the North Highlands.

VALLEY	SITE	RADIOCARBON EVIDENCE			ARCHAEOLOGICAL EVIDENCE[2]			COMMENTS
		SAMPLE #	AGE[1]	REFERENCES	CERAMICS	ARCHITECTURE	REFERENCES	
North Highlands	La Pampa	Tk-193	500 ± 70 (529 ± 80) (AD 1421)	(Terada 1979)	LH	LH	(Terada 1979)	Caserones Period - Inca.
		Tk-173	640 ± 50 (655 ± 58) (AD 1295)	(Terada 1979)	EIP	EIP	(Terada 1979)	Tornapampa period - Terada feels that this date is too late to date the associated white-on-red ceramics (Terada 1979:178).
		Tk-195	2490 ± 60 (2599 ± 121) (649 BC)	(Terada 1979)	EH	EH	(Terada 1979)	La Pampa Period - Chavin.
		Tk-176	2620 ± 70 (2763 ± 86) (813 BC)	(Terada 1979)	EH	EH	(Terada 1979)	La Pampa Period - Chavin.
		Tk-175	2920 ± 70 (3134 ± 76) (1184 BC)	(Terada 1979)	IP	IP	(Terada 1979)	Yesopampa Period - pre-Chavin.
		Tk-174	3090 ± 70 (3360 ± 89) (1410 BC)	(Terada 1979)	IP	IP	(Terada 1979)	Yesopampa Period - pre-Chavin.
		Tk-192	3100 ± 70 (3373 ± 89) (1423 BC)	(Terada 1979)	IP	IP	(Terada 1979)	Yesopampa Period - pre-Chavin.
		Tk-187	3120 ± 110 (3398 ± 123) (1448 BC)	(Terada 1979)	IP	IP	(Terada 1979)	Yesopampa Period - pre-Chavin.
		Tk-186	3350 ± 100 (3998 ± 109) (1748 BC)	(Terada 1979)	IP	IP	(Terada 1979)	Yesopampa Period - pre-Chavin.
	La Galgada	Tx-2464	3440 ± 80 (3817 ± 91) (1867 BC)	(Grieder p.c.)	IP	IP	(Grieder p.c.)	Wood stick stuck in wall of shaft tomb built into a preceramic chamber (Grieder p.c.).
		Tx-3663	3540 ± 50 (3947 ± 139) (1997 BC)	(Grieder 1981)	IP	IP	(Grieder 1981; p.c.)	Pit in floor 9 - latest occupation of mound. Initial Period with Chavin features, earliest ceramics (Grieder p.c.).
		Tx-3166	3660 ± 80 (4105 ± 153) (1945 BC)	(Valastro, et al. 1980)	PC	PC	(Grieder p.c.)	Sample from floor 3,5,7 fire pit - should compare to Tx-2464, late preceramic (Grieder p.c.).

Table 5.1c. Chronological evidence for selected sites in the North Highlands.

VALLEY	SITE	RADIOCARBON EVIDENCE			ARCHAEOLOGICAL EVIDENCE [2]			COMMENTS
		SAMPLE #	AGE [1]	REFERENCES	CERAMICS	ARCHITECTURE	REFERENCES	
North Highlands	La Galgada (continued)	Tx-2463	3740 ± 90 (4210 ± 158) (2260 BC)	(Grieder p.c.)	PC	PC	(Grieder p.c.)	Sample from gallery outside of south temple, should post-date Tx-3167 (Grieder p.c.).
		Tx-3167	3820 ± 60 (4314 ± 112) (2364 BC)	(Valastro, et al. 1980)	PC	PC	(Grieder p.c.)	Sample from floor 25, fire pit - should date early period of building (Grieder p.c.).
		Tx-3664	4110 ± 50 (4689 ± 114) (2739 BC)	(Grieder p.c.)	PC	PC	(Grieder p.c.)	Sample from sector I, floor 30, fire pit - preceramic ceremonial chamber, higher than fire pit dated by sample Tx-3167 (Grieder p.c.).
	Huaricoto	lab # not reported	2310 ± 80 (2382 ± 132) (432 BC)	(Burger and Burger 1980)	EH	EH	(Burger and Burger 1980)	Carbon from a cache of human bone, charcoal, and ceremonial paraphernalia deposited on the original floor. This cache included a pan pipe, a human cranium fragment and a carved bone with Chavin style carving. Both of these samples are from the same context.
		lab # not reported	2330 ± 110 (2406 ± 152) (456 BC)	(Burger and Burger 1980)	EH	EH	(Burger and Burger 1980)	
		lab # not reported	2440 ± 130 (2539 ± 167) (589 BC)	(Burger and Burger 1980)	EH	EH	(Burger and Burger 1980)	Initial phase of the Early Horizon.
		lab # not reported	3970 ± 110 (4508 ± 145) (2558 BC)	(Burger and Burger 1980)	PC	PC	(Burger and Burger 1980)	Sample from late Preceramic hearth.
		lab # not reported	4210 ± 120 (4817 ± 157) (2876 BC)	(Burger and Burger 1980)	PC	PC	(Burger and Burger 1980)	Sample from just above the half-moon hearth, late Preceramic.
		lab # not reported	4770 ± 200 (5505 ± 219) (3555 BC)	(Burger and Burger 1980)	PC	PC	(Burger and Burger 1980)	Initial use of Huaricoto.
		lab # not reported	5240 ± 120 (6042 ± 175) (4902 BC)	(Burger and Burger 1980)	PC	PC	(Burger and Burger 1980)	Initial use of Huaricoto.

Table 5.2a. Chronological evidence for selected sites in the Casma Valley.

VALLEY	SITE	SAMPLE #	AGE [1]	REFERENCES	CERAMICS	ARCHITECTURE	REFERENCES	COMMENTS
			RADIOCARBON EVIDENCE			ARCHAEOLOGICAL EVIDENCE [2]		
Casma	Huaca Moxeque	----				EH,MH(B)	(Kosok 1965; Schaedel n.d.; Tello 1956)	
	Pampa Llama	----			MH(B-C)	MH(B-C)	(Kosok 1965; Schaedel n.d.)	
	Pueblo de Moxeque	----			MH(B-C), LIP,LH	MH(C),LIP	(Kosok 1965; Schaedel n.d.)	
	Manchan	----			EIP,MH(C), LIP.LH	MH(C),LIP	(Kosok 1965; Schaedel n.d.)	
	Cerro Sechin	Tk-105	1100 ± 70 (1083 ± 87) (AD 867)	(Kobayashi et al. 1974)	?	EH?	(Tello 1956)	"Charcoal samples were secured from floors identified outside of the carved stone wall that defined the platform of the principle temple." (Matsuzawa 1978:667).
		Tk-106	2720 ± 60 (2885 ± 78) (935 BC)	(Kobayashi et al. 1974)	?	EH?		
		Tk-107	2940 ± 120 (3165 ± 124) (1215 BC)	(Kobayashi et al. 1974)	?	EH?		
	Las Haldas	Tk-121	2360 ± 90 (2442 ± 138) (492 BC)	(Matsuzawa 1978)	?	?	(Matsuzawa 1978)	Due to the spatial proximity and homogeneity of the formation from which this sample and sample Gak-106 were collected a much closer correspondence of dates was expected, see (Matsuzawa 1978).
		V-901	2492 ± 100 (2601 ± 145) (651 BC)	(Engel 1963)	EH	?		Sample associated with Chavin ceramics similar to Guanape II ceramics from the Viru Valley (Engel 1963).
		NZ-211	2500 ± 100 (2611 ± 145) (661 BC)	(Fergusson and Rafter 1959)	EH	?		Chavinoid (Ravines and Alvarez Sauri 1966).
		NZ-370-1	2500 ± 100 (2611 ± 145) (661 BC)	(Engel 1966)	EH	?		Associated with Chavin ceramics (Engel 1966).

Table 5.2b. Chronological evidence for selected sites in the Casma Valley.

VALLEY	SITE	RADIOCARBON EVIDENCE			ARCHAEOLOGICAL EVIDENCE[2]			COMMENTS
		SAMPLE #	AGE[1]	REFERENCES	CERAMICS	ARCHITECTURE	REFERENCES	
Casma (continued)	Las Haldas (continued)	Tk-122	2520 ± 60 (2636 ± 78) (686 BC)	(Matsuzawa 1978)	IP?	IP?		See Gak-107.
		Tk-123	2590 ± 80 (2723 ± 94) (773 BC)	(Matsuzawa 1978)	IP?	IP?		On the basis of stratigraphic relationships and ceramic associations Matsuzawa (1978: 667) concluded that: "A difference of 560 years between F/3 (sample Gak-4455) and BEX/9 (sample Tk-123) is well over our expectations."
		Gak-106	2680 ± 150 (2836 ± 158) (886 BC)	(Ishida et al. 1960)	EH?	EH?		[3] See Tk-121. This sample is reported as Gak-606 by (Matsuzawa 1978).
		Tx-1011	2730 ± 70 (2898 ± 86) (948 BC)	(Greider 1975)	EH	EH	(Greider 1975)	Greider believes that this date is a reasonable estimate for the terminal occupation (Greider 1975).
		Tx-632	2830 ± 70 (3025 ± 76) (1075 BC)	(Greider 1975)	EH	EH	(Greider 1975)	"This is a plausable date for the beginning of the terminal period..." (Greider 1975:100).
		Tx-648	3140 ± 80 (3424 ± 97) (1474 BC)	(Greider 1975)	IP?	IP	(Greider 1975)	Greider (1975:100) states that this date "...would seem to date the main period of building visible on the surface..."
		Gak-4455	3150 ± 90 (3440 ± 105) (1490 BC)	(Matsuzawa 1978)	IP?	IP?	(Matsuzawa 1978)	See Tk-123.
		Tx-631	3430 ± 80 (3803 ± 91) (1853 BC)	(Greider 1975)	IP	---	(Greider 1975)	Early post Preceramic level.
		Gak-107	3580 ± 130 (4000 ± 184) (2050 BC)	(Ishida et al. 1960)	IP	IP?	(Matsuzawa 1978)	[3] Matsuzawa (1978) reports this sample as Gak-607. He also notes that there is a discrepency between this date and Tk-122 both of which were collected from "what appeared to be a homogeneous matrix." The stratigraphic evidence does not support such an early date (Matsuzawa 1978:667).
		Gak-4456	3600 ± 95 (4027 ± 161) (2077 BC)	(Matsuzawa 1978)	PC	?		Pretemple construction and occupation (Matsuzawa 1978).

Table 5.2c. Chronological evidence for selected sites in the Casma Valley.

VALLEY	SITE	RADIOCARBON EVIDENCE			ARCHAEOLOGICAL EVIDENCE②			COMMENTS
		SAMPLE #	AGE①	REFERENCES	CERAMICS	ARCHITECTURE	REFERENCES	
Casma (continued)	Las Haldas (continued)	V-902	3792 ± 80 (4278 ± 123) (2328 BC)	(Engel 1963)	PC	?	(Engel 1963)	Preceramic with cotton ?
		NZ-370-2	3600 ± 80 (4291 ± 123) (2341 BC)	(Engel 1966)	PC	?	(Engel 1966)	Preceramic with cotton (Engel 1966:82).
	Chancayillo	L-404a	2300 ± 80 (2370 ± 132) (420 BC)	(Olsen and Broecker 1959)	MH(A-B)	MH(A-B)	(Fung and Pimentel 1973; Kosok 1965; Schaedel n.d.)	This date appears to be too early to date the primary occupation of the site and may represent the reuse of material from nearby stylistically older (EH) sites (Schaedel p.c.).
	Pampa Adentro	---			---	MH(B-C),LIP	(Schaedel n.d.)	

Table 5.3. Chronological evidence for selected sites in the Nepena Valley.

VALLEY	SITE	RADIOCARBON EVIDENCE			ARCHAEOLOGICAL EVIDENCE②			COMMENTS
		SAMPLE #	AGE①	REFERENCES	CERAMICS	ARCHITECTURE	REFERENCES	
Nepeña	Panamarca	---			EH?, EIP(C), MH(A-B)	MH(A-C)	(Kosok 1965; Proulx 1968,1973; Schaedel 1951a,1951b; Soriano Infante 1941; Squire 1877)	
	Punkuri-Alto	---			EIP(C), MH(B-C), LIP	MH(C),LIP	(Kosok 1965; Proulx 1968,1973; Schaedel 1951a)	
	Huambacho Viejo	---			EIP(C), MH(B-C)	MH(B)	(Kosok 1965; Proulx 1968,1973; Soriano Infante 1941)	
	Huaca Partida	---			MH(A-B)	MH(A-B)	(Schaedel n.d.)	
	Agua Hedionda (Samanco)	---			MH(B)	MH(B)	(Kosok 1965; Proulx 1968; Schaedel n.d.)	
	Huacatambo	---			MH(C),LIP, LH	LIP	(Bennett 1939; Proulx 1968;1973; Soriano Infante 1941; Squire 1877)	

Table 5.4a. Chronological evidence for selected sites in the Santa Valley.

VALLEY	SITE	RADIOCARBON EVIDENCE			ARCHAEOLOGICAL EVIDENCE[2]			COMMENTS
		SAMPLE #	AGE[1]	REFERENCES	CERAMICS	ARCHITECTURE	REFERENCES	
Santa	Inca Pampa (PV28-161)	---	---		EIP(C), MH(A-C)	EIP(C),MH(B-C), LIP	(Donnan 1973; Kosok 1965; Schaedel n.d.)	All ^{14}C dates from this site are from textiles associated with Moche IV ceramics.
		UCLA-1801	1060 ± 60 (1045 ± 79) (AD 905)	(Donnan 1973)	EIP(C)	---		
		UCLA-1803	1390 ± 60 (1368 ± 64) (AD 582)	(Donnan 1973)	EIP(C)	---		
	Tanque (PV28-161)	---	---		EIP(B-C),MH, MH(A C), LIP,LH,C?	EIP(B-C),MH, LIP?,LH?	(Donnan 1973; Schaedel n.d.)	All ^{14}C dates from this site are from textiles associated with Moche III ceramics.
		UCLA-1806	1220 ± 70 (1199 ± 87) (AD 751)	(Donnan 1973)	EIP(C)	---		
		UCLA-1804	1450 ± 140 (1429 ± 142) (AD 521)	(Donnan 1973)	EIP(C)	---		
		UCLA-1805	1870 ± 50 (1875 ± 62) (AD 75)	(Donnan 1973)	EIP(C)	---		
	PV28-92	---	---		EIP(C), LIP	EIP?,LIP?	(Donnan 1973)	This date is from textiles associated with Moche IV ceramics.
		UCLA-1802	1550 ± 110 (1531 ± 112) (AD 419)	(Donnan 1973)	EIP(C)	---		
	Huacas de Chimbote	---			EIP(C), MH(A-C)	MH(B-C)	(Schaedel n.d.)	
	Choloque	---			EIP(C), MH(B)	MH(B)	(Schaedel n.d.)	
	Entres Cerros	---			MH(B)	EIP(C)	(Schaedel n.d.)	
	El Huabo	---			MH(B-C)	EIP(C)	(Schaedel n.d.)	
	Alto Peru	---			MH(C),LIP	LIP	(Kosok 1965; Schaedel n.d.)	

Table 5.4b. Chronological evidence for selected sites in the Santa Valley.

VALLEY	SITE	RADIOCARBON EVIDENCE			ARCHAEOLOGICAL EVIDENCE [2]			COMMENTS
		SAMPLE #	AGE [1]	REFERENCES	CERAMICS	ARCHITECTURE	REFERENCES	
Santa	Coisquillo	88	AD 1650 ± 50	(M. Cardenas 1979:28)	?	?	(M. Cardenas 1979)	This site is mentioned only in the date list.
	Pejerrey	76	AD 1540 ± 60	(M. Cardenas 1979:28)	PC	?	(M. Cardenas 1979:12)	The only reference to this site other than in the date list is as a Preceramic site near the coast.
	Las Huacas	79	AD 620 ± 60	(M. Cardenas 1979:28)	EIP,LIP	EIP,LIP	(M. Cardenas 1979:10-12)	
		77	AD 110 ± 70	(M. Cardenas 1979:28)	?	?		Edificio de las Pilastras ?
		78	AD 20 ± 70	(M. Cardenas 1979:28)	?	?		Edificio de las Pilastras ?
		96	1250 BC ± 70	(M. Cardenas 1979:28)	?	?		
		97	1620 BC ± 70	(M. Cardenas 1979:28)	?	?		
		98	1680 BC ± 80	(M. Cardenas 1979:29)	?	?		
	Huaca Calvera B	92	AD 440 ± 60	(M. Cardenas 1979:28)	?	?	(M. Cardenas 1979)	This site is mentioned only in the date list.
	Condorcerro A	94	730 BC ± 60	(M. Cardenas 1979:28)	PC	PC	(M. Cardenas 1979:13,24)	This site is described as a Preceramic settlement, this date does not support such a placement.
	Condorcerro B	95	2060 BC ± 70	(M. Cardenas 1979:29)	PC	?	(M. Cardenas 1979:13,24)	
		113	2120 BC ± 60	(M. Cardenas 1979:29)	PC	PC		
	Cerro Urena	89	1010 BC ± 90	(M. Cardenas 1979:28)	?	?	(M. Cardenas 1979)	This site is mentioned only in the date list.
	Cerro Obrero (Tanguche)	93	1740 BC ± 60	(M. Cardenas 1979:29)	EIP	EIP	(M. Cardenas 1979:25)	
	Cerro Yolanda B (Tanguche)	67	1770 BC ± 70	(M. Cardenas 1979:29)	EH,EIP	PC,EH,EIP	(M. Cardenas 1979:11-12)	
		100	4140 BC ± 70	(M. Cardenas 1979:29)	?	?		
	Besique A – La Cocina	90	2020 BC ± 100	(M. Cardenas 1979:29)	PC	?	(M. Cardenas 1979:20)	Preceramic site with maize, if this association is good it represents the earliest dated occurance of maize found on the coast.

Table 5.5a. Chronological evidence for selected sites in the Chao Valley.

| VALLEY | SITE | RADIOCARBON EVIDENCE | | | ARCHAEOLOGICAL EVIDENCE② | | | COMMENTS |
		SAMPLE #	AGE①	REFERENCES	CERAMICS	ARCHITECTURE	REFERENCES	
Chao	Cerro Coronado	74	AD 1130 ± 60	(M. Cardenas 1979:28)	?	?	(M. Cardenas 1979)	This site is mentioned only in the date list.
	Cerro La Cruz	62	AD 880 ± 70	(M. Cardenas 1979:28)	?	?	(M. Cardenas 1979:15)	This site is mentioned in association with a series of agricultural fields.
		61	AD 720 ± 60	(M. Cardenas 1979:28)				
	Huasaquito	63	AD 490 ± 70	(M. Cardenas 1979:28)	?	?	(M. Cardenas 1979)	This site is mentioned only in the date list.
	San Francisco de Lunar	64	AD 200 ± 70	(M. Cardenas 1979:28)	?	?	(M. Cardenas 1979)	This site is mentioned only in the date list.
	Cerro Laramie A	58	AD 30 ± 70	(M. Cardenas 1979:28)	?	?	(M. Cardenas 1979)	This site is mentioned only in the date list.
	El Templo	30	1350 BC ± 60	(M. Cardenas 1979:28)	?	?	(M. Cardenas 1979)	This site is mentioned only in the date list.
		29	1420 BC ± 70	(M. Cardenas 1979:28)	?	?	(M. Cardenas 1979)	
	Las Salinas	2	1350 BC ± 150	(M. Cardenas 1979:28)	PC	PC	(M. Cardenas 1979:6-7, 10,12,17-23,26)	This site is reported as being exclusively Preceramic. An interpretation not supported by the published 14C dates, nor conclusively by the illustrated architecture.
		7	1360 BC ± 60	(M. Cardenas 1979:28)				
		21	1510 BC ± 70	(M. Cardenas 1979:28)				
		8	1540 BC ± 80	(M. Cardenas 1979:28)				
		20	1600 BC ± 70	(M. Cardenas 1979:28)				
		22	1620 BC ± 60	(M. Cardenas 1979:28)				
	Piedras Negras B	1	1900 BC ± 180	(M. Cardenas 1979:28)	PC?	?	(M. Cardenas 1979)	This date and that of sample #4 correspond to the date assigned to the "Geoglyph" at the site of Las Salinas (see Cardenas 1979:21-22), there is no reference to a site by this name (Piedras Negras), however.
		4	1900 BC ± 180	(M. Cardenas 1979:28)				
		5	2020 BC ± 160	(M. Cardenas 1979:28)				
		3	2240 BC ± 110	(M. Cardenas 1979:28)				
		35	2540 BC ± 100	(M. Cardenas 1979:28)				
	Piedras Negras A	36	4150 BC ± 90	(M. Cardenas 1979:28)	?	?	(M. Cardenas 1979)	

Table 5.5b.   Chronological evidence for selected sites in the Chao Valley.

| VALLEY | SITE | RADIOCARBON EVIDENCE | | | ARCHAEOLOGICAL EVIDENCE [2] | | | |
		SAMPLE [4]	AGE [1]	REFERENCES	CERAMICS	ARCHITECTURE	REFERENCES	COMMENTS
Chao (continued)	Los Morteros	27	2610 BC ± 60	(M. Cardenas 1979:28)	?	?	(M. Cardenas 1979)	This site is mentioned only in the date list.
		26	2710 BC ± 60	(M. Cardenas 1979:28)				
	Conchal Viejo	31	3130 BC ± 70	(M. Cardenas 1979:28)	?	?	(M. Cardenas 1979)	This site is mentioned only in the date list.
		28	3320 BC ± 120	(M. Cardenas 1979:28)				
	El Muerto	38	3240 BC ± 150	(M. Cardenas 1979:28)	?	?	(M. Cardenas 1979)	This site is mentioned only in the date list.
		19	3640 BC ± 80	(M. Cardenas 1979:28)				

104

Table 5.6a. Chronological evidence for selected sites in the Virú Valley.

VALLEY	SITE	RADIOCARBON EVIDENCE			ARCHAEOLOGICAL EVIDENCE [2]			COMMENTS
		SAMPLE #	AGE [1]	REFERENCES	CERAMICS	ARCHITECTURE	REFERENCES	
Viru	Castillo de Tomoval (V-51)	----			EIP(A-C), MH	EIP(A-C)	(Strong and Evans 1952; Willey 1953)	
	Huaca de la Cruz (V-162)	----			EIP(B-C), MH, LIP	EIP(B-C)	(Bennett 1939; Strong and Evans 1952; Willey 1953)	
		C-619	1837 ± 190 (1838 ± 193) (AD 112)	(Libby 1951)	EIP(C)	----	(Strong and Evans 1947; 1952)	⑤ This date seems to be too early on the basis of its association with Moche III/IV ceramics. Burial of the Warrior-God.
		L-335a	1300 ± 80 (1277 ± 95) (AD 673)	(Broecker and Kulp 1957)	EIP	EIP		⑤
		L-335b	1300 ± 80 (1277 ± 95) (AD 673)	(Broecker and Kulp 1957)	EIP	EIP		⑤
	V-127	UCLA-1976A	2295 ± 60 (2364 ± 121) (414 BC)	(West p.c.)	EH	EH	(West p.c.; Willey 1953)	Late Early Horizon (Guanape)
		UCLA-1976B	2800 ± 70 (2986 ± 76) (1036 BC)	(West p.c.)	EH	EH	(West p.c.)	Late Early Horizon (Guanape)
	Gallinazo (V-59)	----			EIP(A?-C)	EIP(A?-C)	(Bennett 1939; 1950; Kroeber 1930; Larco Hoyle 1938-39; Strong and Evans 1952; Willey 1953)	
	Puerto Moorin (V-66)	----			EIP(A-B?), MH	EIP(A-B?), MH	(Strong and Evans 1952; West p.c.; Willey 1953)	Type site for the Puerto Moorin Phase.
		UCLA-1975B	1600 ± 60 (1584 ± 66) (AD 366)	(West p.c.)	EIP(B)	EIP(B)	(West p.c.)	
		UCLA-1975A	2035 ± 60 (2061 ± 70) (111 BC)	(West p.c.)	EIP(A)	EIP(A)	(West p.c.)	Late Gallinazo? (West p.c.)

Table 5.6b. Chronological evidence for selected sites in the Virú Valley.

VALLEY	SITE	RADIOCARBON EVIDENCE			ARCHAEOLOGICAL EVIDENCE②			COMMENTS
		SAMPLE #	AGE①	REFERENCES	CERAMICS	ARCHITECTURE	REFERENCES	
Viru (continued)	Guanape (V-71)	---			PC,IP,MH, LIP	PC,IP	(Strong and Evans 1953; Willey 1953)	Type site for the Guanape phase.
	V-434	UCLA-1974D	1600 ± 60 (1584 ± 66) (AD 366)	(West p.c.)	EIP(B)	EIP(B)	(West p.c.)	Late Gallinazo phase (West p.c.).
		UCLA-1974A	1870 ± 70 (1875 ± 79) (AD 75)	(West p.c.)	EIP(A)	EIP(A)	(West p.c.)	Late Puerto Moorin/Early Gallinazo phase (West p.c.).
		UCLA-1974C	1890 ± 70 (1897 ± 79) (AD 53)	(West p.c.)	EIP(A)	EIP(A)	(West p.c.)	Puerto Moorin phase (West p.c.).
		UCLA-1974B	1950 ± 60 (1963 ± 70) (13 BC)	(West p.c.)	EIP(A)	EIP(A)	(West p.c.)	Puerto Moorin phase (West p.c.).
		UCLA-1974E	2260 ± 70 (2323 ± 119) (373 BC)	(West p.c.)	EH	EH	(West p.c.)	Late Early Horizon ? (West p.c.).
	V-358	Tx-3788	950 ± 50 (941 ± 59) (AD 1009)	(Julien 1980)	MH	---	(Julien 1980)	Unit 1, level 2. Tomoval phase habitation and area of sunken fields.(Julien 1980).
		Tx-3790	1020 ± 50 (1008 ± 59) (AD 942)	(Julien 1980)	MH	---	(Julien 1980)	Unit 1, level 4.
		Tx-3789	1040 ± 60 (1026 ± 79) (AD 924)	(Julien 1980)	MH	---	(Julien 1980)	Unit 1, level 1.
		Tx-3787	1060 ± 30 (1045 ± 49) (AD 905)	(Julien 1980)	MH	---	(Julien 1980)	Unit 1, level 5.
	V-432	UCLA-1977	2180 ± 60 (2228 ± 113) (278 BC)	(West p.c.)	EIP(A)	EIP(A)	(West p.c.)	

Table 5.7a. Chronological evidence for selected sites in the Moche Valley.

VALLEY	SITE	RADIOCARBON EVIDENCE			ARCHAEOLOGICAL EVIDENCE[2]			COMMENTS
		SAMPLE #	AGE[1]	REFERENCES	CERAMICS	ARCHITECTURE	REFERENCES	
Moche	Caballo Muerto	----			IP,EH	IP,EH	(Moseley and Watanabe 1974; T. Pozorski 1975,1976; Pozorski and Pozorski 1979)	
		Tx-2181	1560 ± 120 (1542 ± 123) (AD 408)	(Valastro, Davis and Varela 1978)	----	EH?	(T. Pozorski 1976)	"... A sample of junco fiber (Cyperus sp.) taken from a somewhat dubious context of the colonade floor of mound B' at Reyes..." (T. Pozorski 1976:113).
		Tx-1939	2390 ± 70 (2477 ± 126) (527 BC)	(Valastro, Davis and Varela 1978)	----	EH	(T. Pozorski 1976)	Late construction at Huaca Guavalito (T. Pozorski 1976).
		Tx-2180	2800 ± 60 (2987 ± 67) (1037 BC)	(Valastro, Davis and Varela 1978)	----	IP?	(T. Pozorski 1976)	Early construction at Huaca de los Reyes (T. Pozorski 1976). See Tx-1974.
		Tx-1937	3040 ± 60 (3294 ± 81) (1344 BC)	(Valastro, Davis and Varela 1978)	----	IP	(T. Pozorski 1976)	Initial construction at Huaca Herederos Chica (T. Pozorski 1976). From the same context as Tx-1938.
		Tx-1973	3140 ± 60 (3424 ± 81) (1474 BC)	(Valastro, Davis and Varela 1978)	----	IP?	(T. Pozorski 1976)	Early construction at Huaca de los Reyes (T. Pozorski 1976). See Tx-1974.
		Tx-1972	3310 ± 80 (3646 ± 91) (1696 BC)	(Valastro, Davis and Varela 1978)	----	IP?	(T. Pozorski 1976)	Early construction at Huaca de los Reyes (T. Pozorski 1976). See Tx-1974.
		Tx-1938	3450 ± 70 (3828 ± 82) (1878 BC)	(Valastro, Davis and Varela 1978)	----	IP	(T. Pozorski 1976)	Initial construction at Huaca Herederos Chica (T. Pozorski 1976).
		Tx-1974	3680 ± 80 (4132 ± 153) (2182 BC)	(Valastro, Davis and Varela 1978)	----	IP?	(T. Pozorski 1976)	Early construction at Huaca de los Reyes. This sample and samples Tx-2120, Tx-1973, Tx 1972 were all collected from postholes on the summit of mound F of Huaca de los Reyes and were expected to date the first phase of construction (T. Pozorski 1976).
	Galindo	----			EIP(A-C), MH(B C), LIP,LH	EIP(A-C), MH(B), LIP,LH	(Bawden 1977; Kosok 1965; S. Pozorski 1976; Schaedel 1951a, 1951b)	As originally defined by Schaedel (p.c.) this site covered a large area extending from Caballo Muerto to Quebrada Katuay (aprox. 6 kms.).
		?	(AD 570 - 590)	(Shimada n.d.)	EIP(C)	EIP(C)		These dates were reported to Shimada by G. Conrad as a personal communication and are not reported with lab numbers. These dates are dendrochronologically calibrated as reported (Shimada n.d.).
		?	(AD 650 - 670)	(Shimada n.d.)	EIP(C)	EIP(C)		

Table 5.7b. Chronological evidence for selected sites in the Moche Valley.

| VALLEY | SITE | RADIOCARBON EVIDENCE | | | ARCHAEOLOGICAL EVIDENCE [2] | | | COMMENTS |
		SAMPLE #	AGE [1]	REFERENCES	CERAMICS	ARCHITECTURE	REFERENCES	
Moche (continued)	Moche Huacas	---			EIP(C), MH,LIP	EIP(C)	(Kosok 1965; Kroeber 1925; S. Pozorski 1976; Schaedel n.d.; Uhle 1913)	
	Gramalote	Tx-1930A	3050 ± 110 (3307 ± 123) (1357 BC)	(Valastro, Davis and Varela 1978)	IP	---	(S. Pozorski 1976; Pozorski and Pozorski 1979)	Cut 2, natural level 2.
		Tx-1929A	3070 ± 90 (3333 ± 106) (1383 BC)	(Valastro, Davis and Varela 1978)	IP	---	(S. Pozorski 1976; Pozorski and Pozorski 1979)	Cut 2, natural level 3. A flexed Burial with woven textiles was found in this level, but it is not clear as to its relationship to the ^{14}C sample, if any.
		Tx-1929B	3250 ± 120 (3567 ± 124) (1617 BC)	(Valastro, Davis and Varela 1978)	IP	---	(S. Pozorski 1976; Pozorski and Pozorski 1979)	Cut 2, natural level 3.
		Tx-1931B	3280 ± 60 (3607 ± 74) (1657 BC)	(Valastro, Davis and Varela 1978)	IP	---	(S. Pozorski 1976; Pozorski and Pozorski 1979)	Cut 2, natural level 1.
		Tx-1931A	3530 ± 130 (3935 ± 137) (1985 BC)	(Valastro, Davis and Varela 1978)	IP	---	(S. Pozorski 1976; Pozorski and Pozorski 1979)	Cut 2, natural level 1.
		Tx-1930B	3540 ± 80 (3947 ± 91) (1997 BC)	(Valastro, Davis and Varela 1978)	IP	---	(S. Pozorski 1976; Pozorski and Pozorski 1979)	Cut 2, natural level 2.
	Cerro Arena	RI-804	2090 ± 110 (2124 ± 146) (174 BC)	(Brennan 1980)	EIP(A)	EIP(A)	(Brennan 1980)	Nucleated Salinar phase habitation.
	Huaca Dragon	---			MH(C)	MH(C)	(Kosok 1965; Schaedel 1966)	
	Chan Chan	Gx-3253	730 ± 150 (737 ± 153) (AD 1213)	(Moseley 1975)	LIP	LIP	(Day 1974; Kosok 1965; Moseley 1975; Squire 1877; West 1970)	Uhle Compound.
	Padre Aban	Tx-1935	3670 ± 260 (4119 ± 291) (2169 BC)	(Valastro, Davis and Varela 1978)	PC	---	(S. Pozorski 1976)	Cut 1, natural level 5. This date may be too late according to T. Pozorski (see Valastro, Davis and Varela 1978).
		Tx-1933	3850 ± 210 (4354 ± 230) (2404 BC)	(Valastro, Davis and Varela 1978)	PC	---	(S. Pozorski 1976)	Cut 1, natural level 5.

Table 5.7c. Chronological evidence for selected sites in the Moche Valley.

VALLEY	SITE	RADIOCARBON EVIDENCE			ARCHAEOLOGICAL EVIDENCE[2]			COMMENTS
		SAMPLE #	AGE[1]	REFERENCES	CERAMICS	ARCHITECTURE	REFERENCES	
Moche (continued)	Padre Aban (continued)	Tx-1934	3930 ± 120 (4456 ± 152) (2506 BC)	(Valastro, Davis and Varela 1978)	PC	---	(S. Pozorski 1976)	Cut 1, natural level 7.
		Tx-1936	5420 ± 140 (6237 ± 189) (4287 BC)	(Valastro, Davis and Varela 1978)	PC	---	(S. Pozorski 1976)	Cut 1, natural level 3. T. Pozorski is of the opinion that: "Tx-1936 is much too old." (Valastro, Davis and Varela 1978:268).
	Alto Salaverry	---			PC	PC	(S. Pozorski 1976; Pozorski and Pozorski 1979)	
	Choroval	---			LIP	LIP	(S. Pozorski 1976)	
	Cerro la Virgen	---			LIP	LIP	(Keatinge 1975; S. Pozorski 1976)	

Table 5.8a. Chronological evidence for selected sites in the Chicama Valley.

| VALLEY | SITE | RADIOCARBON EVIDENCE | | | ARCHAEOLOGICAL EVIDENCE[2] | | | COMMENTS |
		SAMPLE #	AGE[1]	REFERENCES	CERAMICS	ARCHITECTURE	REFERENCES	
Chicama	Intervalley Canal	---			MH(C)?, LIP	MH(C)?, LIP	(Kosok 1965; Kus 1972)	All 14C samples where collected from cross sections through the Intervalley Canal.
		UCLA-1711I	780 ± 110 (783 ± 114) (AD 1167)	(Kus 1972)	LIP	---	(Kus 1972)	Cross Section 33, aqueduct across the Quebrada de Oso.
		UCLA-1711G	820 ± 60 (820 ± 67) (AD 1130)	(Kus 1972)	---	---	(Kus 1972)	Cross Section 18. "There is no question but that this sample dates to some time during the use cycle of the canal." (Kus 1972:227).
		UCLA-1711H	870 ± 80 (866 ± 86) (AD 1084)	(Kus 1972)	---	---	(Kus 1972)	Cross Section 18. This sample was collected from 20 cm. below UCLA-1711G and presumably dates an earlier period of canal cleaning.
		UCLA-1711E	1990 ± 80 (2009 ± 88) (59 BC)	(Kus 1972)	---	---	(Kus 1972)	Cross Section 16. Kus believes that this sample is from materials redeposited from a Salinar or Moche phase cemetery during canal construction (1972:226)
		UCLA-1711F	2190 ± 90 (2240 ± 132) (290 BC)	(Kus 1972)	EIP(A)?	---	(Kus 1972)	Cross Section 16. This sample was collected from 40 cm. below UCLA-1711E, it is also believed to date materials redeposited from an EIP cemetery.
		UCLA-1711C	9475 ± 110 (7809 BC)	(Kus 1972)	---	---	(Kus 1972)	[6] Cross Section 6. This sample, "... was probably a root washed into the canal during flooding of the adjacent quebrada." (Kus 1972:225).
		UCLA-1711A	9725 ± 640 (8067 BC)	(Kus 1972)	---	---	(Kus 1972)	[6] Cross Section 4, Quebrada del Leon. Kus believes that this sample was old when it was washed into the canal.
		UCLA-1711B	11,175 ± 330 (9560 BC)	(Kus 1972)	---	---	(Kus 1972)	[6] Cross Section 4, Quebrada del Leon. "The sample was from parts of a long branch or root, which was in the middle of a sandy deposit above the lowest floor of the canal. Again it seems likely that the sample was washed into the canal bed during flooding of the Quebrada del Leon," (Kus 1972:225).
	Jaguay	---			EH,MH(C)	EH,MH	(T. Pozorski 1976; Watson 1979)	

Table 5.8b. Chronological evidence for selected sites in the Chicama Valley.

VALLEY	SITE	RADIOCARBON EVIDENCE			ARCHAEOLOGICAL EVIDENCE [2]			COMMENTS
		SAMPLE #	AGE [1]	REFERENCES	CERAMICS	ARCHITECTURE	REFERENCES	
Chicama (continued)	La Laguna	----			EIP,MH(C)	EIP,MH,LIP	(Kosok 1965; Watson 1979)	Includes the Ascope Aqueduct.
	Huaca Pucuche	----			EH,EIP LIP	EH,EIP	(Bennett 1939; Larco Hoyle 1941)	
	Pelenque	----			MH(A-C)	MH	(Donnan 1968; Watson 1979)	
	Mocollope	----			EIP(C), MH(B), LIP	MH(B),LIP	(Kosok 1965; Schaedel 1951a)	
	Pampa Chiquitoy Viejo	----			EIP,MH, LIP,LH	EIP,LIP,LH	(Conrad 1977; Kosok 1965; Schaedel 1951a)	
	Huaca Prieta	----			PC,IP,EH	PC,IP,EH	(Bird 1948,1951)	
		C-318a	1989 ± 196 (2008 ± 199) (58 BC)	(Arnold and Libby 1951)	PC	----	(Bird 1951)	[5] Bird believes this sample was very likely contaminated and as a result dated far too late, since such a late date is not supported by the stratigraphic evidence (Bird 1951).
		C-323	2631 ± 300 (2774 ± 304) (824 BC)	(Arnold and Libby 1951)	EIP(A/B)	----	(Bird 1951)	[5] This date appears to be too old to date the associated Gallinazo ceramics.
		C-75	2665 ± 200 (2816 ± 206) (866 BC)	(Arnold and Libby 1951)	EH	EH	(Bird 1951)	[5] Associated with maize and Cupisnique ceramics.
		C-321	2966 ± 300 (3199 ± 301) (1249 BC)	(Arnold and Libby 1951)	PC	----	(Bird 1951)	[5] This sample is stratigraphically older that C-322 although the ^{14}C dates would indicate otherwise. Bird suggests that C-321 (a digging stick) may have been old when it was discarded, thus accounting for the discrepency.
		C-322	3278 ± 250 (3604 ± 254) (1654 BC)	(Arnold and Libby 1951)	PC	----	(Bird 1951)	[5] This sample was assayed twice. See C-321.
			3333 ± 340 (3676 ± 343) (1726 BC)	(Bird 1951)				[5]

Table 5.8c.   Chronological evidence for selected sites in the Chicama Valley.

| VALLEY | SITE | SAMPLE # | RADIOCARBON EVIDENCE | | ARCHAEOLOGICAL EVIDENCE② | | | COMMENTS |
			AGE①	REFERENCES	CERAMICS	ARCHITECTURE	REFERENCES	
Chicama (continued)	Huaca Prieta (continued)	C-318b	3550 ± 600 (3960 ± 614) (2010 BC)	(Arnold and Libby 1951)	PC	---	(Bird 1951)	⑤ This is a rerun of sample C-318a and is far more consistent with archaeological and stratigraphic evidence, see (Bird 1951).
		C-315	3572 ± 220 (3989 ± 255) (2039 BC)	(Arnold and Libby 1951)	PC	---	(Bird 1951)	⑤ This date is from shell from the same stratigraphic unit as C-316. Neither of these dates is entirely consistent with the stratigraphic evidence, see Bird (1951).
		L-116B (1)	3650 ± 400 (4092 ± 421) (2142 BC)	(Kulp, Feely, and Tryon 1951)	PC	---		⑤ This sample was run on the same material used for C-598.
		L-116A	3780 ± 100 (4263 ± 137) (2313 BC)	(Broecker, Kulp, and Tucek 1956)	PC	---		The same material used for samples C-598 and L-116B (1) was dated twice more by the Lamont Laboratory using an improved CO_2 technique. These two dates should therefore more accurately reflect the true age of this material.
		L-116B (2)	3860 ± 100 (4366 ± 137) (2416 BC)	(Broecker, Kulp, and Tucek 1956)	PC	---		
		C-362	4043 ± 300 (4602 ± 317) (2652 BC)	(Libby 1951)	PC	---	(Bird 1951)	⑤
		C-313	4257 ± 250 (4876 ± 276) (2926 BC)	(Arnold and Libby 1951)	PC	---	(Bird 1951)	⑤ "On the basis of stratigraphy sample 313 is older than 316," (Bird 1951:37).
		C-598	4298 ± 230 (4927 ± 294) (2977 BC)	(Libby 1951)	PC	---	(Bird 1951)	⑤ See L-116B (1), and L-116A.
		C-316	4380 ± 270 (5030 ± 285) (3080 BC)	(Arnold and Libby 1951)	PC	---	(Bird 1951)	⑤ See sample C-313.
	Licapa	---			EH, EIP, MH(B-C)	EH	(Rodriguez Suy Suy n.d.)	

Table 5.9.   Chronological evidence for selected sites in the Jequetepeque Valley.

VALLEY	SITE	RADIOCARBON EVIDENCE			ARCHAEOLOGICAL EVIDENCE[2]			COMMENTS
		SAMPLE #	AGE[1]	REFERENCES	CERAMICS	ARCHITECTURE	REFERENCES	
Jequetepeque	Cerros Kanchape	----			MH(A-C), LIP,LH	MH,LIP,LH	(Eling p.c.)	
	Moro	----			MH(B)	MH(B)	(Eling p.c.; Kosok 1965; Schaedel n.d.)	
	Canoncillo	----			EIP(C), MH(A-C), LIP,LH	EIP,MH,LIP,LH	(Eling p.c.; Kosok 1965; Schaedel n.d.)	
	Pacatnamu	----			EIP(A-C), MH(B-C), LIP	EIP,MH,LIP	(Hecker and Hecker 1977; Kosok 1965; Schaedel n.d. Ubbelohde Doering 1967)	
		Hv- ?	(AD 485)	(Ubbelohde Doering 1967)	EIP?	EIP?	(Ubbelohde Doering 1967)	Average of samples, reported by Ubbelohde Doering (1967:22). Not calibrated.
	Ventanillas	----			EH,EIP, MH,LIP	EIP,MH,LIP	(Eling p.c.; Kosok 1965; Schaedel n.d.)	
	Talambo	----			EH,EIP, MH,LIP	EH,EIP,MH,LIP	(Eling 1978; Kosok 1965; Schaedel n.d.)	
	Farfan	----			EIP(C), MH(B-C), LIP,LH	MH,LIP	(Eling p.c.; Kosok 1965; Schaedel n.d.)	
	Monte Grande-Tembladera	----			EH,MH(B-C), LIP	EH,MH,LIP	(Eling p.c.; Keatinge 1981; Schaedel n.d.)	
	Templete Chavin	----			EH	EH	(Eling p.c.)	

Table 5.10. Chronological evidence for selected sites in the Saña Valley.

VALLEY	SITE	RADIOCARBON EVIDENCE			ARCHAEOLOGICAL EVIDENCE[2]		
		SAMPLE #	AGE[1]	REFERENCES	CERAMICS	ARCHITECTURE	REFERENCES / COMMENTS
Saña	Huaca Teodora	---			MH(B-C)	MH(B-C)	(Kosok 1965; Schaedel n.d.)
	Huaca Quinones	---			EIP(C), MH(A)	EIP	(Schaedel n.d.)
	Cerro Guitarres	---			MH(B-C)	MH(B-C)	(Kosok 1965; Schaedel n.d.)
	Otra Banda	---			MH(B)	MH(B)	(Schaedel n.d.)
	Cerro Corbacho	---			MH(C), LIP,LH	MH(C),LIP,LH	(Kosok 1965; Schaedel n.d.)

Table 5.11. Chronological evidence for selected sites in the Lambayeque Valley.

VALLEY	SITE	RADIOCARBON EVIDENCE			ARCHAEOLOGICAL EVIDENCE[2]			
		SAMPLE #	AGE[1]	REFERENCES	CERAMICS	ARCHITECTURE	REFERENCES	COMMENTS
Lambayeque	Pampa de los Burros	----			EIP(B-C), MH(B)	----	(Schaedel n.d.)	
	Patapo	----			MH(B-C), LIP, LH	MH(B-C), LIP, LH	(Kosok 1965; Schaedel 1951a)	
	Pampa Grande	A-1704	1280 ± 70 (1258 ± 76) (AD 692)	(Shimada 1978)	EIP(C)	EIP(C)	(Day 1976; Kosok 1965; Schaedel 1951a; Shimada 1978)	Moche V.
		SMU-399	1300 ± 60 (1277 ± 79) (AD 673)	(Shimada 1978)	EIP(C)	EIP(C)	(Shimada 1978)	Moche V.
		A-1705	1380 ± 70 (1357 ± 82) (AD 593)	(Shimada 1978)	EIP(C)	EIP(C)	(Shimada 1978)	Moche V.
	Sipan	----			EIP(C), MH(B-C), LIP	MH(B-C), LIP	(Kosok 1965; Schaedel 1951a)	
	Colluz	----			MH(B-C)	MH(B-C)	(Kosok 1965; Schaedel 1951a)	
	Chotuna	----			MH(C), LIP	MH(C), LIP	(Kosok 1965; Schaedel 1951a; Trimborn 1972)	
		Bonn-1958	590 ± 70 (610 ± 80) (AD 1340)	(Scharpenseel and Pietig 1974)	LIP?	LIP?	(Trimborn 1972)	
		Bonn-1957	720 ± 70 (727 ± 76) (AD 1223)	(Scharpenseel and Pietig 1974)	LIP?	LIP?	(Trimborn 1972)	

Table 5.12. Chronological evidence for selected sites in the Leche and Motupe Valleys.

VALLEY	SITE	RADIOCARBON EVIDENCE			ARCHAEOLOGICAL EVIDENCE[2]			COMMENTS
		SAMPLE #	AGE[1]	REFERENCES	CERAMICS	ARCHITECTURE	REFERENCES	
Leche	Batan Grande	----			PC,IP,EH, EIP,MH,LIP LH	EH,EIP,MH,LIP LH	(Donnan 1972; Kosok 1965; Pedersen 1976; Schaedel 1951a, 1951b; Shimada 1979, 1980)	
		GrN-5474	915 ± 50 (909 ± 59) (AD 1041)	(Vogel and Lerman 1969)	MH	MH	(Pedersen 1976)	Sample from a charred bow fragment (Vogel and Lerman 1969).
	Purgatorio	----			MH(C), LIP,LH	MH(C),LIP,LH	(Kosok 1965; Schaedel 1951a,1951b)	
	Mirador	----			MH(B C), LIP?	MH(B-C),LIP?	(Kosok 1965; Schaedel n.d.; Trimborn 1972)	
		Bonn-1141	660 ± 60 (674 ± 67) (AD 1276)	(Sharpenseel and Pietig 1973)	?	?	(Trimborn 1972)	The context and associations of this sample are not clear.
		Bonn-1142	680 ± 50 (692 ± 58) (AD 1258)	(Sharpenseel and Pietig 1973)	?	?	(Trimborn 1972)	The context and associations of this sample are not clear.
	Tambo Real	----			EIP,LH	EIP,LH	(Kosok 1965; Schaedel n.d.; Shimada 1980)	
	Banderas	----			MH(B)	MH(B)	(Kosok 1965; Schaedel 1951a)	
Motupe	Jotoro	----			LH,C	LH,C	(Schaedel n.d.)	
	La Vina	----			LIP,LH	LIP,LH	(Kosok 1965; Schaedel 1951a)	
	Apurle	----			MH(C),LIP	MH(C),LIP	(Kosok 1965; Schaedel 1951a; Trimborn 1972)	
		Bonn-1813	1100 ± 70 (1083 ± 87) (AD 867)	(Sharpenseel and Pietig 1974)	?	?	(Trimborn 1972)	The context and associations of this sample are not clear.
		Bonn-1145	1430 ± 50 (1408 ± 55) (AD 542)	(Sharpenseel and Pietig 1974)	?	?	(Trimborn 1972)	The context and associations of this sample are not clear.

Table 5.13a. Chronological evidence for selected sites in the Piura Valley.

VALLEY	SITE	RADIOCARBON EVIDENCE			ARCHAEOLOGICAL EVIDENCE[2]			COMMENTS
		SAMPLE #[4]	AGE[1]	REFERENCES	CERAMICS	ARCHITECTURE	REFERENCES	
Piura	Bayovar	41	AD 1350 ± 90	(M. Cardenas 1979:27)	MH,LIP, LH,C	?	(M. Cardenas 1979:18,22)	
		40	AD 1180 ± 80	(M. Cardenas 1979:27)				
		37	AD 1040 ± 110	(M. Cardenas 1979:27)				
		47	AD 730 ± 50	(M. Cardenas 1979:27)				
	Quebrada de Chorrillos	34	AD 1050 ± 60	(M. Cardenas 1979:27)	PC	?	(M. Cardenas 1979:18,20, 21)	This site is described only as a Preceramic settlement. Samples 34 & 60 suggest later reoccupations.
		60	AD 560 ± 70	(M. Cardenas 1979:27)				
		33	5020 BC ± 140	(M. Cardenas 1979:27)				
		18	5590 BC ± 90	(M. Cardenas 1979:27)				
	Pan de Azucar	45	AD 1040 ± 90	(M. Cardenas 1979:27)	?	?	(M. Cardenas 1979)	This site is mentioned only in the date list.
	Nunura	15	AD 1010 ± 80	(M. Cardenas 1979:27)	PC,MH	?	(M. Cardenas 1979:9,13, 14)	
		16	1300 BC ± 70	(M. Cardenas 1979:27)				This date is too late to be Preceramic even by Cardenas' chronology (see figure).
	Reventazon III	48	AD 710 ± 80	(M. Cardenas 1979:27)	MH?	?	(M. Cardenas 1979:18,20)	
	Reventazon II	42	AD 620 ± 80	(M. Cardenas 1979:27)	MH?	?	(M. Cardenas 1979:18,20)	
	Avic 1	39	AD 600 ± 90	(M. Cardenas 1979:27)	MH	?	(M. Cardenas 1979:6-7,9, 14,18,20)	
		46	AD 750 ± 80	(M. Cardenas 1979:27)				
	Avic 2	10	750 BC ± 80	(M. Cardenas 1979:27)				
		11	2980 BC ± 70	(M. Cardenas 1979:27)				
		57	3230 BC ± 90	(M. Cardenas 1979:27)				
	Chusis	43	AD 480 ± 90	(M. Cardenas 1979:27)	?	?	(M. Cardenas 1979)	This site is mentioned only in the date list.
		17	AD 470 ± 60	(M. Cardenas 1979:27)				
		44	AD 380 ± 80	(M. Cardenas 1979:27)				

Table 5.13b. Chronological evidence for selected sites in the Piura Valley.

VALLEY	SITE	RADIOCARBON EVIDENCE			ARCHAEOLOGICAL EVIDENCE [2]			COMMENTS
		SAMPLE #	AGE [1]	REFERENCES	CERAMICS	ARCHITECTURE	REFERENCES	
Piura	Vicus	----		----	EIP	----	(Disselhoff 1971; Matos 1965-66)	See Appendix 1.
		Hv-1519	1295 ± 100 (1272 ± 112) (AD 678)	(Disselhoff 1971)	EIP	----	(Disselhoff 1971)	Grave 5.
		Hv-1520	1480 ± 60 (1459 ± 64) (AD 491)	(Disselhoff 1971)	EIP	----	(Disselhoff 1971)	Grave 2.
		Hv-1521	1490 ± 70 (1470 ± 73) (AD 480)	(Disselhoff 1971)	EIP	----	(Disselhoff 1971)	Grave 1.
		Hv-1517	1525 ± 115 (1506 ± 117) (AD 444)	(Disselhoff 1971)	EIP	----	(Disselhoff 1971)	Grave 1.
		Hv-1518	1700 ± 110 (1689 ± 113) (AD 261)	(Disselhoff 1971)	EIP	----	(Disselhoff 1971)	Grave 3.
		Gx-216	2030 ± 105 (2055 ± 111) (105 BC)	(Engel 1966)	EIP?	----	(Engel 1966)	This date is based of materials not recovered from a controlled excavation and has a questionable context. It also appears to be too early when compared to the other available dates.

Table 5.14a. Chronological evidence for selected sites in the Chira/Punta Parinas Region.

VALLEY	SITE	RADIOCARBON EVIDENCE			ARCHAEOLOGICAL EVIDENCE[2]			COMMENTS
		SAMPLE #	AGE[1]	REFERENCES	CERAMICS	ARCHITECTURE	REFERENCES	
Chira/Punta Parinas region	PV7-4	GX-1560	640 ± 90 (656 ± 95) (AD 1294)	(Richardson 1974)	LIP?	---	(Richardson 1974)	Piura phase.
	PV7-18	GX-1562	1445 ± 95 (1424 ± 97) (AD 526)	(Richardson 1974)	EIP?	---	(Richardson 1974)	Sechura phase.
		GX-1561	1675 ± 85 (1663 ± 89) (AD 287)	(Richardson 1974)	EIP?	---	(Richardson 1974)	Sechura phase.
		SI-1419	1810 ± 70 (1809 ± 79) (AD 141)	(Richardson 1974)	EIP?	---	(Richardson 1974)	Sechura phase.
	PV9-8	GX-1564	2010 ± 110 (2032 ± 116) (82 BC)	(Richardson 1974)	EIP?	---	(Richardson 1974)	Sechura phase.
	PV6-5	SI-1418	2535 ± 185 (2654 ± 213) (704 BC)	(Richardson 1974)	EH?	---	(Richardson 1974)	Sechura phase.
	PV8-7	GX-1003	3390 ± 125 (3750 ± 132) (1800 BC)	(Richardson 1974)	IP?	---	(Richardson 1974)	Paita phase.
		GX-1136	3610 ± 145 (4040 ± 195) (2090 BC)	(Richardson 1974)	IP?	---	(Richardson 1974)	Paita phase.
	PV7-16	GX-0993	4850 ± 95 (5599 ± 132) (3649 BC)	(Richardson 1974)	PC	---	(Richardson 1974)	Honda phase, type site.
		GX-0995	5150 ± 105 (5942 ± 149) (3992 BC)	(Richardson 1974)	PC	---	(Richardson 1974)	Honda phase.
		GX-0994	5185 ± 105 (5982 ± 149) (4032 BC)	(Richardson 1974)	PC	---	(Richardson 1974)	Honda phase.
	PV6-3	GX-0999	625 ± 95 (642 ± 100) (AD 1308)	(Richardson 1974)	PC	---	(Richardson 1974)	Estero phase, "contaminated date - should date 3-4,000 B.C. definitely preceramic" (Richardson 1974).

119

Table 5.14b. Chronological evidence for selected sites in the Chira/Punta Parinas Region.

VALLEY	SITE	RADIOCARBON EVIDENCE			ARCHAEOLOGICAL EVIDENCE [2]			
		SAMPLE #	AGE [1]	REFERENCES	CERAMICS	ARCHITECTURE	REFERENCES	COMMENTS
Chira/Punta Parinas region (continued)	PV9-31	SI-1416	7485 ± 120 (5760 BC)	(Richardson 1974)	PC	----	(Richardson 1974)	[6] Siches phase.
	PV8-24	SI-1417	7840 ± 90 (6125 BC)	(Richardson 1974)	PC	----	(Richardson 1974)	[6] Siches phase.
	PV8-13	GX-1563	6655 ± 130 (4905 BC)	(Richardson 1974)	PC	----	(Richardson 1974)	[6] Siches phase.
		GX-1002	8000 ± 140 (6290 BC)	(Richardson 1974)	PC	----	(Richardson 1974)	[6] Siches phase.
	PV7-19	GX-0996	4805 ± 130 (5546 ± 158) (3596 BC)	(Richardson 1974)	PC	----	(Richardson 1974)	Siches/Honda phase.
		GX-1137	5605 ± 95 (6431 ± 203) (4481 BC)	(Richardson 1974)	PC	----	(Richardson 1974)	Siches/Honda phase.
		GX-0998	5990 ± 120 (6820 ± 135) (4870 BC)	(Richardson 1974)	PC	----	(Richardson 1974)	Siches/Honda phase.
		GX-0997	7980 ± 130 (6269 BC)	(Richardson 1974)	PC	----	(Richardson 1974)	[6] Siches phase.
	PV8-26	SI-1414	8125 ± 80 (6419 BC)	(Richardson 1974)	PC	----	(Richardson 1974)	[6] Amotape phase.
	PV8-29	SI-1415	11,200 ± 115 (9586 BC)	(Richardson 1974)	PC	----	(Richardson 1974)	[6] Amotape phase.
	Beach Ridges #2	SI-1424B	1305 ± 100 (1282 ± 112) (AD 668)	(Richardson 1974)	EIP?	----	(Richardson 1974)	Sechura phase.
		SI-1424A	1405 ± 75 (1383 ± 78) (AD 567)	(Richardson 1974)	EIP?	----	(Richardson 1974)	Sechura phase.
	#4	GX-1566	1550 ± 110 (1531 ± 113) (AD 419)	(Richardson 1974)	EIP?	----	(Richardson 1974)	Sechura phase, shell date on Tivella.

Table 5.14c. Chronological evidence for selected sites in the Chira/Punta Parinas Region.

VALLEY	SITE	RADIOCARBON EVIDENCE			ARCHAEOLOGICAL EVIDENCE②			
		SAMPLE #	AGE①	REFERENCES	CERAMICS	ARCHITECTURE	REFERENCES	COMMENTS
Chira/Punta Parinas region (continued)	#5	SI-1423	1955 ± 100 (1969 ± 106) (19 BC)	(Richardson 1974)	EIP?	----	(Richardson 1974)	Sechura phase.
	#6	SI-1422	2685 ± 105 (2842 ± 116) (892 BC)	(Richardson 1974)	EH?	----	(Richardson 1974)	Late Paita phase.
	#7	GX-1565	3500 ± 160 (3896 ± 206) (1946 BC)	(Richardson 1974)	IP?	----	(Richardson 1974)	Paita phase shell date on Tivella.
	#8	SI-1421	3490 ± 80 (3882 ± 153) (1932 BC)	(Richardson 1974)	IP?	----	(Richardson 1974)	Ceramic – Paita phase.
	#9	SI-1420	4255 ± 65 (4874 ± 134) (2924 BC)	(Richardson 1974)	PC	----	(Richardson 1974)	
	?	L-703-D	3000 ± 200 (3243 ± 202) (1293 BC)	(Richardson 1974)	?	?	(Richardson 1974)	
	Lobitos Tablazo	L-703-A	> 30,000 BP	(Richardson 1974)	?	?	(Richardson 1974)	⑥

Table 5.15. Chronological evidence for selected sites in the Tumbes Region.

VALLEY	SITE	RADIOCARBON EVIDENCE			ARCHAEOLOGICAL EVIDENCE②			COMMENTS
		SAMPLE #	AGE①	REFERENCES	CERAMICS	ARCHITECTURE	REFERENCES	
Tumbes	Garbanzal	Gak-55	1730 ± 70 (1720 ± 75) (230 BC)	(Ishida et al. 1960)	EIP?	EIP?	(Izumi and Terada 1966)	Tomb 2.
		N-85	3680 ± 130 (4132 ± 184) (2182 BC)	(Yamasaki, Hamada, and Fujiyama 1966)			(Izumi and Terada 1966)	
		N-84	7510 ± 260 (5785 BC)	(Yamasaki, Hamada, and Fujiyama 1966)			(Izumi and Terada 1966)	⑥ This date is not consistent with its context, it is very much too old (Izumi and Terada 1966).
	Pechiche	N-75	785 ± 120 (788 ± 124) (AD 1162)	(Yamasaki, Hamada, and Fujiyama 1966)	EH?	EH?	(Izumi and Terada 1966	Izumi and Terada feel that this date and those from samples N-72, N-82, and N-83 are all too late, inspite of their internal consistency.
		N-72	810 ± 150 (811 ± 153) (AD 1139)	(Yamasaki, Hamada, and Fujiyama 1966)			(Izumi and Terada 1966)	See N-75.
		N-82	860 ± 110 (857 ± 114) (AD 1093)	(Yamasaki, Hamada, and Fujiyama 1966)			(Izumi and Terada 1966)	See N-75
		N-83	910 ± 120 (904 ± 124) (AD 1046)	(Yamasaki, Hamada, and Fujiyama 1966)			(Izumi and Terada 1966)	See N-75.
		N-80	2260 ± 130 (2323 ± 162) (373 BC)	(Yamasaki, Hamada, and Fujiyama 1966)			(Izumi and Terada 1966)	This sample and sample Gak-? (reported as BC-35) are not consitent with their presumed stratigraphic relationship, see (Izumi and Terada 1966).
		Gak-?	2800 ± 120 (2987 ± 130) (1037 BC)	(Yamasaki, Hamada, and Fujiyama 1966)			(Izumi and Terada 1966)	This sample appears to have been reported using a correction for the 5730 half-life, cf.Izumi and Terada (1966) and Yamasaki, Hamada, and Fujiyama (1966). It has been calibrated accordingly.

References

Arnold, J. R., and W. F. Libby.
1951   Radiocarbon dates, Institute for Nuclear Studies, University of Chicago.   Science 126 (3279): 908-19.

Bawden, B.
1977   Galindo and the nature of the Middle Horizon in northern coastal Peru.   Ph.D. diss., Harvard University.

Bennett, W. C.
1939   Archaeology of the North Coast of Peru: An Account of Explorations and Excavations in Virú and Lambayeque Valleys.   Anthropological Papers of the American Museum of Natural History 37 (2).

1950   The Gallinazo Group, Virú Valley, Peru.   Yale University Publications in Anthropology 43.   New Haven.

Bird, J. B.
1948   Preceramic Cultures in Chicama and Virú.   In Reappraisal of Peruvian Archaeology, edited by W. C. Bennett.   Memoirs of the Society for American Archaeology 4:21-28.

1951   South American radiocarbon dates.   Memoirs of the Society for American Archaeology 8:37-49.

Brennan, C. T.
1980   Cerro Arena: Rise of the Andean elite.   Archaeology 33(3): 6-13.

Broecker, W. S., J. L. Kulp, and C. S. Tucek.
1956   Lamont natural radiocarbon measurements III.   Science 124 (3213): 154-65.

Broecker, W. S., and J. L. Kulp.
1957   Lamont natural radiocarbon measurements IV.   Science 126:1324-34.

Burger, R. L., and L. S. Burger.
1980   Ritual and religion at Huaricoto.   Archaeology 33 (6): 26-32.

Cárdenas, M. M.
1979   A Chronology of the Use of Marine Resources in Ancient Peru.   Publicación del Instituto Riva-Aquero No. 104, Pontifica Universidad Católica del Perú.

Conrad, G. W.
1977   Chiquitoy Viejo: An Inca administrative center in the Chicama Valley, Peru.   Journal of Field Archaeology 4 (1): 1-18.

Damon, P. E., C. W. Ferguson, A. Long, and E. I. Wallick.
1974   Dendrochronological calibration of the radiocarbon time scale.   American Antiquity 39 (2): 350-66.

Day, K. C.
1974 Walk-in wells and water management at Chan Chan, Peru. In The Rise and Fall of Civilizations: An Archaeological Reader, edited by C. C. Lamberg-Karlovsky and J. A. Sabloff. Menlo Park, Calif.: Cummings Publishing Co.

1976 Peru: The land and its people. In Gold for the Gods, by A. D. Tushingham, 21-54. Royal Ontario Museum.

Disselhoff, H. D.
1971 Vicus, eine neu entdeckte alt peruanische kultur. Berlin: Gabr. Mann.

Donnan, C. B.
1968 An association of Middle Horizon epoch 2A specimens from the Chicama Valley, Peru. Ñawpa Pacha 6:15-18.

1972 Moche-Huari murals from northern Peru. Archaeology 25:85-95.

1973 Moche Occupation of the Santa Valley, Peru. University of California Publications in Anthropology 8. Berkeley and Los Angeles: University of California Press.

Donnan, C. B., and C. J. Mackey.
1978 Ancient Burial Patterns of the Moche Valley, Peru. Austin: University of Texas Press.

Eling, H. H., Jr.
1978 Interpretaciones preliminares del sistema de riego antiguo de Talambo en el Valle de Jequetepeque, Perú. In III Congreso Peruano, El Hombre y la Cultura Andina: Actas y Trabajos 1, edited by Ramiro Matos M., 401-19.

Engel, F.
1957 Sites et etablissments sans ceramique de la Côte Peruvienne. Journal de la Société des Américanistes 49:7-35.

1963 Datations de radio carbone 14 et problèmes de la préhistoire du Perou. Journal de la Société des Américanistes, n.s. 53:101-32.

1966 Geografía Humana Prehistórica y Agricultura Precolombina de la Quebrada de Chilca 1. Lima: Informe Preliminar. Oficina de Promoción y Desarrollo, Departamento de Publicaciones, Universidad Agraria. Ed. Juridica S.A.

Fergusson, G. J., and T. A. Rafter.
1959 New Zealand C14 age measurements 4. New Zealand Journal of Geology and Geophysics 2(1): 208-41.

Fung Pineda, R., and V. Pimentel Gurmendi.
1973 Chakillo. Revista del Museo Nacional, Lima, 39:71-80.

Grieder, T.
1975 A dated sequence of building and pottery at Las Haldas. Ñawpa Pacha 13:99-113.

1978 The Art and Archaeology of Pashash. Austin: University of Texas Press.

1981 La Galgada: Peru before pottery. Archaeology 34 (2): 44-51.

Hawkes, C.
1954 Archaeological theory and method: Some suggestions from the Old World. American Anthropologist 56 (2): 155-68.

Hecker, W., and G. Hecker.
1977 Archäologische Untersuchungen in Pacatnamu Nord-Peru. Indiana supp. 9.

Ishida, E., et al.
1960 Andes: The Report of the University of Tokyo Scientific Expedition to the Andes in 1958. Tokyo.

Izumi, S., and K. Terada.
1966 Andes 3: Excavations at Pechiche and Garbanzal, Tumbes Valley, Peru. 1960. Tokyo: Kadokawa Publishing Co.

Julien, D. G.
1980 Ecological stability and maritime adaptation on the north coast of Peru. Master's thesis, University of Texas at Austin.

Keatinge, R. W.
1975 Urban settlement systems and rural sustaining communities: an example from Chan Chan's hinterland. Journal of Field Archaeology 2:215-227.

1980 Archaeology and development: The Tembladera sites of the Peruvian north coast. Journal of Field Archaeology 7 (4): 467-475.

Kluge, M. J., J. B. Rabinowitz, and R. P. Watson.
1976 An archaeological survey in the Chicama Valley, Peru: Preliminary report. Report submitted to the University of Texas at Austin Latin American Archaeological Program.

Kobayashi, H., T. Hirose, M. Sugino and N. Watanabe.
1974 University of Tokyo radiocarbon measurements V. Radiocarbon 16 (3): 381-87.

Kosok, P.
1965 Life, Land, and Water in Ancient Peru. New York: Long Island University Press.

n.d. Chicama valley site map and Huaca list. Unpublished map and field notes.

Kroeber, A. L.
1925 The Uhle Pottery Collections from Moche. University of California Publications in American Archaeology and Ethnology 21 (5).

1930 Archaeological Explorations in Peru. Anthropological Memoirs, Field Museum of Natural History, 2 (4).

Kulp, L. J., H. W. Feely, and L. E. Tryon.
1951   Lamont Natural radiocarbon measurements I. Science 114 (2960): 565–68.

Kus, J. S.
1972   Selected aspects of irrigated agriculture in the Chimu heartland, Peru. Ph.D. diss. University of California, Los Angeles.

Lanning, E. P.
1967   Peru Before the Incas. Englewood Cliffs, N.J.: Prentice-Hall.

Larco Hoyle, R.
1938-
    39   Los Mochicas, Tomos I & II. Lima: Casa Editora.

1941   Los Cupisniques. Buenos Aires: Sociedad Geográfica Americana.

1948   Cronología Arqueológica de Norte del Peru. Buenos Aires: Sociedad Geográfica Americana.

Libby, W. F.
1951   Radiocarbon Dates II. Science 114 (2960): 291–96.

Matos Mendieta, R.
1965-
    66   Algunas consideraciones sobre el Estilo de Vicus. Revista del Museo Nacional, Lima, 34:89–130.

Matsuzawa, T.
1978   The formative site of Las Haldas, Peru: Architecture, chronology, and economy. Translated from Japanese by Izumi Shimada. American Antiquity 43 (4): 652–73.

Moseley, M. E.
1975a   Chan Chan: Andean alternative of the preindustrial city. Science 187 (4173): 219–25.

1975b   The Maritime Foundations of Andean Civilization. Menlo Park, Calif.: Cummings Publishing Co.

Moseley, M. E., and L. Watanabe.
1974   The adobe sculpture of Huaca de los Reyes. Archaeology 27 (3): 155–61.

Olsen, E. A., and W. S. Broecker.
1959   Lamont natural radiocarbon measurements V. American Journal of Science Radiocarbon Supplement 1:1–28.

Pedersen, A.
1976   El ajuar funerario de la tumba de la Huaca Menor de Batán Grande, Lambayeque, Perú. Actas del 41 Congreso Internacional de Americanistas 2:60–73.

Pozorski, S.
1976 Prehistoric subsistence patterns and site economics in the Moche Valley, Peru. Ph.D. diss., University of Texas, Austin.

Pozorski, S., and T. Pozorski.
1979 An early subsistence exchange system in the Moche Valley, Peru. Journal of Field Archaeology 6 (4): 413-32.

Pozorski, T.
1975 El Complejo de Caballo Muerto: Los Frisos de Barro de la Huaca de los Reyes. Revista del Museo Nacional 41:211-251.

1976 Caballo Muerto: A complex of early Ceramic sites in the Moche Valley, Peru. Ph. D. diss., University of Texas, Austin.

1980 The early horizon site of Huaca de los Reyes: Societal implications. American Antiquity 45 (1): 100-10.

Proulx, D. A.
1968 An Archaeological Survey of the Nepeña Valley, Peru. Department of Anthropology Research Report No. 2, University of Massachusetts, Amherst.

1973 Archaeological Investigations in the Nepeña Valley, Peru. Department of Anthropology Research Report No. 13, University of Massachusetts, Amherst.

Richardson, J. B., III.
1974 Holocene beach ridges between the Chira and Punta Parinas, northwest Peru, and the archaeological sequence. Paper presented at the 39th Annual Meeting of the Society for American Archaeology, Washington, D.C.

Rodriguez Suy Suy, V. A.
n.d. Asentamientos prehispánico del hombre en el Valle Chicama y su relación Norperuana. Unpublished proposal.

Rowe, J. H.
1962 Stages and periods in archaeological interpretation. Southwestern Journal of Anthropology 18:1-27.

Rowe, J. H., and D. Menzel, eds.
1967 Peruvian Archaeology: Selected Readings. Palo Alto, Calif.: Peek Publications.

Schaedel, R. P.
1951a Major ceremonial and population centers in northern coastal Peru. Selected Papers, 29th International Congress of Americanists, 232-243. Chicago: University of Chicago Press.

1951b The lost cities of Peru. Scientific American 185 (2): 18-23.

1966 The Huaca el Dragon. Journal de la Société des Américanistes de Paris 50 (2): 383-496.

1978   Permanent and transitory diagnostics of the Middle horizon in the central Andes. Paper presented at the 43rd Annual Meeting of the Society for American Archaeology, Tucson, Arizona.

n.d.   Urbanization on the coast of Peru. Proposal submitted to the National Science Foundation.

Scharpenseel, H. W., and F. Pietig.
1973   University of Bonn natural radiocarbon measurements V. Radiocarbon 15:13-41.

1974   University of Bonn natural radiocarbon measurements VII. Radiocarbon 16:143-65.

Shimada, I.
1978   Economy of a prehistoric urban context: Commodity and labor flow at Moche V Pampa Grande, Peru. American Antiquity 43 (4): 569-92.

1979   Behind the golden mask: The research problems and preliminary results of the Batán Grande-La Leche Valley archaeological project. Report submitted to the National Science Foundation.

1980   Second report, Batán Grande-La Leche archaeological project 1979-80 field season. Report submitted to the National Science Foundation.

n.d.   Cultural interaction and emerging complexity during the Middle Horizon on the north coast of Peru. Proposal submitted to the National Science Foundation.

Smith, J. W., Jr.
1978   The Recuay culture: A reconstruction based on artistic motifs. Ph.D. diss., University of Texas, Austin.

Soriano Infante, A.
1941   Monografía de Ancash: Nepeña (Provincia de Santa). Revista del Museo Nacional, Lima, 10 (2): 263-77.

Squier, E. G.
1877   Peru: Incidents of Travel and Exploration in the Land of the Incas. London: Macmillan and Company.

Strong, W. D., and C. Evans.
1947   Finding the tomb of a warrior-god. National Geographic 91:453-82.

1952   Cultural Stratigraphy in the Virú Valley, Northern Peru: The Formative and Florescent Epochs. Columbia Studies in Archaeology and Ethnology 4. New York.

Stumer, L. M.
1956   Development of Peruvian coastal Tiahuanaco styles. American Antiquity 22 (1): 59-69.

Tello, J. C.
1956 Arqueología del Valle de Casma. Culturas: Chavin, Santa o Huaylas Yunga y Sub-Chimu. Publicación del Archivo "Julio C. Tello", no. 1. Lima: Universidad Nacional Mayor de San Marcos.

Terada, K.
1979 Excavations at La Pampa in the North Highlands of Peru, 1975. Tokyo: University of Tokyo Press.

Trimborn, H.
1972 Nuevas fechas radiocarbónicas para algunos monumentos y sitios prehispánicos de la Costa Peruana. In 40th International Congress of Americanists, Actas 1:313-15.

Ubbelohde Doering, H.
1967 On the Royal Highways of the Inca. New York: Praeger.

Uhle, M
1913 Die Ruinen von Moche. Journal de la Société des Américanistes de Paris 10:95-117.

Valastro, S., Jr., E. M. Davis, and A. G. Varela.
1975 University of Texas at Austin radiocarbon dates X. Radiocarbon 17 (1): 52-98.

1977 University of Texas at Austin radiocarbon dates XI. Radiocarbon 19 (2): 280-325.

1978 University of Texas at Austin radiocarbon dates XII. Radiocarbon 20 (2): 245-73.

Valastro, S., Jr., E. M. Davis, A. G. Varela, and C. Ekland-Olson.
1980 University of Texas at Austin radiocarbon dates XIV. Radiocarbon 22 (4): 1090-115.

Vogel, J. C., and J. C. Lerman
1969 Groningen radiocarbon dates VIII. Radiocarbon 11:351-90.

Watson, R. P.
1979 Water control and land use on the arid north coast of Peru: Prehispanic agricultural systems in the Chicama Valley. Master's thesis, University of Texas, Austin.

West, M.
1970 Community settlement patterns at Chan Chan, Peru. American Antiquity 35 (1): 74-86.

Willey, G. R.
1953 Prehistoric Settlement Patterns in the Virú Valley, Peru. Bureau of American Ethnology, Bulletin 155. Washington, D. C.

1971 An Introduction to American Archaeology. Vol. 2, South America. Englewood Cliffs, N.J.: Prentice-Hall, Inc.

Yamasaki, F., T. Hamada, and C. Fujiyama.
1966 RIKEN natural radiocarbon measurements II. Radiocarbon 8:324-39.

Zevallos Quiñones, J.
1971 Cerámica de la Cultura "Lambayeque" (Lambayeque I). Trujillo, Peru: Universidad Nacional de Trujillo.

6.

Pre-Hispanic Irrigation Sources and Systems in the Jequetepeque Valley, Northern Peru

Herbert H. Eling, Jr.

Geographical Setting

The Jequetepeque Valley is located on the North Coast of Peru between 7° and 7° 45' latitude south and 79° 45' and 78° longitude west. The total area of approximately 115,000 hectares is divided by the easterly flowing Jequetepeque River whose watershed is the eastern slopes of the Andes near Cajamarca. Presently, a maximum of 44,710 hectares is under cultivation (República del Perú 1968, Tomo IV: 1); during pre-Hispanic times the maximum was 81,000 hectares (Kosok 1965; Sutton 1940; Eling 1977). The 2,185 hectares of actual flood plain under cultivation is probably equivalent to that farmed in pre-Hispanic times.

The north bank irrigation system, which is protected by a low coastal mountain range that extends about 20 km north-south and 10 km inland, contains about seventy-five percent of the agricultural land of the valley. The remainder forms the south bank system. The Andes Mountains extend toward the coast on the south bank, thus restricting the amount of land which can be cultivated. Lacking protection similar to that of the north bank, the south bank is subjected to more severe wind and sand erosion caused by the constant 25 kph winds which begin between 10 A.M. and noon each day and originate 50 km to the south from the area around Puerto Chicama (Schweigger 1949:16). With the exception of the small range mentioned above, no mountains rise to impede the winds until the Sechura Desert over 200 km to the north (Broggi 1952:5; Schweigger 1949:7).

Despite the prolonged effects of wind and sand erosion, almost all of the system in use today can be credited to pre-Hispanic builders whose area under cultivation exceeded the modern area by 36,700 ha. With modern agricultural techniques, the present level of 44,710 hectares has risen 8,710 hectares from the 1966 total of only 36,000 ha, but 27,300 hectares on the north bank and 9,400 hectares on the south bank have not yet been reclaimed (Cárdenas and Carnejo 1973: 3).

The area under study includes almost all of the abandoned south bank system (fig. 6.1) and is bounded by the UTMG coordinates of 666.000mE x 9'184.000mN x 680.000mE x 9'170.000mN. This total area of about 16,000 hectares encompasses mountains, sand dune fields, and large washes. Included are the Pampas and Zonas de Dunas de Mojucape, Cañoncillo, Jatanca, and Puémepe; the archaeological sites of Cañoncillo, Jatanca, and Huaca Santa María; and their adjacent zones where associated fields and irrigation networks are variably exposed by sand dune migration. Immediately adjacent, an integral part of the system as it will be reconstructed, is some 10 km of canals and 1,000 hectares of presently irrigated land within the ex-haciendas of Tecapa and Cosquepón to the north and pre-Hispanic agricultural fields of the Pampa de Guereque to the northeast.

The area of Cañoncillo and the Pampa de Mojucape on the southern bank irrigation system of the Jequetepeque River has been continously occupied since the Formative period. This study is concerned only with the occupational periods that are relatable to facets of hydraulic engineering, effectively beginning during the later Moche Period (A.D. 500-750) and continuing through Chimú-Inca times.

Analytic Procedures

The temporal and spatial reconstruction of the pre-Hispanic irrigation, agricultural, and settlement patterns relies upon the use of aerial photo interpretation, data transfer to accurate maps, and ground verification. This approach countermands the inherent liabilities of archaeological survey in an area now covered by migratory sand dunes and subjected to severe wind erosion. Features of the old topography, such as cemeteries, canals, agricultural fields, and habitational areas, now appear as isolates, remote from water sources which might justify their existence. However, projections from these apparently independent constructions may be logically linked to form hypotheses about the overall system. Two separate, but not necessarily unrelated, reconstructions are suggested by the hydrological picture as it is reflected in the archaeological record.

Four separate flights provide the aerial photographic coverage of the Jequetepeque Valley: May 1943 and May 1968 were flown by the Servicio Aerofotográfico Nacional del Perú (SAN) with respective scales of 1:15,000 and 1:20,000; June 1948 and December 1961 were flown by the U.S. Air Force with corresponding scales of 1:40,000 and 1:16,000. The 1968 flight was commissioned by the Ministerio de Agricultura, Comité Especial del Plan Jequetepeque, and Salzgitter Industiebau GMBH for the proposed "Gallito Ciego" Dam project presently underway. Corrected photo composite maps were made from both the 1943 and 1968 flights. The 1943 photomap has a scale of 1:15,000 and the 1968 is set at 1:20,000 and 1:50,000. Stereo pairs of all four flights were utilized for this study. All of the area under consideration is covered in each of the four flights. A series of USAF high altitude obliques, NASA high altitude flights, satellite photographs, and LANDSAT imagery was lightly consulted but was not particularly helpful. Aerial oblique photographs published in Ubbelohde-Doering (1966), taken in 1953, were also used for comparison. Stereographic pairs were viewed with an Adams CF-8 stereoscope and with the more sophisticated Bausch and Lomb Stereo Transfer Scope, with magnifications to 7X, made available by the Department of Geology, University of Texas at Austin.

The topographic maps include the excellent set ordered by Salzgitter of

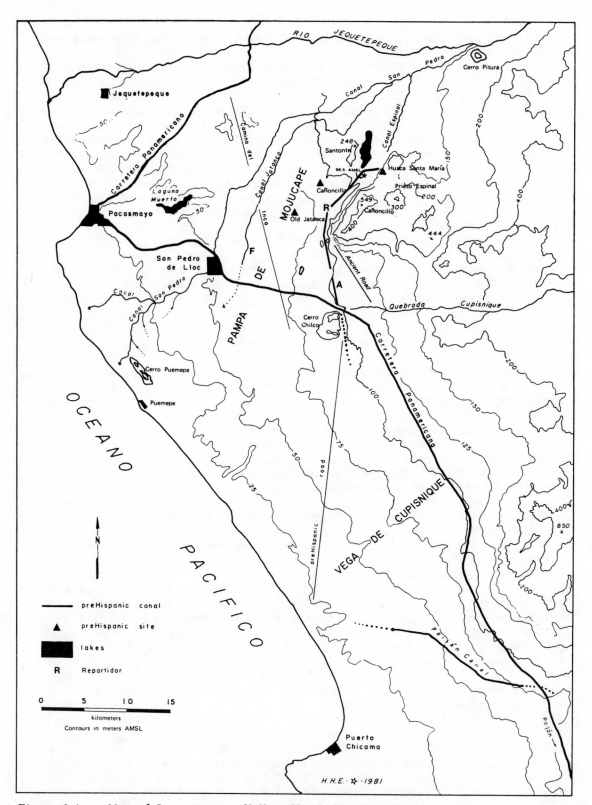

Figure 6.1. Map of Jequetepeque Valley, North Chicama Valley.

1:10,000 with 1, 2, and 10 m intervals which show some major archaeological sites, towns, the abandoned railroad, roads, highways, canals, agricultural plots (chacras), algarroba clumps and stands, sand dunes of 2 m or larger, and the lake area. The 1967 U.S. Army Corps of Engineers 1:50,000 Transverse Mercador Projection, based on the 1961 1:60,000 USAF flight with contour lines to 12.5 m, and the 1966 Instituto Geográfico Militar 1:100,000 TMP, also based on the 1961 USAF flight with contour lines to 25 m, were used. Additional information was obtained from the working field notes and maps of the late Paul Kosok. The latter are based on the 1:100,000 Escuela Superior de Guerra Militar Map of 1938 without the use of aerial photogrammetric methods. These maps were photographed in large format and then converted to larger, more usable scales.

All of the information obtained from aerial photographs was mapped and ground verified. Conversely, the aerials often served as explanatory aids to the surface survey.

The Irrigation System of the Pampa de Mojucape

The Pampa de Mojucape (fig. 6.2a) is situated in the south-central portion of the valley. It presently resembles a palm with four sand-covered fingers up to 30+ m above the floor plain extending northerly into the stable irrigated agricultural lands of the ex-haciendas of Cosquepón and Tecapa. The principal culturally utilized portion of the Pampa is bounded by Cerro Cañoncillo to the east and the present town and adjacent agricultural fields of San Pedro de Lloc 6 km to the west. The northern-central end of the fingers are Cerro Santonte, 304 m AMSL in the center, and Cerro Prieto Espinal, 457 m AMSL to the east. The Lagunas de Cañoncillo are sandwiched between the last two extensions or sand-covered cerros.

The Pampa is the northern extension of a westward sloping alluvial fan caused by the erosional and depositional action of the Quebrada de Cupisnique. The quebrada begins near the 800 m AMSL level where little, if any, rain falls during the normal months of precipitation in the Andes Mountains. The water that is captured is absorbed by the vegetation near the head of the Quebrada, never reaching the Pampa below. During the El Niño rains, the Quebrada de Cupisnique could gather from a watershed of nearly 575 km^2, beginning near the highland town of Trinidad at 2,600 m AMSL and channeling water onto the Pampa. Using stereo pairs of the lower Cupisnique flood plain, it is possible to trace three distinct episodes of downcutting, probably from earlier El Niño rains. Runoff entered the Pampa, altering the topography and destroying segments of the crossing of pre-Hispanic canals.

The profile of the Pampa, at least the first four meters, shows a series of four periods of conglomerate deposition, varying from 0.5 to 1 m in thickness. The strata alternate with loose deposits of eolian sand approximately 20 cm thick (personal observation of bulldozed gravel pit on the Pampa). These eolian sands result from periodic sand encroachment by dune migration, streamer transport, and deflation of the surface. The present flood plain, and that irrigated by the Chimú, was probably the last sand stratum. In those parts where pre-Hispanic agricultural practices have not erased the evidence, the Pampa is a light desert pavement similar to those in south Peru (Hastenrath 1967: 308, figs. 6 and 7; Cooke and Warren 1973: Pl.4.13).

The Pampa is rectangular, beginning at the northeastern edge of the Cupisnique alluvial fan and extending more than 10 km to the south into the central downcut channel (fig. 6.2a). Thus, the contour levels and slope run almost parallel to the long axis of the rectangle beginning at 100 m AMSL and ending 4 km to the west at nearly 60 m AMSL. Irrigation of the Pampa in

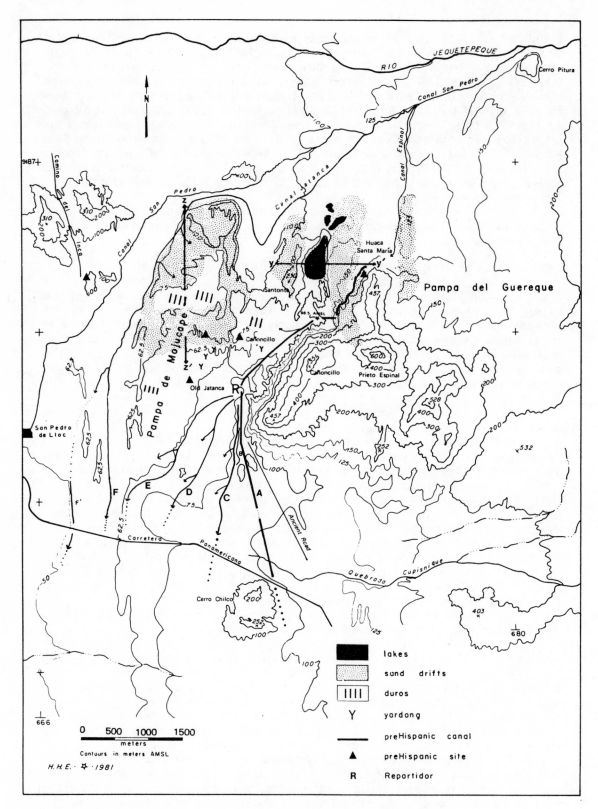

Figure 6.2a. Map of Pampa de Mojucape and related canal systems.

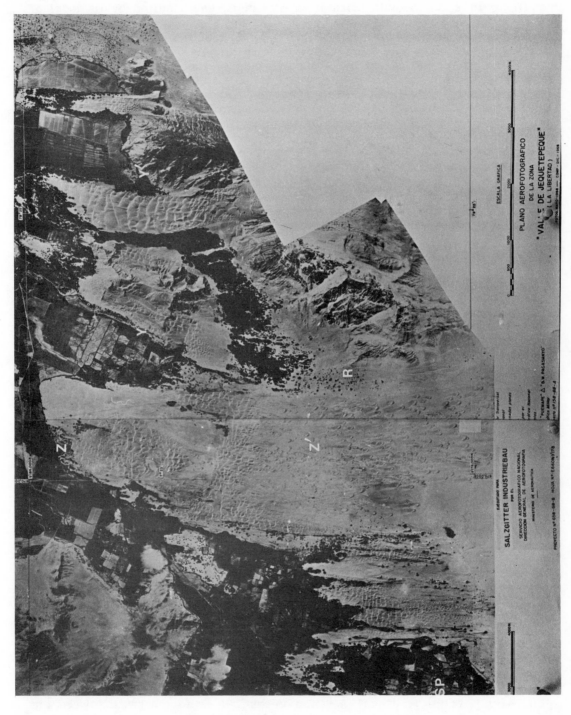

Figure 6.2b.   *Photomap of Pampa de Mojucape, Z–Z′ and Y–Y′ correspond to figure 6.7.   Repartidor shown.*

prehistoric times would have been maximized by following this topography, resulting in a north-south orientation of canals, each limited by its level of entry onto the Pampa. This northern end of the Cupisnique alluvial fan inter-digitates on a perpendicular line with the fanning of the southern edge of the much larger Jequetepeque River Valley to form a coalesced fan or bajada.

The visual and extant hydraulic evidence of the agricultural activity in this area is rendered fragmentary and isolated due to burial by migrating barchan dunes, sand drifts, sand shadows, and to erosion promoted by the Quebrada de Cupisnique and the slot between cerros Prieto Espinal, Cañoncillo, and Santonte (fig. 6.3). The remnant sections of canals and fields are the only hard evidence available and can be plotted on the 1:10,000 topographic maps, but the origins and destinations of many of the canals are eradicated or obscured. The central portion of this system is presented to set the stage for a reconstruction of the potential water sources which fed the plotted canals and fields and the possible destinations of the canal system. Three pre-Hispanic habitational sites in the north central area are also relevant: Huaca Santa Maria, Cañoncillo, and Old Jatanca.

The Aqueduct

The entire canal system on the eastern or higher side of the Pampa was fed through an elevated canal or aqueduct made of stone and a cementlike material known in Peru as argamasa. The highest segment located during field survey lies at an elevation of 96.5 m AMSL (figs. 6.2b, 6.3). From this point, the canal system can only be logically extended eastward to connect with a primary water source. The aqueduct dropped southwest 2.5 km in the slot between three cerros, Prieto Espinal to the east, Santonte to the north, and Cañoncillo to the south, finally linking with the greater Pampa irrigation canal at 93 m AMSL. At this juncture, five canals emanate from what must have been a distribution point (repartidor) of the aquaduct to irrigate and possibly to provide domestic water to the central Pampa (fig. 6.2a). This repartidor is similar to Siete Compuertas on the Talambo canal system in the same valley (Eling 1977: 407). Farrington (1980: 290) has stated "...that Peruvian irrigation systems were of the continuously flowing type, and were regulated only at the field intake." This may have been the case for the smaller Moche Valley, but the Jequetepeque River Valley irrigation systems do not conform to this description.

Canals on the Pampa

The highest and possibly longest canal on the Pampa, Canal A, (fig. 6.2a) leaves the repartidor at 93 m AMSL and continues south for 1 km where it turns southwest for another 6 km. Thereon, any possible continuation has been destroyed by both the Pan American Highway and erosion from El Niño floods coming down the Quebrada de Cupisnique. An indication of the isolation of the Pampa canals from an obvious water source can be gathered by noting the IGN and the U.S. Army Corps of Engineers Topographic Maps designation of this canal as Camino del Inca or Inca Road. Actually, a section of an early pre-Hispanic road, apparently emanating from the Cañoncillo area, runs generally parallel to Canal A, then veers 100 m to the south toward the Chicama Valley; it, too, has been erased by the Cupisnique Quebrada. That the roads of Chimú origin in the nearby Quebrada de Cupisnique are still intact suggests this road is earlier, probably built at the same general time as Cañoncillo, a late Moche-Middle Horizon site. Canal A is almost entirely covered with sand (fig. 6.4) and is breached by the quebrada channel. The

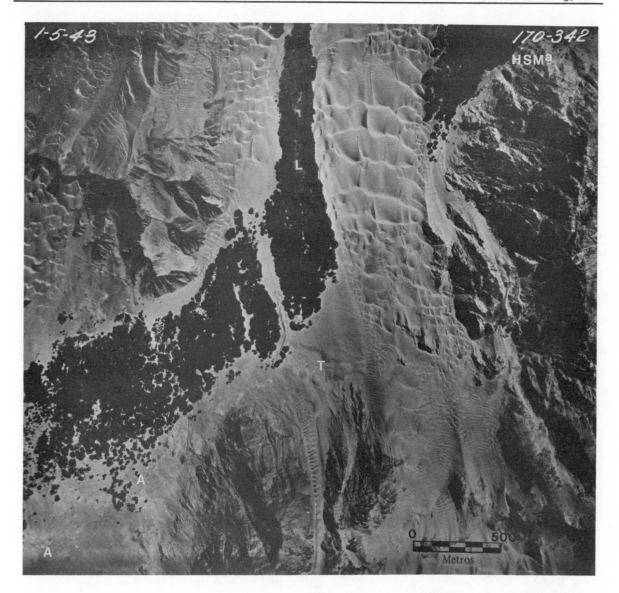

Figure 6.3.   *Cerro Santonte on left, Huaca Santa María upper right; lakes in algorrobal. Trench (T) and aqueduct (A) indicated.*

remnants show the canal was lined with stone and may have carried around 5. m³/sec. of water.   The relationship of the canal to the Pampa irrigation system as a whole can only be inferred.   Canal A has no branch canal to divert water onto the Pampa.

Canal B begins at 93 m AMSL and runs almost parallel to Canal A, but radiates to begin irrigating the 90 m level (fig. 6.2a).   The greater antiquity of this canal is testified to by its trajectory and by its truncation by El Niño–Cupisnique floods whereas the other canals are mainly intact.   This remnant section is only 1.25 km long, but its projected path would have interrupted Canal C.   No evidence of this traverse exists; Canal C is not breached at this point, suggesting it was of later construction.

Canal C irrigates the 80 m level (fig. 6.2a).   Along with Canal A, this canal is well defined and about the same size except that it irrigated both the

137

upper central and probably the lower southern sections of the Pampa.

Canal D, originating at the 93 m level, drops west to the 65 m level, then turns south to parallel the higher canals. Both D and the lower Canal E are in the sand corridor and are obscured most of the time. The lower reaches also irrigate the land around a 40 m hill in the center of the Pampa, where the moving dunes periodically unveil small mamparos, wind shelters formed by stones vertically placed in a semicircle approximately 6 m in diameter. These features are generally associated with Chavín ceramics illustrating the alterations in the agricultural use of the area since that time.

Canal E, the lowest canal to radiate from the aqueduct, drops to the 55 m level to irrigate the land on the western extension. This canal, passing just south of Old Jatanca (Ubbelohde-Doering 1967:104-112), a large pre-Hispanic tapia (rammed earth) walled settlement on the Pampa, is the only canal in this part of the system which could have provided water to the area for domestic use. Also on the lower reaches of Canal E, a few square stone housing structures stand on an eolian sand base between 1.5 and 3 m above the present Pampa floor, indicating a previous level that has since eroded. This phenomenon is similar to that found on the upper Pampa in the form of residual topography, later discussed as yardangs (fig. 6.5).

Each canal was able to irrigate the land between its contour and the next lower level, a configuration also seen on the much larger Pampa de Cerro Colorado to the north in the same valley (Eling 1977). Canals A, C, and sometimes D show the same Cupisnique Quebrada sequence of erosional patterns, wherein the braided steams abrade and break the walls, suggesting the erosional episodes may be contemporaneous. Canal E, which is protected from similar processes by a small rock hill in the center of the Pampa, lies directly in the path of migrating dunes. Canals B through E tend to meander slightly, following their respective contour lines across the Pampa. The straight path of Canal A, cut into small hills and elevated over minor depressions, indicates it was constructed for the mass transportation of water to some point outside the greater Pampa for distribution. These five branch canals service only the southern, lower half of the Pampa de Mojucape.

The aqueduct may also have serviced the central section above Old Jatanca. Taking advantage of the topographic slope, canal water could have been diverted from the repartidor to supply Old Jatanca's domestic needs. Water could have been sent both westward and/or in a northerly direction. This area is directly in the central portion of the dune path; the canals have been eroded by wind action, leaving only those remnants protected by the walls within the old settlement.

The northern section may have also been fed by the aquaduct since this area is within the northern extension of the migrating dunes. The entire width and length are covered by sand drifts and sand shadows up to 35 m high. Eddies produced by wind patterns passing over the drifts have left sand-free areas complete with canals, furrowed agricultural fields, walls, and cultural debris indicating Mochica occupation. These cultural indicators were plotted and then connected with other visible features to project a sand-free topography. Most of the projected topography of the northern area is 75 m AMSL, sloping southward for 4 km to the boundary of the sand field beyond which the flood plain topography can again be definitely determined. All or part of this northern extension could have been irrigated by the aquaduct.

An alternative is water from the Acequia San Pedro passing to the north, then curving to the west of the Pampa; a canal may have entered from the northwestern corner at near the 85 m level. In this manner, water could have also reached the site of Old Jatanca and the western portion of the Pampa. Exact determination is problematical because mountains of sand

Figure 6.4.   *Sand-filled Canal A leading south toward Cerro Chileo.*

Figure 6.5.   *Yardang on the upper Pampa de Mojucape.*

presently cover the projected trajectory into this area.

Vestiges of canals skirt the edges of the eastern Pampa around the modern town of Jatanca and head in a southerly direction toward the southern periphery of the pre-Hispanic agricultural area to distribute water at the lower elevations (fig. 6.2a). The western slope of the topography prevents these canals from playing an important role in the irrigation of the greater Pampa.

Yardangs

In the upper reaches of the Pampa, on the windward side of the sand drifts (fig. 6.3), a series of buttelike features or yardangs (Blackwelder 1934, esp. pl. 7), composed of soft, cohesive river silt between 1 to 1.5 m thick, are perched on the top of up to 6 m of eolian sand (figs. 6.6, 6.7). Yardangs are erosional remnants, residuals of an older topography that are "elongated...parallel to the strongest prevailing wind direction and commonly occur in groups or fields" (Twidale 1968:1237). Yardangs described herein, however, are archaeological features, culturally produced but modified by normal geomorphological processes. The Mojucape yardangs range in size from 5x10 m to 40x75 m. These features evidence an older, elevated occupational floor utilized for agriculture on the northern end of the Pampa. Remnants of canals, furrows, and scattered cultural debris, mainly sherds and lithic agricultural implements, imply a Moche V occupation, terminating before A.D. 750. A second group of yardangs with cultural remains is located within the slot between Cerros Cañoncillo and Santonte (fig. 6.2a). These features are more elongated, only 2 m above the present floor, and were apparently also fed by the elevated canal. Thus, this now uncultivated area was irrigated in the past.

The old topography was formed by irrigating sand drifts with silt-charged river water over a period of time. Dr. Winn Van Immerzeel, a Dutch hydrologist working with our project in 1976, calculated a 1 cm per year buildup of silt from the Jequetepeque River. Thus, 1 to 1.5 m thickness of silt layering implies a 100 to 150 year occupation. Subsequent to the abandonment of the fields, natural erosional processes reduced the old topography, leaving only yardangs as fragmentary evidence of the prior occupational floor 6 m above the level utilized from the Middle Horizon to the present. By implication, irrigation with silt-rich river water of a surface 6 m above the modern plain would require an elevated silt charged water source—the Jequetepeque River.

Duros

The last agricultural area under consideration is the duros, hard, compacted, furrowed agricultural fields, behind the site of Cañoncillo (fig. 6.2a) (see Kosok 1965:115, fig. 1). These lie at 82 to 84 m AMSL, and are attributable to the occupational periods of that site as demonstrated by our excavations in 1975. Moche V utilization of the site was followed by a hiatus of approximately 200 years. The Middle Horizon B reconstruction topped a sterile sand deposit 1 m thick. Terminal abandonment is estimated to have occurred after A.D. 1000. This related duro area was probably irrigated by the elevated canal.

Probable Water Sources

Lakes

Because of their relative scarcity on the north coast of Peru, natural lakes have received little attention in studies of hydraulic agriculture and its impact

Figure 6.6.   Yardang with Moche utilized surface and Chimu surface below.

on cultural development. This scarcity may result from obliteration of the lakes by modern reclamation for agriculture or from the simple lack of recognition by the archaeologist.

The pre-Hispanic use of reservoirs is well documented. Methods utilized were walk-in wells at Chan Chan (Day 1974), earth-filled dams of small capacity (Rodriguez Suy Suy 1972; Watson 1979; Lostaunau 1955), dammed quebradas filled with canal water from the upper end (Eling 1977), and other similar retentive constructions. All these reservoirs held water sufficient for domestic use, but none were adequate for irrigation. The Talambo Reservoirs, with a capacity of around 22,500 m³ would have been depleted in only one hour if diverted into the 8 m³/sec. Talambo canal (Eling 1977). Coastal reservoirs are constructed in the middle of the canal system, whereas in the highlands many systems originate at reservoirs which feed into much smaller (0.5 m³ or less) canals. Thus, in the highlands, a reservoir similar in size to that at Talambo would be able to sustain a flow for at least twelve hours. Additionally, sierra reservoirs need only be used as a backup system because of the coincidence of the agricultural and rainy seasons. Desert agriculture is entirely dependent upon highland rains to fill the rivers which feed the large canals that irrigate and sustain the coastal fields.

In the Jequetepeque Valley, two substantial lake systems were exploited by past or present agricultural populations for irrigation water and economically useful flora and fauna. The first, in use today, is formed by the Laguna del Muerto and its small lateral counterpart, the Laguna del Hornito (figs. 6.2a, 6.3). Their combined capacity of 3,650,000 m³ at a depth of 4 m or 5,475,000 m³ at 6 m depth can irrigate approximately 1,200 ha. This lake region is bordered by sand dunes and drifts.

The second system, the Lagunas de Cañoncillo, is composed of a series of small interlocking lakes also in a sand encroachment area. Situated between Cerro Santonte to the west and the western leg of Cerro Prieto Espinal to the east, the lagunas Sondo, Cañoncillo, Gallinazo, and one unnamed <u>laguna</u> form what may have been one large lake in pre-Hispanic times (figs. 6.2b, 6.3). In the 1943 aerial photographs, three lakes may be seen just to the north: two of these have been reclaimed by agriculture; the third is still protected from the reach of the tractor by migrating sand dunes.

The present-day lake levels and capacities, computed from comparisons of 1943, 1949, 1961, and 1968 aerials, are an unimpressive 300,000 m^3 at 2.5 m depth. In 1943, prior to reclamation, the total capacity would have approached 500,000 m^3. Suspended silt deposition is approximately 1 m on the slopes and may be much thicker in the middle. Presently, the lakes support an algarrobo stand of approximately 2.5 km^2 and over 2,000 head of cattle, but no other agricultural benefits are derived.

A possible sequence of lake formation, based on a discussion with Dr. Miguel Graetzer, an Ecuadorian geologist, has been previously proposed:

> (Lakes) were formed by first, a large accumulation of sand filling in the gap between the cerros Santonte and Prieto Espinal and then, a very large amount of precipitation was deposited. The rock base below, and the sand above, formed a "sponge effect", thus leaving a lake, or as at present, a series of shallow lakes (Eling manuscript).

In the latter half of the 1970s, a team of geologists and archaeologists working with Michael Moseley's Proyecto de Riego Antiguo in the Moche and Chicama valleys, attacking a similar problem, gave the following sequence and description of the process of "ponding":

> In the Moche Valley between about 1500 and 1000 B.C. there was one or more major vertical shoreline displacements...This uplift caused the river to downcut, while the general landscape regime away from the river was aggradational. There was a massive influx of aeolian sands, and sand seas blanketed the landscape, raising surfaces to their highest recorded levels. The sediment input blocked local drainage creating large scale ponding of El Niño runoff. Silt deposited in these entrapments are imbedded with aeolian sands, indicating that ponding lasted through a series of local rains.
> By about 500 B.C. a major cycle of landscape deflation began. Previously occupied surfaces were stripped by desert rains and wind action, creating a very fragmentary archaeological record. Ponding of El Niño runoff was no longer prevalent.
> Around the time of Christ there was another major episode of coastal uplift perhaps of 3 to 6 meters, triggering aeolian deposition. However, the volume of drifting sand seems relatively small and seaward displacement of the coastline may be implicated in some areas.
> Around 400 A.D. there was a major episode of flash flooding and river downcutting. Some 7 kms inland at the archaeological monument Huaca del Sol this REAC episode eroded the land surface from a level about 2 m above to 2 m below today's surface. Passing the valley neck, river downcutting had

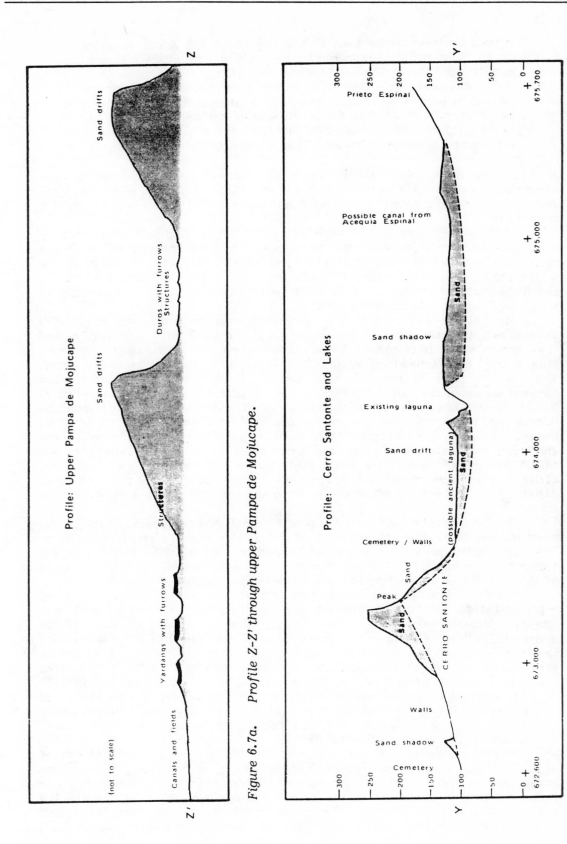

Figure 6.7a. Profile Z-Z' through upper Pampa de Mojucape.

Figure 6.7b. Profile Y-Y' of laguna area.

moved upstream more than 15 kms. by about 600 A.D. A series of El Niño rains then brought normally dry tributaries toward equilibrium through localized radical alteration.

Between 800-1,000 A.D. minor coastal uplift was accompanied by southward river migration. Aeolian input was renewed, but largely restricted to the south side of the valley. Since the large El Niño deluge around 1,100 A.D., there has been relative landscape quiescence (Moseley, Feldman and Ortloff 1981:243).

Although the above refers specifically to the Moche Valley, these events were occurring simultaneously in the Jequetepeque Valley, only 100 km to the north and, given the characteristics of El Niño, were probably of equal or greater magnitude.

Both lake systems in the Jequetepeque Valley appear to have formed by ponding. Similarities between the two systems include: location on the south bank of the river at 7°23' latitude and at the northern extension of the migrating barchan dunes which emanate from the Puerto Chicama area to the south; formation by eolian sand blocking natural drainages; and permanency of water implying an underground source.

Recent studies of the Plan Jequetepeque (República del Perú 1968) determined that the level of the water table ranges from 0.3 to 4.05 m and that ground water is supplied by a subterranean river. Additionally, algarrobo stands rely upon subsurface water equal in depth to the height of the trees. The algarrobal in the area of the Cañoncillo lakes is one of the largest and densest stands in the valley (fig. 6.3); a second is in the old river channel of El Río Seco (or Loco) de Chamán. An elevated water table in the Cañoncillo laguna area would have had a more profound effect in pre-Hispanic times than today. Although the requirements of modern rice cultivation, using both canal and deep well water, have raised the water table in the central valley, the net result has been to reduce the water table in the now "marginal" but previously utilized pre-Hispanic agricultural areas. This also reduces the recharging capabilities of the lakes which lie on the outer edges of the modern cultivated area.

The Cañoncillo lakes are blocked by small hills and sand drifts at the northern end above the 145 m elevation and at the southern end above 120 m. The lake outlet would then have to be higher than the 96.5 m level of the highest canal segment. The last vestige of the aquaduct lies only 250 m south of the lake but no connecting link can be discerned through the sands.

To determine the irrigation potential of this source and present a logical representation of the old topography as it would have existed without sand cover, a cross section derived from stereo pairs was plotted on the 1:10,000 maps at 2 m intervals (fig. 6.7). Based on a lake bed level of 95 m or perhaps lower, a presumed past water level of approximately 115 m (fig. 6.7), and an areal extent of 300,000 m² including a western basin now filled with drift sand, the pre-Hispanic capacity of the four lakes would have been about 6,000,000 m³, or approximately the same capacity as the Laguna del Muerto system in use today. Prior to reclamation, the outside lakes had an estimated capacity of 500,000 m³. It is most likely that all seven lagunas were part of one lake, canal, and irrigation system for the Pampa.

Given the estimated total capacity of 6,500,000 m³ and a canal size of 4 to 5 m³/sec., approximately 450 to 360 hours, respectively, of irrigation could be provided. The lesser demands on subterranean waters in pre-Hispanic times would have enhanced the recuperative capabilities, thus maintaining the lake levels for longer periods. The canals on the Pampa are about equivalent in size to those of the modern community of Pueblo Nuevo on the north bank.

The Pueblo Nuevo branch canal, with a capacity of 5 m³/sec., irrigates 1,330 ha. The community receives 7 min./ha/week for a total of 9,310 min., or 155 hours. Of course, these parallels are not exact because the demands of rice cultivation far exceed those of the pan llevar cultigens such as corn, beans, or even cotton.

In sum, the Lagunas de Cañoncillo could have been tapped to provide an alternative water source for the Pampa de Mojucape analogous to the still operative system of the Laguna del Muerto.

Jequetepeque River Canal Water

A second possible water source for the Pampa de Mojucape irrigation system is by direct linkage with the Jequetepeque River canals. The last vestige of the aqueduct within the slot between the mountains is at 96.5 m AMSL and is less than 300 m west of the remains of a trench dug into an exposure of Cerro Prieto Espinal (fig. 6.2a). The visible, albeit sand obscured, section of 300 m cuts east from 110 m to 122 m AMSL where it is submerged by a sand shadow created by entrapment between the peaks of Prieto Espinal and Cerro Cañoncillo. (fig. 6.3).

The most logical projection to a river source between visible features is a connection with Acequia Espinal, a canal with an intake from the Jequetepeque River (fig. 6.2a). The Acequia Espinal is presently a branch of the Acequia Tecapa and, in pre-Hispanic times, may have been a part of the Acequia San Pedro system (20 m³/sec); the latter is only 25 m from the intake juncture of the Acequia Espinal. Espinal can be traced a distance of 4.5 km from its intake to a point at the 122 m elevation, 1.25 km from the pre-Hispanic trench on the eastern side of Cerro Prieto Espinal, where it disappears into the sand. This canal most probably continued around the sand-covered rock outcrops of the northern side of the mountain to emerge and connect with the trench segment on the Cañoncillo side. Projection of the topography as it would have been without the sand cover would then reveal a contour canal, a construction common in the Jequetepeque Valley, especially in the south bank Ventanillas system.

This route would then explain the size and complexity of the hillside site of Huaca Santa María. Now tucked away in the corner of a small cultivated area and adjacent to the northern spur of Cerro Prieto Espinal (figs. 6.2a, 6.3), this site contains at least two huacas (pyramids), many hillside terraces and buildings, and defensive and boundary walls which are intermittantly exposed through the sand. The 1943 aerial photographs show the complex extended out into the presently reclaimed agricultural area. If the proposed linkage between the Acequia Espinal and the trench remnant passed by this route, Huaca Santa María would become an important control point on a possible level with Ventanillas, Talambo, Moro, and Farfán (Eling 1977: 413). If situated near an important canal bifurcation, controlling the canal water and irrigation system, Huaca Santa María becomes an integral part of the greater Pampa system and the contradiction between its complexity and isolation would be resolved.

Finally, water diverted from the Jequetepeque River by the Acequia San Pedro probably fed the fields in the lower, western portion of the Pampa. Since most of the vestigial canals on the western side run directly south toward, and including, the Cerro Puémepe area to irrigate the 45 and 55 m contour levels, the amount of land cultivated is restricted to that beneath this elevation. Thus, this portion of the system provides only an interlocking segment linked with the Pampa as a whole.

Conclusions

By extrapolation from extant and exposed features, isolated hydraulic constructions can be integrated into the larger irrigation system of the Pampa and then into the Jequetepeque irrigation system as a whole. The two proposed water sources are not alternatives but additives. One primary source is indicated by the formation of yardangs and duros by the deposition of silt transported by the irrigating waters from the Jequetepeque River. Secondly, at present, the Laguna del Muerto serves as a reserve to be tapped only during water shortages. I see no reason why in pre-Hispanic times the Lagunas de Cañoncillo could not have been interconnected with the Huaca Santa María system to augment the available water supply. This conjunction would certainly have provided more stability.

Additionally, the data from this study can be brought to bear upon the unresolved question of a link between the Lambayeque and Chicama drainages. Paul Kosok (1940, 1965) posited two large, interconnecting irrigation systems on the north coast—the Leche-Lambayeque complex including the Jequetepeque on the southern extreme, and the Moche-Chicama complex to the south. Ortloff, Moseley, and Feldman (1982: 573) state "Kosok overlooked a partially preserved irrigation linkage between the Lambayeque and the Chicama drainage which would have united what he considered two distinct multi-valley networks."

Kosok (1965: 116-117) traveled the area between the Chicama and Jequetepeque valleys over the two old "Inca Roads," but found no traces of canals which might have formed this connection. No mention of canals is made in his notes. I, too, have made the trip many times, criss-crossing the entire 35 km distance at least four times with similarly negative results.

I have mapped the northern terminus of the Chicama-Paiján canal which ends around 40 m AMSL in the Vega de Cupisnique (fig. 6.1) where flooding and deflation would have erased all evidence of an irrigation network. Given the topographic constraints, the Paiján area canals could only cross the Vega at a point near the ocean some 23 km from the southernmost Jequetepeque canals. From its terminus at the 85 m elevation at Cerro Chilco, Canal A would need to drop approximately 45 m in 20 km, or at least 2.25 m/km (1:444 or .00225). However, if a gradient greater than 3 m/km (1:333 or .003) was achieved, the canals would have had to cross the well-preserved pre-Hispanic roads on La Pampa. I have observed no evidence of this crossing or vestiges of any canals oriented toward the Vega de Cupisnique in many surveys of the area.

This may, however, be a case where the absence of evidence is not evidence of absence. The Puerto Chicama area is "one of the most pronounced fault bays between Eten and Chimbote, and thus relatively one of the largest dune source beaches on the north coast" (Moseley, personal communication). Therefore, the constant 25 kph winds passing north from Puerto Chicama to the Pampa de Mojucape have resulted in substantial sand influx and wind deflation of the general Jequetepeque-Chicama intervalley area. The yardangs of the Pampa are certainly the result of sand influx, silt deposition by silt-charged irrigation water, wind deflation, and a combination of tectonic and El Niño events. In the near future, these few remnants will disappear and the only evidence of this old topography will be the notes and photographs taken during this project. If similar processes so affected the area south of Cerro Chilco, erasing the prior topography and all evidence of cultural modification, the pre-Hispanic roads may have been constructed on an already eroded and deflated plain where any evidence for earlier canal construction had been eradicated.

A second, and perhaps more serious, concern is canal size and water source, a primary focus of this paper. The lagunas lacked the constant capacity to provide water to the Paiján area. Therefore, the only possible source is the 20 m³ Acequia San Pedro diversion through the proposed Huaca Santa María connection. Since Canal A, the highest canal on the Pampa de Mojucape, has no branches and simply ends in the Quebrada de Cupisnique, it could have provided the link in the intervalley system. However, a canal of the magnitude to effect this transfer should have left some mark of its course on the landscape, and none has yet been detected.

References

Blackwelder, E.
  1934   Yardangs. Geological Society of America Bulletin 45:159-66.

Broggi, J. A.
  1952   Migración de arenas a lo largo de la costa Peruana. Boletín de la Sociedad Geológica del Peru 24:1-25.

Cárdenas Saavedra, Edeson and Arturo Carnejo Taboada.
  1973   Influencia de la Disponibilidad de Agua de Río en la Producción Agrícola del Valle de Jequetepeque. Lima: Dirección General de Aguas.

Cooke, Ronald U., and Andrew Warren.
  1973   Geomorphology in Deserts. Berkeley: University of California Press.

Day, Kent.
  1974   Walk-in-wells and water management at Chan Chan, Peru. In The Rise and Fall of Civilizations, edited by J. Sabloff and C. Lamberg-Karlovsky. Menlo Park, CA: Cummings Publishing Co.

Eling, Herbert H., Jr.
  1977   Interpretaciones preliminares del sistema de Riego Antiguo de Talambo en el Valle de Jequetepeque, Perú. In El Hombre y la Cultura Andena, Actas Y Trabajos, 2, 3 Congreso Peruano, edited by Ramiro Matos. Lima.

  n.d.   Informe de investigaciones sobre el sistema prehispánico de Riego en el Valle del Río Jequetepeque, Perú. A report to the Instituto Nacional de Cultura, Lima, July 20 1977.

Farrington, Ian S.
1980 The archaeology of irrigation canals, with special reference to Peru. World Archaeology 2(3): 287-305.

Hastenrath, Stephen L.
1967 The barchans of the Arequipa region, southern Peru. Zeit. fur. Geom. 11:300-31.

Kosok, Paul.
1940 The role of irrigation in ancient Peru. Proceedings of the Eighth American Scientific Congress 5:169-78.

1965 Life, Land and Water in Ancient Peru. New York: Long Island University Press.

Lostaunau, Oscar.
1955 La zona arqueólogica de Jequetepeque. Chimór 3(1): 4-9. Trujillo.

Moseley, Michael E., Robert A. Feldman, and Charles R. Ortloff.
1981 Living with crises: Human perception of process and time. In The Third Spring Systematic Symposium, 1980: Biotic Crises in Ecological and Evolutionary Time. New York: Academic Press, Inc.

Ortloff, Charles R., Michael E. Moseley, and Robert A. Feldman.
1982 Hydraulic engineering aspects of the Chimu Chicama-Moche intervalley canal. American Antiquity 47(3): 572-95.

República del Perú.
1968 Proyecto Jequetepeque 4. Lima: Ministerio de Fomento y Obras Públicas Dirección de Irregación.

Rodriguez Suy Suy.
1971 Irrigación prehistórica en el Valle de Moche. Cencira. Lima.

Schweigger, Erwin.
1949 Vientos Marinos y su Influencia en el Continente. Sociedad Geológico del Perú, Volumen Jubilar, Fascícula 25:1-22. Lima.

Sutton, Carlos.
1940 A letter to Dr. Paul Kosok regarding pre-Hispanic land use calculations. In possession of the author.

Twidale, C. R.
1968 Yardang. In Encyclopedia of Geomorphology, edited by R. W. Fairbridge, 1237-38. New York: Reinhold Book Corp.

Watson, Richard P.
1979 Land use and water control on the north coast of Peru: Late preHispanic agricultural systems in the Chicama Valley. Masters thesis. University of Texas at Austin.

Ubbelohde-Doering, H.
1967   On the Royal Highways of the Inca.   Switzerland: Plata Co. Ltd.

7.

Pollen Evidence for Economic Plant Utilization in Prehistoric Agricultural Fields of Jequetepeque Valley, Northern Peru

Glendon H. Weir and Herbert H. Eling, Jr.

In the Jequetepeque area of northern Peru, soil sediment samples from pre-Hispanic agricultural fields both with and without preserved furrows were collected during May and August 1978 by Herbert H. Eling, Jr., of the University of Texas at Austin. These samples were analyzed by Glendon H. Weir of Texas A&M University. One objective of the investigation was to determine if fossil pollen types of past economic field crop plants had been preserved in the samples and if a correlation could be established with the types of field and furrow arrangements associated with occupational periods ranging from Gallinazo (A.D. 0-200) through Moche (A.D. 200-750), Middle Horizon (A.D. 750-1250), Chimú (A.D. 1250-1470), Chimú-Inca (A.D. 1470-1532) and a modern field where cotton was grown in the late 1930s. All the samples were taken from four field and furrow systems in the Jequetepeque Valley (fig. 7.1) which could be roughly attributed to one of the occupational periods.

Fields with no furrow patterns but which were irrigated by feeder canals are considered to be of the earliest occupational period. Furrowed fields range from vestiges of early periods in Farfan Sur (fig. 7.2) to the well-preserved Chimu-Inca fields of Pampa de Cerro Colorado. These are usually composed of cohesive but loose soil.

Duros are compact, encrusted, furrowed fields characteristic of the Cañoncillo area and are often covered by sand dunes (fig. 7.3). These fields were formed by silt-charged river irrigation over a desert pavement base; when abandoned, the clay component of the silt, under periodic El Niño rains and alternate baking by the sun, hardens to a ceramic like crust.

Yardangs are residuals of older topography now standing above the current valley floor and generally take the form of elongated platforms aligned parallel to the prevailing winds (Blackwelder 1934; Twidale 1968; Eling, this volume, fig. 6.5). In the Cañoncillo area and on the adjacent Pampa de

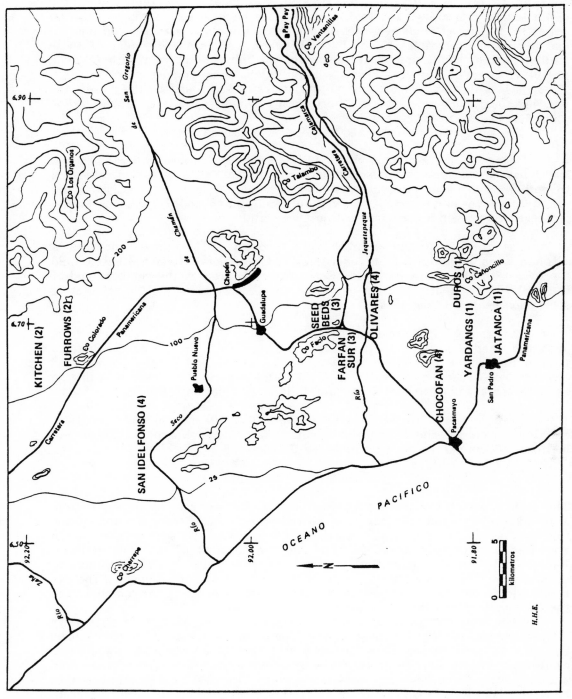

Figure 7.1.   Map of Jequetepeque Valley showing sampled locations.

Mojucape, the upper strata of the yardang is man-made, consisting of silt deposited on as much as 6 m of sand as a result of irrigating with the sediment-laden waters of the Jequetepeque River. This practice of irrigating on sand to create cultivable fields is still used today. The thickness of the deposited layer averages 100 to 120 cm. Since about 1 cm of top soil can be deposited by the silt-rich irrigation in one year, 100 cm of strata could imply a use period of approximately one hundred years. After abandonment of these fields, eolian, sand, and water erosion, probably combined with tectonic activity, reduced the topography, leaving erosional remnants or yardangs. Thus, Moche furrows, canals, and cultural remains are found on the top of the yardangs, and more recent Middle Horizon and Chimú features are found on the plain 6 m below (see Eling, this volume).

The samples are categorized by geographical area as:

Category 1: Seven samples (JV1 through JV7) were collected in the 3000+ ha Cañoncillo area in the southern end of the Valley, a region subjected to both wind and sand erosion and sand deposition. Samples 1 through 5 were taken from yardangs with furrows, and samples 6 and 7 from very well-preserved furrows in a duro area within Cañoncillo.

Category 2: Nine samples (JV8 through JV16) include one from a kitchen area and eight from extremely well-preserved and protected field furrows in the 20,000 ha Pampa de Cerro Colorado area on the northern end of the Valley which contains intact irrigation and field systems and the remains of population centers (Eling 1977).

Category 3: Twelve samples (JV17 through JV28) were collected from probable seed beds (fig. 7.4) and various field furrows in 300 ha of the Sistema Farfan Sur which contained representative canal and field technology as observed elsewhere in the valley (fig. 7.5). This area is considered by Eling to be an important developmental area for field and irrigation technology.

Category 4: Five samples (JV29 through JV33) include one each from canal and field systems in Pampa Chocofan West, Cerro Negro, Frente de San Idelfonso, Puente Olivares, and Pampa de Jatanca.

Methods and Materials

The field sediment samples were collected from furrows ranging in height from 8 to 50 cm by sampling down an appropriate distance from the top of the furrows, after clearing away wind-blown sediments and surface sand which appeared to have been deposited since the abandonment of the field systems. Each sample was then immediately stored in sterile polyethylene containers to avoid ambient wind-borne contamination by modern pollen contained in the atmospheric pollen rain. All samples were then recorded as to provenience, and the field system was photographed.

The sediment samples were processed in the Texas A&M University Palynology Laboratory according to a standard laboratory technique developed by Weir for extraction of pollen from arid land sediments with low organic content. Briefly, this involved removal of carbonates with hydrochloric acid and removal of silicates with hydrofluoric acid. The resulting sample residues, consisting mostly of residual organic materials (including polliniferous material) with some trace minerals, were then treated in an ultrasonic generator to disaggregate these fractions. The heavier organic fraction and the remaining trace minerals were then separated from the lighter, pollen-bearing fraction by

Figure 7.2.   *Well preserved furrows of the Farfan Sur system. These furrows are very similar to those of the Cerro Colorado system.*

Figure 7.3.   *Duros of Cañoncillo with Cerro Santonte on the left and Prieto Espinal in the center.*

a heavy density separation technique using zinc chloride at a specific gravity of 1.90. The remaining pollen-bearing residues containing the fossil grains were oxidized in a 9 to 1 acetolysis mixture of acetic anhydride and concentrated sulfuric acid to separate these residues from the fossil pollen. Finally, the resulting pollen samples were transferred to a silicone oil mounting medium with a viscosity of 1000 centistokes and mounted on microscope slides under 18 mm covers for optical examination.

Identification of the fossil pollen grain types from the samples was based on morphological comparisons with pollen reference material collected over many years in Peru by Weir and others. This special subcollection, in the Texas A&M University Modern Pollen Reference Collection, is believed to be the most complete extant. Pollen grains in the samples were identified between 200 and 1000 x magnifications on a Nikon SuKe II microscope. Use of phase contrast microscopy was necessary on occasion, as when confirming identification of fossil Zea (Span. maiz) pollen types of the Gramineae (grass) family.

Pollen analyses of the sediment samples attempted to include two hundred grain pollen counts wherever possible for each sample. Pollen grains so badly crushed or deteriorated as to be unidentifiable and fungal or other cryptogamic spores were noted but excluded from the pollen counts. Some few well-preserved pollen types not identified at the time of examination were included in the pollen sample counts as unknowns.

Results and Discussion

Sample JV7 contained no pollen, and samples JV12, 13, 15, 19, 21, 24, 25, 31, and 34 contained almost none (ranging from one to nine grains total). A number of reasons may account for the absence of sufficient pollen. Many of the samples were collected from mainly fine-grained alluvial or eolian arid land sediments consisting primarily of sand, silt, and clay-sized particles and with a very low organic content. Generally, the arid coast of Peru is characterized by soils which have a low content of organic matter, coupled with generally low pollen concentrations. This is due to the relatively low density of plant cover in arid lands, prolonged exposure of the pollen rain on the surface to agents of chemical and mechanical weathering before burial by later sedimentation, periodic wetting and drying which speeds oxidation, and normal soil bacterial and fungal acitivity. Many of the sediment samples from the Jequetepeque Valley showed evidence of numerous fungal spores, for example, indicating that this agent of pollen degradation was active. The severity of these agents of pollen degradation, acting alone or in combination, determine the eventual state of preservation or destruction of the fossil pollen grains. As yet, there is no known method by which palynologists can reliably predetermine the state or likelihood of pollen preservation in arid land soils. However, in our laboratory we have found, as a generalization, that the higher the percent of organic content of sediment samples, the greater the likelihood of preservation of statistically significant amounts of fossil pollen.

The fossil pollen and other contents of the samples are appended in tabular form (table 7.1). The presence of the characteristic pollen types of potential economic plants were noted in sample JV5 of the Cañoncillo area (Solanaceae and Typha species); Samples JV8 (Solanaceae and Typha), JV9 (Typha), JV10 (Capparis, Gossypium, Solanaceae, Typha and Zea), JV11 (Gossypium and Typha), JV12 (Solanaceae), JV14 and 16 (Typha) of the Pampa Cerro Colorado area; in Samples JV18 (Typha), JV20 (Capparis, Solanaceae, Gossypium and Typha), JV22 (Capparis), JV23 (Gossypium), JV26 and 27

Figure 7.4.   *Seed beds of Farfan Sur. Modern rice paddies are in the ravine with pre-Hispanic La Calera system in the background.*

Figure 7.5.   *Farfan Sur field systems. Canals in foreground and furrows conform to the topography.*

(Solanaceae), JV28 (Gossypium) of the Sistema Farfan Sur area; and in samples JV30 (Zea) and JV33 (Tillandsia and Zea) of the Pampa Chocofan (Cerro Negro) and Pampa de Jatanca areas.

Potential economic plants are those whose known modern and past uses and distribution, or suspected past uses, are closely associated with man. Such plants are agricultural crops, wild plants used by man, and noncultigens which humans encourage and manage.

In the Jequetepeque Valley area, the fossil pollen types of potential economic or near-economic plants were preserved in approximately fifty percent (seventeen of thirty-three samples) of the sediment samples from agricultural fields in relatively low numbers of a few grains each. However, the herb caper (Capparis) economic variety is of Old World origin and is not reported archaeologically as a field crop in pre-Hispanic Peru. Two wild species, now grown in the Jequetepeque Valley, and native species are used presently as condiments (Soukop 1970:60) and medicines in Peru. They may conceivably have been used, grown, or encouraged prehistorically. Further, the center of diversity and origin for many of the members of Solanaceae (potato, tomato, or nightshade) family is in South and Central America, and many wild genera of the family are now present as weeds in Peru, including the north coast. Nonetheless, the solanaceous fossil pollen types in these samples appear to compare favorably with the genus Solanum, which includes such modern cultivars as potatoes and tomatoes, among others, and possibly the genus Capsicum, which contains the modern aji. Solanum and Capsicum have been documented in archaeological contexts in Peru (Towle 1961).

Somewhat surprisingly, fossil pollen types of cotton (Span. algodon) or Gossypium were present in five of the samples. They are rarely found preserved in prehistoric sites, perhaps because the parent plant is either insect or self pollinated. Thus, relatively few pollen grains are produced as compared to the numerous pollen produced by wind-pollinated plants such as the grasses. The pollen type listed as Gossypium in the tables appears to compare favorably with the G. barbadense type in our reference collections and is well-known archaeologically in Peru. Another pollen type of the Malvaceae (mallow) family, which includes cotton, in the samples also compares reasonably well with the modern pollen type of Gossypium raimondii of northern Peru, which is thought to have figured in the genetic ancestry of the modern cultivar. Zea (Span. sara or maiz) is present in small amounts in three of the samples. Typha or cattail (Span. enea) grows wild in moist areas of coastal Peru today, and its use is archaeologically known; however, its status here may be that of a near-economic plant, grown or encouraged along the edges of the fields and irrigation systems to act as a shield from the wind, as well as for direct or indirect consumption of plant parts as food or as material for matting.

Finally, the fossil pollen type of Tillandsia (Span. cardo or pucahuele) is present in large amounts from one sample (JV33 from a possible floor area in the Pampa de Jatanca) and may well represent economic usage. Tillandsia, an epiphyte, has native Peruvian species endemic to the coast of Peru and was commonly used for stuffing or wrapping of mummy bundles (Towle 1961). Today in Peru it is administered as a treatment for rheumatism, pulmonary diseases, etc. (Soukop 1970), as an antidepressant in folk medicine (Vasquez-Nuñez 1974) and may have been used in the past on the central coast of Peru as firewood (Weir and Dering, this volume).

Whether the fossil pollen types present in the sediment samples from the Jequetepeque Valley represent field crops grown by the ancient Peruvians is, of course, another question. There is certainly solid archaeological evidence for the past use of Zea (Span. sara), Gossypium (Span. algodon), and extensive documentation of the use of Solanum species tubers and fruits, as well as others. Of these examples, fossil pollen types comparing favorably with potential economic parent plants above are present in the Jequetepeque samples in small amounts. Given the qualification discussed above, it is likely that the fossil pollen evidence does indeed represent at least some usage as crop plants in the fields, if only for the reason that, with the exception of corn, very small amounts of pollen are typically produced by these insect- or self-pollinating crop plants. Similarly, Zea pollen, although produced in larger amounts, does not typically travel far from its parent plant. The presence of the pollen in the sediments from the fields suggests that, if not actually grown as crops, they were washed in by irrigation water, thus demonstrating that these now barren areas were once cultivated fields watered by functioning canals.

The Tillandsia, Typha, and Capparis fossil pollen types may or may not be indicative of domesticated crops. More probably they were economic plants in the sense of being used in their wild or encouraged state.

In addition, there is some indication of economic utilization of yet other, probably non-field crop plants contained in the fossil pollen record from the Jequetepeque area samples. Some of these plants, not listed in the tables or sample descriptions as economic pollen types (due to space considerations) are:

Acacia sp. Leguminosae (Span. huarango or faique), which is known archaeologically from Peru, and used medicinally and industrially there today;

Prosopis sp. Leguminosae (Span. algarroba), known archaeologically from Peru, used as food (pods, seeds, "beans") and for construction;

Salix sp. Salicaceae (Span. sauce), known archaeologically from Peru and used in the construction of preceramic (archaic) houses at the Paloma site on the central coast of Peru (Weir & Dering, this volume), and as a folk medicine today;

Schinus sp. Anacardiaceae (Span. molle), although infrequent as an archaeological plant (it occurs at the Paloma site), it is one of the most prominent trees of the western Andes, particularly where underground water is present. The fruits are used medicinally (Cerrate 1979; Horkheimer 1973);

Campomanesia sp. Myrtaceae (Span. palillo), known infrequently from archaeological sites; the fruit is eaten today;

Gramineae spp. (Span. yerba), grass "seeds" (caryopses) of various species were ground and used for food, in construction material for houses, and as mattings for burials and houses at the Paloma site and elsewhere, and are frequently encountered archaeologically in Peru;

Cactaceae spp. Loxanthocereus, Cereus, Opuntia, etc. species are well-known archaeologically in Peru; the tuna and fruits are tasty and still consumed today;

Capparis prisca Capparidaceae, a tree, was common in the past in the lomas of central Peru, and is known archaeologically from the earlier levels of the Paloma site where it was apparently used for construction and firewood;

Leguminosae spp. Caesalpinia species are known archaeologically from the Paloma site where they were used as firewood, were a common lomas tree of the past, and are also used medicinally on the coast of Peru today (Vasquez-Nuñez 1974).

Many other Leguminosae species have well-known economic uses, including Phaseolus species and others which are found both archaeologically and as modern cultigens or economic plants. None of the Leguminosae fossil pollen types in the Jequetepeque samples could be positively identified as representing parent plants such as Phaseolus (Span. pallar), a well-known prehistoric and modern field crop, nor, similarly as Canavalia (Span. pallar de

Table 7.1. Soil sediment samples from pre-Hispanic agricultural fields.

Sample numbers:	Totals:
JV1	50/100
JV2	13/100
JV3	66/100
JV4	52/100
JV5	115/100
JV6	45/100
JV7	NO POLLEN
JV8	303/100
JV9	61/100
JV10	271/100
JV11	11/100
JV12	06/100
JV13	03/100
JV14	110/100
JV15	00/76
JV16	03/100

Key: + = pollen/spore type present
##/% = number of grains/percent of sample
AP - Arboreal pollen types
NAP - Nonarboreal pollen types
PECO - Pollen types of potential economic plants
Other - Spore types of Bryophytes (Mosses), Pteridophytes (Ferns, etc.), & Thallophytes (Fungi, etc.)
UNKNOWN - Unknown pollen types present in samples

Table 7.1. Continued.

PECO — Pollen types of potential economic plants

Sample numbers	cf.Capparis/CAP.	cf.Gossypium/MAL.	SOLANACEAE - 1	SOLANACEAE - 2	SOLANACEAE - 3	Tillandsia/BRO.	Typha/TYP.	Zea/GRA.
JV17		+						
JV18							+	
JV19		+						
JV20		+ + + + +				+		
JV21								
JV22								
JV23			+					
JV24								
JV25								
JV26					+			
JV27					+			
JV28	+							
JV29								
JV30								+
JV31								
JV32								
JV33								+

AP — Arboreal pollen types

Sample numbers	Acacia/LEG.	Alnus/BET.	cf.CORNACEAE	cf.MYRICACEAE	Podocarpus/POD.	Prosopis/LEG.	Salix/SAL.	Schinus/ANA.	cf.Weinmannia/CUN.
JV17	+		+			+			
JV18									
JV19									
JV20									
JV21									
JV22					+			+	
JV23									
JV24									
JV25									
JV26		+							
JV27	+	+					+		+
JV28		+	+	+			+		+
JV29									
JV30									
JV31									
JV32	+	+			+				+
JV33	+	+							+

NAP — Nonarboreal pollen types

Sample numbers	CHENO-Am./CHE.-Amar.	COMP.,"H.S."	COMP.,"L.S."	GRAMINEAE	AGAVACEAE	Alternanthera/AMA.	APOCYNACEAE	CACTACEAE	CAMPANULACEAE	CARYOPHYLLACEAE	CONVOLVULACEAE	CRUCIFERAE	CUCURBITACEAE	CYPERACEAE	ERICACEAE	IRIDACEAE	LABIATAE	LEGUMINOSAE/Caesal.	LEGUMINOSAE/Mimosaceae	LILIACEAE	LOBELIACEAE	MALVACEAE - 1	MALVACEAE - 2	cf.Monnina/POLYGAL.	NOLANACEAE	NYCTAGINACEAE	PAPAVERACEAE	POLEMONIACEAE	PORTULACACEAE	Potomogeton/POT.	PROTEACEAE	RANUNCULACEAE	ROSACEAE	Scirpus/CYP.	UMBELLIFERAE	VERBENACEAE
JV17	+	+	+	+						+		+										+		+												
JV18	+	+	+	+																					+											
JV19	+	+	+	+																		+			+	+									+	+
JV20	+	+	+	+										+				+	+		+				+										+	
JV21			+	+						+												+														
JV22	+	+	+	+						+												+														+
JV23	+	+	+																			+	+													
JV24	+	+	+																				+		+											
JV25		+	+																													+				
JV26		+	+	+				+								+										+										
JV27	+	+	+	+				+						+		+									+											
JV28	+	+	+					+	+							+						+		+ +												
JV29	+	+	+	+												+											+									
JV30		+	+	+	+	+																														
JV31		+	+	+	+																															
JV32		+		+																																
JV33	+	+	+	+	+	+		+																												+

Other — Spore types of Bryophytes (Mosses), Pteridophytes (Ferns, etc.) & Thallophytes (Fungi, etc.)

Sample numbers	CYATHEACEAE	GLEICHENIACEAE	POLYPODIACEAE	SALVINIACEAE	Other Pteridophyta	Fungal spores	UNKNOWN	Totals:
JV17								138/100
JV18						+	+	43/100
JV19							+	05/100
JV20								152/100
JV21								05/100
JV22							+	44/100
JV23					+	+	+	14/100
JV24					+			03/100
JV25					+			02/100
JV26							+	25/100
JV27							+	37/100
JV28								97/100
JV29						+	+	58/100
JV30								13/100
JV31								09/100
JV32						+	+	11/100
JV33								90/100

Key:
+ = pollen/spore type present
##/% = number of grains/percent of sample
AP - Arboreal pollen types
NAP - Nonarboreal pollen types
PECO - Pollen types of potential economic plants
Other - Spore types of Bryophytes (Mosses), Pteridophytes (Ferns, etc.) & Thallophytes (Fungi, etc.)

gentilles). Nonetheless, such plants may have been present, as their pollen types are difficult to identify to the generic or specific level.

Also present were Cyperaceae spp., for example Scirpus sp. (Span. junco), whose use is well-documented archaeologically and was used medicinally and for construction. In addition, some genera and species of the Chenopodiaceae, Amaranthaceae, Compositae as well as other herbaceous and woody species (for example the endemic Nolanaceae) are also well-documented archaeologically and ethnobotanically as economic plants. These fossil pollen types were also present in the Jequetepeque area sediment samples.

Thus, the pollen types of potential economic parent plants which are not necessarily cultigens are present in the fossil pollen spectra of the samples analyzed, although not in sufficient numbers to infer the nature of their exploitation. Although the pollen may well have come from wild species, its presence suggests the possibility that these plants were managed or exploited in conjuction with field crops.

Taken in summary, the fossil pollen evidence preserved in the sediments from the Jequetepeque area demonstrates that certain of the parent plants were likely present as field crops. Unfortunately, the nature of the evidence does not allow a determination of the correlation of the crops grown with the types of fields. Other economic plants were certainly present and may have been grown as food plants, if not as field crop plants, in association with the fields and irrigation systems.

Two factors affect the nature of the fossil pollen data recovered from the fields in the Jequetepeque Valley area. The first and more important factor concerns the nature of the fossil pollen rain and the relative pollen production of different kinds of plants, particularly some field crop plants, which are notoriously low pollen producers. The majority of pollen grains that are produced (and also preserved in the fossil pollen record) came from anemophilous, or wind-pollinated plants, such as the grasses and various trees, which produce prodigious amounts of pollen compared to the relatively low pollen production of most insect- or self-pollinated field crop plants. Thus, in any given sample, well over ninety percent of the fossil pollen grains that are likely to be present will primarily represent the wind-pollinated (usually not field crop) portion of the pollen rain, past or present. Since most field crops are self- or insect-pollinated and, therefore, produce much less pollen than wind-pollinated plants, the likelihood of the fossil pollen being preserved in significant numbers is low. One partial exception, corn, produces numerous pollen grains, but deposits them directly underneath plants, but corn pollen production is still relatively low compared to other wind-pollinated plants. Studies of the pollen content of corn plants in a producing field suggest that only about one percent of the modern pollen rain was made up of Zea grains, even directly underneath the parent plants (Martin 1963: 50). The scarcity of corn pollen in the sediments is compounded by poor pollen preservation in certain kinds of arid land soils. Accordingly, the limited pollen produced by most insect- or self-pollinated field crop plants (since they do not depend on producing vast amounts of pollen by the "hit or miss" wind-pollination method) is even less likely to survive in the fossil pollen record.

The second factor concerns the preservation of fossil pollen grains of any kind in general. Only in anaerobic conditions such as bogs, or in sediments below the water table, are conditions ideal for the preservation of pollen. Under such conditions the pollen is not exposed to the oxidizing effects of the atmosphere, and there is a reasonable expectation that most of the fossil pollen rain and past vegetation will be present. On the other hand, in most surface sediments, especially those of arid lands in general, such as those that exist along the coast of Peru and in the fields of the Jequetepeque area, the probability of pollen being preserved in amounts representative of the past vegetation is not as good.

Another related factor is that of differential preservation of various types of pollen grains from different kinds of plants. Because the biochemical constituents of different kinds of pollen are genetically controlled by the parent plants, certain kinds of grains are differentially resistant to the various agents of degradation. As a result, some pollen grains are more likely than others to be destroyed and leave no trace in the fossil pollen record. For example, the pollen of many water-pollinated plants have an extremely thin, non resistant pollen wall. Other pollen from other plants, such as that of Populus (cottonwood or poplar) and Ilex (holly) are not resistant to pollen degradation and are often not preserved in representative numbers. In Weir's experience, Peruvian crop plants such as Zea (Span. sara, maiz) and certain kinds of Gossypium (Span. algodon) are less likely than other crop plants, for example Chenopodium (Span. quinoa) to be preserved in the same sediments. Due to this consideration alone, the pollen grains that are present in the fossil pollen record in sediments may not be proportionately representative of the parent plants actually present at the time the grains were deposited.

Conclusions

Fossil pollen of potential economic plants were found to be preserved in fifty percent of the samples from the Jequetepeque Valley area fields in relatively low numbers of only a few grains each. Field crops represented by the fossil pollen spectra of the samples include corn (Zea mays—Span. sara or maiz), certain solanaceous species (thought to represent various Solanum species tubers and fruits), and cotton (Gossypium species—algodon). Other potential economic plants, such as the Tillandsia species (Span. cardo or pucahuele) and certain native Capparis species (Span. sapote), may represent plants encouraged to grow along field margins. Other potential economic plants, including Acacia (Span. huarango), Prosopis (Span. algarrobo), Salix (Span. sauce), and Schinus (Span. molle) probably were not grown on a large scale. These may have had some economic value but probably grew in the vicinity of past fields because of the favorable moisture and other conditions.

The relatively low number of fossil pollen grains in some of the samples was probably due to their lack of preservation in aerobic, low organic arid soils and to differential preservation of certain pollen types in the fields aggravated by constant working and irrigation of the soils. However, this presence, regardless of the quantity of pollen grains recovered, suggests that these desert areas in preHispanic times were active field systems irrigated by a complex of functioning canals.

It is believed that the most effective way to carry out a study of this nature is to employ a research design in which fossil pollen data is used in conjunction with analyses of the same sediments for the corroborating presence or absence of representative plant macrofossils such as seeds and various plant parts, or micro-fossils such as phytoliths. A representative, comparative collection of local modern pollen types from the economic field crops under consideration and the local modern flora has been made and is located in the Bruning Museum in Lambayeque, Peru. The degree of comparability of the plant microfossil (pollen) and macrofossil data (plant parts) should provide an additional line of evidence to help confirm or deny the presence of past economic plants in field contexts.

Finally, the data from this study of the fossil pollen from different types of fields in the Jequetepeque Valley of northern Peru is considered to have application in other similar contexts to provide an indication of what plants may have been grown in the past. Of even greater importance, such studies can help to confirm the use of now barren areas as once fertile agricultural fields in the past and resolve controversies over the effectiveness of canal systems.

References

Blackwelder, Elliot.
1934 Yardangs. Bulletin of the Geological Society of America 45:159–66.

Cerrate de Ferreyra, Emily.
1979 El Molle. Boletin de Lima 2:28–32.

Eling, Herbert H., Jr.
1977 Interpretaciones preliminares del sistema de riego antiguo de Talambo en el Valle de Jequetepeque, Perú. In III Congreso Peruano del Hombre y la Cultura Andina, edited by Ramiro Matos M., 2:401–419. Lima.

Horkheimer, Hans.
1973 Alimentación y Obtenación de Alimentos en el Perú Prehispánico. Commentarios del Perú 13. Universidad Nacional Mayor de San Marcos, Lima.

Martin, Paul S.
1963 The Last 10,000 Years: A Fossil Pollen Record of the American Southwest. Tucson: University of Arizona Press.

Soukop, Jaroslav SDB
1970 Vocabulario de los Nombres Vulgares de la Flora Peruana. Lima: Colegio Salesiano.

Towle, Margaret A.
1961 The Ethnobotany of PreColumbian Peru. Chicago: Aldine.

Twidale, C. R.
1968 Yardang. In Encyclopedia of Geomorphology, edited by R. W. Fairbridge, 1237–38. New York: Reinhold Book Corp.

Vasquez-Nuñez, N.
1974 Algunos Aspectos Sobre el Uso de Plantas Medicinales en la Costa Peruana. Anales Científicos 12:32–52.

Weir, Glendon H. and, Philip Dering.
1981 Preliminary Plant Macrofossil Analyses of Paloma Site Deposits. Manuscript.

8.

Batán Grande and Cosmological Unity in the Prehistoric Central Andes

Izumi Shimada

Introduction

In recent years, American archaeologists have ventured out from under the umbrella of strict cultural materialism to voice their opinions on the nature and import of organized religion and ideology in cultural developments in the pre-Hispanic New World. Much uneasiness remains concerning the invoking of religion or ideology as in important causal agent in the change in prehistoric culture and social integration. Recent interest may reflect greater optimism in the competence of modern archaeology to deal with this problematical, "immaterial" domain of prehistory or it may reflect dissatisfaction with current explanatory models. Whatever the motivations, I welcome this upsurge in interest and related research.

Andean archaeologists and ethnologists have played an active and important role in this upsurge. For example, Zuidema (1964, 1972, 1973, 1977, 1978a, b, c, 1980) has been particularly active in exploring the various dimensions and implications of ethnohistorically reconstructed Inca social and cosmological systems. In various publications, he has demonstrated the intricate and close relationships among ritual calendars, cosmologies, kinship systems, ancestor cults, mortuary practices, and architectural organization. Inca models figure heavily in other recent publications on prehistoric Andean ideology and symbolism. These models serve as the cornerstone of Isbell's (1978a; cf. Williams 1978-80) analysis of U-shaped ceremonial/religious structures dating from the Initial Period to the Late Horizon; a strong continuity in Andean cosmology is indicated by his study. Similarly, Conrad (1981) combines archaeological and ethnohistorical Inca models in his reconstruction of the Chimú Kingdom in which he argues for the importance of split inheritance and ancestral worship. Based on architectural study of

Pacatnamú, at the mouth of the Jequetepeque Valley and Chimú sites, Keatinge (1977, 1978; Keatinge et al. 1975) has explored the transition from a sacred to a secular power structure on the North Coast during the Middle Horizon and Late Intermediate Period. These studies, taken together, document the productivity and necessity for archaeological research into Andean cognitions and religion.

In an important publication, "A Reappraisal of Peruvian Archaeology," Bennett (1948:1) proposed the concept of the Peruvian Co-Tradition, which, seen as an improvement over the "Culture Area", was defined as the "overall unit of culture history of an area within which the component cultures have been interrelated over a period of time." Underlying each area co-tradition was a set of overall characteristics, both material and immaterial, which distinguish it as a whole. Although this concept can be criticized in a number of respects, it provides a point of departure: "what cultural (and natural) features and processes gave rise to the unity that is implicit in this concept?" This paper examines the question of the unity of prehistoric Andean cosmology by focusing on archaeologically and/or ethnohistorically documented "temple entombment" and the concepts of ceque and ushnu from the advantageous viewpoint of the northern North Coast.

I begin with a brief characterization of the Batán Grande archaeological complex in the central La Leche Valley on the North Coast (figs. 8.1, 8.2); data from the complex are then compared with those from other areas and time periods.

The Batán Grande Archaeological Complex

Immediately below the extensive Sechura Desert and near the northern end of Peru's arid coast, the Leche River forms a narrow triangular alluvial valley. This small, perennial river drains abruptly into the unusually flat coastal plain of the Sican Valley zone which is composed of four contiguous valleys linked by a series of massive intervalley canals. Where the Leche Valley leaves the Andean piedmont, there is a remarkable concentration of massive adobe pyramids and platforms surrounded by extensive cemeteries built up over some three thousand years of prehistory (fig. 8.1). This is the Batán Grande archaeological complex, the focus of our interdisciplinary investigation since 1978.

Our attention first focused on this complex because of its religious and sociopolitical importance during the Middle Horizon and Late Intermediate Period (ca. A.D. 600-1400), prior to Chimú and Inca conquests of the area. When Pizarro passed through this complex on his way to Cajamarca, there was, however, little to attract his attention.

Physically, the Leche Valley is relatively insignificant compared to the adjacent coastal valleys farther south. Nevertheless, there are some fifty major pyramids, platforms, and cemeteries scattered throughout approximately 55 km² of fertile alluvium. We estimate that the majority of prehistoric Peruvian gold objects now in museums around the world were looted from elaborate tombs in Batán Grande. Four seasons of extensive excavation and survey since 1978 have yielded sufficient data to characterize the Batán Grande complex as the major religious and burial center of North Peru during the Middle Horizon and the first half of the Late Intermediate Period (Shimada 1981a, b; 1982; Shimada et al. 1981).

One of the distinguishing features of the complex is the nonagricultural utilization of fertile valley bottom alluvium. Even the careful archaeological-geomorphological examination of a 3 to 5 m deep, 5 km long canal cut in 1979 through the middle of the complex by the Ministry of Agriculture, to link the

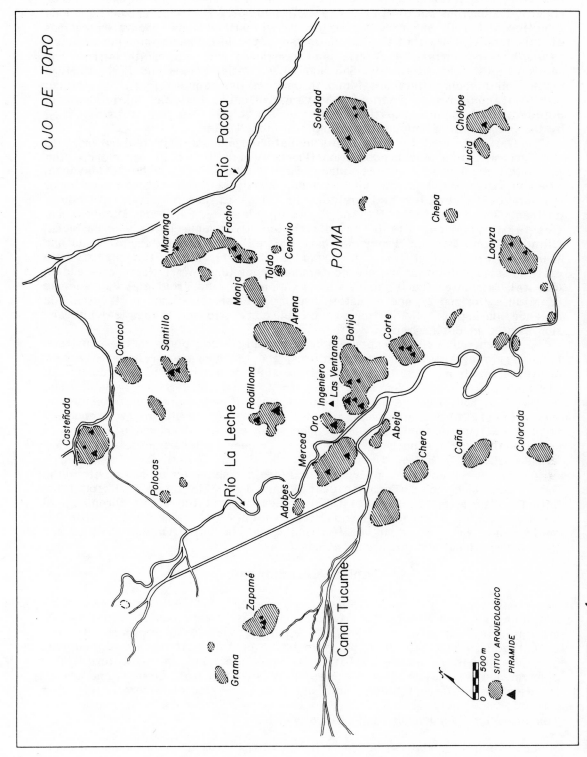

Figure 8.1. The Batán Grande Archaeological Complex with major construction and cemetries.

Pacora and the Leche rivers, failed to show any evidence of extensive or intensive prehistoric agriculture. On the other hand, this transect survey revealed numerous burial pits. In fact, the complex is characterized by a long tradition of burials and religious architectural constructions. Some indications of this tradition are that the burials began in the late Preceramic Period (e.g., semispherical burials in sterile sand associated with anthracite mirrors and semiprecious stone ornaments; Shimada 1979), Initial Period and Early Horizon burials and architecture are found throughout the complex (e.g., La Merced, Las Ventanas, Tordo, Facho-La Mayanga, Corte, Loayza, Lucía-Cholope, Soledad, etc.). The occupation at the Lucía-Cholope Complex is distinguished by the presence of a monumental temple discussed later.

The picture of the Early Intermediate burials and architecture prior to the intrusion of a Moche population (Phase IV and V) is still not clear. The late Moche burials occur at Huacas Soledad, Lucía and Facho-La Mayanga. Starting with the early Middle Horizon, burials at Batán Grande cemeteries become quite complex and include, in terms of ceramic styles previously defined, Moche-Wari, Wari Norteño A and B, paleteada, Early and Middle Sicán, Coastal Cajamarca, Middle and Late (kaolin) Cajamarca, Cajamarca-Sicán, Chimú, Chimú-Inca and Provincial Inca, as well as Provincial Pachacamac and Wari Robles Moqo styles. In terms of stratigraphic position and stylistic criteria, some of the above are contemporaneous (e.g., Wari Norteño A and B, Coastal Cajamarca, Early Sicán, Middle Cajamarca, and Provincial Pachacamac of Middle Horizon 2), and stylistic blending is clear in a number of cases. In essence, during the Middle Horizon, complex stylistic and ideological interaction existed in Batán Grande.

Concurrent with the above, a major upsurge took place in the construction of monumental religious structures, and the enormous religious-funerary precinct (at least 1,600 m east-west x 1000 m north-south) flanked by the pyramids of Corte, Las Ventanas, Ingeniero, Oro and La Merced was established during A.D. 850-1100 (fig. 8.2). An elite tomb within the precinct described by Pedersen (1976) had dimensions of 14 x 14 x 20 m (depth) and was endowed with quantities of gold, arsenical copper and wooden offerings in addition to seventeen "sacrificial burials." The tomb has been radiocarbon dated at 915 ± 50 BP (A.D. 1035; GrN-5474).

Various elaborate, polychrome murals discovered at sites within the Batán Grande complex (Bonavia 1974; Donnan 1972; Florian 1951; Kosok 1965; Shimada 1981a, b; cf. Schaedel 1978) further support the above chronological placement and inferred religious importance of the precinct. With this background, we now turn to specific findings at the Batán Grande complex and their interregional and diachronic comparisons.

Temple Entombment

Temple entombment, coined by Izumi and Terada (1972:304), describes the intentional and careful burial of part or all of a religious structure with a minimum of destruction. Although it cannot be said with any certainty that the structure was buried to preserve it for posterity, it can be argued that entombment is an indication of deference accorded the structure. This phenomenon was observed at three religious structures at Batán Grande, each representing a different time period, and is also reported elsewhere.

Templo de las Columnas at Huaca Lucía

Huaca Lucía, an Initial Period-Early Horizon construction, is an elongated oval-shaped mound situated near the center of the Batán Grande complex. The

166

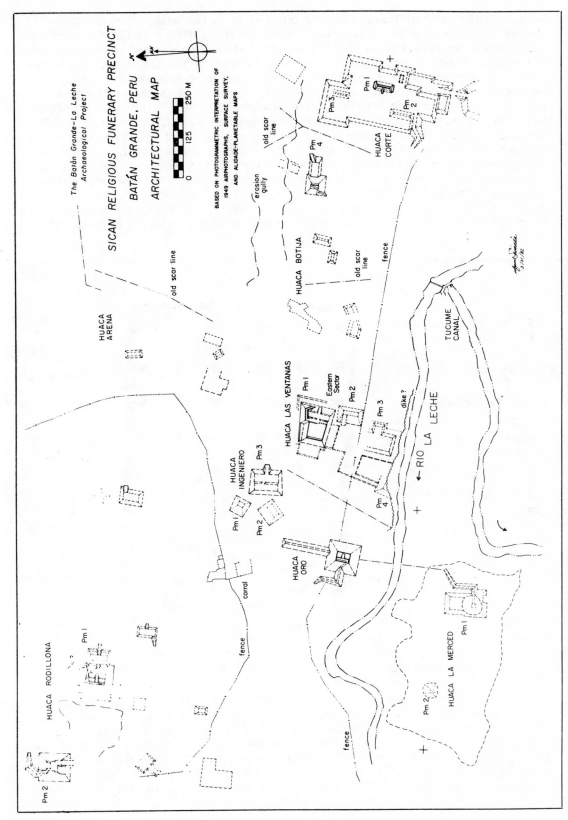

Figure 8.2. The principal religious-funerary precinct of the Batán Grande Archaeological Complex, ca. A.D. 850–1150 flanked by the monumental constructions of Huaca Corte, Las Ventanas, Ingeniero, Oro and La Merced. This photogrammetric map is based on 1949 aerial photographs.

larger oval mound of Huaca Cholope lies 150 m to the east. The north end of Huaca Lucía, leveled by looters' bulldozer(s) in the 1960's, was the focus of our large-scale excavation of 1979 through 1981. Here, we uncovered the monumental adobe construction of the Templo de las Columnas which was buried in sand. It is named for an impressive colonnade of twenty-four painted, circular columns, each measuring 1.2 m in diameter. Construction techniques and characteristics of the enclosure, columns and platforms have been described elsewhere and need not be repeated here (Shimada 1981a, 1982; Shimada et al. 1981). Figure 8.3 shows the symmetrical layout of these columns along the north-south axis. The columns are set within a U-shaped enclosure facing north and a formal entry to the south. Although the enclosure wall originally had a polychrome mural, due to later constructions, intrusive burials, and modern disturbance, most of the mural and the wall are gone. The solid clay floor and the columns within the enclosure were spared from a similar fate. This fine preservation, as we see later, is not coincidental.

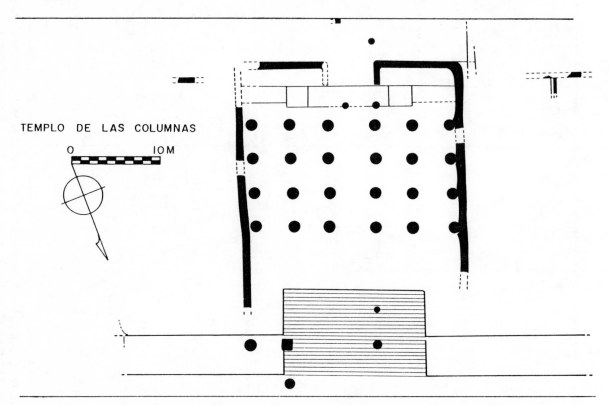

TEMPLO DE LAS COLUMNAS

0   10 M

Figure 8.3.   *Plane map of the Templo de las Columnas at Huaca Lucía. Some wall remnants situated west of the U-shaped enclosure are not shown.*

Much of the above was elucidated in 1979. In 1980, the central trench of the preceding season was extended farther north and south based on our belief that the U-shaped enclosure was part of a larger, formal religious construction and that there should be a central ramp or stairway north of the enclosure. We found a magnificently preserved twenty-three-step stairway 5 m high, 10 m deep, and 16 m wide buried in 5 m of clean sand (figs. 8.4, 8.5). Additional excavations in 1981 revealed that the stairway was set into a two-level platform with an east-west dimension of at least 52 m. The northeast

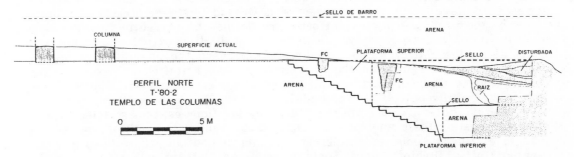

Figure 8.4. *Profile view of the north-south central axis through the Templo de las Columnas. Note the two clay seals covering the stairway.*

Figure 8.5. *The stairway that leads to the Templo de las Columnas atop the two-tier platform from an inferred sunken court. Note the horizontal bipartitioning of the sand fill by the lower clay seal.*

Figure 8.6. *The northeast corner of the stairway. The student at the top is cleaning the upper clay seal, while the worker below exposes the lower clay seal at the thirteenth step of the stairway.*

corner of the platform is not yet securely located, while the northwest corner appears to have been eroded away or destroyed by the looters. The north faces of the upper and lower platforms are defined by perfectly vertical walls of 3 m and 2 m, respectively. Because of the limited extent of our excavations along the platform faces, we cannot disregard the possibility of adobe-clay sculptures or reliefs on the wall faces as found at Huaca Moxeke in the Casma Valley (Tello 1942, 1943, 1956), and at Punkuri and Cerro Blanco in the Nepeña Valley (Bennett 1939; Tello 1942, 1943, 1956).

At the bottom of the stairway, a solid clay floor continues at least 15 m north, suggesting there may be additional buried structures north of the present margin of Huaca Lucía. Considering the overall configuration of other well-mapped Initial Period-Early Horizon ceremonial-religious centers on the Peruvian coast, such as Garagay (Ravines 1975; Ravines and Isbell 1975), Sechin Alto (Fung and Williams 1977), Huaca de los Reyes (Pozorski 1975, 1980), and Huacas Florida and San Jacinto (Williams 1978-1980), the buried structure is most likely a rectangular sunken court.

Although the floor continues south of the U-shaped enclosure, our excavation thus far has been limited by 3 m of overlying cultural remains, much of which belongs to the Middle to Late Horizons. The enclosure was also surrounded on both the east and west sides by additional structures. Here, looters wreaked havoc and only sections of conical adobe-mortar walls can be identified. I believe additional constructions of the same period exist in the unexplored southern portion of Huaca Lucía.

A stratigraphic cut made by M. Shimada in 1979 and 1980 at the adjoining Huaca Chólope yielded a good sample of incised and painted ceramics that overall suggest a late Initial Period to early Early Horizon date (Shimada et al. 1982). This dating is reasonable in light of the radiocarbon date available for the construction of the Templo de las Columnas, 3273 ± 163 B.P. (1323 B.C.; SMU-834).

Several lines of evidence document the entombment of the Templo. The ritual burial of the stairway consists of 5 m of undifferentiated, clean, light-buff, fine-grained sand horizontally bipartitioned and capped by clay "seals." The first seal corresponds to the floor of the Templo; the second occurs at the thirteenth step (counting from the top), corresponding to the top of the lower platform (fig. 8.6). Figure 8.6 shows the lower seal articulates with the lower platform top and hides the stairway below. Although their thicknesses vary from 2 to 10 cm, both seals are perfectly level. In this sand fill, we did not see the grain size sorting and complex bedding that would be expected from water or wind deposition. The characteristics of the sand suggest that it was brought in from the extensive sand sheet that blankets much of the southern margin of the Leche Valley some 3 km away. It would appear that the sand was deposited in a single episode, perhaps within a span of a few months with a tremendous outlay of labor. Our excavation indicates that the sand covered not only the entire stairway but also adjoining areas to the east and west along the north faces of the platforms, an area of about 10 m (north-south) x over 52 m (east-west) x 0.1-5 m (depth). Excellent preservation of the stairways at Cerro Sechin and Garagay is also notable.

A trench placed at the inferred northeast corner of the upper platform in 1981 revealed what is believed to be part of a pit for mixing the clay used for the lower seal. Apparently they piled clay, sand, and water on the top of the lower platform and prepared the clay cement. We can still discern the grooves of implements used for mixing. The overall appearance of this "pit" resembles those seen at any modern adobería. In situ production of clay cement was indeed expected as the seals clearly showed human finger and foot marks as workers applied wet cement over the sand. The cement used for the seals is matched perfectly in color, texture, and composition to that found in the "pit."

There is no apparent evidence of use-related damage or deterioration due to weathering on the stairway or various surfaces of the platforms. On the vertical faces of the steps, one can still recognize "brush marks" from the finishing operation. One has the distinct feeling that the stairway was not intensively used and was maintained in a perfect state. Alternatively, we cannot exclude the possibility that the stairway was refinished before its ritual burial.

The colonnade and U-shaped wall enclosure atop the upper platform were also entombed with the same sand that buried the stairway. Overlying the stairway was yet another thick layer of sand—probably capped by a clay seal as well—that covered the entire U-shaped enclosure and colonnade. This uppermost sand layer was at least 2 m thick, as revealed by a photograph taken by the man who directed the limited looting of the U-shaped enclosure in the 1960s. Leveling by bulldozer(s) reduced the sand cover to the present thickness of about 1.3 to 1.5 m.

Scattered among the standing columns within the U-shaped enclosure are their well-preserved upper segments of about 1.0 to 1.7 m in length, apparently intentionally taken down and placed on the Templo floor. There is hardly any evidence of the fragmentation one would expect from the fall of heavy segments from even a minimal height of about 1.3 m above the floor. I estimate the segments weigh 500 to 800 kg. Further, the columns were built by stacking low cylindrical modular units which were then covered with layers of mortar and thin plaster (see Shimada 1981a; Shimada et al. 1982). This construction technique would have been particularly vulnerable to disintegration upon such falls. The fragmentation we observed was caused by huaquero activities, roots, and our excavation. Thus, the columns that originally stood at an estimated 3.5 to 4.0 m appear to have been taken down for ritual burial. It should also be noted that there is no evidence of a superstructure, although the U-shaped notches at the ends of columns suggest they supported large beams (see the ceramic representation of a Cupisnique temple from the Chicama Valley in Shimada 1981a:43). I suspect the roof was carefully dismantled.

The ritual temple entombment did not end with the deposition of sand and the laying of the clay seals. A set of massive "floating columns" made purely of clay were erected along the north-south central axis of the buried Templo and stairway, as well as along the edge of the upper platform. Some sort of "offering fire" was set in the centers of these columns, as damaged columns show a charcoal deposit in their center surrounded by a heat-discolored zone. A charcoal sample from one of the columns has been dated to 2520 ± 40 B.P. (570 B.C.; SMU-898). We tentatively place the abandonment of the Templo at ca. 600-550 B.C.

Unlike the painted cylindrical columns described earlier, the "floating columns" were unpainted, made of pure clay (identical to that used for the seals) and placed in the middle of sand without solid foundation. Those placed above the stairway and along the north face of the upper platform protrude through the upper seal. The "floating columns" are cylindrical, conical, or quadrilateral (square in cross section) and were built in situ by packing wet, soft clay into preexcavated pits probably lined with some woven material. I suspect the clay was also prepared in situ much like the situation described earlier. Although some columns still have about 1.5 m of the basal portions intact, leveling by bulldozer removed an indeterminate portion of the upper segments and consequently we cannot fully reconstruct the original appearance. Varied sizes and forms of the basal portions, however, suggest that the upper segments were similarly diversified in appearance. Different sectors of the regional population that participated in the operation of the Templo may have been responsible for erection of different columns. ·

Just as significant as the act of entombment are observed differences in the post-entombment history of buried and unburied areas of Huaca Lucía. The sand cover rapidly tapers off south of the U–shaped enclosure, and the clay floor that extends south from the enclosure is covered by later architecture and occupational debris, and pockmarked by intrusive burial pits. We find a similar situation in areas immediately east and west of the enclosure. Within the enclosure and above the buried stairway, we find only a few intrusive burials datable to the Middle Horizon and Late Intermediate Period based on associated ceramics. This notable difference argues that the "sacred" importance of the buried Templo lingered on, perhaps until the Middle Horizon.

Interregional Comparison

Different degrees of temple entombment have been recognized at the geographically and chronologically distinct sites of Kotosh (Central Highlands), Huaricoto (Callejón de Huaylas), Cerro Sechin (Casma) and, possibly, Huacaloma (Cajamarca). I suspect there are other Initial Period-Early Horizon sites in North Peru that manifest varying degrees of temple entombment. The superimposed temples at Kotosh (Initial Period to Early Horizon) offer an excellent comparative case (cf. Burger and Salazar Burger, this volume). The successive White Temple, Temple of the Crossed-Hands, and Temple of the Niches were built one atop the other, each carefully and thoroughly buried with stones and earth (Izumi and Terada 1972). The temple buried under the Temple of the Crossed-Hands has not yet been excavated. The nearby, excavated temple of Shillacoto (Izumi et al. 1972) appears to have been built over another, earlier temple. The particular importance attached to the buried temples and their precise locations is apparent.

Another important comparative case is provided by the superimposed temples at Cerro Sechin. Bischof (1981, personal communication) speaks of a thick sand layer capped with a clay seal that effectively buried and preserved a temple. Further similarity with Lucía is seen in the erection of wooden columns with clay basal supports set into the sand. Apparently these columns were burnt. The latter are reminiscent of the "floating columns" at Lucía. These features and similarities cannot be dismissed as coincidental.

Burger (1981, personal communication; Burger and Salazar Burger 1980:27-28; Burger and Salazar Burger, this volume) also notes a similar series of superimposed religious structures at the late Preceramic-early Initial Period site of Huaricoto. Although not as large or elaborate as the preceding sites, care was taken to thoroughly bury the floors and associated features of earlier temples.

A recently excavated Early Huacaloma temple (early Initial Period?) in the Cajamarca Basin is similar in size and form to the religious structures at Huaricoto and is well preserved, but whether or not it was carefully buried is not clear (Terada and Matsumoto 1980). The late Preceramic North Temple of Galgada (Grieder and Bueno 1981) in the upper Santa Valley may well be yet another example of temple entombment. A preliminary report of its excavation (ibid.), however, describes various rebuilding and expansion without careful, total burial of earlier temples.

Overall, our superficial examination of North Peruvian sites spanning the late Preceramic Period to Early Horizon showed that temple entombment and its approximations, as well as repeated use of the same locus for new temples, were widespread. The cases of Lucía and Cerro Sechin may be regarded as substantially the same. Although Kotosh, Huaricoto, and perhaps Huacaloma and Galgada may have participated in what Burger and Salazar Burger (1980:27) call the Kotosh Religious Tradition, at Lucía, and perhaps Cerro Sechin, we seem to have a religious organization with a considerably broader demographic base and more formalized iconography and ideology. The latter may be tentatively referred to as the Cupisnique Religious Tradition. At the same time, this tradition may prove to have evolved out of even earlier, pan-North Peruvian-Southern Ecuadorian religious tradition(s), such as the Kotosh Tradition.

Temple Entombment at Huaca Soledad: Regional Continuity

During the Early Intermediate period we see numerous adobe pyramids built by the Moche people but the earlier tradition of temple entombment seems to have disappeared from much of the North Coast. The incremental growth documented for the "Pyramid of the Sun" at the site of Moche (Hastings and Moseley 1975; Moseley 1975) physically buried earlier forms but does not constitute a temple entombment. There was nothing that assured preservation of earlier constructions with a minimum of damage. The expansion and modification of extant construction were at a premium.

At Batán Grande the continuity of temple entombment is clearly seen at Mound II, Huaca Soledad, which has at least four successive carefully buried temples. Huaca Soledad is a large conical mound (900 x 600 x 22 m) with a long occupational history situated 1.5 km north of Huacas Lucía and Chólope. Mound II is a conical mound about 10 m high and 55 m in diameter, occupying the highest point of Huaca Soledad, affording an excellent view of the surrounding cemetery. The 1979 excavation showed that there were at least five (perhaps as many as seven) construction phases represented in the mound. Characterization of these phases appears elsewhere (Shimada 1981a; Shimada et al. 1981).

Two discoveries made here are particularly pertinent to the issues at hand: (a) continuation of the tradition of temple entombment and (b) incised marks on a terrace wall that may represent the ceque system (to be discussed later). The constructions of each phase at the Mound were carefully covered first with an "organic protective layer," consisting of leaves, fruits and tiny branches of locally growing algarrobo (Prosopis chilensis), faique (Acacia macracantha), and, to a lesser extent, zapote (Capparis angulata). This layer was laid out evenly not only on horizontal surfaces, but also on the vertical faces of platforms, sloping ramps, and an "undulating" plastered floor. Its thickness varied from 10 to 15 cm to 1 cm. This layer was, in turn, covered by light-buff, sterile, lumpy silt and sand that must have been brought in from nearby water sources such as the Pacora and Leche rivers (1.2 km and 3.5 km away, respectively). The silt-sand fill was also consistent in thickness for the given surface or construction it covered. But, as in the case of the organic cover, thickness varied from one surface to the other. The thickest layer, about 1.5 m., was that covering the Fourth Phase sloping floor and platform.

Elsewhere I (Shimada 1981a; Shimada et al. 1981) described the alternating layers of floor, dark brown organic material and light-buff silt-sand fill, as a "layer-cake effect" (fig. 8.7). This label effectively characterizes the visual effect on the stratigraphy at Mound II. It should be noted that even the exterior surfaces of the basal platform of the first phase construction were buried under the organic layer and silt-sand fill. Downslope movement and erosion have, however, removed much of the protective cover from the peripheries of the Mound.

Figure 8.7.   Mound II, Huaca Soledad. The "layer cake" effect created by the dark brown organic protective layer that covers architecture, and the sterile silt-sand mixture that, in turn, covers the organic layer.

Figure 8.8.   Crenellated wall exposed in the 1981 excavation of Huaca Las Ventanas. This wall had been carefully covered with adobe bricks in order to create a platform at a higher level. The manner in which the crenellations were fitted with bricks implies burial to preserve the architectural detail of the wall.

Charcoal mixed in the organic protective layer covering the First Phase Construction was radiocarbon dated to 1450 ± 60 B.P. (A.D. 500; SMU-833), while the decayed algarrobo that formed the core of one of the eight plastered and painted columns of the third phase construction was dated to 910 ± 50 B.P. (A.D. 1040; SMU-903). These dates indicate that the tradition of temple entombment and building at the same locus continued for a long time after the Lucía burial. Although the A.D. 500 date roughly matches the intrusion of a Moche (Phase IV) population and it is tempting to suggest they carried out initial temple construction at the Mound, the continuity of the temple entombment tradition argues that the maintenance and burial of the initial temple was conducted within local religious canons. Because of the limited extent of our excavation at the Mound, the possibility of yet another earlier temple below the present first phase temple remains strong. Little can be said about the cultural affiliation of the various temples at the Mound due to the absence of diagnostic artifacts. As in the case of the Templo de las Columnas at Lucía, the temple proper was kept clean. Considering the fact that the distinct Middle Sicán style had become clearly established by ca. A.D. 900, the construction, maintenance and disposal of the temples dating perhaps from the second phase was in the hands of the Middle Sicán religious polity.

In regard to the preceding point it is significant that looted Middle Sicán elite tombs recorded thus far had a layer-cake effect created by white sand alternated with ground mineral powders. Pedersen (1976:61), for example, describes the layering created by white sand and about a 1 m thick cinnabar powder within the 14 x 14 m shaft tomb mentioned earlier. Part of a wooden bow in the tomb was radiocarbon dated to 915 ± 50 B.P. (A.D. 1035; GrN-5474). Perhaps the special burial treatment formerly reserved for religious structures was adapted for human burials as if to attribute the sacredness and deference formerly accorded only to religious structures.

Careful burial of a crenellated wall in the eastern sector of Huaca Las Ventanas (fig. 8.8) provides yet another example of Middle Sicán temple entombment. The wall, exposed by looters some time ago, was excavated in 1980 and 1981. The wall was built around A.D. 850-900 and represents one of the earliest monumental constructions at Las Ventanas. The wall is solid, carefully finished, and crowned with a series of five-step crenellations. It undoubtedly enclosed an important ceremonial-religious area attached to the pyramid of Las Ventanas immediately to the west. As part of an architectural expansion sometime around A.D. 900-1000, the wall in its entirety was carefully buried with adobe bricks and organic refuse fill. The space between crenellations was carefully and thoroughly filled with adobes and mortar. The exterior faces (east side) of the crenellations were meticulously covered by vertically placed adobe bricks, rather than simply piling loose fill, to minimize destruction and to preserve the structure in its original state.

Overall, the preceding discussion illustrates over two thousand years of continuity in temple entombment in Batán Grande. Although this practice may have been localized to Batán Grande during the Middle Horizon and Late Intermediate Period, it had its roots in what appears to be a pan-North Peruvian religious tradition dating from the Initial Period-Early Horizon, if not earlier.

Pan-Andean Nature of the Ceque System

The earlier reference to incised marks found in Mound II at Huaca Soledad provides a good point of departure for considering a second feature of cosmological unity in the Central Andes.

The Ceque System

The ceque or seqe (in Quechua, line or ray) system has been most systematically investigated by Zuidema (e.g. 1964, 1972, 1977, 1978b) through fieldwork and analysis of sixteenth century documents. My discussion here of the ceque system is heavily based on the works of Zuidema and his colleagues, Aveni and Urton. Although it is no easy matter to understand all dimensions of the system, we can define it, following Zuidema (1977:231), as a representation of the spatial, temporal, and hierarchical aspects of the Central Andean cosmology that was adopted and perhaps elaborated by the Inca. The noted seventeenth century writer Bernabé Cobo ((1663) 1964 II: 169), for example, informs us that in Inca Cuzco there were forty-one imaginary straight lines which radiated out from the ceremonial center of the city to the horizon around the city and beyond. The forty-one lines, or ceques, were delineated by a number of huacas, each entrusted to perform specific rituals at specific times of the year. Two of these lines, of course, served to divide the Inca Empire (Tawantinsuyu) into four suyu, or quarters. In addition to organizing the space within Cuzco, the Valley of Cuzco, and to a lesser extent the empire, the ceque and huacas were associated with different sociopolitical groups and marriage classes (Zuidema 1964). They also embodied various calendars, the primary one being the lunar.

The Pre-Incaic Ceque System

Numerous lines and huge ground drawings, etched into the desert floor of the extensive Nazca Plateau and adjoining areas to the north and south, have long generated interest among scholars and laymen. The pioneering works of Kosok (1947a, b, 1965; Kosok and Reiche 1947, 1949), Mejía (1939), and Reiche (1949a, b, 1959) are well known. In spite of a relatively long history of research, there are various competing theories as to the function of these lines and drawings. Mejía Xesspe (1939) was the first to identify the lines as seqe but did not explain the grounds for this attribution. Did he use the term only as a physical description or did he intend to imply cultural and behavioral significance? This is not clear in his publication. Kosok (1965:48-59) argued for an astronomical function of the Nazca lines and pointed out stylistic similarities between the ground drawings and the representational iconography seen in Nazca polychrome pottery. Kosok (1965:52) believed the "sight lines" to be intimately related to astronomical observations and calendrical calculations vital to regulating agricultural activities in the arid Nazca region. Reiche (1949a, b, 1959) elaborated upon this astronomical/calendrical argument. Hawkins (1973), using a computer, tested the astronomical/calendrical thesis, arguing that the proportion of lines with demonstrated astronomical significance was not much higher than what one would expect from random matching (39 out of 186 orientations tested). However, Aveni and Urton (1980) pointed out sampling problems associated with the work of Hawkins. Isbell (1979:38-39) turned the tables and argued that the 39 matched alignments support the astronomical/calendrical theory of Kosok and Reiche.

Recent and ongoing investigation by Aveni, Urton, and Zuidema (field research 1977-present) has attempted to narrow the range of possible interpretation of the South Coast lines. One hypothesis is that the lines have astronomical and cosmological significance. Central to this view is the concept of the ceque systems and the fact that most lines radiate from single points. Some of these points with radiating lines are interlinked (fig. 8.9). Aveni, Urton and Zuidema point out that the ceque system and many of the Nazca lines (in addition to the Inca quipus; cf. Kosok 1965:59-60) manifest radial patterning. As in the case of the ceque system in Inca Cuzco, Aveni and Urton (1980:11) argue that certain of the Nazca lines may be astronomically aligned, but an astronomical argument alone will not be adequate to explain the orientation and patterning of lines. Cosmological significance of the lines must be considered.

Figure 8.9.   Photograph, taken June 22, 1955, of a radial pattern on the Nazca Plateau taken from 400 ft. above the ground. Courtesy of the Servicio Aerofotográfico Nacional del Perú, Negative No. 0-17155.

As further support of the pre-Incaic nature of the ceque system, Zuidema (1977:221-226) has shown that a Wari textile now at the Museum of Anthropology in Munich has a calendrical design with organizational principles characteristic of the ceque system. Zuidema (1977:237) also suggests that the organization of the legendary Naymlap Dynasty (Cabello (1586) 1951; Rowe 1948) was based on the ceque system.

Incised Radial Patterns at Mound II, Huaca Soledad, and Pan-Andean Nature of the Ceque System

The three-level platform occupying the focal point of the U-shaped enclosure and assigned to the third phase of construction (tentatively dated A.D. 1000-1100) revealed a set of intriguing incised and punched geometric marks (figs. 8.10a, b). They are found on the north and a portion of the east faces of the platform. The majority of these marks can be described as isolated and interlinked sets of lines radiating from center points. One set of interlinked radial patterns appears to be organized by a ladderlike framework. There are eleven clearly recognizable radial patterns. In addition, there is a 67 cm long straight line of punched circular holes (approximately 1 cm in diameter) on the north face of the platform. Depending on how one counts the lines, the radial patterns have anywhere from eleven to fourteen lines separated by different angles.

These are not graffiti as most of the lines are clearly organized into recognizable geometric patterns and spatial orders. Aveni (1980, personal communication) and I agree that the individual radial patterns and the larger structural pattern created by their interlinkage closely resemble the radial patterns and their larger configurations found on the Nazca Plateau and the adjacent areas some 1200 km to the south (compare figs. 8.9 and 8.11). Although the difference in scale is enormous (the south coastal radial patterns typically separated by 1 to 5 km while those at Mound II are separated by 5 to 12 cm), the similarities of their geometry are undeniable. Elsewhere I (Shimada 1981a,b; Shimada et al. 1981) hypothesized that the incised marks at Mound II are small graphic representations of the pre-Incaic ceque system.

Plausibility of this argument depends largely on the broader architectural and cultural contexts of these marks. There are several pertinent considerations. The third phase construction at Mound II is quite well defined and consists largely of a U-shaped enclosure defined by niched walls. The three-level platform is centrally placed against the west wall. Where the platform abuts, the west wall becomes noticeably thicker. If the niched wall at Huaca La Mayanga situated due west of Mound II (Bonavia 1974; Donnan 1972) serves as any indication, the thick portion of the west wall may have had the focal feature of the mural. Immediately west and below the west wall is a rectangular platform with a two-row colonnade of plastered, painted columns with algarrobo cores mentioned earlier. The open east end of the enclosure has a remarkable, intentionally undulating plastered floor that provided access to a large platform that extended east with good visibility of the interior Leche Valley. This platform served as an excellent sighting place for sunrise and moonrise. As with the preceding and following phases of construction, the third phase architecture was carefully entombed. The formality, symmetry, elaborateness of the construction (as well as total absence of artifacts or floor features that suggest domestic or manufacturing activities), and the association of an extensive contemporaneous cemetery all argue for a ceremonial/religious function of third phase construction.

As described earlier, during A.D. 850-1100, numerous religious buildings and cemeteries within the Batán Grande archaeological complex served the influential Middle Sicán polity whose seat was the huge religious-funerary precinct flanked by the pyramids of Huacas Corte, Las Ventanas, La Merced and Oro. Coordination of ritual activities through a comprehensive calendar would be expected among these contemporary temples. Systematic identification of all contemporaneous "huacas" and their spatial patterns is a major task for future fieldwork. Data from a systematic transect survey of the Batán Grande complex conducted in 1979 do not permit precise delineation of the spatial patterns critical to testing of the above hypothesis.

The final consideration is evidence of "influence" from the Wari and Pachacamac cultures to the south. The ceramics and murals discovered thus far at Batán Grande clearly attest to iconographic and ideological ties to these cultures during Middle Horizon 1B and 2 (Shimada 1981b; Shimada and Elera 1983). For example, the "Pachacamac eagle" of Middle Horizon 2 (Menzel 1968) is found on the base of single spout blackware jars. Textiles excavated and looted from Pacatnamú (Keatinge 1978; Ravines 1980:76; Eling 1981, personal communication) also show the association of Pachacamac and Middle Sicán styles. These lines of evidence suggest a possible mechanism and timing of the transmission of the ceque system from the south, assuming that it originated earlier there.

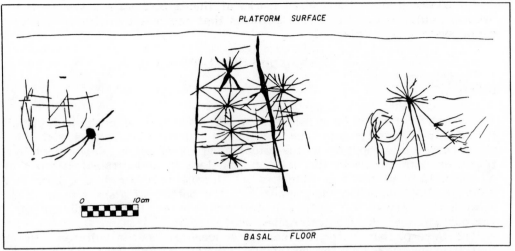

Figure 8.10a. *Incised marks found on the north face of a three-level platform at Mound II, Huaca Soledad. Note linkage among radial patterns.*

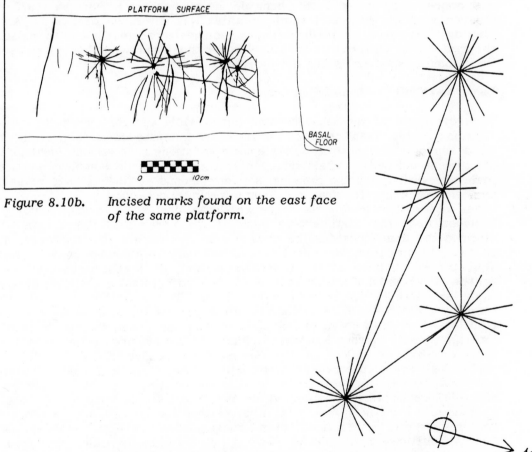

Figure 8.10b. *Incised marks found on the east face of the same platform.*

Figure 8.11. *Linkage of radial patterns found on the Nazca Plateau. Redrawn from figure 3 of Aveni and Urton (1980). Compare with figures 8.10a and 8.10b.*

Overall, when the incised marks at Huaca Soledad are seen within their broader cultural context, the hypothesis that the marks represent a pre-Incaic ceque system seems plausible.

Ushnu and Shaft-Tombs

Ushnu

The final feature to be considered in our discussion of cosmological unity in the Central Andes is the ushnu. Zuidema (1978a:161) explains that the word ushnu originally "applied to the ritual complex of altar, platform or pyramid together with the basin and hole or tube leading underground in front of it." At least in some parts of Chinchasuyu, the ushnu referred to a tube, pipe or conduit that connected the surface with the bottom of a shaft tomb (ibid). In Zuidema's analysis of sixteenth and seventeenth century documents from various areas of the Central Andes, shaft tombs and ushnu were conceptually united in respect to water, the central concern of Andean cultures. He argues that they are linked to the mythical beginnings of the irrigation canal and to the water basin, ocean and muddy flood waters of the rainy season (Zuidema 1978a:162, 170; Rowe 1967). At the coastal site of Pachacamac, during Inca occupation, the pyramid dedicated to the Creator of the Earth was physically and conceptually linked to the bano de las mamaconas. Zuidema (1978a:133) also notes that the shaft tomb complex was a "crucial part of an Andean ideology that heavily influenced Inca political concepts in the formation of their state in Cuzco." Overall, close physical and symbolic linkage among shaft tombs, ushnu and water is indicated.

Ushnu and Shaft Tombs in Batán Grande

The relevance of the ushnu became immediately apparent when the work of Zuidema (1978a, 1980) came to my attention following completion of the 1980 field season. Prior to this, systematic questioning of various local looters, concurrent independent field survey of the Batán Grande complex, and large-scale excavation atop the principal platform mound at Huaca Corte revealed a number of puzzling features. Various informants described long, narrow metal tubes vertically placed in the centers of large, deep shaft tombs, including one situated near the northeastern base of the pyramid of Huaca Oro. They claimed the tube connected the surface with the bottom of a tomb over 15 m below. In addition, they described a well-built rectangular conduit starting near the south base of the platform mound of Huaca Ingeniero running southwest toward the southeast base of the Oro pyramid and ending at a rectangular basin (a distance of over 300 m; Shimada 1979). Importantly, a recently completed (1981) photogrammetric map of the area under consideration (based on 1949 aerial photographs taken prior to large-scale, mechanized looting) shows a narrow, shallow, ditchlike feature running northeast-southwest between the two major constructions mentioned above (fig. 8.2). Excavated and surface-collected ceramics, architectural forms, murals (including the panel reported from Huaca Oro) and tombs all clearly attest to pre-Incaic occupation and religious-funerary activities within the extensive plazalike area where the conduit occurs (fig. 8.2). I hypothesize that the conduit and its associated features are pre-Incaic ushnu used in rituals related to ancestor worship, water, and agricultural productivity. Similarities between the ushnu at Cuzco and Pachacamac on one hand, and the conduit as well as its broader architectural context in Batán Grande on the other, cannot be dismissed as coincidental.

The sherd-lined conduit found near the top of the multilevel T-shaped principal platform mound at Huaca Corte (fig. 8.12) constitutes an important line of evidence for the above hypothesis. The mound, along with two companion platforms to the northwest and southwest, occupies the center of the extensive religious-funerary complex of Huaca Corte. The area in and around the U-shaped architectural complex was used for elite burials. Architectural modifications and a radiocarbon date for a charcoal sample from the burnt roof atop the platform suggest that the principal mound was in use ca. A.D. 800–1000. The elongated top (7 m wide x 40 m long) had an impressive superstructure supported by forty-eight painted square columns arranged in twelve rows of four columns each. The colonnade had a backdrop wall immediately to the east that ran the full length of the platform top and was painted with what must have been a striking polychrome mural.

The conduit also ran north–south the full length of the platform top, slightly below the floor of the platform with a slight incline to the north. If ritual libations were, indeed, poured into the conduit, they would have flowed south. It was well built with carefully fitted sherds laid over a layer of clay and covered by clay plaster. The resultant channel with a trapezoidal cross section is solid and impermeable. I know of no reported structure of this kind; however, the local informants, who earlier described the conduit between Huacas Ingeniero and Oro, were shown photographs of the Huaca Corte conduit and claimed it was nearly identical to the former in size, shape, and construction technique. Unfortunately, the north and south ends of the Corte conduit have been obliterated by erosion.

Figure 8.12.   *Photograph showing construction technique of the conduit atop the platform mound at Huaca Corte. The sherd-lined conduit runs immediately west of the 48 square column colonade. The arrow on the scale does not indictate north.*

Certainly, architectural features of this platform, when taken together, would argue for its use in public ceremonies. Activities atop the mound were easily visible due to its relatively low height and open colonnade construction. At the same time, the backdrop wall, the colonnade, and narrow width of the mound top would have constrained physical movement. I suspect the mound served a public display function.

One alternative interpretation of these conduits is that they served as a drainage system. But why would such a feature be limited to one part of the plaza and the Corte platform? Further, one would expect that a drainage system would show certain predictable relationships with the contemporaneous architecture and extant topography. This expectation has not been born out thus far. The conduit at the Corte mound appears to have been roofed and would not have gathered water along its length. If so, why was it laid so as to run the full length of the platform? Drainage could have been far more effectively carried out by channeling water to the north or south ends of the platform.

Another alternative is that the conduits served as special acoustic devices during ceremonies. If so, why is the conduit in the plaza so long and with a basin? Overall, the ushnu hypothesis emerges as a plausible explanation of the conduits and associated features at Batán Grande.

Discussion and Conclusions

Ethnohistorically-derived Inca models figure heavily in my discussion of the pre-Incaic and pan-Andean nature of the ceque and ushnu. To establish the plausibility of functional analogies to Inca models, I identified and showed the similarities of specific physical features and structural patterns among them. In addition to the above step, however, one must assess other "plausible" explanations and the broader cultural contexts in which the phenomena under consideration operated. In regard to the inferred pre-Incaic ceque at the Huaca Soledad mound, I demonstrated (1) their pre-Incaic date on the basis of radiocarbon dates and "entombment" by later, pre-Incaic constructions; (2) similarities of the geometry and broader structural patterns between radial patterns at Soledad and on the Nazca Plateau; and (3) association with religious and funerary architecture and activities. Alternative explanations such as "graffiti" and "playing game" marks were refuted on the basis of the formality, elaborateness, and well-maintained quality of the associated architecture and its association with an extensive cemetery, as well as the presence of definite spatial order among the marks. The plausibility of a comprehensive ritual calendar was also argued on the basis of numerous contemporaneous religious structures in Batán Grande. We now await testing of the pre-Incaic ceque hypothesis with an independent body of data such as would show a set of astronomically significant alignments within and between sites. Conclusive verification will be, however, very difficult.

The case for the pre-Incaic and pan-Andean nature of ushnu also stands at a similar point in our investigation. Further demonstration of physical and functional similarities or even equivalence of the Batán Grande "conduits" and other associated features to the Incaic ushnu is expected with the planned excavation of the plaza area between Huacas Ingeniero and Oro.

The case of temple entombment, however, differs in a number of respects from the preceding two phenomena. The pre-Incaic and pan-Andean (certainly northern Peruvian) nature of the act was clearly established. Although the specific technique and scale of burial differed, it was practiced over a long period of time in different geographical locations as if it were standard procedure in given situations. Minimally, we can speak of the act as a physical manifestation of reverence (positive or negative) that people held toward their temples and the sacred locations they occupied.

What prompted people to perform the costly act of temple entombment? Some possible reasons may be suggested: (a) astronomical phenomena such as passage of a major comet or the occurrence of a total eclipse which may have been regarded as omens indicating the loss of sacred power; (b) prevention of desecration by intrusive populations with distinct ideologies; (c) death of key religious figures, or (d) arbitrary stipulation that important sacred architecture be overhauled or rebuilt on a periodic basis to reassure its physical soundness and sacredness (similar to certain historic Japanese Imperial and Shinto structures). Possibility (a) is difficult to deal with archaeologically, while (b) and (c) offer testable implications. In Batán Grande, Chavín-influenced ceramics that appear to postdate the Templo de las Columnas occur at Huacas Corte and Facho and not at Lucía, suggesting the occupational and funerary loci shifted. Could the shift have been occasioned by an intrusion of the Chavín ideology? Changes seen in the superimposed temples at Kotosh tend to refute possibility (d). Overall, these possibilities are still "plausible" at this stage of our investigation. One interesting future research task would be comparison of North Peruvian temple entombment with the Olmec burial of serpentine mosaic pavements showing feline characteristics (La Venta) and "colossal heads" (e.g. La Venta and San Lorenzo).

In my consideration of the pre-Incaic ceque and ushnu, Batán Grande's long tradition of special religious and funerary importance, particularly during the Middle Horizon and Late Intermediate Period, was evident. I suggested elsewhere (Shimada 1981a, b; Shimada et al. 1981; Shimada and Elera 1983) that major religious (and perhaps burial) centers of the Central Andes such as Tiwanaku, Pachacamac, Batán Grande and Pacatnamú shared important ideological and sociopolitical features during the Middle Horizon to Late Intermediate Period. In a certain sense, we can speak of Batán Grande as the Pachacamac of the North. At both Batán Grande and Pachacamac, Wari (and indirectly Tiwanaku) ideological input at the onset of the Middle Horizon seems to have played a key role in subsequent cultural developments. Both outlasted the Wari culture and remained primarily burial and religious centers. Both developed distinctive art styles and iconographies. Products such as ceramics, metal, and textiles bearing their iconography are found on much of the Peruvian coast. Just as we see Derived-Pachacamac pottery in Batán Grande, Middle Sicán style ceramic vessels are found on the Central Coast, including the famous Ancón burial ground (e.g. Reiss and Stübel 1880-87). Pacatnamú, situated between Pachacamac and Batán Grande, contains textiles and pottery imported from these two centers. Both centers apparently had small permanent resident populations <u>but</u> were surrounded by intensively cultivated and densely occupied sustaining regions. I believe Pachacamac and Batán Grande (and probably Tiwanaku and Pacatnamú) were in constant contact with each other, primarily through religious missionaries and pilgrims who made the rounds of these centers. Transmission of the knowledge and practice of ceque and ushnu may well have been effectively implemented through these mechanisms.

Although the arguments presented thus far may be criticized as little more than additional documentation of ideological commonalities in the prehistoric Central Andes, we must identify and elucidate the structural principles that unified varied ideologies that, in turn, underlay the cultural unity of the Central Andes. The ceque and ushnu may have been just such principles. The U-shaped configuration may be yet another—one that expressed the place of humans within the Andean cosmological structure (Isbell 1978a). Temple entombment appears to be an epiphenomenon of a structural principle or ideology as yet unidentified.

Acknowledgments

I thank A. Aveni for his observations on the incised marks at Huaca Soledad and for permitting me to cite an unpublished manuscript and redraw one of its illustrations here. I am also grateful to F. A. Hildebrand of Hildebrand Aerial Surveys, Austin, for his expert rendering of the photogrammetric map (figure 8.2), as assisted by J. Vreeland. M. Shimada, as usual, provided editorial expertise. Data used in this paper were gathered during the seasons of 1979 through 1981. The first season was supported by the National Science Foundation (BNS-790674) and the second season by the National Geographic Society (No. 2374-81).

References

Aveni, A. F., and G. Urton.
　1980　A preliminary investigation of geometric and astronomical order in the Nazca lines. Report submitted to the National Geographic Society.

Bennett, Wendell C.
　1939　Archaeology of the North Coast of Peru: An account of exploration and excavation in the Viru and Lambayeque valleys. Anthropological Papers of the American Museum of Natural History 37(1).

　1948　The Peruvian co-tradition. In A Reappraisal of Peruvian Archaeology, assembled by Wendell C. Bennett. Society for American Archaeology, Memoir 4:1-7.

Bonavia, Duccio.
　1974　Ricchata Quellccani: Pinturas Murales Prehispánicas. Lima: Eanco Industrial del Perú.

Burger, R. L., and L. Salazar Burger.
　1980　Ritual and religion at Huaricoto. Archaeology 33(6): 26-32.

Cabello Balboa, Miguel.
　1951　Miscelánea Antártica: Una Historia del Perú Antiguo. Lima:
　(1586)　Instituto de Etnología, Universidad Nacional Mayor de San Marcos.

Cobo, Bernabé.
　1964　Historia del Nuevo Mundo, part II. Biblioteca de Autores Españoles,
　(1653)　92. Madrid: Ediciones Atlas.

Conrad, G. W.
　1981　Cultural materialism, split inheritance, and the expansion of ancient Peruvian empires. American Antiquity 46:3-26.

Donnan, C. B.
　1972　Moche-Huari murals from northern Peru. Archaeology 25:85-95.

Eling, Herbert H., Jr.
　1981　Personal communication. University of Texas at Austin.

Florian, Mario.
　1951　Un Icono Mural en Batán Grande. Lima: Imprenta "Amauta".

Fung Pineda, Rosa, and Carlos Williams Léon.
1977 Exploraciones y excavaciones en el Valle de Sechin, Casma. Revista del Museo Nacional 43:111-55.

Grieder, Terence, and Alberto Bueno Mendoza.
1981 Peru before pottery. Archaeology 34(2): 44-51.

Hastings, C. Mansfield, and M. Edward Moseley.
1975 The adobes of Huaca del Sol and Huaca de la Luna. American Antiquity 40:196-203.

Hawkins, G. S.
1973 Beyond Stonehenge. New York: Harper and Row.

Isbell, William H.
1978a Cosmological order expressed in prehistoric ceremonial centers. Actes du XLII Congrès International des Américanistes 4:269-97.

1978b Prehistoric ground drawings of Peru. Scientific American 239:140 ff.

1979 A review of the Final Scientific Report for the National Geographic Society Expedition: Ancient lines. Archaeoastronomy 2(4): 38-40.

Izumi, Seiichi, Pedro J. Cuculiza, and Chiaki Kano.
1972 Excavations at Shillacoto, Juánuco, Peru. University Museum, University of Tokyo Bulletin 3.

Izumi, Seiichi, and K. Terada, eds.
1972 Andes 4: Excavations at Kotosh, 1963 and 1966. Tokyo: University of Tokyo Press.

Keatinge, Richard W.
1977 Religious forms and secular functions: The expansion of state bureaucracies as reflected in prehistoric architecture on the Peruvian North Coast. Annals of the New York Academy of Science 293:229-45.

1978 The Pacatnamú textiles. Archaeology 31:30-41.

Keatinge, Richard W., D. Chodoff, D. P. Chodoff, M. Marvin, and H. I. Silverman.
1975 From the sacred to the secular: First report on a prehistoric architectural transition on the North Coast of Peru. Archaeology 28:128-29.

Kosok, Paul.
1947a Desert puzzle of Peru. Science Illustrated 2(9): 60-61, 92.

1947b Pre-Inca markings in Peru. Life 23:75-76 (July 28).

1959 El Valle de Lambayeque. Actas y Trabajos del II Congreso Nacional de Historia del Perú: Epoca Pre-Hispánica 1:49-66. Lima.

1965 Life, Land and Water in Ancient Peru. New York: Long Island University Press.

Kosok, Paul, and Maria Reiche.
1947 The mysterious markings of Nazca. Natural History 56(5): 200-07, 237-38.

1949 Ancient drawings on the desert of Peru. Archaeology 2(4): 206-15.

Mejía Xesspe, Toribio,
1939 Acueductos y caminos antiguos de la hoya del Río Grande de Nasca. Actas y Trabajos Científicos del 27 Congreso Internacional de Americanistas: 559-70. Lima.

Menzel, Dorothy.
1968 La cultura Wari. Las Grandes Civilizaciones del Antiguo Perú 4. Compania de Seguros y Reaseguros Peruano-Suiza, S.A., Lima.

Moseley, M. E.
1975 Prehistoric principles of labor organization in the Moche Valley, Peru. American Antiquity 40:191-96.

Pedersen, A.
1976 El ajuar funerario de la tumba de la Huaca Menor de Batán Grande, Lambayeque, Perú. Actas del 41 Congreso Internacional de Americanistas 2:60-73. Mexico City.

Pozorski, Thomas.
1975 El complejo de Caballo Muerto: Los frisos de barro de la Huaca de los Reyes. Revista del Museo Nacional 41:211-51.

1980 The Early Horizon site of Huaca de los Reyes: Societal implications. American Antiquity 45:100-10.

Ravines, Rogger.
1975 Garagay: Un viejo templo en los Andes. Textual 10:6-12.

1980 Chanchan: Metrópoli chimú. Lima: Instituto de Estudios Peruanos.

Ravines, Rogger, and William H. Isbell.
1975 Garagay: Sitio temprano en el valle de Lima. Revista del Museo Nacional 41:253-72. Lima.

Reiche, Maria.
1949a Mystery on the desert: A study of the ancient figures and strange delineated surfaces seen from the air near Nazca, Peru. Lima.

1949b Los dibujos gigantescos en el suelo de las Pampas de Nazca y Palpa. Lima.

1959 Interpretación astronómica de la figura del mono en la pampa al sur del Río Ingenio. Actas y Trabajos del 2 Congreso Nacional de la Historia del Perú: Epoca Pre-Hispánica 1:285-86. Lima.

Reiss, Wilhelm, and Alphons Stübel.
1880- The necropolis of Ancon in Peru, 3 vols. Berlin: A. Asher and Co.
87

Rowe, J. H.
 1948   The kingdom of Chimor.   Acta Americana 6:26-59.

 1967   What kind of a settlement was Inca Cuzco?   Ñawpa Pacha 5:59-76.

Schaedel, Richard P.
 1978   The Huaca Pintada of Illimo.   Archaeology 31:27-37.

Shimada, Izumi.
 1979   Behind the golden mask: The research problems and preliminary
        results of the Batán Grande-La Leche Archaeological Project.
        Paper presented at the 44th Annual Meeting of the Society for
        American Archaeology, Vancouver.

 1981a Temples of time: The ancient burial and religious center of Batán
        Grande, Peru.   Archaeology 34(5): 37-45.

 1981b Final report of the Batán Grande-La Leche Archaeological Project.
        Report submitted to the National Geographic Society Foundation.

 1982   Horizontal archipelago and coast-highland interaction in North Peru:
        Archaeological models.   In El Hombre y su Ambiente en los Andes
        Centrales, edited by L. Millones and Y. Tomoeda.   Suita, Japan:
        National Museum of Ethnology.

 n.d.   Integration and segregation of urbanism and ceremonialism on the
        North Coast during the Middle Horizon.   In Cultural Unity and
        Diversity in the Andes: Defining the Middle Horizon, edited by R. P.
        Schaedel, I. Shimada, and J. M. Vreeland, Jr.

Shimada, Izumi, and colleagues.
 1981   The Batan Grande-La Leche Archaeological Project: The first two
        seasons.   Journal of Field Archaeology 8:405-46.

Shimada, I., Carlos G. Elera A., and Melody J. Shimada
 1982   Excavaciones efectuadas en el centro ceremonial de Huaca Lucía-
        Chólope del Horizonte Temporano, Batán Grande, Costa Norte del
        Perú, 1979-1981.   Arqueólogicas 19:109-210.   Lima: Museo Nacional
        de Antropología y Arqueología.

Shimada, Izumi, and Carlos G. Elera A.
 1983   Batán Grande y la emergente complejidad cultural en el norte del
        Peru durante el Horizonte Medio: Datos y modelos.   Boletin del
        Museo Nacional de Antropología y Arqueología 8:41-47.   Lima.

Tello, Julio C.
 1942   Origen y desarrollo de la civilizaciones prehistoricas andinas.   Actas
        y Trabajos Científicos del 27 Congreso Internacional de Americanis-
        tas 1:589-720.

 1943   Discovery of the Chavín culture in Peru.   American Antiquity 9:135-
        60.

1956   Arqueología del Valle de Casma, Culturas: Chavín, Santa o Huaylas, Yunga y sub-Chimú.   Lima: Universidad Nacional Mayor de San Marcos.

Terada, Kazuo, and Ryozo Matsumoto.
   1980   Excavation at the site of Huacoloma, Peru: The chronology (in Japanese).   Minzokugaku 14:21-29.

Williams Léon, Carlos.
   1978-   Complejos de pirámides con planta en U: Patrón arquitectónico de la
   80   costa central.   Revista del Museo Nacional 44:95-110.

Zuidema, R. T.
   1964   The ceque system of Cuzco: The social organization of the capital of the Inca.   Leiden: E. J. Brill.

   1972   A model for the study of Andean art and architecture.   Verhandlungen des 38 Amerikanisten Kongresses.   Munich.

   1973   Kinship and ancestor cult in three Peruvian communities: Hernandez Principe's account in 1662.   Bulletin Institut Francais des Etudes Andines 2(1):16-33.   Lima.

   1977   The Inca calendar.   In Native American astronomy, edited by Anthony F. Aveni, 219-59.   Austin: University of Texas Press.

   1978a Shaft tombs and the Inca Empire.   Journal of the Steward Anthropological Society 9(1-2): 133-78.

   1978b Mito, rito, calendario y geografía en el antiguo Perú.   Actes du 42 Congrès International des Américanistes 4:347-57.

   1978c Mito e historia en el antiguo Perú.   Allpanchis Phuturinga 10:15-52.   Cuzco.

   1980   El ushnu.   Revista de la Universidad Complutense 28:317-62.   Madrid.

9.

Emergence of City and State at
Wari, Ayacucho, Peru, during the Middle Horizon

William H. Isbell

The uneven distribution of archaeological research in the Central Andes has vastly affected our interpretations of the past. Tiwanaku and its elaborate stone carvings were described by Max Uhle (Stübel and Uhle 1892) before the beginning of this century. Years later, related icons were discovered by Uhle (1903) at Pachacamac and named after Tiwanaku. Subsequent generations of archaeologists have assumed that the source of the art named after Tiwanaku was the Tiwanaku site itself, even though Alfred Kroeber (1944) warned that this had never been demonstrated.

Wari was not discovered by archaeologists until the 1940s, and research by the Wari Urban Prehistory Project is in very early stages. Consequently, Wari is still poorly known. The purpose of this paper is to discuss some of the data collected by the Wari Urban Prehistory Project and to suggest what they might mean. Most specifically, it is hoped that this discussion will help to reveal the importance of Wari as a prehistoric center and as representing an evolutionary stage in Andean prehistory.

Four topics are addressed. First, evidence concerning the size of Wari is presented. Two different estimates of its aggregate population are discussed. Although significantly different in themselves, both estimates confirm the interpretation that Wari was an urban center. Second, the political unity of the sphere of Wari influence, as it is indicated by the distribution of art, is re-examined. Specifically, the iconic and political independence of Pachacamac and the central coast are questioned on the basis of new discoveries at Wari. Third, it is shown that Wari probably developed both the administrative system and the corresponding facilities on which revenue collection by the subsequent Chimú and Inca states was based. Fourth, interactions between Wari and Tiwanaku, as revealed in Wari ceremonial architecture, were complex. In each of these dimensions, Wari was innovative and progressive, establishing a new stage of sociocultural complexity in the Central Andes. It achieved urbanism, as well as hierarchical and centralized administration based on a secular bureaucracy.

Two of my colleagues have recently compared Wari and Tiwanaku, and both concluded that Tiwanaku was the larger site. Moseley (1978) states that the size of Tiwanaku has not been firmly established. He points out that Bennett's sketch map of Wari suggests it covered only about 120 to 150 hectares and concludes that Tiwanaku was larger. Browman (1978) employs Ponce's (1969, 1971, 1972, 1979) figures of 420 hectares for Tiwanaku, as well as Isbell and Schreiber's (1978) estimate of 300 hectares for Wari, to conclude that Tiwanaku was the larger site. He failed, however, to note that Isbell and Schreiber had stated:

> Research at Wari is only now beginning to reveal the changes in its size through time, but our provisional estimates of its area range between 260 and 400 hectares. Three-hundred hectares seems to be a conservative estimate for terminal Middle Horizon I. (Isbell and Schreiber 1978:376)

The estimate of 300 hectares was based on the distribution of monumental architecture revealed in air photographs and on surface reconnaissance during which impressionistic observations of refuse density were made. Subsequently, surface survey was begun at Wari, including areas outside that with visible architectural remains. It was found that sherds and other refuse extend far beyond what can now be recognized as the architectural core of the city. From the center of this core, refuse extends for about 3 km to the south and the east, about 1 km north and .75 km to the west. This implies that the Wari archaeological zone includes 1,000 to 1,500 hectares.

Surface collections of sherds from slightly fewer than 100 collection units within a 50 m² sample area, located to the south of Wari's architectural core, provide some indication of the density of occupation in the past. If sherd density is converted to population as indicated below, we have an area of 38.12 hectares that possessed a population of between 743 and 1,604 persons.

Wari Surface Collections

Sherds per m²		Population per Hectare		Sample Area in Hectares	Population Estimated Min.—Max.	
0.2	2	2	10	4.98	10	50
2	20	10	25	17.71	177	443
20	100	25	50	12.32	308	616
100	200	50	100	1.45	73	145
200+		100	200	1.75	175	350
			total	38.21 hectares	743 persons	1,604

Correlations between population and sherd densities in the above chart have been based on values developed by archaeological surveyors working in the Valley of Mexico (Blanton 1972; Parsons 1971). Very high sherd densities, however, have been associated with higher population densities than those used in Mexico. The justification for this is the deep, stratified refuse that generally underlies surface artifacts at Wari.

Seriation of Wari and Middle Horizon ceramics by Dorothy Menzel (1964, 1968, 1977) has been substantially confirmed by stratigraphic excavations (Knobloch 1983). Many of the diagnostic features and themes of Middle Horizon epochs 1A-2B, however, are common only on highly decorated pottery, and the Early Intermediate Period ceramic styles are only beginning to be divided chronologically. Consequently, much of the surface pottery at Wari cannot be securely assigned to a single epoch of the Early Intermediate Period or Middle Horizon until more detailed analyses are completed. Until then, the dynamics of Wari's urban growth remain obscure. As a provisional measure, it may be supposed that one-third to one-half of Wari, about 500 hectares, was occupied at its peak. Population density may be considered to have been equal to that in our survey samples <u>outside</u> the architectural core, which averaged between 19.5 and 42 persons per hectare. These assumptions indicate that at its peak, Wari possessed between 9,715 and 20,985 inhabitants.

This estimate of about 10,000 to 20,000 inhabitants on five hundred simultaneously occupied hectares at Wari is probably conservative. It does not allow for a denser population at the center of the settlement. Two fairly extensive excavations have been conducted within Wari's architectural core. At Cheqo Wasi, Mario Benavides (1979) exposed an architectural zone of about 0.5 hectares. It appears to have been strictly ceremonial. The buildings may have been devoid of residents, having been constructed exclusively for elite tombs and their associated shrines. At Moraduchayoq, the Wari Urban Prehistory Project has mapped and excavated another sample of rooms also in an architectural enclosure of about 0.5 hectares. The excavations clearly show that Moraduchayoq housed people, even though specialized activities were probably carried out as well. If this tiny sample indicates the ratio of habitation units to public, or non-residential, space it can be suggested that about half of Wari's core was public space while the other half was residential.

The most common architectural form in the Moraduchayoq compound is a square or trapezoidal enclosure with an open patio at its center and four elongated rooms, one on each side of the patio. Archaeological remains preserved in the rooms confirm that at least some were residential. It is also clear that the elongated rooms consisted of more than one floor level, having at least second, if not third, levels. Although the sample of these patio units at Wari is still limited to the Moraduchayoq specimens, it would appear that the average patio contained about 100 m² of floor area while the elongated rooms averaged about 20 m² each. If each patio had only two stories of elongated rooms around its four sides, that would total eight such rooms, or an average of 260 m² of floor space in the rooms and patio of each unit. If it is assumed that the ratio of occupants to floor space was about one person per 10 m², there was an average of about 26 occupants per patio unit.

Another estimate of the number of inhabitants residing in each patio unit can be reached by assuming that each of the eight galleries belonged to a nuclear family with five members. This implies an average of 40 persons per patio unit. These figures suggest that 20 to 40 persons resided in each patio unit. The six patio units at Moraduchayoq represent a resident population of 120 to 240 persons, even if all other architectural forms within the enclosure were non-residential.

The estimated 500 hectares of occupied settlement at Wari during its peak may be provisionally divided into 250 hectares of core and 250 hectares of periphery. Between 120 and 240 persons resided on 0.5 hectares of core area, but only about half of the core was dedicated to residential compounds.

This would imply that an aggregate population for the core of the site was between 30,000 and 60,000 persons. If 250 hectares of periphery carried a residential density between 19.5 and 42 per hectare or 4,875 to 10,500 on the 250 hectares, the total population of Wari ranged between 35,000 and 70,000 at its peak.

The two estimates of Wari's aggregate population, 10,000 to 20,000 and 35,000 to 70,000 are significantly different. Both are based on approximations and surmises which, although reasonable, are without proof. What they do reveal is that, even at the lowest range of the lower estimate, Wari had the necessary number of inhabitants to be considered urban and also to exercise a great deal of influence and power during the Middle Horizon. At the upper end of the larger estimate, the population size overlaps with the estimate of 50,000 to 100,000 inhabitants at Wari made by Richard MacNeish (MacNeish, Patterson and Browman 1975). Wari may have been the largest city in aboriginal South America; perhaps this fact is related to the brevity of its success.

These new estimates of Wari's population do not demonstrate securely that Wari was larger than Tiwanaku but they do place Wari in a new perspective. Carlos Ponce Sangines (1979) asserts that Tiwanaku carried 100,000 residents. Apparently he assumes that all of the 420 hectares he claims as Tiwanaku's residential area was occupied simultaneously with an average density of 238 persons on each hectare. Both of these assumptions are unlikely in light of prehistoric urban research in other New World settlements.

Iconography and style have been the principal sources of information in terms of which the Wari and Tiwanaku spheres of influence have been defined. Menzel (1964, 1968) feels that Tiahuanacoid iconography was introduced into Ayacucho at the beginning of the Middle Horizon 1A, making its appearance on the Conchopata-style offering urns from the Conchopata site, about 10 km from Wari. In epoch 1B of the Middle Horizon, the Nieveria ceramic style appeared on the central coast, which combined Tiahuanacoid and Ayacucho's Chakipampa style features with local stylistic attributes. Menzel (1964, 1968) argues that this introduction was accomplished by conquest and incorporation of the central coast. It does appear that the large site of Maranga collapsed at about this time and a shift up the valley to Cajamarquilla took place. This sequence of events so closely parallels the collapse of Moche's Huacas del Sol and Luna in favor of the site of Galindo, also located well up the valley, that a single process does appear to have been involved.

Subsequently, in epoch 2 of the Middle Horizon, Pachacamac emerged as the power center on the central coast, but its rise was accompanied by an icon almost unknown in Ayacucho—the Pachacamac Griffin. Noting the importance of the Pachacamac Griffin on the central coast, Menzel (1964, 1968) proposed that this iconic independence reflected political independence, and it has been inferred that, after brief subjection to Wari, the Pachacamac site emerged as a new and independent capital for the central coast. The distribution of the Pachacamac Griffin may indicate that subsequently Pachamac conquered a territory of its own, extending far into the highlands of Huancayo, north at least to Supe, and perhaps farther. Historical linguists such as Torrero (1964) have seized upon the Pachacamac iconic spread as a mechanism for the expansion of Quechua speakers from a coastal hearth. In addition, Torrero and others have viewed the independence of Pachacamac as a testimony that the diffusion of Wari-Tiahuanacoid iconography did not involve conquest and incorporation by Wari, but was achieved through trade among independent polities. Shimada (personal communication) has employed this model to argue that during the Middle Horizon the North Coast retained its political independence and maintained intensive exchange with equivalent polities centered at

Cajamarca, Wari, and Pachacamac (see Shimada, this volume). In this interpretation, these latter two centers were introducing new and adaptive ideology that was accompanied by the Wari and Wari-Pachacamac iconography.

About fifteen years ago, I photographed a textile fragment in the collection of the Lucanamarca school in southern Ayacucho that is decorated with a Pachamac Griffin. More recently our excavations at Wari in the Moraduchayoq compound have revealed ceramics with the classic epoch 2B Griffin, as well as other ceramic forms and icons best known at Pachacamac.

Discovery of the Pachacamac Griffin and other Pachacamac-related icons at Wari deflates the case for the iconic independence of Pachacamac. The rest of the interpretations associated with Pachacamac's independence must be questioned too. If Pachacamac was not an independent polity, then Cajamarca's independence is less likely, and it becomes apparent that the north coast, even if it were not conquered, faced a centralized Wari state powerful enough to exercise decisive control in any encounter between the two. Shimada's model of trade and religious interchange between a number of equivalent Middle Horizon states comes into question.

I find it tempting to propose that the Pachacamac Griffin was associated with a social group at Wari, perhaps some sort of specialist class or high status kin group, that was specially associated with Pachacamac and the central coast. If the Griffin is limited to the Moraduchayoq compound, or a small number of compounds at Wari, its distribution would support its association with a particular social group and suggests that the mythical icons played an important role in social processes as well.

The preceding discussion of Wari's aggregate population and its regional political hegemony have been based on archaeological remains. Before attempting to infer Middle Horizon developments in administrative organization it will be instructive to examine Inca political practices in the sixteenth century for which both archaeological and historical information exist. The "Inca Mode of Production" is the term coined by Maurice Godelier (1977) for the system of taxation through control of labor employed by the Incas. He argues that it masked exploitation of the peasants by dressing corvee labor in the trappings of reciprocal exchange, which characterized domestic production throughout the Andes. When working for the state, peasants were obliged to dress in fiesta clothes and were given abundant food and drink by the state, just as in kin and community-based minka. Morris's (1972, 1974, 1978) research at Huánuco Pampa, an Inca provincial administrative center, has shown that this kind of revenue management had heavy costs in administrative facilities. Vast complexes of storehouses were required to insure sufficient food and drink to demonstrate the generosity of the state. Specialized great kitchens were employed in preparation of edibles, as well as immense quantities of chicha beer. Large culinary vessels and innumerable serving bowls would also have been required at administrative centers that collected revenue in this fashion. Housing was provided for administrators in charge of the corvee workers, as well as for cooks, accountants, and various other specialists. Barrackslike quarters were required for the laborers themselves. The distinctive characteristics of such administrative facilities are obvious even in archaeological remains.

Keatinge (1974) has described several archaeological sites from the Moche-Chicama area which he considers to have been Chimú rural administrative centers from the immediate hinterland around Chan Chan. All the sites have three-sided audiencias believed to have been administrators' offices. Large communal kitchens are present in some of the complexes, but the most convincing data come from the Quebrada del Oso site where abundant surface sherds came primarily from open bowls. The exceptionally high frequency of open bowls implies that food was served to large numbers of people, an activity best associated with corvee labor controlled by the "Inca Mode of Production". This conclusion is supported by the near standardization of the Chimú architectural compounds described by Keatinge.

Little is known of other Chimú administrative centers, especially larger installations which may have been provincial capitals. This problem is currently under investigation by Carol Mackey and associates. We may anticipate new information soon. It is clear, however, that the "Inca Mode of Production" was at least one, if not the principal, means of collecting revenue by the Chimú state.

Administrative facilities, such as the Quebrada del Oso installation or the Huánuco Pampa center, are lacking in the Moche polity that preceded Chimú on the north coast. This fact has not been fully appreciated by Moseley (1978:523) who argues for an Inca-style administrative system at this early date. He writes:

> The Moche Valley site of Huacas Sol and Luna is the largest monumental construction project for its time in Tawantinsuyu... Building was done in multiple stages interspersed with periods of use, and a mitalike labor system was used to mobilize workmen from communities scattered over a broad area (Hastings and Moseley 1975).

Subsequently, Moseley (1978:524) states:

> During the third and fourth phases of the (Moche) ceramic sequence, each valley from Chicama to Nepeña contained at least one sizable monument built in the architectural canons expressed at Huaca del Sol and Luna. Although the monuments do not approach Sol in scope, each is generally the largest construction in its valley for the period, and each is associated with expressions of Moche corporate style in ceramics and occasionally murals and other media. The two southernmost sites, Pañamarca in Nepeña (Proulx 1968, 1973) and Tembladera in Santa (Donnan 1973), can be interpreted as intrusive phenomena that were spread by means of conquest and served as satellite administrative centers to a polity based at Sol and Luna.

It is apparent that Moseley feels Moche was a hierarchically-organized state, with provincial and rural administrative facilities where corvee labor was concentrated and employed in mitalike fashion. That is to say, the "Inca Mode of Production" already existed in the later part of the Early Intermediate Period on the north coast. Moche administrative facilities, however, are ceremonial platforms. There is no evidence for large storage facilities, great kitchens, barrackslike quarters, or concentrations of serving utensils which are demonstrable archaeological correlates of the "Inca Mode of Production." In fact, I am not aware of any such facilities anywhere in the Central Andes during the Early Intermediate Period. Moche lacks administrative facilities associated with the conspicuous generosity that permitted the Inca state to disguise its compulsory labor tax. This may mean that the Moche polity also lacked compulsory labor tax, depending instead on voluntary support of prestigious policies and decisions. That prestige was an important motivation for construction is indicated by the apparent lack of task specialization in building. Each construction gang carried out all of the steps necessary to build its own specially-marked section of the great pyramid. This insured that its contribution was clearly apparent and easily compared with that built by other groups.

The first archaeologists to describe the two immense highland sites of Pikillaqta and Viracochapampa believed them to be Inca administrative installations. Smaller but similar settlements have been studied at Jargampata and Jincamocco. Isbell and Schreiber (1978) have shown that they are very similar to one another with respect to room shape. Wari style pottery has been found in, or in the immediate vicinity of, each compound, and the compounds have already been compared to Wari in general plan (Isbell 1977). If this is not enough to demonstrate that the centers represent Wari provincial and rural administrative facilities, it is now possible to show that all employ the same specific layout (Schreiber 1978). Great rectangular-to-square enclosures were divided into room blocks, each with a central patio. The central patio was surrounded by low benches, and behind these were elongated corridorlike rooms that usually consisted of two or more stories. This pattern is documented in the Moraduchayoq compound at Wari, constructed during epoch 1B of the Middle Horizon, and virtually all of the component architectural features existed in Ayacucho prior to the Middle Horizon (Spickard 1983). A somewhat similar pattern was employed in the Putuni and Kherikala palaces at Tiwanaku, but these are dated to late Tiwanaku IV or V, which is significantly later than Middle Horizon I. If a diffusional relationship is indicated, Wari was the source of the invention rather than the recipient.

Pikillaqta, Viracochapampa, Jargampata, and Jincamocco have not been investigated extensively, but they provide barrackslike quarters that could have been occupied by specialists as well as workers. Kitchen areas are known, although it is not clear whether they are large enough to have served entire labor parties. Some of the architectural features present have been interpreted as storage facilities, although this, too, remains to be confirmed by careful excavation. If the oval buildings arranged in long lines at Pikillaqta are storehouses, their capacity in cubic meters approached that of the Inca administrative center at Huánuco Pampa. These numerous indications of the "Inca Mode of Production" as Wari's basic administrative form are all overshadowed by data from the smallest known Wari installation which, in terms of relative sample size is the best investigated. Jargampata is located only about 25 km from Wari, in its immediate hinterland; it is easily compared with Quebrada del Oso, and the other Chimú rural administrative stations reported by Keatinge (1974).

At Jargampata, the construction of a rectangular administrative enclosure was accompanied by a dramatic increase in the frequency of open bowls. After the collapse of Wari, a reoccupation of the rectangular enclosure at Jargampta was accompanied by bowls, jars and other vessel forms in approximately the same relative frequency that characterized occupation of the site before the state installation was constructed (Isbell 1977). Consequently, it is clear that serving food and drink was a major activity in the Jargampata administrative compound, documenting the "Inca Mode of Production."

Finally, I want to deal with new evidence for relations with Tiwanaku and other distant areas. Until now, relationships between Wari and Tiwanaku have been manifested only in iconography (Cook 1983; Isbell 1983). No item from Wari has been found at Tiwanaku, and nothing from Tiwanaku has been found at Wari. Only a single copy of a Tiwanaku vessel, a feline effigy pot, is known from the Wari sphere of influence. Recently, Wari Urban Prehistory Project excavations have revealed a semi-subterranean temple at Wari, covered by the Middle Horizon 1B Moraduchayoq compound.

Semi-subterranean temples are not associated exclusively with Tiwanaku. They are known in the south highlands from the Early Horizon at Pucara and probably earlier in the north at Chavín de Huantar and many other sites. It is also possible that the Early Horizon Ayacucho Valley site of Wichqana possessed a platform with sunken court at its center; so the tradition of semi-subterranean temples may be very old in Ayacucho.

The temple at Wari is perfectly square and constructed of cut stones precisely fitted to one another. The dressed blocks are rectangular, trapezoidal or polygonal. The masonry contrasts with the tall ashlars, imperfectly-fitted rectangular blocks and decorative tenoned heads in the semi-subterranean temple of Tiwanaku. The stonework of the Wari temple finds closer parallels in the facing of the Akapana at Tiwanaku, but even the facades of these two are far from identical. Consequently, there is no precise antecedent for either the square form of the Wari temple or its beautiful masonry at Tiwanaku. With these points in mind, I still suggest that the semi-subterranean temple of Wari reveals Tiwanaku influence. It did not, however, retain the functions of similar temples in the Tiwanaku sphere.

Mujica (in press) has argued that during Tiwanaku III times, Tiwanaku controlled a polity at the south end of Lake Titicaca. The evidence is supportive. At Tiwanaku, the impressive monuments were the semi-subterranean temple, the Kalasasaya, Pumapuncu, and the Akapana. At several sites, 10 to 20 km from Tiwanaku (e.g., Chiripa, Callamarca, and Jesus de Machaca), smaller ceremonial buildings were constructed, employing the pattern of the semi-subterranean temple or the Kalasasaya. At more distant sites, as much as 50 to 60 km away, even smaller but similar ceremonial buildings were erected.

These ceremonial buildings were probably links in a centralized theocratic administrative hierarchy much like that which Moseley (1978) has described for the broadly contemporary Moche polity. Subsequent to Period III, Tiwanaku's expansion of its sphere of influence beyond the south end of the Altiplano in Tiwanaku IV and V times was accomplished without constructing temples in the newly-colonized areas. A shift to a more secular form of administration is implied by the construction of the palacelike Putuni and Kherikala at Tiwanaku during these late periods.

The semi-subterranean temple of Wari probably dates to the final years of Tiwanaku III or the beginning of Tiwanaku IV. Its construction phase is C14 dated to AD 580 ± 60, and later remodeling yielded the date of 720 ± 60. As other evidence for Tiwanaku influence is not present, it seems unlikely that a Tiwanaku colony, such as those believed to have been established on the coast of Chile or the Cochabamba Valley, was established at Wari. Wari did not become a Tiwanaku-style theocratic center either. It never consolidated a core territory administered through lower order ceremonial complexes that employed the semi-subterranean temple form. This form of religious architecture is virtually unknown in the Middle Horizon archaeology of Ayacucho except for that of Moraduchayoq.

Even before the construction of the semi-subterranean temple at Wari, Ayacucho influence had appeared in the distant Nasca Valley. Allison Paulsen (1983) has shown that the Early Intermediate period 7-8 site of Huaca del Loro had ceramics with Ayacucho influence and a circular building whose form and construction lacked antecedents on the south coast. Paulsen has noted that similar circular buildings were present at the Nasca sites of Pacheco, where a Middle Horizon 1B cache of Wari offering pots was found, and at Tres Palos II, demonstrating the presence of a line of Wari centers paralleling the coast in three of the major tributaries of the Nasca drainage. Such site locations imply a north-south coastal highway under Ayacucho control.

Circular structures are known at Wari, and two have been found near the semi-subterranean temple at Moraduchayoq. It may be that they were associated with a primitive form of theocratic regional organization by Wari.

At any rate, it appears that when Wari and Tiwanaku met and exchanged cultural information, probably in Middle Horizon 1A between AD 500 and 600, Wari had already been experimenting with the colonization of distant ecological zones. The strategy of expansion may have been theocratic although the general lack of religious buildings in Ayacucho during the Early Intermediate Period suggests kin-based authority that was not hierarchical. Tiwanaku, on the other hand, had developed a strong, centralized theocratic hierarchy that governed a small territory in the southern Altiplano.

Following the exchange of information, Wari experimented for a century or so with Tiwanaku religion and organization, but a Tiwanaku system never materialized. Rather, Wari produced a novel combination of its own control of distant and contrastive ecological areas with Tiwanaku's centralized and hierarchical religious structure. By Middle Horizon 1B, the administrative compound characteristic of Wari had been developed. An old, probably secular, decentralized form of vertical ecological control had been successfully combined with centralized and hierarchical governmental structure. The "Inca Mode of Production" was institutionalized, appropriate architectural facilities were invented, and the Andean pattern of state and empire administration was initiated.

Tiwanaku must also have gained something from its contacts with Wari. I would suggest that its development of more secular government, the design and functions of the Putuni and Kherikala palace compounds, and the formation of a policy for colonizing distant environments without the temple monuments characteristic of its core territory all sound like responses to organizational stimuli that could have come from Ayacucho about AD 600.

Much remains to be learned about Wari, its role in city and state evolution, and its relationships to Tiwanaku. It is apparent that Wari became a huge settlement with an urban-sized population. It is also clear that it administered a large and unified territory employing elaborate provincial facilities designed for centralized control of citizen labor: the "Inca Mode of Production," in Godelier's terms. Tiwanaku's impact on Wari seems to have come after Wari had developed a form of colonization in distant areas. Tiwanaku's religious organization was employed only long enough to adapt its hierarchical and centralized structure to Wari's more secular government. The product was a strong, centralized form of bureaucratic administration that ushered in a new stage of political development in the Andes. Wari's invention of compulsory labor tax that appeared to be sanctioned by secular, reciprocal relations of production probably laid the foundation for the successful rise of the Inca Empire and determined the unique form of organization generally attributed to Andean peoples.

References

Benavides, Mario.
    1979   Notas sobre excavaciones en Cheqo Wasi, Huari. Investigaciones 2(2): 9-26. Ayacucho, Perú: Universidad Nacional de San Cristobal de Huamanga.

Blanton, Richard E.
    1972   Pre-Hispanic settlement patterns of the Ixtapalapa Peninsula region, Mexico. Department of Anthropology, Pennsylvania State University, Occasional Papers 6.

Browman, David L.
1978 Toward the development of the Tiahuanaco (Tiwanaku) State. In Advances in Andean Archaeology, edited by David L. Browman, 327-349. The Hague: Mouton.

Cook, Anita G.
1983 Aspects of state ideology in Huari and Tiwanaku iconography: The central deity and sacrificer. In Investigations of the Andean Past, edited by Daniel H. Sandweiss, 161-185. Ithaca: Cornell Latin American Studies Program.

Godelier, Maurice.
1977 Perspectives in Marxist Anthropology. New York: Cambridge University Press.

Hastings, C. Mansfield, and M. Edward Moseley.
1975 The adobes of Huaca del Sol and Huaca de la Luna. American Antiquity 40:196-203.

Isbell, William H.
1977 The Rural Foundation of Urbanism. Urbana: University of Illinois Press.

1983 Shared ideology and parallel political development: Huari and Tiwanaku. In Investigations of the Andean Past, edited by Daniel H. Sandweiss, 186-208. Ithaca: Cornell Latin American Studies Program.

Isbell, William H., and Katharina Schreiber.
1978 Was Huari a state? American Antiquity 48:372-89.

Keatinge, Richard W.
1974 Chimu rural administrative centers in the Moche Valley, Peru. World Archaeology 6(1): 66-87.

Knobloch, Patricia J.
1983 A study of the Andean Huari ceramics from the Early Intermediate Period to the Middle Horizon epoch 1. Ph.D. diss. Department of Anthropology, State University of New York at Binghamton.

Kroeber, Alfred L.
1944 Peruvian archaeology in 1942. Viking Fund Publications in Anthropology 4. New York: Wenner-Gren Foundation.

MacNeish, Richard, Thomas C. Patterson, and David L. Browman.
1975 The central Peruvian prehistoric interaction sphere. Papers of the Robert S. Peabody Foundation for Archaeology 7. Andover: Phillips Academy.

Menzel, Dorothy.
1964 Style and time in the Middle Horizon. Ñawpa Pacha 2:1-105.

1968 New data on the Huari empire in Middle Horizon epoch 2A. Nawpa Pacha 6:47-114.

1977 The Archaeology of Ancient Peru and the Work of Max Uhle. R. H. Lowie Museum of Anthropology, University of California, Berkeley.

198

Morris, Craig.
1972 State settlements in Tawantinsuyu: A strategy of compulsory urbanism. In Contemporary Archaeology, edited by Mark. P. Leone. Carbondale: Southern Illinois University Press.

1974 Reconstructing patterns of non-agricultural production in the Inca economy: Archaeology and documents in institutional analysis. In Reconstructing Complex Societies, edited by Charlotte B. Moore, 49-68. Supplement to the Bulletin of the American Schools of Oriental Research 20.

1978 The archaeological study of Andean exchange systems. In Social Archaeology, edited by Charles L. Redman, et al., 315-27. New York: Academic Press.

Moseley, Michael E.
1978 The evolution of Andean civilization. In Ancient Native Americans, edited by Jesse D. Jennings, 491-541. San Francisco: W. H. Freeman and Company.

Mujica, Elias.
in Desarrollo de las culturas prehistóricas en el área Centro-Sur Andina.
press Paper submitted for translation and publication in the Precolumbian Time of Troubles in the Andes, edited by R. P. Schaedel, I. Shimada and J. M. Vreeland.

Parsons, Jeffrey R.
1971 Prehistoric settlement patterns in the Texcoco region, Mexico. Museum of Anthropology, University of Michigan, Memoirs 3.

Paulsen, Allison C.
1983 Huaca del Loro revisited: The Nasca-Huarpa Connection. In Investigations of the Andean Past, edited by Daniel H. Sandweiss, 98-121. Ithaca: Cornell Latin American Studies Program.

Ponce Sangines, Carlos.
1969 Descripción Sumaria del Templete Semisubterraneo. 4th ed. La Paz: Los Amigos del Libro.

1971 Tiwanaku: Espacio, tiempo y cultura. Pumapunku 3:29-44.

1972 Tiwanaku: Espacio, tiempo y cultura. Pumapunku 4:7-24.

1979 Nueva Perspectiva Para el Estudio de la Expansión de la Cultura Tiwanaku. La Paz: Instituto Nacional de Arqueología.

Schreiber, Katharina J.
1978 Planned architecture of Middle Horizon Peru: Implications for social and political organization. Ph.D. diss. Department of Anthropology, State University of New York at Binghamton.

Spickard, Lynda E.
1983 The development of Huari administrative architecture. In Investigations of the Andean Past, edited by Daniel H. Sandweiss, 136-60. Ithaca: Cornell Latin American Studies Program.

Stübel, Alfons, and Max Uhle.
  1892 Die Ruinenstaette von Tiahuanaco im Hochlande des Alten Peru. Leipzig: Verlag von Karl W. Hiersemann.

Torrero, Alfredo.
  1974 El Quechua y la Historia Social Andina. Lima: Dirección Universitaria de Investigación, Universidad Ricardo Palma.

Uhle, Max.
  1903 Pachacamac: Report of the William Pepper, M.D., L.L.D., Peruvian Expedition of 1896. Philadelphia: Department of Archaeology, University of Pennsylvania.

10.

Wari Experiments in Statecraft: A View from Azángaro

Martha B. Anders

In recent years, archaeologists have shown increased interest in the development of Andean statecraft, that body of institutions or organizational principles that represents an attempt to create social, political, and economic mechanisms by which control was imposed on other ethnic groups in wider and wider geographical areas (Anders 1979, 1981; W. H. Isbell 1977; Lumbreras 1980; Morris 1974; Moseley and Day 1982; Shimada 1978). Remarkable historical documentation exists for the last of the Andean experiments in statecraft, the Inka state. Weighing the documents in terms of the various filters through which information passed before being recorded, an extremely complex vision of the nature of this state and its meteoric rise emerges. While the Inka experimented with institutions based on organizational principles that appear to have operated at all levels of Andean societies, these developments moved increasingly toward a break with the spirit of the underlying principles of reciprocity, redistribution, and verticality (Murra 1972:468; 1980:181).

The Inka state was the last and most successful of a long line of Andean states. How were the Inka able to expand and consolidate power so quickly over such a large area? It is argued that they were able to do so because they had available to them a body of statecraft—knowledge about the art of governing—which had evolved over centuries and which had been preserved and passed down from one generation to the next of awkui, wise and experienced men. Antecedents to Inka administrative strategies should be sought, then, in earlier Andean states.

The Wari state is one probable source of these antecedents. It was also highland-based, in the Central Andes, and it attained control, or at least strong influence, over an area second in size only to that governed by the later Inka state. Until recently, the political organization and growth of Wari have been inferred from iconographic and stylistic studies of ceramics and ceramic distributions (Benavides 1965; Bennett 1953; Cook 1979; González 1966; W. H. Isbell 1977; Knobloch 1976; Kroeber and Strong 1924a, 1924b; Larco Hoyle 1948; Lumbreras 1959; Menzel 1964, 1968; Paulsen 1968; Ravines 1977; Rowe 1956; Rowe, Collier, and Willey 1950; Strong 1957; Thatcher 1977; Wallace 1957; Uhle 1903). In contrast to this long tradition of ceramic studies, the investigation of Wari sites has lagged behind.

With the emergence of Wari as an imperial power, urbanism arose in the Andean highlands (see Isbell, this volume). A network of sites developed throughout the area under Wari influence. Since these centers appear to have been intrusive and their planning and construction seem to have been directed by a central authority, it has been assumed that they were established to administer provinces subjugated by the Wari state. Despite the obvious importance of understanding these centers, studies of these sites have been restricted largely to surface reconnaissance and notation of formal architectural characteristics (Collier 1955, 1960; Benavides 1976; Harth-Terré 1959; McCown 1945; MacNeish 1969; Rowe, Collier, and Willey 1950; Sanders 1973; Schaedel 1966; Stumer 1956; Tello 1931; Thompson 1964, 1966; Willey 1953). Functional investigations of Wari sites are recent and relatively few (W. H. Isbell 1977, 1980, this volume; McEwan, personal communication; Schreiber 1978). Much remains to be done to elucidate further the nature and growth of Wari's governing structure.

In discussing the Inka state, Morris (1972) argued that administrative structures were required to mediate between local communities and the state and to sustain the conquest. The administrative centers established by the Inka were "nodes of the elaborate communication and logistic system which enable the movement of armies, workers, officials, goods, and information over long distances . . . " (Morris 1972:398). In other words, these centers were the materialization of an administrative hierarchy responsible for the implementation, operation, and maintenance of state decisions. In like fashion, Isbell and Schreiber (1978) compiled available data on Wari administrative centers and defined at least three modes of site size that they argued reflect an administrative hierarchy. While beginning to give some definition to Wari administration, their model is a coarse-grained and static one. The model assumes homogeneity of administrative functions and decision-making activities in sites of the same size. It does not address the significance of varying formal architectural configurations and their probable correspondence to different functions with different spatial requisites. Furthermore, the model assumes near-contemporaneous construction and operation of all centers. It does not accommodate the dynamics of state growth and consolidation nor consider the constellation of administrative centers as probable relics of different stages in an ever-increasing, centralized managerial complex.

Elucidation of the nature of Wari administration must consider not just site size and the existence of a hierarchy but also functional, regional, and temporal differentiation of Wari administrative centers. For example, how do these centers vary in terms of the kind and number of functions both within a single administrative level as well as between levels? How does function vary among sites of the same level but located in different parts of the state (e.g., core vs. periphery)? How does the function of these administrative sites change through time as the state expands and consolidates its authority? Addressing such questions will lead to a finer definition of the administrative hierarchy. At the same time, however, other dimensions of the governing structure require attention. For example, what is the composition of the population living and working in these administrative centers? What social and political hierarchy can be detected within these centers? How are these centers maintained? To what degree is there craft specialization? How great is the disjuncture between rural and urban production? Finally, how centralized is state control vis-à-vis social, economic, and political organization? How are the state and local population articulated in these centers?

With these questions in mind, research was carried out from 1978 to 1980 at Azángaro, a Wari administrative installation near the present-day town of Huanta (Department of Ayacucho) (fig. 10.1). This report presents a summary of that work, together with tentative interpretations based on analysis of the data to date.

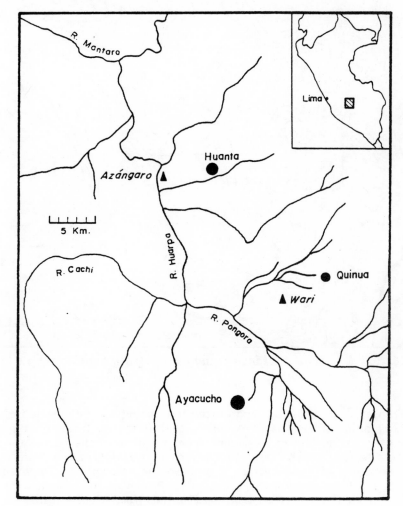

Figure 10.1.   Map of Ayacucho Basin.

The Setting and Layout of Azángaro

The site of Azángaro is located 15 km northwest of the site of Wari, on a broad plain near the bottom of the Cachi (Huarpa) River valley in the lower end of the Ayacucho Basin at 2,390 m above sea level (fig. 10.2).

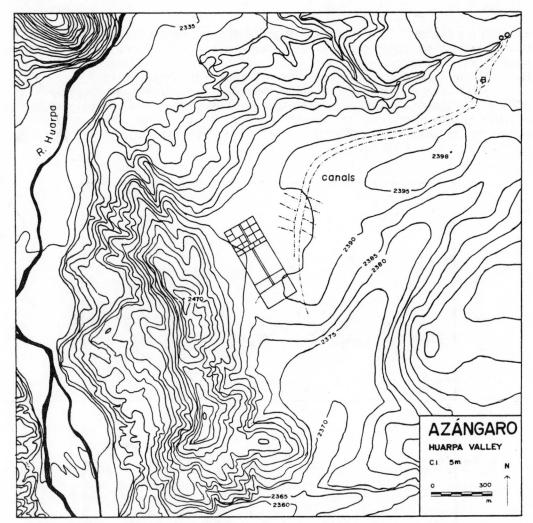

Figure 10.2.   Location of Azángaro and associated irrigation canals in Huarpa Valley.

The plain was irrigated and cultivated during the occupation of the site. There are remains of two parallel canals that irrigated fields on the plain and carried water to the site of Azángaro from a spring in the ravine on the north side of the site (fig. 10.2). Irrigation makes cultivation of the plain possible in this otherwise dry valley bottom. A multiroomed structure is located between the canals, just below two seepage collection tanks at their heads; the size and layout of the structure, which conform to the Wari architectural style, along with pottery of the Huamanga style from the surface of these ruins, point to a Middle Horizon 2 date for the irrigation/water supply system.

Ravines to the north and south of the plain are also extremely fertile areas, fed year-round by springs at several points along their course. A local resident reported seeing remnants of terracing and canals along the southern ravine; they were destroyed as new fields were opened and the present-day irrigation network was installed during the past decade. Disturbance of the other systems makes it difficult to date the use of this ravine. Yet, it seems likely that this ravine and the one to the north were used during the Middle Horizon.

Thus it appears that one of the reasons for the founding of Azángaro in this locale was to facilitate and oversee expansion of irrigation networks and cultivatable lands in this part of the valley bottom. No evidence of prior habitation or use of this plain was found in survey of the area. Furthermore, this zone where Azángaro is located is particularly favorable to the cultivation of corn, a crop of great prestige during the Inka period and probably much earlier (Murra 1960), suggesting that these lands were devoted to cultivation of this highly-valued crop.

The Installation: Regular and Irregular Buildings

The site itself comprises buildings of two architectural forms: regular and irregular. The regular, or formal, installation, easily visible on aerial photographs, is a large rectangular enclosure measuring 175 m x 447 m, occupying an area of 7.5 hectares (fig. 10.3). The enclosure is divided into three major sectors by massive east-west walls, and each sector follows a distinctive pattern of internal subdivision. The South Sector is subdivided into three units. The Central Sector is dominated by nineteen rows of equal-sized rooms and a twentieth row of smaller rooms. The North Sector is divided into three subsectors: the south with five equal-sized courts with galleries (long, narrow rooms) on three sides; the west with six court-and-gallery units of variable size and arrangement; and the east with six enclosures with virtually no internal subdivision.

Not visible on the aerial photographs are two zones of irregular structures of considerable extent. One cluster of buildings is located outside the great enclosure but adjacent to, and built into, the entry to the site (fig. 10.4); the other is found in the southern unit of the South Sector (fig. 10.5). The spatial layout of these structures departs radically from the orderly, symmetrical character of the formal installation. Though their appearance suggests construction through agglutination, the pattern of wall bondings and abutments shows some form of planning, and the integrity of most spatial units there (as in the formal structure) depends upon the simultaneous construction of a number of room complexes. Moreover, these same data show that the site was constructed in stages from north to south and that the south enclosure wall was built only after the irregular buildings within the South Sector were installed. Not only formal or regular structures but also irregular ones were part of the preconceived plan for the physical layout and composition of the site (Anders n.d.).

Controlled Access

Access to the site and between spatial units within the site was complex, and the full pattern has yet to be unraveled. Generally, traffic was closely supervised and restricted. Buildings of both architectural forms were involved in this system of control. The only detected entry to the enclosure was uncovered in the south wall; no corresponding entry/exit was found in the north enclosure wall where it might have been expected at the end of the long corridor. All movement into the site was channeled through a multiroomed, irregular structure (Complex I) that was built in the gap in the south enclosure wall (fig. 10.4). Once inside, access to the irregular buildings located in the south unit of the South Sector was relatively unrestricted. From there, traffic moving toward the Central Sector was once again restricted and channeled by a double-doored room or hall and a narrow corridor leading to the Central Sector (fig. 10.3). Like the south entry to the site, this access point appears to have been overseen by an irregular building (Complex II) located just to the

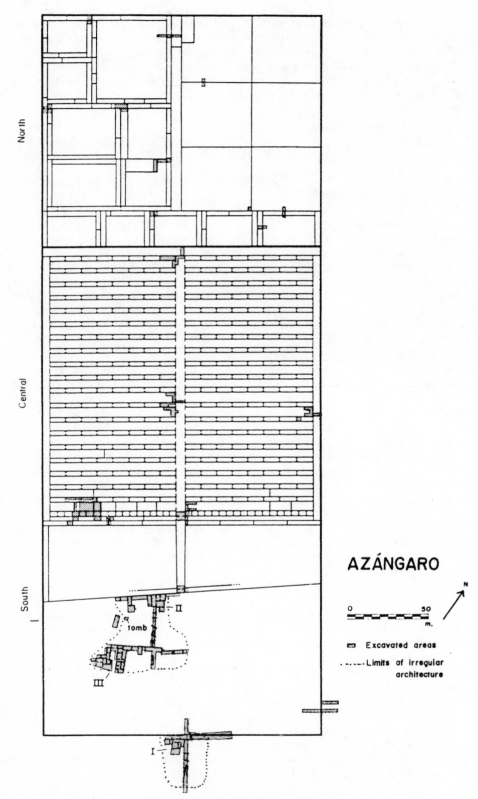

Figure 10.3.   Preliminary map of Azángaro.

Figure 10.4. *Irregular architecture (Complex I) at entry to Azángaro.*

west of the room at the foot of the corridor. Both building and room have security features not found elsewhere in the site—door jambs fitted with barholds designed to secure barriers (fig. 10.6).

Upon reaching the Central Sector, traffic was diverted to east or west side corridors by a crosswall at the head of the access corridor. Additional control was placed on movement into the maze of rooms and corridors by intermittently spaced double-doored rooms in the southernmost row of rooms (fig. 10.7). These rooms were part of larger bounded spaces: groupings of large and small rooms created by crosswalls in the nineteenth corridor; these complexes appear to have been constructed and used serially. Once past these points, a number of crosswalls in central, side, and peripheral corridors directed and complicated movement even further.

No point of access between Central and North Sectors was found. The wall dividing the two stands to a height of 3 m at points and shows no breaks.

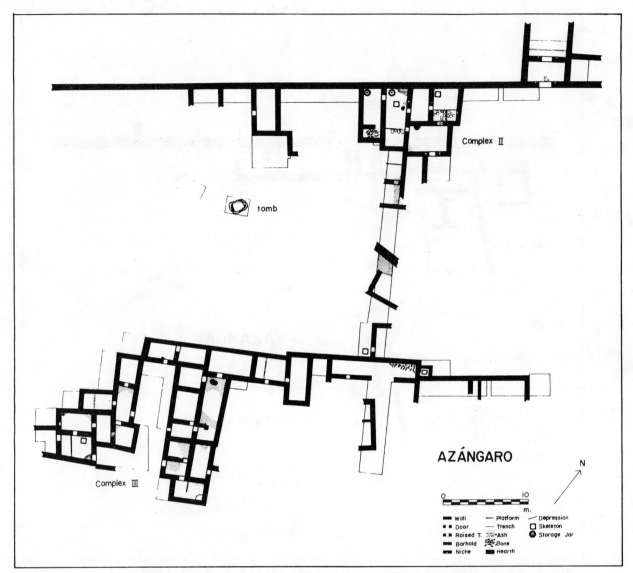

Figure 10.5. *Irregular architecture (Complexes II and III) inside south enclosure wall.*

The only conceivable passage through this wall would seem to have been through very low, narrow doors of the kind found in the large rooms of the Central Sector (80 cm tall x 60 cm wide). Such doors would not be readily visible since rubble from the sector wall would cover them easily. Once in the north sector, traffic was channeled by a series of corridors and passage through galleries into inner courts; details of access in this sector are still problematic.

Access patterns and the dichotomy between formal and irregular structures begin to give some profile to administrative dimensions at Azángaro. Access was repeatedly constricted at a series of checkpoints. This control appears to have been supervised at two different levels. Two irregular structures controlled entry into the enclosure as a whole, and then again at the core of the formal installation, the Central Sector. At the south end of that sector, a number of complexes of formal architecture took over supervision of access within the sector.

Figure 10.6.   Barholds at south end of access corridor to Central Sector.

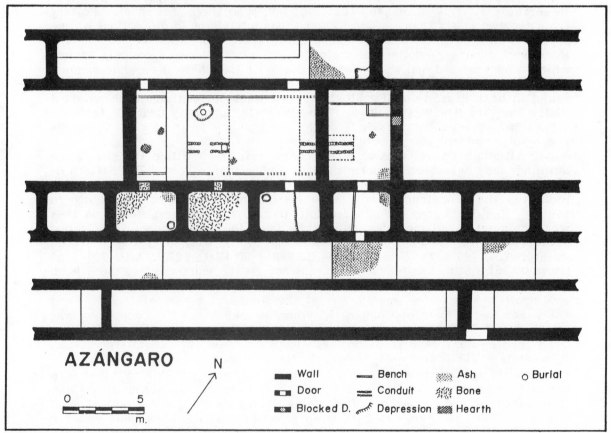

Figure 10.7.   Southwest corner of Central Sector showing detail of one control unit.

Results of Excavations at Azángaro

Excavations at Azángaro were designed to test the widest range of spatial contexts possible as well as to provide a sample of thoroughly excavated units to give a more accurate picture of functional variability within and between buildings. The sampling strategy operated on the assumption that different spatial configurations housed different activities. Thus, visible architecture served as the principal guide to excavation location and layout. In all, 166 units of varying size, totaling approximately 2,045 m² (1.8% of formal structures, 37.7% of irregular buildings), were excavated. These units are grouped into twenty zones of excavation: ten relatively small zones (24 units) located in the north sector; six zones of larger extent (38 units) in the Central Sector and adjoining parts of the South Sector; the two largest zones sampling irregular buildings inside the enclosure (63 units) and outside the enclosure adjacent to the south entry (35 units); and finally, one zone (6 units) in a midden at the southeast corner of the enclosure (fig. 10.3).

Length and Dating of Occupation

Excavation data point to a brief and not so intensive occupation at Azángaro. Stratigraphic evidence shows a single occupation level throughout the site with the exception of the south end of the site. There, a building underlies the later entry complex (Complex I), and one or two other structures belonging to this earlier phase are located to the south of this complex (fig. 10.4). Nevertheless, it is estimated that the time span there was short. Pottery from the two layers shows no significant shifts in style or in proportions of one style to another, which would indicate any appreciable time depth. Middle Horizon 2 Huamanga pottery comprises 97.6% of the Phase I ceramic sample which was analyzed and an average of 94.7% of the Phase II ceramic sample. Wari, Black Decorated C, Blackware, and Caja pottery of the same period are found in both Phase I and II contexts in comparable quantities. It seems most likely that the buildings of Phase I functioned as temporary quarters for construction supervisors and workers during the building of the formal enclosure and regular and irregular structures within it.

Although no occupation levels are superimposed within the site, some buildings may have been occupied a little earlier than others. The pattern of wall bondings and abutments in buildings of formal and irregular architecture indicates that construction of large spatial units progressed from north to south. Residents may have moved into these larger integral spaces as they were completed. Radiocarbon dates (two from the south end of the Central Sector, one from Complex II in the south end of the site) suggest such a possibility: A.D. 760 ± 75 (Beta-1876), A.D. 880 ± 50 (Beta-1874), A.D. 990 ± 65 (Beta-1875). Still, this temporal range is not great. Furthermore, there is no large or extensive accumulation of garbage within or around the site. Only two small middens were located, one at the southeast corner of the site, and the other to the south of Complex I. Thus, it seems that the occupation was relatively brief and essentially contemporaneous throughout the site.

Preliminary results of pottery analysis sustain such an interpretation. Huamanga-style pottery of Middle Horizon 2 comprises 85.0 to 97.9% of samples throughout the site. Wari pottery is regularly low (0.8 to 2.0%) with varying frequencies of Blackware, Black Decorated C, Warpa II/C, Caja, Cajamarca IV, and four unidentified styles making up the complement of each sample. Thus, the evidence (stratigraphy, midden accumulation, and ceramic composition) points to a period of perhaps 10 years of construction within a 100 year maximum occupation from the early ninth to early tenth centuries.

The Abandonment of Azángaro

Azángaro was abandoned abruptly. The end of occupation there coincided with the rapid decline of the Wari state in the Middle Horizon 2B period. Several aspects of the remains reflect a violent, unsettled period in which this site was quickly vacated.

Numerous storage jars were found in situ. Other vessels were found where they had been dropped, not yet kicked aside or swept up. A few deposits of luxury items were found but, unlike ritual caches, appear as if their owners intended to return to claim them. At a number of points throughout the site, walls had been breached; the south enclosure wall was almost completely demolished. Tombs in the south end of the site were looted, and flagstone floors were ripped up; undisturbed post-occupation fill places this looting at the time of abandonment. Finally, the remains of individuals were left uninterred. A child died crouched in front of a doorway in a protected corner of one complex; an adult lay curled up on a bench in the corner of a corridor in the Central Sector. A third individual, who had died of a head wound, received a hasty burial in a shallow grave near the entry to the site.

Diffused Domestic Activities

A variety of materials representing a range of activities was recovered in the excavations. Little was found in the North Sector and most of the Central Sector; remains increased greatly in the south end of the Central Sector and were heavy in the irregular buildings. The density of pottery, which was the most common artifact (128,500 sherds representing an approximate 6,563 vessels) illustrates this pattern: 1.5 sherds per square meter of excavation in the North Sector, 2.6 in most of the Central Sector, 32.6 in the south end of the Central Sector, 44 in the irregular buildings in the south end of the enclosure, and a high of 160.3 among the buildings adjacent to the south entry.

The artifacts reflect a number of activities carried on at the site and in the vicinity: cultivation (8 stone hoes, 3 stone clodbreakers, 2 reaping blades); hunting (7 projectile points, 1 sling shot, 1 bola stone); food preparation and consumption (3 grinding tables, 10 rocker-grinders, 6 mortars, 9 pestles, 38 scraper-knives, 2 bone degrainers for shelling corn, 2,116 neckless cooking and brewing jars, 711 necked carrying and serving jars, 3,328 serving and eating bowls, 285 drinking cups, 14 spoons); tool maintenance (and perhaps manufacture) (41 hammerstones, 714 waste flakes of obsidian and other siliceous materials, 2 obsidian gravers); spinning and weaving (36 ceramic spindle whorls, 1 bone batten, 2 bone beaters, 6 bone pick-up sticks, 2 bone spindles); sewing (13 copper and bone needles); leatherworking (2 pumice scrapers, 3 bone awls); pottery manufacture (2 ceramic scrapers, 5 polishing stones, 1 pigment pot); woodworking (1 axe, 2 copper chisels); metalworking (1 ceramic axe mold); and gaming (166 ceramic disks). Artifacts which may be grouped as ritual paraphernalia are: 25 ceramic vessels, 19 ceramic figurines, 3 stone tablets, 1 ceramic tablet, 2 small pumice cones, 9 turquoise seed effigies (corn, bean, pacae pod, gourd, 2 unidentified seeds), 12 geometric turquoise forms, 32 geometric shell forms, 24 shell fragments (mostly Spondylus princeps spines), and a handful of verdigris from a small ritual cache. Finally, among objects of adornment, perhaps status markers, were 17 copper women's clothing pins, 2 copper pendants, 66 pendants of a silver-copper alloy, 10 turquoise beads, 6 Spondylus princeps beads, and one bone bead.

The inventory is varied but, given the area excavated, there are not many artifacts overall (only 585, excluding ceramic vessels and waste flakes). With the exception of ceramic vessels used in the preparation, serving, and consumption of food and drink, artifacts representing any given activity are few. Furthermore, there are no heavy concentrations of these objects that could be interpreted as a result of specialized craft production. Even though the dichotomy of regular and irregular buildings suggests that, at least in these two contexts, there should be distinctive functional differences, artifact distributions point to generalized domestic activity throughout buildings of both types. Of eleven activity categories, only objects for cultivation, metalworking, and woodworking were <u>not</u> found in both areas; evidence for these activities was retrieved from irregular buildings.

Differentiation in the Handling of Food and Drink: Hospitality and Generosity

The one exception to this diffused, household-level production occurs in the handling of food and drink. Evidence of cooking, serving, and consumption together was found throughout the site, along with evidence of other domestic activities. However, in the four completely excavated residential units, the emphasis shifts. Variation in the proportion of different vessel forms, in the density of osteological remains, and in the number of hearths, suggests that the level of preparation and consumption differed from unit to unit and that individuals outside the household were served (see discussion in Isbell, this volume). It is argued that the differences from household to household reflect different degrees and kinds of involvement in state-sponsored hospitality, including the provision of food and drink to those working at the site or visiting the site on official business. This information, along with contextual information of architectural form, location, accessibility, and associated artifacts that might indicate status or ethnic differentiation for each household, thus becomes the means by which administrative dimensions (social, economic, and political differences) can be inferred for Azángaro.

Individuals in both irregular and regular buildings were involved in the dispensing of hospitality and displays of generosity. Those in irregular buildings, however, appear to have been preeminent for two reasons. First, drinking, probably of <u>chicha</u>, was heaviest there. As in later Inka times (Morris 1979), consumption of this corn beer would have been consistently associated with political and religious ceremonies, as well as used in gestures of hospitality in reciprocal exchange for access to labor services. The second indicator of the importance of residents in these buildings is the frequency of luxury goods. Items of rare and valued material (turquoise, shells such as <u>Spondylus princeps</u>) used for adornment and in ritual paraphernalia and caches, were more frequent in these buildings (83.4%). Also, the greater part (76.2%) of prestige pottery at the site was found there (Wari, Black Decorated, Blackware, Caja, Cajamarca).

Complex II (fig. 10.5) stands out as the most important of the three excavated irregular buildings and was most likely the residence of the chief authority of the site. As discussed above, this complex supervised access to the core of the formal installation, the Central Sector, and exhibited an extra security feature—barholds. Further, the status of its occupants is signaled by its spacious layout, with the largest average room size of any irregular building, and by its elaborate flagstone floors in at least two rooms. Also, more prestige items (turquoise, shell, obsidian) were found there than in other irregular buildings, as was a high proportion of prestige pottery (7.8%).

Complex II contained the highest frequency of drinking cups (6.6%), which, together with serving jars, formed the largest drinking assemblage (15.0%). The highest frequency of eating bowls (57.7%) and serving bowls (5.1%) also occurred in this building. This prominence of drinking and eating vessels reflects a focus on hospitality in this building greater than in any other.

Interestingly, this same building contained the lowest frequency of cooking and brewing vessels (17.2%). It appears that while Complex II was the primary locus of serving and consumption of food and drink, some of the preparation of food and drink for this building took place in another locale.

Complex I (fig. 10.4) seems to have been where a surplus of food and drink was prepared and then distributed to buildings like Complex II. There, 44.4% of the pottery vessels were devoted to brewing and cooking. This building also contained two very large hearths and the second highest quantity and density of faunal remains (8.5 kg, 0.11 kg/m^2). Eating bowls were least common there (31.4%), seemingly indicating the distribution of food and perhaps drink from this building to other locations. Nevertheless, the second highest frequency of serving bowls (4.2%) and drinking cups (6.2%) occurred in this building and points to its importance in the reception of people at the site. The building received all traffic entering the site, and was equipped with the largest single room of an irregular building. That room had benches along at least two sides, probably to seat those given food and drink before being allowed to move on into the enclosure. Finally, though prestige items are not quite as frequent as in Complex II, the occupants did have access nevertheless (6.3% prestige pottery), and the status difference does not seem great.

Complex III is made up of five room clusters facing a common patio (fig. 10.5). Each cluster has its own hearth, and the proportion of vessel forms in each cluster does not appear to emphasize any one activity over another as in Complexes I and II. Serving of food and drink is not marked by a high frequency of vessels (6.0% jars, 2.0% bowls) as is found in the other two irregular buildings, or in the control complex (Complex IV) at the south end of the Central Sector. However, cooking and brewing vessels (29.0%), eating bowls (54.7%), and drinking cups (5.0%) are frequent enough to suggest that those in this complex prepared their own food and drink and that consumption was important. The lack of emphasis on serving per se points to a less public context for food consumption. Finally, the status of those residing in this complex was not markedly different from that of residents in Complexes I and II, despite the difference in handling of food and drink. Comparable quantities of luxury goods and a slightly smaller proportion of prestige pottery (4.7%) were found in this complex.

In contrast to irregular buildings, Complex IV, a control unit in the south end of the Central Sector, shows greater emphasis on the serving of liquids (10.6%) and food (4.0%), although cups (1.4%) and bowls (50.4%) are a little less prominent than in Complexes II and III. While cooking and brewing vessels are only third highest in frequency (23.3%) of the four complexes, eight hearths and the highest density of faunal remains (36.1 kg, 0.22 kg/m^2) attest to the importance of preparing and serving food there. Given the location of this complex, it is likely that food was served to individuals residing in rooms of the Central Sector as well as to those living in the control units. The status of the residents in this unit is not radically different from that of those living in irregular buildings. Although prestige items are far fewer, there is a higher proportion of prestige pottery (9.3%).

Short-Term Housing

Remains in the greater part of the Central Sector were scarce. A few small hearths and light scatters of pottery, faunal, and floral remains were located in corridors, while little was found in the rooms. The regularity of these rooms, their bareness, low doorways (80 cm tall x 60 cm wide), and low second floors (100 cm above the floor) (fig. 10.8), might suggest a storage function (Anders 1981:399). However, a number of features preclude such a reading. Besides some domestic refuse in corridors, the water supply system in the southwest quadrant (fig. 10.9), the floor paving (not connected here with storage technology) in all rooms (fig. 10.8), and benches along all corridor walls indicate the likelihood of a residential function over a storage one. Moreover, the small doors and low ceilings do not necessarily rule out human occupation; similar proportions have been noted in contemporary high altitude buildings in nearby Huancavelica (Freddy Ferrua, personal communication) and in Puno to the south (Felix Palacios, personal communication).

The remains of the Central Sector instead suggest a light or brief domestic occupation, perhaps as the result of temporary or rotational residency. Also, the highly restricted access to this residential zone points to one of two things. Either the individuals residing in this area were detained there by force, guarded by control units at the south end of the Central Sector, or they performed a function of such importance that they and their residences were kept under tight security.

The large open spaces of the North Sector imply differential use, yet materials from that area were even more scarce than in the Central Sector. The few artifacts found there reflect domestic activities similar to those found elsewhere in the site; nothing among the finds distinguishes the handling of food and drink or the function of this area from that in other buildings, regular or irregular. However, since security of the North Sector was strict, it may be that the use of this area was on the same basis as that of most of the Central Sector—by temporary residents coming to the site on a rotational basis.

This suggestion of short-term, rotational residency is based on four lines of evidence. The first three—scarce diffused domestic refuse, at least partial provisioning by control units in the south end of the sector, and highly restricted access to both areas—have been noted already. The fourth line of support is based on ceramic data. A greater proportion of rare, nonprestigious wares and a large number of such jar and bowl forms were found in the North and Central Sectors; some forms were exclusive to those areas. This pottery appears to be from other areas in the Ayacucho Basin.

The Organization of Authority and Agriculture

To this point, differentiation of the residents and their activities has been based on what access points these people controlled, what kinds and degrees of hospitality they offered, and what amounts of luxury goods their houses contained. From these contrasts, inferences may be made about administrative organization, the articulation of those in regular and irregular buildings, and why the state established Azángaro.

At the most general level, there were two kinds of authority at the site. One is represented by those residing and working in irregular buildings; the other is represented by those in control units at the south end of the Central Sector within the formal installation. Each is related to what appear to be the two major purposes for the foundation of Azángaro. The former presided over the site in general and specifically over agricultural activities. The latter supervised an activity more closely regulated by and associated with state authority—observation of two calendrical and ritual cycles.

Irregular Complexes I and II played important roles in controlling all access to the formal installation and in dispensing hospitality through food and drink. But what other duties might be inferred for the residents of these buildings? Since agricultural tools come only from areas of irregular buildings, it seems logical that these folk were responsible for cultivation of nearby fields. Furthermore, they probably maintained and operated the canal systems,

Figure 10.8. Large room at north end of Central Sector showing small door, corbels, and flagstone paving.

Figure 10.9. Subfloor water conduit excavated in corridor of Central Sector.

Figure 10.10. Tomb to southwest of Complex I.

irrigating those fields which were worth little without water. The fields and their produce may have belonged to these households, although it seems more likely that they were destined to support people engaged in state-related activities, given the amount of time and labor invested in constructing the formal installation. Other people probably assisted in these agricultural tasks. They might have been drawn from people outside the site, but more probably from the available pool of short-term residents in the Central Sector. By analogy to ethnohistoric data on agricultural service on the North Coast of Peru (Netherly 1977:213), it is argued that although there were no caches of agricultural tools like those noted for the North Coast, the residents of irregular buildings probably issued implements to laborers and gave them food and drink (particularly in Complexes I and II) in exchange for their services.

What hierarchical organization is there among these irregular buildings? Complexes I and II are preeminent in the dispensing of hospitality, control of crucial checkpoints of access, and the use of prestige items. This duplication of duties and status is also mirrored in the two canals on the plain. These unnecessarily duplicate one another where a single channel with feeder canals would have served just as well. These various arrangements seem to reflect a dual authority system, an organizational pattern well documented for later Precolumbian times (Murra 1967; Netherly 1984; Zuidema 1964), up to the present day (Albó et al. 1972; B. J. Isbell 1978; Mitchell 1976; Palomino Flores 1971). Moieties of a dual system often are spatially separate, operate and maintain separate irrigation and agricultural systems, and mobilize labor through separate networks of reciprocal relations, exchanging hospitality and generosity for services. These three aspects are reflected in the remains at Azángaro. Further, Complex II seems the predominant of the two households by virtue of the level of hospitality offered (both food and drink), control of the most crucial point of access to the state part of the installation, and access to luxury goods. Complex II would have housed the lord of the upper moiety, while Complex I the lord of the lower.

Who were these authorities and from what region did they come? The irregular buildings housed approximately sixty-five people on a full-time basis (calculation based on an estimated 10 m² residential space per person). These folk were drawn from the surrounding Huanta Valley. Three lines of evidence point to this identification. The first argument is based on architectural form. It seems unusual that the state officials who authorized the construction of Azángaro would incorporate irregular buildings within the formal installation. If those who were to administer the site were sent from Wari or other regions, it is likely that they would have been housed in buildings of more regular design. In conceding to the construction of irregular buildings at the site, state officials perhaps deferred to the preference of the Azángaro authorities precisely because they were drawn from the local region. These buildings are similar in size and layout to others in the valley.

The second argument is based on pottery. Of the ceramic assemblage at Azángaro, 94.7% is of the Huamanga style. While this secular style is broadly distributed in the Ayacucho Basin in the Middle Horizon 2 period, the Huamanga-Huanta style, a local variant, dominates the Azángaro assemblage (Anders n.d.). The form of utilitarian vessels (cooking, brewing, and water-carrying jars) is local while the decoration on eating bowls, the so-called Wari Cursive design pattern, is one which seems to be most common in the Huanta Valley.

The final argument for identifying the administrators housed in irregular buildings as locals rests on the presence of tombs in the south end of the site among these buildings (figs. 10.5, 10.10). Ancestor cults were widespread in the Andes during the late pre-Hispanic period (Zuidema 1973, 1978) and probably long before (Hocquenghem 1977). The preservation of the bodies of the dead was considered vital to the well-being of a community. If a body were removed from its burial place among the other ancestors of a community, then the community would suffer (Duviols 1977:319-320). Indeed, during the colonial period, bodies of the dead which had been improperly interred in Christian cemeteries were removed by stealth and returned to the burial place of the other ancestors of its home community (Arriaga 1920:61).

At Azángaro one of several looted tombs was excavated. No pottery or other objects, except badly decomposed bones, remained in the tomb; the surface scatter of sherds in the vicinity could not be assigned specifically to looted burial property. However, the very presence of tombs in this zone points to identification of the administrators as locals. The bodies of the dead were left in place, albeit greatly disarticulated. No one came to claim them. It seems probable that the residents considered Azángaro and the surrounding plain to be home, part of lands traditionally within the domain of the local polity. Thus, they buried their dead there. Indeed, whoever disturbed the tombs may have wished to render a symbolic and demoralizing blow to this installation, its authorities, and the continuing productivity of its agricultural fields by destroying all burials. Such was the effect of the Spanish destruction of mummies in their efforts to extirpate idolatries in the Andean area (Allen 1982:83).

The Organization of Authority and the Calendar System

Complementing the authorities residing in the irregular buildings were those in the control units of the Central Sector. Although residing in the formal, most obviously state-oriented part of the site, these folk also appear to be local. First, their pottery was 90% local Huamanga-Huanta. The slightly higher proportion of other pottery (prestige and nonprestige) perhaps reflects the closer association with more strictly state-directed or state-sponsored activities. Second, despite this closer association, access to luxury items was not substantially greater for these authorities than for those in the irregular buildings. Finally, as above, the burial in the court/partitioned corridor of Complex IV (fig. 10.7) points to identification of these authorities as locals.

These control units could accommodate approximately sixty-five full-time residents. However, these units may have been used sequentially or on a rotating basis. At some point in time, Complex IV was sealed off (fig. 10.7); perhaps related to the death of one of its residents who was buried in the court formed by the partitioned corridor. Other crosswalls partitioning this corridor were placed periodically to coincide with every third room of the southernmost row of rooms (fig. 10.3). In the case of sequential or rotational use, about five persons would be working at a time.

What were the responsibilities of these authorities? As already discussed, they restricted access to the Central Sector and fed those living there. Since these authorities were closely linked to that area, probably supervising activities of residents there, the function of those in the Central Sector must be examined in order to understand what other specific duty the authorities performed.

Occupation of the Central Sector was rotational. The residents may have worked in the nearby fields, but why they were given such special housing and why their homes were under such close watch is not immediately apparent. To answer these questions, one must consider possibilities beyond the more obvious and immediate "utilitarian" interpretations of the Central Sector.

Researchers studying Andean settlements, both Precolumbian and contemporary, recognize increasingly that the spatial layout of these centers is meaningful and symbolically expresses various dimensions or structural principles of Andean social and cosmological order (W. H. Isbell 1978; Morris 1983; Zuidema 1966, n.d.). Social, political, economic, and cosmological orders are mapped out simultaneously in space.

It is with this understanding that the Central Sector was reexamined. Various aspects of the sector—highly restricted access, rotational occupation, the number of rows of rooms, of rooms in each row, of large versus small rooms, anomalies in the water supply system in the southwest quadrant—show intriguing possibilities when compared with the ceque and huaca system of Inka Cuzco. This system comprised 41 ceques, or invisible lines, radiating from the Coricancha, the Temple of the Sun, and 328 huacas, or shrines, situated on these lines. Zuidema (n.d.) continues to explore the multiple functions of that system with respect to the social, political, economic, and religious organization of Cuzco. What is most pertinent to interpreting the function of the Central Sector of Azángaro are his efforts to reconstruct the Inka calendar.

It is argued here that the Central Sector of Azángaro was an analogous construct, though more compact and concrete, and that the authorities in the control units and the individuals housed temporarily there engaged in the ritual observation and regulation of a dual calendrical system—solar and sidereal-lunar. The appropriateness of using this analogy to the later ceque system as calendar is strengthened by Zuidema's (1977:221-225) analysis of a Wari textile in which he has identified numerical data that appear to denote solar and lunar calendars. Space does not permit full elaboration of this interpretation here, but the reader may find full treatment of the argument in Anders (n.d.).

Conclusions

During the Middle Horizon, the Wari state expanded its influence and control over a large part of the Central Andes. In the process, Wari officials sought ways to articulate and integrate local polities, with their different social, economic, and religious systems, within a much larger political unit. The role of religion has frequently been posited as a major integrating force in the Wari state (e.g., see Menzel 1964). Work on Wari iconography indicates that these Wari authorities drew on powerful symbols pervasive and long-embedded in Andean thought (e.g., staff gods, winged attendant figures, felines, snakes) (Cook 1979; Rowe 1971). Through the co-option and manipulation of these symbols, state officials gave legitimacy and sanctity to the Wari state while giving unity to the many polities or ethnic groups which made up the state.

At Azángaro, this feat was accomplished by translating shared ideological constructs into practical and material agricultural/calendrical terms. By means of symbolically constituted buildings, architectural layout, water system, burials, and organization of authority and rotational labor, two calendar systems were coordinated--solar and sidereal-lunar. As in later Inka times (Zuidema 1977:228), it appears that the solar calendar was dominant and more political in purpose, whereas the local-level sidereal-lunar calendar was subordinate and agricultural in nature. Through ritual observance of the calendrical round, authorities of this state center sought to ensure plentiful rains and agricultural abundance, thereby providing for the well-being of the region and of the state as a whole.

The coordination of state and local agricultural/calendrical cycles was facilitated by officials appointed by the state but drawn from the local Huanta region. The local dual authority system was preserved in the supervision of the site and the working of cult lands on the plain, and probably in the regulation of calendrical activities as well. These authorities were substantially self-supporting, though they drew on rotational, or mit'a, labor to work in the fields devoted to the Wari cult and to perform rituals connected to the agricultural/calendrical round. They were able to do so by offering food, drink, and a place to sleep in exchange for labor services.

These mit'a workers were drawn largely from the Ayacucho Basin. Furthermore, they were probably mobilized according to different sociopolitical units within this region. The organization of living space in the Central Sector of Azángaro for these workers hints at both idealized and real divisions. The organization of the housing there into forty rows of rooms recalls Zuidema's (1977:233-238) suggested reconstruction of the number of Inka political units outside Cuzco: forty. He finds a comparable organization in the Kingdom of Nampallec in the Lambayeque Valley (1977:237). The evidence at Azángaro suggests that organization of the Ayacucho area was considerably more complex and the division into forty an idealized version of that order. Multiple crosswalls in the central and side corridors of the Central Sector may divide this area into units that correspond to real sociopolitical divisions of the basin. Unfortunately, lack of complete information on this aspect of the Central Sector does not permit clarification of this tantalizing dimension of the sociopolitical organization of the core area of the Wari state.

Much remains to be discussed regarding the temporal, regional, and functional variation in Wari's administrative hierarchy, as well as the nature of state-local relations in the larger Ayacucho Basin and further afield. Analysis of the materials from Azángaro is ongoing, and a fuller picture of Azángaro and its position in Wari's governing system is forthcoming.

Acknowledgments

Fieldwork at Azángaro was funded by grants from the Fulbright-Hays Doctoral Dissertation Research Abroad Program and the Social Science Research Fellowship Program, under permit of the Instituto Nacional de Cultura of Peru (Acuerdo No. 05/06.06.78). The author is grateful to Thomas F. Lynch, Craig Morris, and Patricia J. Netherly for their many constructive comments on this paper.

References

Albó, Javier y equipo CIPCA.
   1972   Dinámica en la estructura inter-comunitaria de Jesús de Machaca. América Indígena 32:773-816.

Allen, Catherine J.
   1982   Body and soul in Quechua thought. Journal of Latin American Lore 8 (2): 179-96.

Anders, Martha B.
   1979   Diseño para la investigación de las funciones de un sitio Wari. Revista Investigaciones 2 (1): 27-44. Ayacucho, Perú: Departamento de Ciencias Histórico-Sociales, Universidad Nacional de San Cristóbal de Huamanga.

   1981   Investigation of state storage facilities in Pampa Grande, Peru. Journal of Field Archaeology 8:391-404.

   n.d.   Dual organization and calendars inferred from the planned site of Azángaro--Wari administrative strategies. Ph.D. diss., Cornell University.

Arriaga, Pablo Joseph de
1920
(1621) La Extirpación de la Idolotría en el Perú.   Lima: Imprenta Sanmartí y
Ca.

Benavides, Mario
1965 Estudio de la cerámica decorada de Conchopata.   Tesis para optar al
grado de Bachiller en Ciencias Antropológicas, Universidad Nacional
de San Cristóbal de Huamanga.   Ayacucho, Peru.

1976 Yacimientos Arqueológicos en Ayacucho.   Ayacucho, Peru:
Universidad Nacional de San Cristóbal de Huamanga.

Bennett, Wendell C.
1953 Excavations at Wari, Ayacucho, Peru.   Yale University Publications in
Anthropology 49.

Collier, Donald
1955 Cultural chronology and change as reflected in the ceramics of the
Viru Valley, Peru.   Fieldiana, Anthropology 43.   Chicago: Field
Museum of Natural History.

1960 Archaeological investigations in the Casma Valley, Peru.   Acts, 34th
International Congress of Americanists, 411-17.

Cook, Anita Gwynn
1979 The iconography of empire: symbolic communication in Seventh
Century Peru.   M.A. thesis.   State University of New York at
Binghamton.

Duviols, Pierre
1977 La Destrucción de las Religiones Andinas (Conquista y Colonia).
Mexico: Universidad Nacional Autonóma de México.

González Carré, J. Enrique
1966 Investigación Arqueológica en Ñawimpukio.   Ayacucho: Consejo
General de Investigaciones, Universidad Nacional de San Cristóbal de
Huamanga.

Harth-Terré, Emilio
1959 Piki-Llacta: Ciudad de pósitos y bastimentos.   Revista del Museo e
Instituto Arqueológico 18:41-56.   Cuzco: Universidad Nacional de
Cuzco.

Hocquenghem, Anne Marie
1977 Quelques projections sur l'iconographie des Mochicas: Une image de
leur monde d'après leurs images du monde.   Baessler-Archiv N.F.
25:163-91.

Isbell, Billie Jean
1978 To Defend Ourselves: Ecology and Ritual in an Andean Village.
Austin: University of Texas Press.

220

Isbell, William H.
1977 The Rural Foundation for Urbanism: Economic and Stylistic Interaction Between Rural and Urban Communites in Eighth-Century Peru. Urbana: University of Illinois Press.

1978 Cosmological order expressed in prehistoric ceremonial centers. Actes du XLIIe Congrès International des Américanistes 4:269-97.

1980 La evolución del urbanismo y del estado en el Perú tiwanacoide. Estudios Arqueológicos 5:121-32. Universidad de Chile, Sede Antofagasta.

Isbell, William H., and Katharina J. Schreiber
1978 Was Wari a state? American Antiquity 43:372-89.

Knobloch, Patricia J.
1976 A study of the Huarpa ceramic style of the Andean Early Intermediate Period. M.A. thesis, State University of New York at Binghamton.

Kroeber, Alfred, and William D. Strong
1924a The Uhle collections from Chincha. University of California Publications in American Archaeology and Ethnology 21 (1).

1924b The Uhle pottery collections from Ica. University of California Publications in American Archaeology and Ethnology 21 (3).

Larco Hoyle, Rafael
1948 Cronología Arqueológica del Norte del Perú. Hacienda Chiclín-Trujillo, Perú: Biblioteca del Museo de Arqueología "Rafael Larco Herrera."

Lumbreras, Luis G.
1959 La cultura de Wari, Ayacucho. Etnología y Arqueología 1:130-227. Lima: Universidad Nacional Mayor de San Marcos.

1980 El Imperio Wari. In Historia del Perú, Tomo II, edited by Juan Mejía Baca, 9-91. Lima: Editorial Juan Mejía Baca.

McCown, Theodore D.
1945 Pre-Incaic Huamachuco. Survey and excavations in the region of Huamachuco and Cajabamba. University of California Publications in American Archaeology and Ethnology 39 (4).

MacNeish, Richard S.
1969 First Annual Report of the Ayacucho Archaeological-Botanical Project. Andover: Phillips Academy.

Menzel, Dorothy
1964 Style and time in the Middle Horizon. Ñawpa Pacha 2:1-106.

1968 New data on the Huari empire in Middle Horizon epoch 2B. Ñawpa Pacha 6:47-114.

Mitchell, William P.
  1976 Irrigation and community in the central Peruvian highlands. American Anthropologist 78:25-44.

Morris, Craig
  1972 State settlements in Tawantinsuyu: a strategy of compulsory urbanism. In Contemporary Archaeology, edited by Mark P. Leone, 393-401. Carbondale: Southern Illinois University Press.

  1974 Reconstructing patterns of non-agricultural production in the Inca economy: archaeology and documents in institutional analysis. In Reconstructing Complex Societies, edited by Charlotte B. Moore. Bulletin of the American Schools of Oriental Research, Supplement 20:49-68.

  1979 Maize beer in the economics, politics, and religion of the Inca empire. In Fermented Food Beverages in Nutrition, edited by Clifford F. Gastineau, William J. Darby, and Thomas B. Turner, 21-34. New York: Academic Press.

  1983 The sacred architecture of Huánuco Pampa, an Inca administrative center. Paper presented at the Symposium on the Inca Empire: New Perspectives, December 1-2, Cornell University.

Moseley, Michael E., and Kent C. Days, eds.
  1982 Chan Chan: Andean Desert City. Albuquerque: University of New Mexico Press.

Murra, John V.
  1960 Rite and crop in the Inca state. In Culture in History: Essays in Honor of Paul Radin, edited by Stanley Diamond, 393-407. New York: Columbia University Press.

  1967 La visita de los Chupachu como fuente etnológica. In Visita de la Provincia de Léon de Huánuco en 1562, edited by Iñigo Ortiz de Zúñiga, 1:381-406. Huánuco, Perú: Universidad Nacional Hermilio Valdizán.

  1972 El control vertical de un máximo de pisos ecológicos en la economía de las sociedades andinas. In Visita de la Provincia de León de Huánuco en 1562, edited by Iñigo Ortiz de Zúñiga, 2:427-76. Huánuco, Perú: Universidad Nacional Hermilio Valdizán.

  1980 The Economic Organization of the Inka State. Research in Economic Anthropology, Supplement 1. Greenwich: JAI Press Inc.

Netherly, Patricia Joan
  1977 Local level lords on the north coast of Peru. Ph.D. diss., Cornell University.

  1984 The management of late Andean irrigation systems on the north coast of Peru. American Antiquity 49 (2): 227-54.

Palomino Flores, Salvador
1971 La dualidad en la organización sociocultural de algunos pueblos del area andina. Revista del Museo Nacional 37:231-60. Lima, Peru.

Paulsen, Allison C.
1968 A Middle Horizon tomb, Pinilla, Ica Valley, Peru. Ñawpa Pacha 6:1-6.

Ravines, Rogger
1977 Excavaciones en Ayapata, Huancavelica, Perú. Ñawpa Pacha 15:49-100.

Rowe, John H.
1956 Archaeological explorations in southern Peru, 1954-1955. American Antiquity 22:135-51.

1971 The influence of Chavin art on later styles. In Dumbarton Oaks Conference on Chavin, edited by Elizabeth P. Benson, 101-23. Washington, D.C.: Dumbarton Oaks Research Library and Collection.

Rowe, John H., Donald Collier, and Gordon R. Willey
1950 Reconnaissance notes on the site of Huari, near Ayacucho, Peru. American Antiquity 16:120-37.

Sanders, William T.
1973 The significance of Pikillacta in Andean culture history. Occasional Papers in Anthropology, Pennsylvania State University 8:380-428.

Schaedel, Richard P.
1966 Incipient urbanization and secularization in Tiahuanacoid Peru. American Antiquity 31:338-44.

Schreiber, Katharina Jeanne
1978 Planned architecture of Middle Horizon Peru: implications for social and political organization. Ph.D. diss., State University of New York at Binghamton.

Shimada, Izumi.
1978 Economy of a prehistoric urban context: commodity and labor flow at Moche V Pampa Grande, Peru. American Antiquity 43:569-92.

Strong, William D.
1957 Paracas, Nazca, and Tiahuanacoid cultural relationships in south coastal Peru. Memoirs, Society for American Archaeology 13.

Stumer, Louis M.
1956 Development of Peruvian coastal Tiahuanacoid styles. American Antiquity 22:59-69.

Tello, Julio C.
1931 Las ruinas de Wari son, por su extensión, el enorme material arquitectónico, la piedra tallada, los edificios subterraneos, estatuas, etc. superiores en ciertos aspectos a las de Tiahuanacu y semejantes a las de Chavín. El Perú. Diario de la Mañana, 27 agosto. Lima.

Thatcher, John P.
1977   A Middle Horizon 1B cache from Huamachuco, north highlands, Peru. Ñawpa Pacha 15:101-10.

Thompson, Donald E.
1964   Postclassic innovations in architecture and settlement patterns in the Casma Valley, Peru. Southwestern Journal of Anthropology 20:91-105.

1966   Archaeological investigations in the Huarmey Valley, Peru. Acts, 36th International Congress of Americanists, 541-48.

Uhle, Max
1903   Pachacamac. Report of the William Pepper, M.D., L.L.D., Peruvian Expedition of 1896. Philadelphia: University of Pennsylvania.

Wallace, Dwight T.
1957   The Tiahuanaco Horizon styles in the Peruvian and Bolivian highlands. Ph.D. diss., University of California, Berkeley.

Willey, Gordon R.
1953   Prehistoric settlement patterns in the Virú Valley, Peru. Bureau of American Ethnology, Bulletin 155.

Zuidema, R. T.
1964   The Ceque System of Cuzco: The Social Organization of the Capital of the Inca. Leiden: E.J. Brill.

1966   La relación entre el patrón de poblamiento prehispánico y los principios derivados de la estructura social incaica. Actas, 37° Congreso Internacional de Americanistas 1:45-55.

1973   Kinship and ancestor cult in three Peruvian communities. Hernandez Príncipe's account of 1622. Institut Français des Etudes Andines, Bulletin 2:16-33.

1977   The Inca calendar. In Native American Astronomy, edited by Anthony F. Aveni, 219-59. Austin: University of Texas Press.

1978   Shaft tombs and the Inca Empire. Journal of the Steward Anthropological Society 9:133-78.

1982   The sidereal lunar calendar of the Incas. In Archaeoastronomy in the New World, edited by Anthony F. Aveni, 59-107. Cambridge: Cambridge University Press.

n.d.   Hierarchy, space and time in Cuzco: a reconsideration of the ceque system. Manuscript, University of Illinois.

11.

Notes On Ancient Exchange:
A Plea for Collaboration

Susan E. Ramírez

During the last two decades, pioneering efforts on several fronts have significantly revised our understanding of the economic organization of the Inca empire. John V. Murra, one of the recognized leaders in the field of ethnohistory and most responsible for these advances, describes the preHispanic highland economy in terms of complementarity and redistribution. He concludes that non-commercial exchanges and the exploitation of multiple ecological tiers by a single polity suggest the drive toward self-sufficiency of ethnic groups or chiefdomships (señoríos) from Huánuco in the north to the Lake Titicaca region in the south. María Rostworowski de Diez Canseco, another pioneer in the field and, more recently, Frank Salomon call the universality of this conclusion into question, however, with their evidence of the existence of specialized traders or merchants on the Peruvian coast and in the highlands around present-day Quito.[1] My purpose is to discuss the issues of self-sufficiency and exchange for the señoríos of the north coast between Pacasmayo and Jayanca on the eve of the Spanish conquest in an effort to assess the adaptability of Murra's model to the area.[2]

Complementarity and redistribution were demonstrably operative on the coast at this time. Therefore, my discussion of the local economic and political situation will be summarily brief. It is included only as introduction and background material, a context or benchmark within or against which to judge the evidence of exchange within the various coastal groups and between these and their highland counterparts.[3]

The area of inquiry is the modern provinces of Lambayeque and Pacasmayo, which, according to archaeologists, had once been part of the united Kingdom of Chimor. When the Incas conquered the coast in the fifteenth century, they subdivided the area. This process of divide and conquer was repeated again at the time of the Spanish invasion, making the reconstruction of the polities of 1530 an extremely difficult task. Based on the encomienda grants of Francisco Pizarro, which represent the first of many changes made by the Spanish in the administrative structure of the Inca system, and other documents written within the first decade or so of the conquest, it appears that the area was divided into six señoríos: Jayanca, Túcume, Sinto, Collique, Saña, and Pacasmayo, from north to south.[4]

All six were similar in structure. A paramount lord (curaca or cacique principal) exercised supreme authority on the local level over the masses, the so-called indios parques y mitayos.[5] The curaca was the dueño de indios with power over life and death. He personified his people, representing them and, in so doing, his own interests, within the Inca empire. Tempering his potential to abuse power was the fact that his status and prestige were based on the number of his subjects and the wealth their labor could produce. Measures of this were the general well-being of his people and the hospitality--the sumptuousness of his banquets or his generosity in providing cloth and chicha (maize beer)--exhibited to visitors.[6]

His subjects worked for him in exchange for ceremonial redistribution, mediation with the supernatural, and access to the natural resources he controlled. Most lived apart from his administrative and ceremonial center in relatively small hamlets, usually under the rule of a lesser or secondary lord (principal) and his lieutenants (mandones). By far the greatest number of his subjects were farmers, who lived in close proximity to the fields in which they cultivated cotton and foodstuffs. Others were fishermen, who lived separate from the farmers in hamlets situated for easy access to specially designated beaches and areas of shellfish collection. On his periodic junkets to their scattered villages and hamlets, the curaca assigned specific tasks to these commoners in the form of tribute, in addition to farming and fishing. They might be asked to cultivate a field, clean an irrigation canal, guard herds, serve at the tambo or inn, repair roads or bridges, guide travelers, carry messages, or deliver their produce to his administrative center, warehouses, or other villages under his control. Sometimes whole villages (parcialidades) left home to comply with these temporary labor obligations, giving a sense of movement to this otherwise sedentary population.[7]

In a more privileged position, in that they might be exempt from some or all of these duties, were the few skilled craftsmen—perhaps no more than 5 to 6 percent of the total population--who served the lord.[8] Table 11.1 summarizes the available data on the existence of over twenty different types of specialists in the six señoríos by the year of the first documentary reference to them.[9] Some, such as the hamaqueros, quickly became obsolete with the mid-1560s prohibition of transportation by litter. The existence of others, such as tejedores, cumbicos, tintoreros, pintores de mantas, and roperos, suggests a great deal of expertise and division of labor, especially in the weaving, decoration, and storage of cloth.

Some of these specialists, such as the chicha brewers, the cooks and the bearers, along with pages and other servants, made up the curaca's court and lived and worked at his center of administration. They depended on him for subsistence and probably for at least part of their raw materials. Other specialists, like the farmers and fishermen, lived in their own villages, often near the source of the raw material that they used, for example, the salt makers near salt pans and the potters near clay sources.[10]

From the variety of these craftsmen, their spatial distribution, and the geography of the river valleys inhabited by the people of the different señoríos, we know that each curaca had a similarly wide range of resources at his disposal. They all had access to marine life. The lords of Saña, Collique, and Tucume controlled marshlands behind the beaches where their people caught freshwater fish and aquatic fowl and cut reeds (totora, junco and carrizo) for

Table 11.1.   Summary of specialists in the six señoríos.

SPECIALISTS	Túcume	Jayanca	Collique	Pacasmayo	Saña	Sinto	Unknown
Albañiles		n.d.	1566				
Cabesteros		1566					
Carpinteros	1573	1566	1566				
Cocineros	1566		1530s	1582		pre 1532	
Cumbicos		1566					
Chicheros	1560	1540	1566		1566		
Esteros/Petateros		1739	1611		1549	1566	1566
Hacheros/Leñadores		1540					
Hamaqueros		1566	1530s		1566	pre 1532	
Huseros	1566	1566					1566
Mercaderes	1560	1563	1566			1566	
Olleros	1566	1540	1566	1566		1566	
Ovejeros/Pastores		1540		1582		1566	
Pescadores	1541	1540	1565	1566	1549	1566	
Pintores (de mantas)	1558	1566	1558			1566	
Plateros	n.d.	1566	1566			1566	
Roperos		1566				1566	
Salineros	1566	n.d.			1549	n.d.	
Sapateros/Alpargateros	1566	1566					
Sastres		1566					
Silleros	1566				1549	1751	
Tejedores	1576	1540	1582			pre 1532	
Tintoreros	1566	1566					
Venaderos	1566						

Note: I believe the lack of data for Pacasmayo and Saña to be few documentary sources rather than an undifferentiated population.

Sources: BAH/9-4664, 1549, 24; ANP/R: 1. 3, c. 7, 1582, 106v-7, 111, and 154; 1. 22, c. 57, 1611, 164v; ART/CoO: 13-VII-1570; 11-VIII-1582; CoJ: 29-III-1558; and Mata: 1565; CoR: 30-VI-1576; BNP/A157, 126; ANCR/1739; Polo: 20-X-1751; and 1740, 3v; AGI/J: 418; 457, 717, 785v, 786v, 832, 1057v, 1163, and 1240; 458, 1800v, 1898, 1919v, 1920, 1922, 1935-35v, 2025v, 2053v, 2088; 461, 1028v, 1042v-43, 1102v, 1466-68, 1470, 1481v, 1486, and 1514v; Patronato: 1. 189, r. 11, 1566; AL: 133; Miguel Cabello de Valboa, Miscelanea antártica (Lima, 1951), 327; Maria Rostworowski de Diaz Canseco, Curacas y sucesiones (Lima, 1961), 14-15, 77 and 105; Carlos Valdez de la Torre, Evolución de las comunidades indígenas (Lima, 1921), 117; Sara Delia Farroñán Vidaurre, et al., "Breve estudio del Distrito de Morrope," Escuela Normal Superior Mixta Enrique Lopez Albujar, Ferreñafe, 1970, 15; Sebastian da Gama, "Visita hecha en el Valle de Jayanca (Trujillo), Historia y cultura VIII (1974), 215-28; Marcos Jiménez de la Espada, Relaciones geográficas de Indias, 1885, t. 1, App. II, cxl.

mat-making, canoe and raft construction, and building.   Inland from these swamps were montes and forests, jealously guarded as a source of firewood and poles.   Four of the six señoríos included specialized salt producers, although the location of their sources has not yet been determined.[11]

Metal ore, heretofore frequently believed to have been imported from the highlands, was available within the jurisdiction of at least some of these coastal lords.   Colonial documents mention gold and silver mining at Sinpallpon (Sanpallpon?) in the Túcume area in 1562, and an eighteenth-century document reports an early source of silver in the Saña Valley.   Archaeologists have found sources of copper in Jayanca and Túcume, and at least one student of the problem states that there were sources of copper ore in nearly every valley between 200 and 2,000 m.[12]

The documentary record also indicates that the curacas controlled lands and peoples in their mountain hinterland. The lord of Túcume claimed lands in Guambos (near Cajamarca) in 1540. A lord of Saña used lands bordering those of the highland noble of Niepos in the foothills of the Andes near present-day Oyotún.[13]

Much more frequent than reports of distant land holdings in different ecological zones are reports of subjects living apart. One curaca in 1566 reported having a group of his subjects in a town more than 30 leagues inland from the sea. This was common. Table 11.2 shows that five of the six señoríos are known to have had what the Spanish labeled <u>mitimaes</u> ("foreigners" or Indians that reside permanently outside their community of origin) associated with them, dating at least from the Inca conquest and reorganization of the area.[14]

Table 11.2. Señoríos having "foreigners"

Date	Spanish Señorío	Repartimiento	Function	Location
1566	Pacasmayo	Moro		Cajamarca
1566	Pacasmayo	Chepén		Chontal, Cajamarca
1616	Collique	Callanca		
1564	Saña	Saña	shepherds, weavers	Chontal, Cajamarca
ca. 1550 -1560s	Sinto	Lambayeque	shepherds	
1590	Sinto	Sinto		
1590	Sinto	Chiclayo		
1540	Jayanca	Jayanca	potters	Guambos
1561-82	Túcume	Túcume		Cajamarca

Sources: AGI/J: 458, 1746, and 1871; 460, 377v, and 457v; 461, 1256, 1257v, and 1534v; 462, 1860v, and 1875; 509A; and Patronato: 1. 108, r. 7, 1562, 48; and 1. 185, r. 24, 1541, 78; BNP/A157, 110-10v; ART/Mata: 18-IV-1564; Rostworowski, "Plantaciones prehispánicas de coca en la vertiente del Pacífico," in <u>Etnía y sociedad</u> (Lima, 1977), 191; and Espinoza, 269-70.

The literature suggests several functions for mitimaes. Some had a garrison function of fortifying a newly conquered area with people subject to the Inca. Others were transferred from densely populated areas to less densely populated or uninhabited ones to reduce population pressure and better utilize natural resources. A third type were colonists situated in an area to provide access to resources unavailable in the home region. The last seems to have been one of the functions of several of the mitimae groups under discussion. Finally, some of the mitimaes who lived in the nine towns (<u>pueblos</u>) in Cajamarca subject to the curaca of Saña must have included shepherds and weavers, because they periodically sent him cloth. The mitimaes of Lambayeque also served as shepherds. Although we do not know their function, it is clear from early manuscripts that the rather large number of 200 mitimaes of the Spanish repartimiento of Moro in the señorío of Pacasmayo remained loyal and subject to their coastal lord into the

1560s.[15] The contact between the lord of Jayanca and his highland colonists, tenuous and deteriorating in 1540, revived thereafter. Jayanca potters in Guambos continued to serve their coastal lord at least until Cuenca's visit in 1566.[16]

The coastal señoríos, in short, included persons living at various altitudes from sea level on up into the Andes. The range of inhabited ecology suggests that the señoríos were self-sufficient in basic subsistence needs, thus supporting Murra's assertion that his model works on the coast. However, if the señoríos tended to be self-sufficient, how can the existence of the "merchants" in table 11.1 be explained?

That specialized groups of merchants existed in the 1560s on the north coast cannot be doubted, if we accept uncritically our primary documents. As early as 1560, Melchior Osorno, an encomendero of the area, was given formal possession of the merchant lord Don Pedro Blo of Lodifac in the community of Ferreñafe (which itself was part of what had been the pre-Hispanic señorío of Túcume). More documentary evidence comes from petitions of other merchants which were presented to Doctor Gregorio González de Cuenca, the judge of the Real Audiencia in Los Reyes who visited the district six years later, charged with the task of regulating Indian life. Among the ordinances he wrote were several which prohibited Indians from riding on horseback with saddle and bridle and traveling freely within the district. Such rulings prompted Indian traders to ask for exemption. They had to be able to travel freely in the area, they reasoned, to exercise their professions of "buying and selling," "trading," "bartering," or "exchanging" with other Indians. Yaypen of Illimo, for example, came forward saying:

> yo soy mercader con mys mercaderias tratos y granjerias me
> sustento y pago my tributo andando conprando y vendiendo como
> es uso y costumbre entre los yndios.

Lechec, another "merchant" of Túcume, petitioned Cuenca for freedom to exchange his clothing, wool, shell beads, and other things among the Indians of the surrounding repartimientos. Indians from Sinto and Collique petitioned likewise. Pochoc, born in the village of Pololo, asked to be able to barter (rescatar) the items the Indians used and needed in nearby villages. He went on to state he had no land or irrigation water with·which to plant, suggesting that he was a full-time specialist.[17]

Other petitions from artisans show that a few of them traveled to exchange their products with others. Potters of Pacasmayo and Collique "sold" and "traded" their pots (tinajones grandes and medianos) in nearby towns. Salt was the article of exchange which provided the livelihood for twenty or so salt makers from Túcume. Carpenters of Collique and Túcume produced goods (obras) to "sell" within their own area and in towns along the coast.[18]

Among the most frequent petitioners were the lords of groups of fishermen from Collique, Sinto, and Túcume, who asked to be allowed to sell their catch in nearby towns.

> Don Alonso Eten principal y alcalde del pueblo de Eten que esta
> en la mar deel rrepartimiento de collique digo q[ue] yo y los
> yndios de la dha my parcialidad tenemos pocas tierras para
> senbrar e sustentarnos y ansi nuestro trato es pescar y vender
> pescado en los pueblos comarcanos. . . .

Pedro Corina of Sinto stated:

> Don Pedro Corina principal de unos pescadores digo que yo vivo
> de tratar y contratar con los yndios deste rrepartimiento y de los
> demas comarcanos vendiendo, conprando y trocando por pescado
> lana chaquira y algodon y otras cosas con lo qual me sustento y
> pago my tributo y sustento my cassa e hijos porque no siembro ni
> tengo tierras para ello[.]

Don Diego Mocchumi, principal of the repartimiento of Túcume, told the same
story:

> yo e mys yndios somos pescadores y nuestra granjeria y donde
> procede el tributo es el pescado q[ue] vendemos asi para nuestra
> comida y nunca tenemos costumbre de hazer sementeras de maiz
> ny tenemos tierras para ello[.]

In a separate petition he reiterated these facts:

> Don Diego Muchumy digo que los yndios de my parcialidad son
> pescadores y tienen rrescate con los yndios de los
> rreparty[mient]os comarcanos vendiendo les el dho pescado por
> mayz y algodon y otras cossas [frijoles.]

He complained that Indians ate his fish without paying for it and asked Dr.
Cuenca to establish an exchange rate or equivalency between fish and corn.[19]

By the 1560s, periodic markets, which were frequented by Indians,
existed. The *tianguez* of Jayanca every Thursday was one such market where
artisans sold their produce.

> por que de tratar y contratar los yndios unos con otros vienen a
> tomar horden y se proveen de lo que no tienen en sus tierras y
> venden sus comidas rropa lana algodon ganados frutas y otras
> cosas[.]

By 1578 Ferreñafe had become known as a center of cotton trade. There and
elsewhere, farmers, fisherfolk, and artisans met at the plaza and exchanged
chicha, corn, wool, shell beads, cotton, ceramics, and other goods.[20]

In other parts of Peru, trade was not only local, but extraregional and
long-distance. Rostworowski reports that Chinchanos carried salted seafood to
Cuzco and maintained commercial relations with the peoples of present-day
coastal Ecuador. Puerto Viejo, in the north, was a major interregional
exchange center, especially for conch shells. The chronicler Arriaga reported
that these were traded by Indians of the coast with those of the sierra. Coca
leaves were another important item exchanged between the mountains and the
coast. Trade between the six señoríos with polities of the sierra hinterland,
however, is not directly mentioned in the testimonies reviewed to date.
Petitions from residents of the highland "province" of Guambos also suggest
that, although they exchanged foodstuffs among themselves, they did not trade
with the coast.[21]

Although we have no evidence of pre-Hispanic exchange in the
commercial sense with the sierra, we know that coastal polities did send
"tribute" (presentes) to lords who controlled the headwaters of the rivers of the
region. Augusto D. Barandiarán reports that the Morropanos delivered cargoes
of salt, chili pepper, and cotton cloth to the cacique of Penachi in return for

water rights. A mid-seventeenth-century manuscript, possibly the source of Barandiarán's information, adds that Jayanca's cacique "bought" the quebrada of Canchachalá from the cacique of Penachi years before the Spanish invasion and continued to pay tribute until Cuenca's visit. Indeed, Dr. Cuenca himself confirms this version in a progress report to the king when he mentions settling a water dispute involving Jayanca with a new regulatory code that may have ended this practice in 1566.[22]

However, this evidence of pre-Hispanic exchange between polities and the presence of specialized "independent" traders in this part of the north coast in the 1560s need not necessarily imply that merchants (as defined above) existed before the Spanish invasion. "Traders" may represent the breakdown of the pre-Hispanic order based on complementarity and redistribution, controlled, on the local level, by the curaca and his agents. Changes made by the Spanish in the area rapidly destroyed the basis of the traditional economic order. The mere act as early as 1534 of subdividing señoríos to create encomiendas to satisfy the conquerors' needs for an economic base and status greatly reduced the number of a lord's subjects and the range and diversity of the natural resources at his disposal. European diseases, harsh treatment, rebellions, and wars also took their toll on the native population.

Dr. Cuenca's ordinances further weakened the system. In order to alleviate the excessive tribute burden of the Indians, for example, Dr. Cuenca replaced the fixed amounts of goods and services owed by each community as a whole with a specific amount of items and labor services that each household head should provide to the curacas and encomenderos. Then, as the population declined, so would the tribute owed. No Indian would, at least in theory, be expected to make up the tribute for another who had died or left the community. As a result of this tribute reassessment, lords complained vociferously that their share was too little. They grumbled of being impoverished to the point of being reduced to the level of commoners. They argued that they would not be able to maintain the same levels of hospitality and exchange as before, which would cause their status and position to decline. They would lose respect and their ability to govern. For the curacas who had already suffered some status loss as a result of the demographic decline and the Spanish practice of appointing Indian officials for their own purposes, sometimes without due regard to their ancient custom of succession, a significant decline in their material wealth meant another serious limitation on the exercise of power.[23]

Dr. Cuenca's other disposition restricting the use of chicha had the same effect. Many petitions from perplexed lords asked for special license to provide chicha to subjects engaged in communal tasks. Don Christóval Payco, principal and tercera persona of the Spanish repartimiento of Jequetepeque and principal of the town of Lloco, asked Cuenca for permission to serve chicha to workers on community projects, explaining

> . . . por que la principal causa porque los yndios obedescen a sus caciques e principales es mediante aquella costumbre que tienen de dalles de beber que a el como a principal del dho rrepartimiento se manda por la tasa que los yndios de su parcialidad le hagan una chacara de maiz como hasta aqui la an hecho y que sino obiese de dar de beber a los yndios que la obiesen de beneficiar y a los demas que an de hacer la sementera de la comunidad para pagar el tributo no se querrian juntar para ello. . .

The lords of the repartimiento of Moro and several others also asked for licenses to distribute chicha at communal gatherings. [24]

Such regulations effectively undermined the authority and ability of the curacas to lead by destroying the material base of the traditional economic system. Already some Indians refused to serve their lords, perhaps because the lords could no longer fulfill their subjects' expectations. The cacique of Túcume complained that his Indians did not obey him as they once obeyed leaders in the time of the Incas. In 1540, the subjects of Jayanca in the mountains no longer served the lord because he had not called on them. Perhaps this was his way of reducing his obligations. Contemporaries described Don Juan, cacique principal of Collique, as a "cacique de los viejos que avia en los valles al qual sus yndios temian." The cacique of Túcume, who himself was identified with the fast-disappearing, old-style caciques, said that "Don Juan cacique se hazia respetar de los yndios como en tiempos pasados lo solian hazer." The implication of both of these statements is that their replacements were parvenus, even impostors, who did not enjoy the same legitimacy or authority associated with predecessors. [25]

As the traditional, pre-Hispanic system broke down, then, the Indians would have been forced to supply their needs through the mechanism of the market. Those left outside the purview of the curaca's reciprocal exchange network as his resources dwindled would have been the first to become dependent on the market for their needs. It is significant that farmers, perhaps the most independent group of subjects in terms of their subsistence, did not ask Dr. Cuenca for permission to travel and trade. It was the specialists, those most dependent on their lord for food, drink, and raw materials, who petitioned him. The chicheros, who made it clear that they were not "merchants" or "farmers," came to trade with the latter in the plaza—their chicha for corn (their raw material), wool, shell beads, and other goods. They were also dependent on the market by the 1560s to supply them with the clay jars in which they brewed their beer. The metal workers, weavers, and carpenters of Jayanca also frequented the markets to supply their needs. The breakdown of the traditional system created a need for an alternative mechanism of exchange. By the 1560s, some Indians had become merchants to meet the need. In undermining the lord's authority, establishing equivalencies between products, setting tribute in terms of silver pesos, and designating specific market days, Dr. Cuenca hastened the spread of a modified "market" economy. [26]

That the Spanish did not understand the system that they were destroying, perhaps inadvertently, is also evident from the language they used to describe it. The situation of 1560, the date of our first documentary proof of traders and the start of a decade of major administrative changes on the coast, was still one of difficult communication between the Spanish and the Indian groups. Interpreters, called lenguas or "tongues," were the key to an imperfect understanding between the Indians on the coast and those of the sierra and between both of these groups and the Spanish. Lizarraga, referring specifically to the Chicama Valley directly to the south of the area under consideration, states that between 1555 and 1560

> Los indios deste valle tienen dos lenguas, que hablan: los pescadores una, y dificultosísima, y otra no tanto; pocos hablan la general del Inga; . . .

Joel Rabinowitz suggests that speech peculiarities within coastal señoríos might have complicated communication even more. Spaniards, even priests who had lived in the area for decades, who could converse directly with the Indians were still a rarity. Cuenca's visita (inspection tour) was conducted in almost every area with the help of interpreters.[27]

Bilingual Spanish and mestizo scribes wrote the petitions presented by the Indians. Their attempts at finding the proper Spanish words to describe the exchange "a modo indio" may account for the wide range of words used in the petitions to describe the transaction. The verbs trocar and cambiar were used often and perhaps most faithfully describe the activities of the Indians. Another favorite, the verb rescatar, connotes "ransoming": recobrar por precio lo que el enemigo ha robado. Rescatar in this respect might mean "to win back or obtain what had previously been taken or denied them by the enemy" or "to win their freedom by obtaining what they needed." It is significant that da Gama uses the word rescatar to describe the transactions by which the Indians of Jayanca obtained the gold and silver demanded by their Spanish encomenderos in 1540. Granjear, another term found frequently in the documents of the period, means "to get, to obtain, to win, to conciliate or to gain the good will of another." The last definition is precisely the basis of exchange under the traditional system. Although the verbs comprar ("to buy") and vender ("to sell") also frequently appear, we have no evidence that money was used. The so-called Indian merchants and traders of the 1560s were exchanging as they had in the past. However, instead of the vertical or hierarchical exchange patterns between lord or his agent and commoner, the exchange was horizontal among commoners. The impersonal marketplace was replacing the personal and reciprocal exchange with the lord.[28]

Given the language problem and the fact that the Spanish interpreted the native reality according to their own cultural heritage, it is also feasible that those whom the Spanish identified early as merchants really might have been mitayos or porters, retainers of the lords, carrying tribute and supplies between the various settlements within a lord's jurisdiction for distribution or storage. The Indians, parroting Spanish as they learned the language over the next two or three generations, may have called themselves merchants when in this capacity, without necessarily implying being full-time specialists engaged in trade for personal gain.[29]

One explanation, then, of the apparent contradiction between Murra's model and Rostworowski's evidence of merchants is that traders represent a symptom of the breakdown of the traditional system and the transition to a "market" economy. Porters were mistaken as merchants. Murra's model, by extension, would seem to apply to the polities of the pre-Hispanic north coast as well as to those in the highlands.

However, given the data at the present time, this is only one, perhaps the best, of the possible explanations. It does not answer all of the questions. For example, it does not explain the existence of the Chincha merchants, although it is possible, as Rostworowski herself suggests, that they may have been a vestige of an older, pre-Inca pattern. After the Inca conquest of the area, the formerly "independent" traders may have been granted "concessionaire" status and incorporated into the empire as state agents, charged with procuring the goods otherwise unavailable within the imperial system.

Tentativeness is also indicated because the explanation is based primarily on manuscript records that are far from complete. There is always the possibility that ongoing archival exploration may turn up additional evidence that might alter the conclusions. Until that happens, historians should utilize the available information more fully. One could argue, for example, that a discussion of state-administered exchange within and between señoríos is premature, pending a more definitive outline of the jurisdictional limits of these units. This definition implies mapping the settlements, lands, and other natural resources known to have been under the control of each local lord. This task is beyond the capabilities of most individual historians. It can only be accomplished by close collaboration between historians, archaeologists, anthropologists, and others familiar with the coast and the highland hinterland. The detailed knowledge and perspective of such specialists would help test and refine the interpretations based on early colonial sources and, thus, lead to a more accurate vision of the ancient indigenous economy and the role of exchange.

Notes

Abbreviations-
    Archivo Castillo Muro Sime (ACMS)
    Archivo del Fuero Agrario (AFA)
    Archivo General de la Indias (Seville) (AGI):
      Justicia (J)
      Audiencia de Lima (AL)
    Archivo Nacional del Perú (ANP):
      Residencia (R)
    Archivo Notarial Carlos Rivadeneira (ANCR)
    Archivo del Departamento de La Libertad (ART):
      Corregimiento Justicia (CoJ)
      Corregimiento Ordinario (CoO)
      Corregimiento Pedimento (CoP)
      Corregimiento Residencia (CoR)
      Intendencia Asuntos de Govierno (IAG)
      Intendencia Compulsa (IC)
      Intendencia Ordinaria (IO)
      Intendencia Pedimento (IP)
    Biblioteca del Real Academia de Historia (BAH)
    Biblioteca Nacional del Perú (BNP)
    Colección Vargas Ugarte (Lima) (CVU)

1. My definition of merchant or specialized trader implies an independent group a la pochteca of Mexico, who lived in their own sector apart from other specialists and who traded to accumulate personal wealth. María Rostworowski de Diez Canseco uses the term in this sense in regard to Chincha. See her book, Etnía y Sociedad (Lima, 1977), 108, 138, and 253.

2. John V. Murra, "El 'control vertical' de un máximo de pisos ecológicos en la economía de las sociedades Andinas," in: Iñigo Ortiz de Zúñiga, Visita de la Provincia de León de Huánuco en 1562 (Huánuco, 1972), 427-68; Rostworowski, "Mercaderes del Valle de Chincha en la época preHispánica," in Etnía y Sociedad, 97-140; and idem, "Pescadoros, artesanos y mercaderes costeños en el Perú prehispánico," in Etnía y Sociedad, 211-63.

3. Susan E. Ramírez-Horton, "La organización económica de la costa norte: Un análisis preliminar del período prehispánico tardio," in Etnohistoria y Antropología Andina, comp. Amalia Castelli et al., (Lima, 1981), 281-97.

4. Rostworowski, Curacas y sucesiones: Costa norte (Lima, 1961), 121; John Howland Rowe, The Kingdom of Chimor, Acta Americana 6 (1-2), 1948, 26-59; and Waldemar Espinoza Soriano, "El Valle de Jayanca y el reino de los Mochica Siglos XV y XVI," Bulletin de L'Institut Français D'Etudes Andines 4 (3-4), 1975, 243-74.

5. "Un yndio parque que en castellano es hombre bil y bajo y sujeto a pagar mita y tributo." AGI/AL 167 (1648).

6. AGI/J: 461, 857, 1521; and Nathan Wachtel, The Vision of the Vanquished (New York, 1977), 80.

7. Rostworowski, Curacas 8; AGI/J: 458, 1778v-79; 461, 866v, 1400v, 1521, 1524, and 1553; Patronato: 1. 189, r. 11, 1566; and ART/Mata: 25-IV-1565; and 16-V-1565.

8. This estimate is based on the relative proportions for Chincha reported by Rostworowski, "Chincha," 137, and Ramírez-Horton, footnote 14.

9. Not included are tamberos, pajes, porteros, labradores and other specializations that may have been mitayos and, therefore, only temporarily employed in such tasks.

10. AGI/J: 461, 1468v; 1481, 1482v; and 1484v-87.

11. AGI/J: 461, 1028v and 1234v; ART/IC: 11-XII-1787; IO: 18-I-1800; IAG: 12-III-1802; AFA/1. 2, c. 1, 1599-1802; Hda. San Luis, 191; and table 11.1.

12. In 1566, many of the subjects of the coastal lords were absent from their villages because they were working in the mines. AGI/J: 461, 1019; ART/Mata: 1-VII-1562; and CoP: 26-VI-1782; Heather Lechtman, "Temas de metalurgía Andina," in Technología Andina, comp. Rogger Ravines (Lima, 1978), 409; Patricia J. Netherly, "On Defining the North Coast of Peru" (Paper presented at the Society for American Archaeology 4th Annual Meeting, New Orleans, LA., April 28-30, 1977), 5; Izumi Shimada, "Behind the Golden Mask" (typescript, Princeton University, 1979), 17; and Shimada, "Coast-Highland Interaction in North Peru: An Archaeological Perspective" (Paper presented at the Fourth International Symposium on Ethnology, "El hombre y su ambiente en los Andes," Japan, December 19-26, 1980).

13. Espinoza, 270; AFA/1. 1, c. 4, 1613 and c. 19, 1694, 142v, and 176.

14. AGI/J: 458, 1829v; Patronato: 1. 185, r. 24, 1541, 78; and ART/Mata: 18-IV-1564.

15. Some of these probably were shepherds in charge of llama herds, because an Indian official (governador) of Moro owned llamas and wore sandals made of their wool in 1582. ART/CoO: 11-VIII-1582.

16. Dr. Cuenca's ordinances for Jayanca indicate that it was common for coastal caciques to have mountain-dwelling Indians as subjects to them. AGI/Patronato: 1. 189, r. 11, 1566; J: 461, 1452, and 1527v; Espinoza, especially 256 and 269-70; Margarita Gentile, "Mitimaes de Nasca en Arequipa siglo XVI," in Etnohistoria y antropología Andina, comp. Marcia Koth de Paredes and Amalia Castelli (Lima, 1978), 135-40; and Wachtel, 74, 80, and 99.

17. AGI/J: 458, 1830v and 1920v; 461, 1454v, 1456v-57v; 1464; and 1466v-67.

18. AGI/J: 457, 786v; 458, 2053v; 461, 1028v; 1459; 1461v-62; 1467; and 1468; and 462, 1871.

19. AGI/J: 456, 1922v; 1928; 1936v; 457, 716; 840; 843v; 1460; 461, 1091v; 1458v; 1462v; 1464v-65; and 1517v; and 462, 1871.

20. AGI/J: 461, 1567; Patronato: 1. 189, r. 11; and BNP/A538, 1580.

21. Rostworowski, "Chincha," 99, 108; "Pescadores," 254-55; idem, "Plantaciones prehispánicas de coca en la vertiente del Pacífico," in Etnía y sociedad, 177; AGI/J: 461, 1481v; and Arriaga (Cap. IV, 211) as cited by Ravines, 60. The documents reviewed include twenty-two grants of encomiendas in the sixteenth century for Túcume (1536-49); Saña (1548-62); Jayanca (1545); Jequetepeque (1535-90); Sinto and Collique (1590); Illimo (1539-60); and Ferreñafe (1536-97).

22. Augusto D. Leon Barandiarán, Mitos, leyendas y tradiciones Lambayecanos (n.p. [Lima], n.d. [1938]), 235-36; ACMS/1654-1765, 7v-8; and AGI/AL: 92.

23. Rostworowski, "Curacas," 104; AGI/J: 458, 1261; BAH/9-9-2-1644.

24. AGI/J: 458, 2550v and 1799; and 461, 1769-71.

25. AGI/J: 459, 3085v-86; and 461, 1407 and 1521v.

26. AGI/J: 458, 2090v; and 461, 1481v.

27. AGI/J: 461, 1043v; AL: 92; Lizarraga (1916, 67) as cited by Joel Rabinowitz, "La Lengua Pescadora . . . " MA Thesis, University of Texas, Austin, 1980:46.

28. AGI/J: 457, 871; 462, 2172v; and Sebastián De Covarrubias, Tesoro de la Lengua Castellana o Española (1611) (Barcelona, 1943), 906.

29. CVU, 1-1: Carta de Santo Tomás, 1-VII-1550.

Translation of Quotes for "Notes on Ancient Exchange"
By Susan Ramírez

Page	TRANSLATION
229a (1st extract)	I am a merchant[.] with my merchandise[,] negotiations [tratos][,] and gains [granjerias] I sustain myself and pay my tribute[,] going along [andando] buying and selling as is the use and custom among the Indians.
229b (2nd extract)	[I,] Don Alonso Eten[,] principal person [lord] and mayor of the town of Eten that is located near the sea and is part of the community [repartimiento] of Collique say that my Indians and I of said community [parcialidad] have few lands on which to plant and sustain ourselves and therefore our occupation [trato] is to fish and to sell fish in nearby towns. . . .
230a (1st extract)	[I,] Don Pedro Corina[,] principal person [lord] of some fishermen say that I live by negotiating [tratar] and bargaining [contratar] with the Indians of this community [repartimiento] and of those [the communities] of the area selling, buying and exchanging [my] fish for wool[,] beads [chaquira] and cotton and other things with which I sustain myself and pay my tribute and sustain my house [family] and children because I do not plant nor do I have lands on which to plant.
230b (2nd extract)	My Indians and I are fishermen and our livelihood [granjeria] and from where proceeds the tribute is the fish that we sell and that we eat ourselves and we never customarily plant corn nor do we have lands on which to plant [corn].
230c (3rd extract)	[I,] Don Diego Muchumy say that the Indians of my community [parcialidad] are fishermen and they exchange [tienen rescate] with the Indians of the communities [repartimientos] of the area selling them fish for corn and cotton and other things [beans].
230d (4th extract)	because by negotiating and bargaining [de tratar y contratar] with one another the Indians come to establish [tomar] order and provide themselves of that which they do not have in their own lands and they sell their food[,] clothing[,] wool[,] cotton[,] cattle[,] fruits[,] and other things.
231 (extract)	because the principal reason why the Indians obey their chiefs and lords is because of the custom that they [the chiefs] have of giving them [the Indians] drink[,] the Indians of the lord's community [parcialidad] are ordered in the tribute list to plant for him a field of corn as they have always done up to the present[,] and if it was not for giving drink to the Indians who were to do the work and to the others that are to make the [common] field of the community to pay the tribute[,] they [the Indians] would not want to gather to do it [the work].

232, line 10   a chieftain of these valleys representative of the old ones whom the Indians feared

232, line 13   Don Juan chieftain made the Indians respect him as they [the chieftains] used to do in the past

232
(extract)   The Indians of this valley have two languages [lenguas] that they speak: the fishermen speak a very difficult one, and another not as difficult; few speak the general language of the Inga; . . .

233, line 4   in the Indian manner

233, line 5   trocar [to exchange]
cambiar [to change or exchange]

233, line 7   rescatar [to ransom or redeem]

233, line 7   retake [recobrar] for a price what the enemy has stolen